D1329465

The Use of Force after the Cold War

NUMBER THREE

Foreign Relations and the Presidency
H. W. Brands, General Editor

In association with
The Center for Presidential Studies
George Bush School of Government and Public Service

The Use of Force after the Cold War

Edited by H. W. Brands
with Darren J. Pierson and Reynolds S. Kiefer

TEXAS A&M UNIVERSITY PRESS
COLLEGE STATION

The paper used in this book meets the minimum requirements
of the American National Standard for Permanence
of Paper for Printed Library Materials, z39.48-1984.
Binding materials have been chosen for durability.

Texas A&M University Press gratefully acknowledges the support and
cooperation of the Center for Presidential Studies, George Bush School of
Government and Public Service, Texas A&M University, in making possible
publications of distinction on the presidency. The Center and its director,
George C. Edwards III, have brought energy, prestige, and funding that make
possible this book and others in this and related Press series. The Center's
contribution helps both the Press and the University accomplish their missions
of promoting and disseminating the highest quality scholarly research, analysis,
and reflection.

Library of Congress Cataloging-in-Publication Data

The use of force after the Cold War / edited by H. W. Brands.—1st ed.
        p. cm.— (Foreign relations and the presidency ; no. 3)
    Includes index.
    ISBN 0-89096-928-0 (cloth)
        1. United States—Military policy.   2. United States—Foreign
    relations—1989–   3. World politics—1989–   4. Security, International.
    I. Brands, H. W.   II. Series.
    UA23.U82   2000
    355'.033573—dc21

                                                          99-058775

Contents

Figures

Tables

The Use of Force after the Cold War

Introduction

H. W. Brands

THE END OF THE COLD WAR raised hopes that military force, the actual and implied arbiter of international affairs during most of the twentieth century, would lose some of its salience. For forty-five years the struggle between the superpowers had engendered tensions around the globe, tensions that in many cases erupted into war. The disintegration of the Soviet Union terminated the superpower struggle, and in its wake an era of peace—if perhaps not perfect or perpetual peace, then at least a closer approximation than had heretofore obtained—did not appear out of the question.

Events soon dashed the higher of these hopes. Iraqi aggression in Kuwait triggered the Gulf War of 1991. The dissolution of Yugoslavia precipitated organized violence that included "ethnic cleansing" and other forms of armed brutality. Long-suppressed resentments in the former Soviet Union touched off a ruthlessly suppressed uprising in Chechnya and less spectacular turbulence elsewhere. Civil wars tore apart several African countries; in Rwanda the bloodshed crossed the line of gruesomeness into genocide. If the ultimate war that had threatened humanity since the dawn of the nuclear age now appeared less likely than before, smaller wars that added up to tragedy enough for any generation were not only likely but were occurring all too frequently.

This said, the nature of military force and the uses to which it might be put did appear to be changing. The unification of Germany and the collapse of the Warsaw Pact precluded the land battle for Central Europe that had been the focus of North Atlantic Treaty Organization (NATO) planning since 1949. The Soviet Union's demise rendered redundant most of the large cadre of nuclear strategists who had made their living off the Cold War. The resultant confusion led to such diverse applications of military force as Panama, where American troops formed a posse to capture Pres. Manuel Noriega; the Persian Gulf, where American technology won a brilliantly painless (for the United States and its coalition partners) victory over Iraq; Somalia, where American forces followed the imperatives of humanitarianism only to find themselves in a quagmire of anarchy; and Bosnia, where a belated deployment of U.S. and other troops tentatively enforced a precarious peace. Yet what the new paradigm for the use of force was—if there was one—remained open to question.

The contributors to the present volume examine this question and others related to it. The authors include some of the most distinguished and thoughtful analysts of international conflict and American politics. J. Bryan Hehir, head of the Harvard Divinity School and a faculty associate at Harvard University's Weatherhead Center for International Affairs, begins by asking a fundamental question confronting any policy maker tempted to employ military force: Is such employment morally justified? This question is hardly new; policy makers—and the theologians, philosophers and other kibitzers looking over the policy makers' shoulders—have been asking it for centuries. Father Hehir identifies three different viewpoints: that of the pacifists, who contend that it is never justified; of the political "realists," who do not bother trying to justify it but simply consider it a fact of international life; and of the just-war theorists, who draw distinctions between permissible and impermissible uses of force, depending on the degree of provocation and the degree of force employed. The Cold War, with its omnipresent danger that small wars would escalate into a single, world-destroying conflict, placed a special burden of proof on those persons willing to permit war under certain circumstances. The end of the Cold War, Hehir suggests, has eased that burden somewhat. Additionally, by increasing the possibility of eliminating nuclear weapons, the end of the Cold War has placed a new burden on those concerned with the morality of force—namely, to banish the threat of nuclear war entirely. At the same time, the reduced post–Cold War risk of nuclear war changes the moral balance between arguments for and against American intervention abroad, allowing—perhaps requiring—intervention in circumstances that would have been too dangerous before.

Tony Smith elaborates on the intervention issue. A political scientist at Tufts University and the author of the provocative *America's Mission,* Smith has long advocated intervention abroad to promote democracy and human rights, and he does so here. Where many other observers detect worrisome complexity and danger in the post–Cold War world, Smith perceives an unprecedented opportunity for the assertion of American values. While he grants that confusion and unpredictability might surround the use of force on behalf of democracy and human rights, he contends that both national security, broadly defined, and simple humanity require the United States to take some chances.

Both Hehir and Smith explicitly cite morality as a basis for American foreign policy; for Bruce Russett morality is more implicit. A political scientist at Yale University and the editor of the *Journal of Conflict Resolution,* Russett examines two scenarios for international relations after the Cold War. The first is based on American hegemony—the United States as the sole superpower. The second is based on American cooperation with other nations—that is, multilateralism. The former is tempting, Russett says, but the latter offers a more stable basis for dealing with such necessary and inevitable changes as the integration of China into the international system. However, the two scenarios need not be mutually exclusive, for even during the Cold War U.S. hegemony rested as much on democracy and other values it shared with its allies as on raw American power. Something similar must take place in the post–Cold War world. Following this line of reasoning, Russett winds up near the point where Hehir and Smith start.

If Hehir, Smith, and Russett explore the intersection of morality and force, the next three essays examine the implementation of force by diplomats. Alexander L. George's *Force and Statecraft* (written with Stanford colleague Gordon A. Craig) has long been a primer on the subject. Here he examines the struggle by American diplomats to devise rules or guidelines for the use of force after the Cold War. Despite their best efforts, diplomats have encountered a paradox: At a time when American power, relative to other nations, is greater than ever, American willingness to use that power has been less than it often was before the end of the Cold War. George investigates why this is true, adducing various theoretical and practical arguments. He concludes that although the use of force—including its use as the threat behind coercive diplomacy—has not gone out of style, any effort to write a set of rules to govern the use of force is bound to fail. This is especially true in the complicated wake of the Cold War, where each case is unique.

Williamson Murray and Susan L. Woodward also investigate the interrelationship of force and diplomacy. Murray, of the Marine Corps Research Center and a longtime student of airpower, assesses the application of American force during the 1991 Gulf War. Murray sees the war as a stunning success for American arms following a dismal failure of American intelligence. Unfortunately for the United States, intelligence failures in the frequently anarchic environment of the post–Cold War world are apt to be unavoidable. Because the use of force is inextricably linked to intelligence, this places serious prudential constraints on the use of force. Consequently, Murray finds the victory of high-tech arms in the war itself less impressive—especially as a model for other interventions—than have some other observers.

Susan Woodward is a senior fellow at the Center for Defence Studies, King's

College London and the author of *Balkan Tragedy*. Here she applies her expertise to a subset of that regional tragedy: Bosnia. With Alexander George, Woodward sees two camps having formed in American decision making regarding the use of force: one centered in the comparatively interventionist State Department, the other in the more cautious Defense Department. The two sides took shape after the Vietnam War, while the Cold War was still on; unexpectedly, the end of the Cold War made resolution of their contest not easier but harder. The high stakes in any international crisis during the Cold War required U.S. presidents to reach decisions for or against force quickly; the low stakes (for the United States) in such places as post–Cold War Bosnia allow presidents the luxury of procrastination. What this suggests to Woodward is that posing diplomatic questions narrowly in terms of the use of force puts things backward. What matters is not whether force ought to be used, but what force, or any other instrument of diplomacy, ought to be used for.

In any political system, decisions on the use of force involve politics. In the American political system those decisions call into play distinctive aspects of democracy. James M. Lindsay, a political scientist at the University of Iowa and former staff member of the National Security Council, traces the historical tug-of-war between the executive and legislative branches over the use of force, thus providing context for the similar contest in the post–Cold War period. During the Cold War, presidents not only proposed, they often disposed—primarily because the high risks and limited time for decisions made legislators reluctant to challenge assertive executives. The end of the Cold War changed the calculus, encouraging legislators to insist on a greater decision-making role. This will probably result in fewer decisions to use force—an outcome Lindsay appears to find satisfactory.

Andrew Kohut looks beyond the Washington Beltway for checks on the use of force. The director of the Pew Research Center for the People and the Press, Kohut tracks popular opinion regarding the use of force and finds striking similarities between public attitudes after the Cold War and public attitudes during the 1930s—the most isolationist era in modern American history. The ideologically charged nature of the Cold War kept Americans attuned to foreign affairs in a historically anomalous manner; after the Cold War, attention has largely reverted to its traditional low level. This being the case, American policy makers will have a harder time generating support for the use of force than at nearly any time during the last half-century.

Politics impinges on the use of force in other ways, as Charles Moskos demonstrates. A sociologist at Northwestern University, Moskos has spent much of his career examining the evolving nature of military society. He concludes that social issues in the military, which themselves reflect social and political issues in American society as a whole, will strongly influence decisions on the use of force. The increasing role of women in the military appears to Moskos to be one of the most significant developments in recent American military affairs—and one of the most thorny. Moskos compares the integration of women into the military with the earlier integration of African Americans. He sees certain similarities but also critical differences, which lead him to wonder whether gender integration can ever match the success of racial integration. This cannot but have effects on when and how the military is employed. Moreover, he notes the growing gap between the elites who make the decisions on the use of force and the working-class men and women who must carry out those decisions. He suggests that this gap may have as much influence on the use of force as questions of armaments and doctrine.

Armaments and doctrine are the particular province of Andrew F. Krepinevich, Jr., and Stephen Biddle. Krepinevich—a career army officer before becoming executive director at the Center for Strategic and Budgetary Assessments, and the author of *The Army and Vietnam*—contends that a technology-driven revolution in military affairs is well under way. If the United States hopes to maintain its present edge over its potential rivals, American leaders need to recognize the revolution for the transforming event it is, and to invest the political, economic, and intellectual resources necessary to ensure that the nation remains at the forefront of the revolution. During the Gulf War the United States was able to strike Iraq with impunity. However, absent the necessary commitment to radical change, there is no guarantee that America will be able to do so in a similar conflict even a decade from now.

Biddle, of the Institute for Defense Analysis, takes strong exception to this view. He contends that analyses that ascribe the low American losses during the Gulf War to the technological advantage of U.S. forces are incomplete. He believes Iraqi incompetence played a large part as well. The United States cannot expect to encounter such incompetence in future conflicts. From this starting point Biddle proceeds to argue that far too much is made of the so-called revolution in military affairs. He advances arguments from technology, economics, and politics as evidence that evolution, not revolution, is what is taking place in military affairs—and will likely continue. In his view, the radical changes in force structure and doctrine urged by proponents of the revolutionary school are not only unnecessary but will probably be counterproductive.

The foregoing synopses merely touch upon the detailed, subtle, and sophisticated arguments presented by the authors. As the opposing views of Krepinevich and Biddle illustrate, the authors are hardly of one mind regarding what the past implies and the future promises regarding the use of American force. The topic is a multifaceted and contentious one. None of the authors would be so bold as to claim to offer definitive answers to the questions surrounding the use of force after the Cold War. But if they have moved the debate forward—or, in Alexander George's formulation, provided a framework for future discussion of this vital issue—they will have accomplished their purpose.

Part I

Morality and Force

Chapter 1

The Moral Dimension in the Use of Force

J. Bryan Hehir

THE USE OF FORCE has been the core issue in the history of empires, nations, and states. Diplomatic history, strategic theory, and the narratives of specific nations are informed by the story of war and peace. Tolstoy's *War and Peace* and Raymond Aron's *Peace and War* tell the story artistically and analytically. They are now joined by Michael W. Doyle whose monumental study *The Ways of War and Peace* is devoted to the philosophical foundations of this ancient problem. The issue has never been simply a matter of war and politics, rising powers versus declining empires, or winning and losing. War—because of its methods, its stakes, and its costs—has always been a moral reality. It is a phenomenon to be judged as well as waged, to be evaluated as well as recorded. Those responsible for war and for its conduct—the diplomats and the generals, the citizens and the soldiers—are judged not only on the end result but on the means they used to achieve it. The primary discourse of war is politics and strategy, but both must pass the test of moral argument and analysis even if that which is tested is often resisted or rejected in the midst of the campaign.

My purpose here is to describe how this ancient enterprise can be carried out on the cusp of a new century in human history. More analytically, I intend to show how moral argument relates to the fabric of the post–Cold War world. First, I will review the ways of evaluating the use of force, focusing particularly on how an earlier stage of development in moral teaching provides insight for assessing the changing political and moral demands of this age. Second, I will analyze the status of one dimension of war and peace that absorbed the time and effort of Pres. George Bush during his entire term of office: the nuclear question as it stands today. Third, while the nuclear challenge was focused on the moral means of warfare, a different dimension of the moral doctrine is engaged by the multilateral use of force. My argument thus reviews the moral methods of assessing war and tests what they contribute to two areas of international politics today.

Moral Arguments about Killing, Conquering, and Rescuing

Killing and conquering have negative moral connotations, whereas rescuing carries the aura of moral merit. The use of force in world politics involves all three terms. More precisely, killing is a means of both conquest and rescue, and has served the ends of aggression and justice. The assessment of war carries with it an intrinsic ambiguity. Jesuit theologian John Courtney Murray captured the inherent tension of moral arguments about the war this way: "In fact the whole Catholic doctrine of war is hardly more than a Grenzmoral, an effort to establish on a minimal basis of reason a form of human action, the making of war, that remains fundamentally irrational."[1]

In response to the persistent complexity of war and politics, three dominant perspectives have shaped the ancient argument about the morality of war. The first is the tradition of pacifism or nonviolence. Its roots are primarily in religious traditions, but it can be held as a purely philosophical position. Essentially, it asserts that the intentional taking of human life, in individual cases or in the social institution of warfare, is never justified. Two characteristics of this position should be noted. On one hand, while this view of war has ancient roots and is persistently present in any discussion of the morality of war, its dominant role has been as an ethic for individuals or a basis for social protest. It has rarely come close to being an ethic of statecraft. On the other hand, it is unfair and inaccurate to criticize the nonviolent tradition as one that is passive in the face of aggression or injustice. The nonviolent position seeks to oppose both by all means short of the use of lethal force, even to the point of self-sacrifice in defense of the rights of others.[2]

The second perspective is a variant of political realism. I say variant purposefully because the position I am about to describe should not be equated with all forms of realism. It is, rather, the version described by Michael Walzer in *Just and Unjust Wars*. Using the discourse of the victorious Athenian generals in Thucydides' history of the Peloponnesian Wars as the basis for his argument, Walzer describes a view of war that places it outside the normal standards of restraint and obligation binding persons to their political communities.[3] Such a view essentially argues that both the nature of warfare and the stakes involved in its conduct are incompatible with the standards of human morality. The only moral imperative of war is to pursue victory so society can return to normalcy and moral standards can again regulate human behavior. The comment required for fairness to this position—in addition to recognizing it as only one view of realism—is that it does not necessarily assert an amoral position for individuals or within societies. It is precisely the issue of war, and by extension international relations as a whole, that is excluded from moral analysis and moral imperatives.

The third position in the moral assessment of warfare is the most well known, the just war (or just defense) ethic. Its fundamental assertion is that some—but not all—uses of force are morally justified. In one sense, it redefines itself in terms of the other two positions. It shares a skepticism with the pacifist position regarding the moral role of lethal force, but does not translate that skepticism into an absolute prohibition against war of any kind. It recognizes the possibility that some use of force may be necessary lest massive injustice ensue, but it refuses to accept the realist claim that the necessities of statecraft excuse warfare from the demands of the moral order.

Having framed a position that is prepared to evaluate the resort to war case by case, this moral tradition then structures its judgments in terms of an evaluation of the ends of policy, the means used, and the intention that animates the decision to resort to force. To summarize the structure of the argument, it evaluates the decision to resort to war in terms of *jus ad bellum* categories of cause, proper authority, right intention, last resort, and proportionality of the enterprise of war as an instrument of justice. It also evaluates means within war *(jus in bello)* in light of the principles of discrimination (noncombatant immunity) and proportionality of means.[4]

The function of the moral doctrine is meant to provide both a policy ethic and a personal ethic. The structure of ends, means, and intention is designed to assess the content of public policy. It thus provides a set of questions and criteria capable of being brought into policy discourse to engage the political purpose and strategic plan proposed by a state as its rationale for resorting to war. The policy ethic is designed for use in two forums: within the structure of a government as it seeks to formulate a policy, and in public debate as a society assesses the action of the state. This latter forum—the arena in which citizens, the media, universities, and policy institutes debate not only the wisdom, effectiveness, or purpose of policy but also its moral content— leads to the role of the just war ethic as a personal ethic. It thus serves as a guide for the conscience of the citizen, including the citizen under arms, to assess the ultimate question of whether to support or oppose state policy. This final forum of conscience opens the possibility that while a state may be able to convince a majority of the population that its decision to undertake the use of force is wise and just, individual citizens may refuse to support that decision or to serve in the armed forces.

It is notable on this occasion to recall that, in the midst of the Gulf War crisis, President Bush made a speech in which he sought to establish the moral foundation of his administration's policy. "The war in the Gulf," he explained, "is not a Christian war, a Jewish war or a Moslem war—it's just a war."[5] His speech reflected his conviction that the policy already had been tested against moral criteria within the confines of government. However, he made the statement at the beginning of the societal debate on war rather than at its conclusion. That debate found citizens on both sides of the moral question of whether to go to war and, if so, how to fight it. The retrospective analysis of the war now being conducted by historians and policy analysts continues that moral debate.[6]

Of the three responses to the moral question of warfare, the realist position outlined here denies the possibility of moral analysis. Of the remaining two positions, only the just war ethic has maintained an ongoing engagement with both statecraft and strategy. The narrative of how this dialectic of morality and policy has evolved far surpasses the scope of this discussion. However, history illustrates that the moral doctrine itself had to develop and then be reassessed and restructured in order to maintain its viability as a normative constraint and guide for diplomacy and conscience. One moment in the evolution of the tradition helps to illuminate the challenges faced by the moral doctrine in the post–Cold War era.

That moment was created by the rise of the nation state, the successor to the medieval political order, in which the just war ethic had been the dominant moral doctrine. The transition from the medieval commonwealth to the modern era of sovereign nation states was an evolutionary process that occurred from the fourteenth through the seventeenth centuries.[7] This transition from medieval to modern politics involved three kinds of change: political, religious, and moral. The eighteenth century intellectual and political changes brought about by the Enlightenment and democratic revolutions later augmented the changes that occurred during the transition period. The cumulative effect of these changes was to fragment the medieval norms of authority, legitimacy, and standards of conduct.

Political change was rooted in the consolidation of political power geographically in the hands of individual rulers. The dynamic involved the diffusion of power away from a single authority—whether political or religious—and toward the several sovereigns who had previously held power but under some sense of obligation to the empire. Even in the work of Thomas Aquinas, the foremost medieval exponent the just war ethic, one senses recognition that political change prefigured a restructuring of the medieval order.[8] The rise of "the lay state" in the fourteenth century—symbolized by Francis I of France—and the continuing process of consolidation of power in nation states constituted a major structural change by itself. However, it did not stand alone. The political universalism of the medieval period was symbolized by the emperor, but the more substantive ties of the medieval order rested in religious conviction and institutions embodied in the Catholic Church. The medieval model was that of the *Respublica Christiana,* with spiritual and temporal unity embodied in the pope and emperor. The fact that these two representations of unity often were locked in mortal combat over the limits of their powers, prerogatives, and roles did not erase the notion of an overarching unity.[9]

It was the profound shattering of religious unity during the Reformation that complemented the political diffusion of power already well underway by 1517. Once again, this time in the sphere religious authority, ministry and doctrine, the center did not hold. By the middle of the sixteenth century the two bonds that had held the *Respublica Christiana* together since the tenth century had been ruptured. The concept of a single political-religious community with a shared conception of authority, legitimacy, and fabric of duties running from the emperor to the peasant had been dissolved.

One decisive consequence of this political and religious collapse was in the moral order—more precisely, the public moral order that specified the duties and rights of states and citizens. The structure of the *Respublica Christiana* yielded both a moral code and a recognized moral authority. In spite of multiple breaches of the code by ruler and ruled alike—and in spite of persistent conflicts between secular and temporal authorities—the medieval church was both the source of moral norms and an acknowledged center of executive moral authority. By the sixteenth century it was clear that, along with the collapse of the medieval political and religious order, the ecclesial structure of authority that had sustained public morality also had been severely eroded. Faced with this reality in a time of deep transformation of international relations, three figures separately undertook the task of restructuring the moral foundations of international relations, specifically the just war ethic. They were Francisco de Vitoria (1486–1546), a Dominican theologian from Spain and a successor in the moral tradition of Aquinas; Francisco Suarez (1548–1617), a Spanish Jesuit theologian; and Hugo Grotius (1583–1645); a Protestant theologian-jurist from Holland.

The first two, often called "the Spanish Scholastics," were integral parts of the Counter Reformation, seeking to renew Catholic doctrine and restore the life of the Catholic community. Grotius in a sense represented some of the intellectual and moral change that had dealt the final blow to the medieval order. While it was not his intent or design to recapture that pattern of religion and politics, like Vitoria and Suarez he saw the absolute need to fill the moral vacuum created by the erosion of the church's authority. All three relied upon a version of the natural-law ethic that had been the foundation of public morality in the Middle Ages and from which the just war ethic was drawn.[10] While each approached the subject in a different manner, their work converged around key ideas that illustrate how the just war ethic was sustained and adapted to a quite different setting than the one in which it had flourished for centuries. Each of the three theologians sought to preserve the substance of the just war ethic (legitimizing and limiting war) by changing its structure. Grotius was more willing to ground the moral argument in secular soil, acknowledging its separation from religious authority. Yet all three sought to sustain the premise of an international ethic: that some form of moral community, held together by a fabric of rights and duties, is a reality whether a political expression of that community exists or not. In brief, the universalist claims of the medieval order were to be sustained in spite of the collapse of the Respublica Christiana.

The change in structure required to address the facts of political change involved coming to terms with the rise of the sovereign state. The essential move made by all three was to acknowledge the fact of the new political entity, providing legitimacy for some of the claims of sovereignty while denying moral legitimacy to the notion of absolute sovereignty. The fact could not be ignored, save at the price of relegating moral arguments to a purely theoretical position. The legitimacy of the sovereign state was rooted in the way it provided for the needs of a defined political community, guaranteeing order, security, and the framework for pursuit of economic welfare. However, claims for an absolute conception of sovereignty, which implied both a freedom from moral restraint and an ability to limit the moral and political duties of citizens to their own political community, were unacceptable to the three theologians. Such claims posed a mortal threat to the idea of a universal moral community rooted in a shared conception of human nature and reason. Their refusal to adapt this broader conception of human community to the new claims of the sovereign state led to a degree of tension between the ideas they advanced and later conceptions of international law that were more willing to accept the broader demands of sovereign rulers.

How did the moral acknowledgment of the emerging sovereign state change the just war ethic? To reiterate, the essence of the just war argument is that force may legitimately be used only when it is limited to specific purposes and the means necessary to achieve those purposes. In the medieval model of the just war ethic, best exemplified by Aquinas, resort to war is made in a penal model. Political authorities go to war in the service of the wider community. Since a single normative doctrine governs public life, an assault on the order of justice can be clearly defined and political authorities are mobilized to restore the legal and moral order. By the sixteenth century sovereign rulers assumed that the right to use force was an attribute of sovereignty. This *droit de guerre* was not reserved for instances of preserving public order. It was assumed to be at the service of the state, so no higher legitimization was needed.

As with the concept of sovereignty itself, the custodians of the just war ethic conceded some of the claims of the rulers, but not all. They acknowledged that in the emerging order of states devoid of any higher authority some legitimacy must be accorded to specific instances of resort to force (hence "just cause"). However, they refused to acknowledge the *droit de guerre* as a right that could simply be invoked at the will of the sovereign power.

This shift in moral legitimization of the right to resort to war required a second change in moral teaching. In Aquinas's penal model, war could be initiated in situations where justice was clearly on one side of the case, hence the idea of war as an instrument of justice. Once all sovereign rulers were granted the moral right to resort to force, the question arose of who had justice on their side. The sixteenth and seventeenth century authors invoked a distinction between objective justice (where in principle one could distinguish clearly the just side) and what they called "simultaneous ostensible justice." The phrase meant that citizens and rulers alike might be convinced they possessed a just claim and thus were subjectively justified in pursuing it, but this did not necessarily mean they had an objective claim to a just cause.

Both of these moves eroded the moral strength of the "just cause" and "proper authority" criteria of the traditional ethic. This, in turn, led to the third change in how the just war ethic was invoked. Because of the concessions made over *when* war could be invoked, the moral tradition in the era of the sovereign state shifted its emphasis to the *jus in bello,* seeking to place restraints on *how* war should be fought. This trend continued into the late twentieth century, reaching its apogee in the nuclear age, which produced an enormous amount of literature focused exclusively on the means of warfare and strategy.

The reason this capsule analysis of how the ethic of war adapted to the rise of sovereignty is of interest to our inquiry is that the challenge posed by the politics of the 1990s involves the shifting status of sovereignty today. The shift is in the direction of a more limited role for sovereignty (at least operationally) in world politics.[11]

This shift in sovereignty's status is rooted in older and broader processes of change in international relations. These processes have been examined at length in the literature of the last twenty years.[12] A synthetic statement of the forces that have set limits on the theory and practice of sovereignty involves moral, economic, and political factors. Morally, the human rights regime of the United Nations (UN) system, rooted in the Universal Declaration and accompanying covenants, directly challenged the scope of "domestic jurisdiction" that sovereign states have jealously guarded. Economically, the web of relationships that compose interdependence and now globalization require a strong role for states, but also set limits on state discretion. Politically, the process of "pooling" sovereignty in Europe (the home of the sovereign state) illustrates how states themselves accept new limits in order to gain new benefits.[13]

Cumulatively, these changes in how sovereignty is understood and exercised are best summarized as erosion of operational sovereignty but no threat to eliminate it. Moreover, security questions—issues of war and peace—have been those most directly connected to sovereignty and least likely to be open to change. The argument proposed here, however, is that the present era is a time to re-think the ethic of war as it has been received from the adaptations made by the Scholastics and Grotius. The shifting status of sovereignty and the post–Cold War configuration of politics open two roads of inquiry about the content of the just war ethic. The first would continue the modern emphasis on an ethic of means by examining the nuclear question in its post–Cold War setting. John Courtney Murray's comment that the ethic of war was always a *grenzmoral*, an assessment of the outer limits of moral conduct, was given new meaning by the invention and use of nuclear weapons. The political configuration of the Cold War, with the deep ideological division it involved, led many to provide a marginal moral justification for nuclear arsenals. But the change in political relationships raises new questions about the legitimacy or lack of it of nuclear arsenals as instruments of defense. The second inquiry involves a return to *jus ad bellum* issues of cause, authority, and sovereignty. The rising incidence of intrastate violence particularly raises the question of the responsibilities of other states and/or institutions for violence and injustice within states. Whereas the *jus in bello* issues point toward the possibility of further restricting the claims of sovereignty, the *jus ad bellum* issues could lead to an expansion of the authority to use force. It is these two questions I wish to pursue.

Nuclear Weapons: Must the Past Shape the Future?

The advent of the nuclear age had an equally powerful effect on traditional conceptions of strategy and ethics. The revolutionary quality of nuclear weapons lay in their destructive capability, their speed, and the decisive primacy they bestowed on offense over defense. The long history of strategic doctrine had recorded change in all these issues previously, but the nuclear era constituted a moment of qualitative difference from all that had preceded it. Morally, the character of both the weapons and the strategy that directed them created a frontal challenge to the essential premise of the ethic of war: that legitimate use of force must be a limited use of force.

Neither the strategists nor the moralists adapted readily to this new reality in the history of war and peace. The strategic consensus coalesced first around the concept of deterrence, joined with the idea of a firebreak between nuclear and conventional weapons and tied to a conception of arms control that sought to limit—but not eliminate—the dangers of the strategic competition. Essentially, the strategic consensus sought to find a way to live with nuclear weapons rather than pursue a world free them. The strategic consensus was theoretically complete by the early 1960s and institutionalized during the Kennedy-Johnson years under the direction of Secretary of Defense Robert S. McNamara.[14] Subsequent policy debates involved variations on theoretical and operational themes that were set in place between 1958 and 1968.

Nuclear weapons drove the moral debate back to its foundations. The original question of the moral argument (Could war and morality ever be compatible?) surfaced again. Three moral positions structured the Cold War debate. One amounted to a retreat from just war principles: Moralists who had espoused a position that some use of force was morally legitimate concluded that nuclear weapons could never fit within the traditional criteria of limitation. From this conclusion arose the position of "nuclear pacifism," which rejected both the use of nuclear weapons and the strategy of deterrence.[15] A second position was that nuclear weapons and strategy did not constitute a qualitative break with conventional warfare. The moral task thus remained constant for adherents of this position, who sought to morally justify both the use of nuclear weapons and the strategy of deterrence as "conventional."[16] A third position, identified with Michael Walzer, was that the use of nuclear weapons was immoral but deterrence was not.[17] Other variations soon developed from this spectrum of views, and tension was evident in every moral argument.[18] The doctrine of limited war faced a fundamental challenge in nuclear weapons. Strategic literature, even after the 1960s, was contested terrain, but the higher standards of the moral order deepened the skepticism about the feasibility and legitimacy of using settled principles of prior ages to define, direct, and evaluate the nuclear age.

For both the strategists and the moralists the dual dilemma of the nuclear age was the political context of an intense ideological conflict and the strategic content of the nuclear relationship. Strategists and moralists alike adopted the perspective of "the long peace": a seemingly unending condition of constant competition without war, but always under the shadow of the catastrophic risk of nuclear war.[19] Fundamental change, as late as the mid-1980s, seemed impossible. But change came—profound, pervasive political change that recast the familiar strategic landscape.

However, the post–Cold War era is not post-nuclear. While the nature of the nuclear threat has changed—and the possibilities for reducing that threat are the most favorable they have been in fifty years[20]—the focus today is on the proliferation of weapons of mass destruction (including chemical and biological weapons) and the systems to deliver them. The new possibility involves very deep cuts in nuclear weapons, including the idea of eliminating them completely. A synthetic (but hardly exhaustive) sense of the character of the post–Cold War chapter of the nuclear age can be grasped by examining the new problem and possibility.

The problem of proliferation has been an essential aspect of nuclear policy since the 1940s. In the Cold War, however, it fitted securely into the broader bipolar structure of politics and strategy. Proliferation was always a danger, but a secondary danger. The focus was always on the problem of "vertical proliferation" between the superpowers. The dominant strategic and moral problem for fifty years was to avoid a "rational" choice with irrational consequences. Deterrence was the prescribed answer: a strategy often characterized as "the rationality of irrationality." The logic of this strategy had less salience in preventing the spread of nuclear weapons. The Nonproliferation Treaty (NPT) sought to complement deterrence with a range of benefits, guarantees, and restrictions that would contain nuclear politics among the permanent members of the UN Security Council. The 1995 Review and Extension Conference of the Treaty on Nonproliferation of Nuclear Weapons (NPTREC) was a moment to assess the results of the strategy. The record of restraint was impressive but not perfect. President John F. Kennedy expressed fear in the 1960s that there would be fifteen nuclear states by 1975, but the actual count in 1995 was only five declared powers and three well-known undeclared nuclear states: Israel, India and Pakistan. There was one recorded reversal (South Africa), as well as some close calls (Iraq and North Korea).[21]

The successful NPTREC gave new life to the effort to constrain nuclear expansion while highlighting the new role of proliferation.[22] Although the United States and Russia still control the overwhelming majority of nuclear weapons, the dramatically altered political relationship between them has transformed the strategic danger. The new danger arises from a combination of post–Cold War elements: reduced control by the superpowers over other states, greater accessibility to nuclear materials, a pluralistic structure of power that gives regional disputes greater importance and embattled states reasons to reach for nuclear weapons. A post–Cold War assessment of proliferation is found in the Canberra Commission on the Elimination of Nuclear Weapons: "The proliferation of nuclear weapons is amongst the most immediate security challenges facing the international community. It is a palpable threat to the security of both nuclear weapon states and non-nuclear weapons states."[23]

The commission wrote from a systemic perspective, but its assessment is complemented by Michael Mandelbaum's view of U.S. national interest: "Thus the major military danger now facing the United States in the post-Soviet world is not a particular country but rather a trend: nuclear proliferation."[24]

The enhanced status of proliferation changes the structure of policy priorities. The superpower relationship presumed that little could be accomplished in the political relationship of the US and USSR, and it placed primary attention on regulating the strategic relationship through deterrence and arms control. Preventing proliferation is primarily a political task: Convincing sovereign states that it is in their best interest to spurn the most potent weapons available. In a world of sovereign states, nonproliferation embodies a fundamental tension: maintaining equal sovereignty among dramatically unequal states with regard to nuclear weapons. The intensity and danger of the Cold War superpower struggle diverted attention from this underlying problem, but post–Cold War politics exposes the difficulty of simply extending the previous proliferation policy. The heart of the effort has been to classify nuclear weapons as being unacceptable as instruments of war but irreplaceable as instruments of safety through deterrence, and then confining their possession to a handful of major powers. The logic of the policy is plainly evident: Because nuclear weapons are uniquely dangerous, control over them should be as centralized as possible in an anarchic system. But the questionable long-term prospects of the policy are equally evident: It is a system perceived as discriminatory in intent and consequences, sustained by an argument about systemic safety but not always pertinent to the goals of individual states. The NPT's long-term argument has been that the discriminatory system is not permanent. Article VI of the treaty commits the possessing states to a process of nuclear disarmament. However, the superpowers have been slow to comply with Article VI. In part their defense has been that any sudden disruption of the deterrence relationship would be more dangerous than any benefit sought in the name of sovereign equality. Maintaining stable deterrence thus has prevailed over all other considerations.

The post–Cold War era will place increasing strain on the inherited policy of nonproliferation. The improved political character of U.S.-Russian relations will erode arguments about the necessity of maintaining strategic forces at anything near the levels of the past. Connections between the nuclear arsenals of the five major powers and systemic safety will come under increasing scrutiny, while the status conferred by nuclear weapons will be more visible. Pressure on the nuclear "social contract" as it was conceived in the NPT will likely intensify.

Three responses to this prospect of pressure on nonproliferation are conceivable. First, the shape of a classical realist response is readily evident. States are equal in sovereignty but not in power. Power yields perquisites, among them nuclear status in a nuclear age. Power also brings responsibility for maintaining order in the system. The record of the past thirty years testifies to the wisdom of a radically discriminatory system in which deterrence is secure and challengers can be dealt with effectively. From both political and moral perspectives, therefore, arguments about discrimination and the dangers of maintaining nuclear arsenals should be resisted.

Second, an argument about the irreducible or permanent necessity of nuclear deterrence, even under the new conditions of world politics, remains a possibility. This position would have substantial continuity with the past thirty years, but it would have to address more effectively a series of issues. On one hand, like the realist position, it would have to defend the past record of effective deterrence and the continuing need for nuclear deterrence in maintaining the peace. Next, if the role for deterrence is to serve a systemic function—peace in the system—then the question of who should have authority over deterrent forces becomes an issue. As in the earliest days of the nuclear age, the role of an international authority to act in the name of the international community would at least have to be considered in any case for maintaining nuclear weapons in the post–Cold War system. Finally, if deterrent forces are to be maintained, how will the two-tiered status of world politics (nuclear vs. non-nuclear) be addressed? An international authority would point toward a resolution, but if the authority is heavily dependent on some states for an effective deterrent force, then challenges to the NPT will take on new forms.

The third response to the future of nonproliferation points to the greatest possibility of the post–Cold War era: the total elimination of nuclear weapons. Both the Canberra Commission and the U.S. National Academy of Sciences support this position.[25] Calls for disarmament have been persistent but have had little impact on the analysis and formulation of nuclear policy. The two reports cited here are notable because their signers have been prominent voices in the academic, policy-making, and military communities, which in the past have kept disarmament proposals at the margin of public attention and policy discourse. Beyond personalities, however, both texts show a thorough familiarity with all aspects of the nuclear equation and both are rooted in the political and strategic character of post–Cold War world politics. The Canberra Report states: "The end of the Cold War has created a new climate for international action to eliminate nuclear weapons, a new opportunity. It must be exploited quickly or it will be lost."[26]

Both documents see nuclear disarmament as clearly superior to any other way of coping with a world of states in which the knowledge of how to make nuclear weapons cannot be erased. The sense of ambiguity and tragedy that often accompanies the argument about the irreducible need for deterrence is absent in these texts, although both acknowledge that the conditions of the Cold War rendered deterrence a necessary if risky strategy. Both texts exhibit high confidence that a regimen of progressive disarmament, carried out at an agreed upon pace with phased reductions by all parties, can produce a world without nuclear arsenals. The language and logic of the texts is not utopian; they have the careful, rational tone of standard arms control literature.

The Canberra Report, while it answers the usual criticisms made of disarmament proposals, tends to isolate nuclear weapons from the larger issues of international relations. This document so specifies the extraordinary character of nuclear weapons that its case rests upon the ability to carry off this major change in world politics without transforming the political order itself. The National Academy of Sciences report acknowledges that totally eliminating nuclear weapons would require not a political utopia, but "a substantial positive evolution in international politics."[27]

Proponents of the zero option argue that nuclear weapons have no utility save as deterrents to other nuclear systems. The zero option would remove the rationale for deterrence, eliminate the risk of use, and be the best long-term defense against proliferation. The dominant argument in support of the zero option is made in terms of political strategic wisdom, but there are references to its morally imperative quality woven through the case.

The traditional ethic of war has been stretched to the breaking point by the nuclear age. The judgment of marginal acceptance of deterrence, which predominated in the moral literature, was usually tied to imperatives to move beyond the strategic stalemate that characterized the Cold War. At the same time, the paradox of deterrence—preventing use by threatening to use—has carried a certain moral weight. What then of these responses to the now dominant problem of proliferation?

The realist case dismisses too easily arguments about the continuing danger of the present order and its discriminatory character. It usually fails to grapple with the inherently problematical character of nuclear strategy and rests its case with the maintenance of hierarchy and order. Given the fact that some possibilities to move away from nuclear deterrence exist, simply reaffirming the Cold War policy is an inadequate moral response. The second and third arguments constitute more of a moral debate. The case for an irreducible need for deterrence, particularly if tied to some form of international authority, responds to three aspects of the traditional ethic. First, the justification of the right to use force, even after the seventeenth century, has been tied to an argument that no higher authority exists that can guarantee the security of states. If nuclear weapons are classified as uniquely dangerous and, therefore, placed under international authority, then sovereign states would not be the legitimate possessors of these weapons. In brief, one could conceive of limiting the role of sovereign states regarding nuclear weapons and other weapons of mass destruction without denying other traditional security functions of the state.

Second, by arguing that a nuclear deterrent is necessary, but not in the hands of a few states, this approach addresses the discriminatory aspects of existing nonproliferation policy. The third question that must be addressed is the character of the deterrent force—regardless of who possesses it. The paradox of the post–Cold War nuclear debate is that the commonly recognized possibility of achieving very deep reductions in nuclear forces can produce a "minimum deterrent" in the sense of a small number of weapons aimed at civilian targets. This is not the inevitable product of a small deterrent force, but it must be specified as a possibility and opposed on the basis of noncombatant immunity. Throughout the era of Cold War deterrence policy this principle was the primary instrument of restraint on strategy.[28] Its defense and enforcement is all the more necessary in the post–Cold War era. Deterrence may be necessary, but not the targeting of civilians.

The zero-option position denies the premise that nuclear deterrence is a permanent necessity in global politics, a necessary mechanism of security that we must learn to live with and manage effectively. In holding this view, zero-option advocates reflect a position taken on ethical grounds by those moralists who joined justification for deterrence with an obligation to seek other forms of state security. In various ways during the nuclear age, deterrence was justified as an "interim ethic."[29] The zero option is, in a sense, a response to this position: It recognizes the legitimate role deterrence played during the Cold War and now finds it unjustifiably dangerous as a means of security.

In addition to this general affinity with moral positions taken during the past fifty years, the zero option is based on three convictions that find parallels in the moral literature. They are:

(1) that the only legitimate function of deterrence is to deter other nuclear forces;
(2) that nuclear use against a non-nuclear state lacks justification; and

(3) that maintaining the two-tiered world embodied in the NPT will be an incentive to nuclear proliferation.[30]

These propositions are reflected in the ethical literature but they also illustrate the need to test such ideas against contending views. Lawrence Freedman, for example, argues against the first, claiming that it distorts the role nuclear deterrence plays.[31] Michael Mandelbaum bases his opposition to the third proposition on the belief that the zero option would inspire others to possess nuclear weapons.[32]

These are empirical differences of judgment to be sure, but the debate among strategists on the nature of deterrence, its uses, and the consequences of dissolving it have to be part of the argument shaping the moral assessment of the zero option.

As a goal to be pursued, the zero option finds resonance in much of the moral literature. Faced with the debate among strategists about the risks of going to zero and how they should be balanced against the risks of simply maintaining deterrence, the dominant themes in moral analysis would, in my view, tilt decisively toward running the risk of going to zero. Both the objectives of just war theory—limiting the use of force as narrowly as possible and the means tests of the ethic—drive it to seek ways to transcend the pattern of nuclear politics characteristic of the Cold War.

But the just war ethic has multiple tests, and the salient one to use in assessing the zero option is the moral possibility of success. It is used in warfare to prevent political authorities from causing senseless, needless deaths. In the context of the zero option, the possibility of success criterion corresponds to the debate among strategists about comparable risks attached to strategies for the nuclear age. Can a zero option be attained and sustained?

There are multiple criteria for success. Chief among these is to sustain the taboo against nuclear use that has been laboriously constructed during the nuclear age. Others include preventing superpower conflicts, protecting small states from threat or conquest, and restraining military spending in a world of multiple needs. These criteria can be used to judge both the realist position and the necessary deterrence position.

Bringing them to bear upon the zero option involves three questions. First, does it expect more from state behavior than it is reasonable to assume? The zero option, as noted, so focuses on nuclear danger that it sees in it an incentive for states to act in ways that seem a step beyond the pattern of international politics—even in a nonrealist conception of politics. Second, can it outline a structure of political authority that would at least facilitate the choices individual states would have to make in going to zero? Third, does it have a proposal for addressing cheating, breakout, or subversion of the zero-option security order?

My own sense is that the traditional just war ethic can never rest easily with a world order that accepts nuclear deterrence as a permanent fact of life. Hence, proposals to move beyond a method of security that promises to violate the means test of the just war ethic if ever used should find a predisposition to acceptance. The reason for testing these proposals of the zero option stringently is not because they move in the wrong direction, but because the direction they propose has one great risk. In search of absolute restrictions on nuclear weapons, the zero option must substitute for the fragile relative restrictions provided by deterrence thus far. The risk is worth running in my view, but only if its advocates are as aware of the dangers as its critics.[33]

Multilateral Use of Force: An Unfinished Agenda

The proposal to limit sovereign states access to nuclear weapons follows the logic of the modern history of the just war ethic. The emphasis has been primarily focused on setting limits on the means of warfare. In the period since World War II, limits on means have been accompanied by some efforts to set limits on the purposes for which force can be used. Not all just war theorists have seen this as a productive path to follow. Paul Ramsey, the preeminent architect of limits on means, had little confidence that just cause restraints could be constructed for sovereign states. A counterexample, however, is John Courtney Murray's commentary on contemporary Catholic thinking on just war theology. Murray argues that Pius XII reduced the three traditional reasons for just cause (to vindicate rights, to reconquer what had been unjustly taken, and to repel attack) to the third reason: War undertaken in self-defense or the defense of others.[34] To some degree this effort by Pius XII and others can be seen as an attempt to recoup from the sovereign state the relatively free hand it had acquired in the sixteenth and seventeenth century. When viewed in light of the experiences of two world wars, and faced with the prospects of the technological character of modern war in general, the thrust of moral theory increasingly has been on setting limits on both the ends and means of war.

One of several surprises of the post–Cold War period serves as a counterpoint to the theme of limitation. It is the willingness of a range of authors to expand the sovereign state's responsibility to resort to force in response to intrastate violence, accompanied by human rights violations and/or the collapse of state authority. This movement to expand the justification for the use of force arises in the context of the renewed debate on military intervention.[35]

To define precisely the content of this new debate on an old topic, it is necessary to distinguish intervention from war. At first glance the distinction can seem trivial since both involve the conscious, systematic use of force and the taking of life. But it is precisely when intervention and war are placed in a multilateral setting, specifically the UN system, that the difference is evident.

President Bush's name will always be joined to the leadership he displayed in creating a coalition of forces under the auspices of the United Nations to resist Iraqi aggression against Kuwait. As many have observed, U.S. leadership made it possible for the UN collective security system to function as it had been designed in the 1940s but never effectively employed until the Gulf War. The UN system is an organization of sovereign states designed to protect the security and territorial integrity of these states and their populations. While the UN charter goes to great lengths to rule out war as a means of resolving conflicts of interest, it mandates the collective use of force to oppose aggression across recognized international boundaries. It also allows for individual states to respond to aggression. This model, particularly the collective security provisions, is similar to the penal model for the use of force that existed in the Middle Ages: The international community responds to a recognized violation of law. Such a response to the external activity of other states is warfare. The United Nations seeks to limit war in the international system by containing it within the authorizing structure of the UN charter.

However, the UN system is much less prepared to act when intervention is deemed necessary. Intervention means the use of force to address problems within the boundaries of a sovereign state. The dominant theme of the UN system, following closely the Westphalian legacy of international order, is to rule out intervention by the United Nations (see Article 2[7]) or individual states. As an institution founded on the cornerstone of sovereignty, the United Nations seeks to protect sovereign states from either aggression or intervention.

To some degree this perspective on intervention is one of the reasons for the gap between expectation and performance of the United Nations in the post–Cold War period. I hasten to add that the institution is responding to the wishes of the majority of its members in maintaining a great reserve on the question of intervention. Yet the problem of intrastate conflict and catastrophe has surfaced as one of the dominant characteristics of the post–Cold War era. The question of whether the collapse of the Soviet Union caused or occasioned the rise of intrastate violence or whether the world is simply more aware of a phenomenon that has been present but not addressed is beyond the scope of this discussion. It is enough to cite the cases—Bosnia, Haiti, Somalia, Rwanda, Burundi, the Sudan—that have dominated much of the foreign policy debate of the 1990s, to recognize how different this is from the policy agenda of the Cold War years.

In the framework of the Westphalian legacy of international relations, reflected both in international law and the practice of the United Nations, the single agreed upon justification for overriding the norm of nonintervention has been genocide. The policy debates of the 1990s are noticeable for two reasons. First, in spite of moral and legal obligations to act, the international community stood by while genocide was committed in Bosnia and Rwanda. Second, the policy debates—normative and empirical—have been pressing in the direction of expanding the reasons for intervention beyond the single exception of genocide. From those closely linked to the UN system itself—the voices of Boutros Boutros-Ghali and Brian Urquhart—have come calls to give less weight to sovereignty and more to the cries of suffering people in violent or failed states.[36]

The just war ethic is primarily a moral rather than a legal tradition. On the question of intervention the moral tradition has always been more interventionist than modern international law. The interventionist rationale has to be tested against the criteria of last resort, proportionality, limited means, and the possibility of success. In light of this, the premises of the just war ethic require broadly defined responsibilities for states.[37]

It would take an extensive review of the explosion of recent literature on intervention to analyze the details of the arguments calling for states to reconsider and revise the nonintervention norm. However, my purpose here is to highlight another dimension of the intervention debate: Who should fulfill an expanded interventionary role in the contemporary international system? In the first instance, a redefinition of the justifying reasons for intervention should be joined to the responsibilities of sovereign states. They are the primary moral agents obligated to respond to intrastate violence. But states should act through multilateral institutions when fulfilling these expanded duties of intervention. The reasons for relying upon multilateralism in the case of intervention run from normative to institutional concerns.

At the normative level, the evident need to provide a broader justification for intervention must be weighed against the reason that shaped the Westphalian tradition's restrictive view of intervention. The historical record of states in an anarchic system contains multiple instances when intervention was simply an act of self-interested power politics shrouded in a humanitarian rationale. Intervention is a notoriously ambiguous concept. The wisdom of Westphalia involved protecting small states in a system dominated by large powers. The contemporary debate is focused on humanitarian intervention, but most interventions have not been humanitarian in motive or method. The limitation of Westphalia is that it paralyzes action in the name of the sanctity of sovereignty. There is, however, good reason to go beyond inherited conceptions of nonintervention. Expanding the right or duty of states to inter-vene without first determining how such action shall be limited, constrained, and channeled toward specific ends provides an inadequate moral framework.[38]

States do bear moral responsibility for events within other states, but chan-neling that responsibility through multilateral institutions (regional as well as universal) is a prudent restraint on state interests in an endeavor that should not simply be an extension of power politics. The normative rationale for multilateralism thus is to restrain states.

A second reason for multilateralism is to enhance the possibility that the most urgent cases requiring humanitarian intervention are addressed. The pattern of post–Cold War politics is highly segmented. During the Cold War almost every nation had a certain "strategic value" in the bipolar global com-petition. Today some of the most violent internal conflicts occur in regions and nations with little if any connection to the pattern of global politics and economics. Basing a policy of humanitarian intervention on the premise that states will see an interest in these situations is a very risky gamble. Multilateral institutions—which of course require state support—can and should be desig-nated to play a role in a division of labor that will provide an international re-sponse even when there is little or no discernible national interest at stake. The premise behind this proposed division of labor is that major states will be more likely to provide political and financial support for multilateral institutions than to act on their own when demonstrable vital interest is not present.

This leads to a third comment on multilateral policy: It must be effective, particularly when military action is taken for humanitarian reasons, if it is to be sustained. Failure in the execution of policy will erode confidence in the institutions authorizing it. Humanitarian interventions rarely involve major military engagements. They are instead a complex blend of diplomatic, mili-tary, and relief activities. Once a situation reaches the point where military ac-tion is required, the complexity of the case is evident. Hence, a division of labor policy cannot be seen as multilateral institutions taking on simple operations. For this policy to succeed, highly trained fighting forces, hopefully with other skills as well, must be ready to be deployed when needed. It is not clear that major states, even if persuaded to provide political and financial support for a division of labor policy, will also provide well-trained military forces—either consistently or on a case-by-case basis.

This is a major obstacle for a successful multilateral strategy, even if, as I believe, it is not wise to have troops from the major powers in highly visible operations on a regular basis. The major states tend to politicize the situation; their presence is catalytic rather than stabilizing. But major power logistical, transport, and satellite communications support is often a sine qua non for those operations. The effect of both Bosnia and Somalia on key members of the Security Council has created a major psychological and political obstacle to meeting the criterion of effectiveness in multilateral humanitarian interventions.

That reminder leads me to make a final comment. This has not been an essay on U.S. foreign policy. Nevertheless, if one looks at both the nuclear future of the international system and future possibilities of a more effective means of addressing the problems of intrastate violence, it is clear that the United States will play a leading role. America's example, understanding, and participation in both arenas will be a major determinant of how the post–Cold War order joins morality and politics, ethics and strategy, and values and interests.

Notes

1. J. C. Murray, *We Hold These Truths: Catholic Reflections on the American Proposition* (New York: Sheed and Wand, 1960), p. 263.
2. Examples of the nonviolent position can be found in R. H. Bainton, *Christian Attitudes Toward War and Peace* (New York: Abington, 1960); S. Howards, "The Nonresistant Church: The Theological Ethics of John Howard Yoder," in *Vision and Virtue: Essays in Christian Ethical Reflection* (Notre Dame, Ind.: Fides Publishers, 1974), pp. 197–222; J. H. Yoder, *Nevertheless: Varieties of Christian Pacifism* (Scottdale, Pa.: Herald, 1971); Lisa Sowle Cahill, *Discipleship, Pacifism, and Just War Theory,* The Albert Cardinal Meyer Lectures (Mundelein, Ill.: University of Saint Mary of the Lake, 1995).
3. Michael Walzer, *Just and Unjust Wars: A Moral Argument with Historical Illustrations* (New York: Basic, 1977), p. 5.
4. The history of the just war ethic can be found in multiple sources: J. Childress, "Moral Discourse about War in the Early Church," and L. B. Walters, "The Simple Structure of the Just War Doctrine," in *Peace, Politics, and the People of God,* ed. P. Peachly (Philadelphia, Pa.: Fortress, 1986), pp. 117–34, 135–48; F. H. Russell, *The Just War in the Middle Ages* (Cambridge: Cambridge University Press, 1977), pp. 16–39; J. T. Johnson, *Ideology, Reason, and the Limitation of War: Religious and Secular Concepts 1200–1740* (Princeton, N.J.: Princeton University Press, 1975); and Murray, *We Hold These Truths.*
5. The White House (Office of the Press Secretary), Remarks by the President in Address to the National Religious Broadcasters Convention, The Sheraton Washington Hotel, Washington, D.C. (Jan. 28, 1991), p. 2.
6. Examples of the Gulf War debate include: M. Walzer, "Perplexed: Moral Ambiguities in the Gulf Crisis," *New Republic,* Jan. 28, 1991, pp. 13–15; G. Weigel, "From Last Resort to Endgame," and S. Hauerwas, "Whose Just War? Which Peace?" in *But Was It Just?* ed. D. DeCosse (Garden City, N.Y.: Doubleday, 1992), pp. 19–42, 83–105.
7. S. Krasner, "Westphalia and All That," in *Ideas and Foreign Policy: Beliefs, Institutions, and Political Change,* ed. J. Goldstein and R. O. Keohane (Ithaca, N.Y: Cornell University Press, 1993), pp. 235–64.
8. Cf. T. Gilbey, *Between Community and Society* (London: Longmans, Green, 1953), p. 58. In tracing this evolution I draw from J. B. Hehir, "The Ethics of Interven-

tion: U.S. Policy in Vietnam, 1961–1968" (Ph.D. diss., Harvard University, 1977).

9. G. B. Ladner, "Aspects of Medieval Thought on Church and State," *Review of Politics* 9 (1947): 403–22; G. Tellenbach, *Church, State, Society at the Time of the Investiture Controversy* (New York: Harper and Row, 1970).

10. The most detailed comparison of the three is found in LeRoy B. Walters, "Five Classic Just War Theories" (Ph.D. diss., Yale University, 1971).

11. Robert Keohane is the source of the very helpful distinction between "formal sovereignty" (the supreme legal status of the state) and "operational sovereignty" (legal freedom of action). See R. O. Keohane, "Sovereignty, Interdependence, and International Institutions," in *Ideas and Ideals: Essays on Politics in Honor of Stanley Hoffmann,* ed. L. B. Miller and M. J. Smith (Boulder, Colo.: Westview, 1993), pp. 91–107.

12. Cf. R. O. Keohane and J. S. Nye, *Power and interdependence: World Politics in Transition* (Boston, Mass: Little, Brown, 1977); H. Bull, "The Theory of International Politics 1919–1969," in *International Theory,* ed. J. D. Derian (New York: New York University Press, 1995), pp. 181–211; S. Hoffmann, "An American Social Science: International Relations," in *Janus and Minerva: Essays in the Theory of International Politics,* ed. Stanley Hoffmann (Boulder, Colo.: Westview, 1987), pp. 3–24.

13. In addition to the works cited in notes 11 and 12, cf. J. B. Hehir, "Just-War Theory in a Post–Cold War World," *The Journal of Religious Ethics* 20 (fall, 1992): 243–46; and S. Hoffmann and R.O. Keohane, eds., *The New European Community: Decision-Making and Institutional Change* (Boulder, Colo.: Westview, 1991), pp. 7–8, for a discussion of "pooling" sovereignty.

14. The history of strategic thought can be found in several good studies. Exceptionally helpful is L. Freedman, *The Evolution of Nuclear Strategy* (New York: St. Martin's, 1981), chapters 12, 13, 15, 16. A more journalistic but solid account is F. Kaplan, *The Wizards of Armageddon* (New York: Simon and Schuster, 1983). A retrospective account is M. Howard, "Brodie, Wohlstetter, and American Nuclear Strategy," *Survival* 34 (1992): 107–16.

15. Cf. The collection of British authors, *Nuclear Weapons and Christian Conscience,* ed. W. Stein (London: Merlin, 1961).

16. The preeminent representative was Paul Ramsey of Princeton. See P. Ramsey, *The Just War: Force and Political Responsibility* (New York: Charles Scribner's Sons, 1968).

17. Cf. M. Walzer, *Just and Unjust Wars,* pp. 269–83.

18. Examples include J. S. Nye, *Nuclear Ethics* (New York: Free Press, 1986); National Conference of Catholic Bishops, *The Challenge of Peace* (Washington, D.C.: U.S. Catholic Conference, 1983); D. Hollenbach, "Ethics in Distress: Can There Be Just Wars in the Nuclear Age?" and W. V. O'Brien, "The Failure of Deterrence and the Conduct of War," in *The Nuclear Dilemma and the Just War Tradition,* ed. W. V. O'Brien and J. Langan (Lexington, Mass.: D. C. Heath, 1986), pp. 13–30, 153–97.

19. The phrase is drawn from J. L. Gaddis, *The Long Peace: Inquiries into the History of the Cold War* (New York: Oxford University Press, 1987), pp. 215–46.

20. Cf. McG. Bundy, W. J. Crowe, S. D. Drell, *Reducing Nuclear Danger: The Road Away from the Brink* (New York: Council on Foreign Relations, 1993), pp. 1–2.

21. Since 1995 India and Pakistan have become declared nuclear powers while the close calls in Iraq and North Korea now appear to have been very close indeed.

22. In addition to Bundy et al., cf. M. Mandelbaum, "Lessons of the Next Nuclear War," *Foreign Affairs* 74 (1995): 22–37; L. S. Spector, "Neo-Nonproliferation," *Survival* 37 (1995): 66–85; F. C. Ikle, "The Second Coming of the Nuclear Age," *Foreign Affairs* 75 (1996): 119–28; S. Sagan, "Why Do States Build Nuclear Weapons?" *International Security* 21 (1996–97): 54–86.

23. *Report of the Canberra Commission on the Elimination of Nuclear Weapons* (Canberra, Australia: National Capital, 1996), p. 24.

24. Mandelbaum, "Lessons," p. 22.

25. Canberra Commission, *Report;* National Academy of Sciences, *The Future of U.S. Nuclear Policy* (Washington, D.C.: National Academy, 1997).

26. Canberra Commission, *Report,* p. 21.

27. National Academy of Sciences, *Future of U.S. Nuclear Policy,* p. 89.

28. Both P. Ramsey in *The Just War,* pp. 157–65, 211–58, and the Catholic Bishops in *The Challenge of Peace,* pp. 43–48, used noncombatant immunity as the central moral principle in addressing nuclear strategy.

29. Both *The Challenge of Peace* and John Paul II tied acceptance of deterrence to political steps to move beyond deterrence: *The Challenge of Peace,* p. 80; John Paul II, "Message to United Nations Special Session on Disarmament," published in *The United Nations Disarmament Yearbook,* vol. 3 (1978), Department of Political and Security Council Affairs (New York: United Nations Publications, 1979).

30. L. Freedman, "Nuclear Weapons: From Marginalization to Elimination," *Survival* 39 (1997): 187.

31. Ibid.

32. "Steep reductions in and the ultimate abolition of the arsenals of the nuclear 'haves' would promote rather than discourage nuclear proliferation" (Mandelbaum, "Lessons," 25).

33. "Attention has to be paid constantly to the political effects of particular disarmament measures; if they are misjudged, then the consequences could be dire" (Freedman, "Nuclear Weapons," p. 189).

34. Murray, *We Hold These Truths,* p. 256

35. A sampling of the intervention literature includes S. J. Stedman, "The New Interventionists," *Foreign Affairs* 72 (1993): 1–16; S. Hoffmann, "Out of the Cold: Humanitarian Intervention in the 1990s," *Harvard International Review* (fall, 1993): 8–9, 62; A. Roberts, "The Road to Hell: A Critique of Humanitarian Intervention," *Harvard International Review* (fall, 1993): 10–13, 63; L. W. Reed and C. Kaysen, eds., *Emerging Norms of Justified Intervention* (Cambridge, Mass.: American Academy of Arts and Sciences, 1993); J. B. Hehir, "Intervention from Theories to Cases," *Ethics and International Relations* 9 (1995): 1–13.

36. Boutros Boutros-Ghali, "Empowering the United Nations," *Foreign Affairs* 71 (1992–93): 98–99; B. Urquhart, "Sovereignty vs. Suffering," *New York Times,* Apr. 17, 1991.

37. For an elaboration of the moral and legal traditions, cf. "The Ethics of Intervention: Two Normative Traditions" in *Human Rights and U.S. Foreign Policy: Principles and Applications,* ed. P. G. Brown and D. MacLean (Lexington, Mass: D.C. Heath, 1979), pp. 121–34. I have drawn on this article and my own dissertation (see n. 8) in summarizing the transition from the medieval to the modern system of politics.

38. Cf. Hehir, "Intervention."

Chapter 2

Good, Smart, or Bad Samaritan

*A Case for U.S. Military Intervention
for Democracy and Human Rights*

Tony Smith

CURIOUS, IS IT NOT, that virtually no one writing in the United States today is making a general case for American military intervention for the sake of human rights and democratic government abroad? Of course, there are appeals for selective interventions based on warnings that unless the international community is ready to act with force—in Haiti, the former Yugoslavia, or Africa, for example—avoidable humanitarian disasters will occur. And, at least rhetorically, no one appears ready to accept genocide. However, by refusing to use that word, which would automatically have triggered intervention, the United States and France abandoned the Rwandan Tutsi in April, 1994. Yet, so far as I have been able to establish, no one in the academy (human rights activists aside) is so bold as to make a general case that the United States and other like-minded states should be far more aggressive in the promotion of human rights and democracy.

The fact is curious for the obvious reason that such appeals have been the basis of U.S. action abroad on repeated occasions since the Spanish-American War (itself prompted in good measure by stories of outrages perpetrated by the Spanish on the citizens of Cuba). Securing democratic governments for foreign peoples has always been understood to be more difficult than protecting human rights, yet since the time of Pres. Woodrow Wilson, Washington has repeatedly sounded the theme. Indeed, the democratization of Germany and Japan during the occupation period after World War II was arguably the greatest success in the history of American foreign policy—except for winning the Cold War, to which those occupations handily contributed. The question that begs to be answered is why America is so reluctant to make such appeals today, when U.S. power is greater than it has ever been in its history? To be sure, the intervention in Kosovo that began on March 24, 1999, might be seen to herald a wider scope for intervention in the future. But the costs and the difficulties of this operation were such that it may as plausibly be argued that only in select cases will military force be used for the sake of human rights and democracy abroad—and even then with great reservation.

Certainly for a time after the Cold War it seemed Washington would take up just such a crusade. President George Bush talked about a "new world order" that would protect democracy in the Philippines and promote it in Panama and especially Eastern Europe after the collapse of first the Soviet empire in 1989, then the Soviet Union itself in 1991. He then rallied allies to come to the defense of Kuwait. President Bill Clinton was even more explicit, agreeing during his first term with National Security Adviser Anthony Lake, Secretary of State Warren Christopher, and UN Ambassador Madeleine Albright that the "enlargement of democracy" would replace the "containment of communism" as America's foreign policy compass.

Despite these fine sounding words, the answer as to why so little was done about them is fairly easy to come by. America learned from its experience in Vietnam. Despite strenuous American efforts, Vietnam would be politically what its internal forces decided it should be. Talk of "democratizing" Kuwait, Iraq, and later the Palestinian movement was based on a shallow understanding indeed of the logic of the Arab world politically. The biggest blow to post–Cold War American opinion was struck by tiny Somalia, which lashed back fiercely when the United States attempted to sponsor a nation-building effort there. The U.S. experience in Somalia raised doubts as to whether or not America should proceed under the assumption that human rights and democratic government are easily fostered among peoples unfamiliar with Western values and ways.

In short, if foreign peoples—as in Eastern Europe—are ready to practice human rights as they are understood today in the West and prepared to work for democratic government, then the United States stands prepared to help. However, it cannot *force* a people to be free. This is a contradiction in terms. America cannot oblige a people to be other than their history and culture allows them to be, except at a cost to both parties that would be totally disproportionate to the end being pursued. Thus, America should not expect the peoples of Cambodia, Haiti, Bosnia, or most of Africa, for example, to be likely candidates for such development. Let us provide them humanitarian assistance if we can, and peacekeeping forces if they are requested in circumstances that persuade us our own people will not be killed. But let us not engage in will-o'-the-wisp dreams about "nation building" of a sort that will make these people over in our image.

Both the American public and American elites charged with executing U.S. foreign policy are essentially of this conviction. Since the days when Caspar Weinberger was secretary of defense under Pres. Ronald Reagan (and reasoning from the death of U.S. servicemen in Lebanon especially), the United States has adhered to a military doctrine that distinguishes among levels of importance foreign affairs have to this country. The conclusion was that the armed forces should not be engaged where there is no threat to a vital American national interest. Exceptions might be made in cases where armed resistance could be anticipated to be slight (as in Panama in 1989) or in extreme instances such as genocide, where the international community felt it had to act.

However, as the Bush and Clinton administrations have demonstrated, America's foreign policy executors are virtually immune to appeals to act with military force solely on the basis of human rights abuses or to promote democratic government abroad when there is no compelling U.S. interest at stake and when there is a real risk that Americans might be put in harm's way.

According to respected public opinion polls conducted in 1994 and again in 1999 by the Chicago Council on Foreign Relations, the use of force to promote human rights or democratic government for others ranked at or near the very bottom of foreign policy priorities.[1] Not surprisingly, these rationales did not figure prominently as motivation for involvement in Haiti or Bosnia. To be sure, both foreign policy elites and the population at large show themselves to be quite willing to act when there is a clear and present danger to U.S. interests. America is neither pacifist nor isolationist. But Americans high and low are much more likely to see a need for force when one state crosses the border of another with troops than in anything that has to do with a civil conflict. They are also willing to act for what they see as humanitarian purposes—as long as the loss of American life is not in the balance. But force for the sake of human rights and democracy abroad where local resistance can be expected (as is almost inevitably the case)? Very few subscribe to any such proposition, although the apparent success of NATO's military intervention in Kosovo under the leadership of the United States means the door has by no means been closed on such operations in regions of importance to Washington and where a loss of prestige might well follow a reluctance to act.

Their reason for this reluctance is straightforward. The empirical evidence is overwhelming when we look at the failure of U.S. efforts to try to promote such change. In Somalia, disaster struck as we moved from humanitarian assistance to ill-considered efforts to promote nation building. Look also at the popularity of demagogic racists in Serbia, Croatia, Bosnia, and Kosovo. Or consider Cambodia, where a coalition government disintegrated into bloody civil war. Or analyses of the prospects for democratic government in Haiti—damaged by none other than Jean Baptiste Aristide himself, once the paragon of reformist hopes. One success story appears to be Northern Ireland. Yet consider the ingredients of that success: thirty years of bloody conflict, and the intervention of a combination of powerful actors including the United States, the Republic of Ireland, and Great Britain (especially under Prime Minister Tony Blair), and yet despite all this, in the summer of 1999 it once again appeared that there were serious grounds for believing the peace accords signed on Good Friday, 1998, might fail under extremist pressures. In sum, common sense tells us that the gifts of human rights and democratic government such as we enjoy are not easily achieved, they are the product of long historical evolution and struggle, as our own story with African Americans so painfully reveals. How can we presume to do for others what they must do for themselves, as the democratic ethos itself mandates? Reality thus confirms what common sense as held at both an elite and popular level suspects: that America has better things to do with its blood and treasure than to try to turn sows' ears into silk purses.

What case can then be made that this thinking has jumped to too hasty conclusions that more consideration might revise? Although America most certainly cannot go charging everywhere around the world promoting human rights and democratic government with the use of its armed forces, there is nonetheless more it can do for these goals than is generally recognized today.

The Good Samaritan

A certain man went down from Jerusalem to Jericho, and fell among thieves, which stripped him of his raiment, and wounded him, and departed, leaving him half dead.

And by chance there came down a certain priest that way: and when he saw him, he passed by on the other side.

And likewise a Levite, when he was at the place, came and looked on him, and passed by on the other side.

But a certain Samaritan, as he journeyed, came where he was: and when he saw him, he had compassion on him,

And went to him and bound up his wounds, pouring in oil and wine, and he set him on his own beast, and brought him to an inn, and took care of him.

And on the morrow when he departed, he took out two pence, gave them to the host, and said unto him, Take care of him; and whatsoever thou spendest more, when I come again, I will repay thee. (Luke 10:30–35, *KJV*)

The moral seems clear: When we can do for others something that is valuable for them at relatively little cost to ourselves, then we have an obligation to do so. Accordingly, for example, we have laws that a person witnessing an accident has a legal responsibility to assist the victims, even though the witnesses themselves are in no way guilty of the harm that has occurred.

But there are real objections to using this parable as the basis for foreign policy objectives, for the parable assumes that the Samaritan is acting in a humanitarian way at slight expense to himself but with enormous benefit for another. Yet nation building is no such easy affair: it is long, costly, and unsure of success. The Samaritan presumably would not have been obligated to help the man if the cost to him would have been a trial of his character and a risk to his reputation in the event a difficult and protracted undertaking had gone less than perfectly.

These reservations accepted, there may nonetheless be cases where the effort to help others is warranted in the spirit of the biblical text. Consider the recent occupation of Haiti. None of the reservations of the "strict-constructionists" denying the relevance of the Good Samaritan example here clearly pertains. The human rights abuses and the destruction of democratic government by the military leaders who launched a coup in 1991 against the Aristide government were palpable. Aristide himself had been elected months earlier by nearly 70 percent of the Haitian people in a democratic vote. The weakness of Raoul Cedras's military tyranny was equally palpable: sheer sadism and opportunism dictated the recruitment of an armed force that was poorly armed and less numerous than the Boston police force (some six thousand men in all). Given the mood of the public, the Haitian forces under Cedras—fearing summary execution by citizens thirsting for revenge—had every incentive to surrender immediately to the Americans.

If ever there was a case of a Good Samaritan operation, this was it. The costs were minimal (not a single American was killed by hostile fire), and the benefits for a sorely oppressed people have been manifest. Only time will tell. By 1999 it appeared that, despite the period of grace bestowed by the American intervention, Haiti would fail to develop the kind of political institutions that would give its people a greater measure of justice and freedom. But the U.S. occupation cannot be faulted if ultimately that sad outcome prevails.

The Haitian case does not establish a blank check to endorse American interventions elsewhere. The same mathematics of means to ends may not function in Cambodia or Kosovo. Still, in historical terms, the costs of the Haiti operation were low and the benefits presumably high. Here at least is one instance when Good Samaritanism meant something in foreign affairs.

The Smart (Self-Interested) Samaritan

But suppose we "out" our Good Samaritan and demonstrate that his apparently honorable purposes had a self-interested motive. Suppose we find that he thought he recognized the victim as a rich man with a bachelor son, and had calculated, even if ever so dimly, that his penniless (but, of course, beautiful) daughter, might at long last find a husband as a suitable reward for an act of virtue.

Or suppose that our reputedly "Good" Samaritan had been thinking for some time of setting up a private police force. Suppose that when he saw the half-dead victim lying there that he saw intervention as a means of gaining publicity, of enhancing his reputation in a way that would serve not only his own interests but those of his town and kinfolk.

Cannot Haiti be seen in such a light? After the military coup there in September, 1991, the fortunes of democratic governments elsewhere in the hemisphere dimmed at least momentarily thanks to coup attempts in Peru, Guatemala, and Venezuela. If democracy in the western hemisphere serves American national interests—and there is a large and compelling body of literature that says it does—then to draw a line in the sand in Haiti serves notice to the entire hemisphere that America took seriously the regional shift toward democratic government that began in the late 1970s and continues today (as Mexico's July, 1997, elections demonstrate).[2]

Those who cannot find dead Americans to lament the occupation of Haiti will cite the bottom line: at least $1 billion a year in public expenditures. But this is well under one-half of 1 percent of our annual national defense budget! And look what that money is being spent on. It is trying to buy freedom for the Haitian people and hemispheric solidarity in support of a form of political evolution favorable to American interests. It is ensuring that basic human rights are served and gaining less-often noted advantages, such as keeping potential refugees who might otherwise wind up in the United States at home. Surely this criticism is misdirected.

Can an analogous argument apply to Bosnia? The risks there have been higher, no doubt about it, but so too are the stakes. Where Haiti has only a tenuous relationship to the rest of Latin America, Bosnia is a proxy for all the difficulties that can befall Eastern Europe and the Caucasus after the fall of the Soviet Union. A settlement there that is both peaceful and equitable would set a standard and serve as a model in a region of substantial importance to America's national interests. A similar argument can be made for the intervention in Kosovo. Here Washington demonstrated its leadership of NATO in a region of strategic importance to the Western world. If the Balkan Stability Pact outlined by President Clinton in July, 1999, should prove successful, then the Kosovo intervention may have positive implications for NATO and American claims to have a leadership role in Europe.

Could Bosnia and Kosovo turn out to be "splendid little wars"—as Theodore Roosevelt called the 1898 war with Spain—a chance to test ourselves and prove our international stature? There are good reasons to be skeptical. One should beware the temptation to imitate the Texas Rangers, who brought peace to a frontier where no governmental authority held sway. Yugoslavia was a nightmare for Adolf Hitler. Given the terrain and the passions, might it not be the same for Washington? Initially, the U.S. probably underestimated how little power was needed to bring about major changes in this arena. In the spring of 1995 Croatian forces showed how weak Serbian power actually was. It was only thereafter that NATO finally overcame the inhibitions that had sadly—criminally, in the eyes of many—saddled its resolve, and acted with a resolution that finally brought about the Dayton peace accords that November. Of course, American troops were still in place there four years later, and the Bosnia precedent was used as an argument for the 1999 NATO air campaign against Serbia when Slobodan Milošević began "ethnic cleansing" in Kosovo. Still, on balance, the policy of intervention could be deemed a success.

It is difficult in these circumstances not to see America's role in the world to some extent as a function of its own will. If and when the United States is portrayed as being indecisive, then its writ will correspondingly wither. The pusillanimous trip of Secretary of State Warren Christopher in May, 1993, when rather than rallying European support he "consulted" with the various allied capitals on measures to take with respect to Bosnia, sounded the tocsin: America would not lead. Then came the equally pusillanimous mishandling of the situation in Somalia that fall, followed only days later by the craven pullback of a military occupation force (with orders to be peacekeepers and trainers, not fighters) in Haiti. George Bush at least had offered the plausible explanation that he was waiting for the Europeans to act with respect to the former Yugoslavia as they claimed they would, while making it clear that for the moment he was not concerning himself with Haiti. What the Clinton administration demonstrated by contrast was its trademark: an indecisiveness that cost the lives of tens of thousands in Haiti and Bosnia who naively believed that the cavalry was coming when Clinton announced a resolve to act (a decision typically to be reversed shortly thereafter).

Historians may shake their heads in disbelief. The United States, at the apex of its power after the collapse of the Soviet Union and at the beginning of a new administration, when the tide is running in, hesitated in the unsure hands of the Clinton administration. Events in Somalia, mismanaged by the United States itself in an utterly insignificant place for American interests, went on to determine the course of American policy in what has traditionally been the most important sphere of U.S. foreign policy: Europe.

Years later, the question remained to haunt Washington: was Radovan Karadzic the virtual reincarnation of Mohammed Farah Aidid? If America acted to enforce the Dayton peace accords in a way commensurate with the expansion of human rights and democratic government in this region and prosecuted indicted war criminals, would the equivalent of eighteen Americans be killed, and one dragged through the streets naked and reviled? How would America respond? Would it allow itself to be humiliated? Or would it act with purpose and resolve to redeem the loss of its martyred heroes by redoubling its commitment to a Western understanding of human rights and democracy in a part of the world where it is reasonable to make such a stand?

One need not argue that America should anywhere or everywhere champion human rights and democratic government. There are, however, some instances where it makes sense. In Cambodia, Sri Lanka, much of Africa, Tibet, the Caucasus, and Afghanistan, for example, America simply lacks the ability and the interest to commit the blood and treasure needed to bring about change—assuming it could be achieved at all. By contrast, Haiti, Bosnia, and Kosovo are of some importance to the West strategically, politically, and morally, and they are susceptible to the exercise of U.S. power in ways that appear to be lacking in other areas farther away geographically (and more distant politically, culturally, and in terms of historical ties as well).

It is sometimes remarked that a conventional problem with democracies is that they lack a sense of identity and purpose unless they are under attack. After the collapse of the Soviet Union, it is a fair question to ask of the United States. In terms of establishing a collective identity—not just for America but for the democratic world in general—the support of human rights and democratic governments in those parts of the world where such an ambition is realistic makes sense from both a moral and practical standpoint.

Such a position does not mean a worldwide crusade. Where U.S. power is limited and cultures quite foreign, any such efforts are likely to be quixotic.

But such ambitions do make sense in Haiti, in Bosnia, in Kosovo, in Guatemala—anywhere a combination of U.S. influence and indigenous internal development creates real possibilities for change. In the process, the West stands to gain as well for we all may come to have a sense of who we are not so much by what we oppose (as during the Cold War) but by what we support.

The Guilty Samaritan

There is yet another category of cases that the United States should consider in terms of its responsibility to support human rights and democratic government, even though the road may often be hard: peoples it has damaged in the past and to whom it owes reparations. Guatemala is a case in point.

Americans do not have a difficult time understanding reparations made by others for the crimes they have committed. We build a Holocaust museum to commemorate the Nazi murder of the Jews. We lament the Japanese failure to follow the German example and purge themselves of their past crimes against humanity. However, like other peoples, we are more aware of the crimes of others than those we commit ourselves. Small surprise, then, that we wait until 1996 to recognize Vietnam—claiming that *they* were the offending party because they did not account for all our MIAs—while there is not yet a museum on the Washington Mall for Native or African Americans.

If, after Vietnam, Guatemala is the most extreme example of our self-interested destruction of other peoples to secure our own interests in the Cold War (a point established by the nine volume report published in February, 1999, by the independent Historical Clarification Commission), it is not isolated. In Africa we changed the internal balance of power in Zaire, Liberia, Somalia, and Angola—all of which are suffering terrible civil conflicts today that at least in part have to be linked to these earlier interventions. And elsewhere in Central America besides Guatemala we were intimately involved in the political evolution of El Salvador and Nicaragua (and to a lesser extent Honduras). But like those who dump toxic waste in the United States itself, we walk away from the human disasters we created, citing either the requirements of political expedience or local venality for what has occurred, with little effort to contribute to the healing. Is the "malign neglect" we have shown toward these countries not morally reprehensible, whatever the concordance between the thinking of the foreign policy elite and the general public as reported above? What possible excuse can a great power without rivals offer for its failure to make amends for past harm to others?

Of course, we cannot right every wrong we have helped commit. The turmoil in Africa and Afghanistan seems to me to be only partially related to the events of the Cold War. In any event they are on a scale that we can do little to master—although the idea Secretaries of State Christopher and Albright advanced of an African peacekeeping force equipped and logistically supported by the United States is worth pursuing. So too the tragedy besetting Cambodia, related as it is to the events surrounding the Vietnam War a generation ago, has apparently now proven itself intractable despite sustained outside intervention. Surely even those who back American support for human rights and democratic government abroad have to realize that there are limits to either U.S. influence or culpability once a good faith effort is made.

But Central America is different. Both our influence and the damage we inflicted are manifest there. Not to be a part of the process of bringing our own understanding of human rights and democratic government to this region—difficult though it may be—is to be guilty of a moral failure that no amount of elite reasoning or public opinion polling can convince me is acceptable. We expect, as we should, German reparations to Israel (and we see today the hypocrisy of the Swiss, as earlier the Austrians). We await, as we should, Japan's recognition of the wrongs it inflicted on Korea and China. But what of ourselves? In Guatemala especially, but also in El Salvador, Nicaragua, and Honduras, the United States is engaged not as a Good, but as a Guilty, Samaritan. "A man fell among thieves"—and they were us.

In such circumstances, it is not a matter of cost and benefit, but a matter of justice and honor that a wrong be righted. In September, 1997, for example, the United States gave $1 million to a Truth Commission in Guatemala. However, it was a group that lacked power to compel testimony, had no ability to plea bargain, worked under a prohibition on naming names (although groups could be identified), and had scarcely a year to complete its work.

Is anyone surprised when we do much less than we might? In 1996, Richard Nuccio, the State Department official who was lied to by the Central Intelligence Agency (CIA) about its connection with assassinations in Guatemala reported the truth, lost his security clearance and was forced out of government with no protest from the president. Today, have we no greater obligation to human rights and democratic government in Guatemala than the paltry contribution of $1 million after repeated abuses of CIA power there not only a generation ago but consistently since have been disclosed? Why was there no outcry from Washington when Jose Serrano, the Guatemalan president who led a 1993 coup attempt against the constitutional order that elected him, moved on to Panama? Today he lives a privileged life not only immune from prosecution for his crimes in his native land but safe with the millions of dollars he looted from the public treasury before leaving.

When next we congratulate ourselves on our progressive role in world affairs and compare ourselves favorably with others who have forgotten the crimes they have committed, let us not forget Guatemala.

Conclusion

Reading the documents that purport to lay out what U.S. military intervention policy should be—particularly in a case where national interests are not vital—we see that any such action should: (1) occur where American interests are real, (2) come as a last resort, (3) be massive, and (4) have an exit strategy.[3]

But from a human rights/democratic government perspective, such a set of recommendations is largely faulty. *First, the definition of what an interest is needs reconsideration.* If we derive purpose and identity from realistic and at times imperative moral pursuits, then it is the job of our leaders to articulate a vision of the United States commensurate with the undertaking. It can only be regretted that, true to form, once the Clinton administration found through its pilot polling that Americans did not endorse support for human rights and democratic government abroad, it downplayed the slogan that hitherto was to be this presidency's hallmark in world affairs. In short, leaders define interests, and if democracy promotion is not as obvious a national concern as economic growth or strategic invulnerability, it nonetheless is worthy of the nation's attention.

Second, intervention—if it is feasible at all, and it may not be—should come early, not late, before blood is spilled and the situation becomes badly polarized politically. This observation directly contradicts today's military doctrine (backed by public opinion), which has the disadvantage of waiting so long before using force that large amounts of it are required and the political operations needed to bring about peace are even more difficult to establish. Even worse, of course, was the policy of the Clinton administration, which promised intervention in Haiti and Bosnia and then changed its mind, leading to the deaths of thousands of people who naively believed that the American cavalry would any minute be coming around the hill. Only in the Kosovo intervention did the Clinton administration act with relative dispatch, winning with an air war that many critics thought could only succeed with a massive land invasion.

Third, military intervention should indeed be "massive" in order to demonstrate resolve, a critical element in local political thinking. There is widespread agreement on this point. The kind of tentative, half-hearted peacekeeping mission that occurred originally in Bosnia received from the Serbs a lesson not to be forgotten.

Fourth, regrettable though it may be, a clear exit strategy is not always possible, and to wait for one to materialize before acting is most usually not to act at all.

"Mission creep" that leads from military intervention for humanitarian purposes to nation building is an ineluctable process that should be recognized as having a dynamic difficult to avoid and that must therefore be anticipated and dealt with. In the cases I have indicated are proper for action, the presumption is that Western power is extensive in a variety of ways—not only militarily—and that important local forces welcome Western intervention. Latin America and Eastern Europe—where conditions are relatively favorable—should thus not be confused with Africa, the Middle East, the Caucasus, and Asia—where they are generally far less positive.

What is called is for leadership that will do two things. First, it needs to articulate America's responsibility to promote human rights and democratic governance in those areas where the West has influence and local forces would respond positively to such initiatives. Such an undertaking should involve informing the American public on why such developments are in the national interest—and not left to be interpreted as being simply "humanitarian," as if this country had nothing directly to gain from the process. From the standpoint of stability, prosperity, and international security cooperation, the democratic evolution of Latin America and Eastern Europe matters—difficult as making the case may be. Accordingly, a concern for human rights and democratic government need not mean a global commitment, but it does mean a reasoned analysis—which inevitably involves some speculation—of where U.S. power can make a difference.

Second, in many circumstances, a commitment to promote human rights and democratic government means a commitment to multilateralism. In cases like Zaire or the Congo or Africa in general, America cannot and should not undertake unilateral initiatives. If Africans themselves—in the Organization of African Unity or the UN—cannot agree on action, then unilateral U.S. action alone is almost surely uncalled for. However, one should note Washington's efforts to short-circuit UN action. An excellent example is the April, 1994, decision to avoid calling the Rwandan situation "genocide" so as not to trigger an automatic intervention. In contrast, the Clinton administration's talk about equipping and deploying an all-African peacekeeping force is a promising idea. Elsewhere, NATO or an Organization of American States (OAS) more forcibly committed to democratic government (that is, possessed of an agreement that multinational intervention forces may be called on) is a more appropriate venue for these ambitions than unilateral action by the United States.

The point should be not only to rectify wrongs in foreign lands but also to create a constituency in both the United States and the democratic world in general that upholds certain practices in regions where such expectations are culturally appropriate and where Western power (including Japanese and Australian) is real. If there is a "democratic peace," then it must be enforced by military means. This may not be possible everywhere, but it is desirable wherever history, culture, and power make such an undertaking a reasonable and worthwhile undertaking. Such a policy is ultimately defensible not only in moral but also practical, self-interested terms.

It is curious indeed that—at the height of America's power, and faced with clear evidence of the positive impact the promotion of human rights and democracy can have on American national interests—both leaders and the public are so reticent.

Notes

1. John Reilly, ed., *American Public Opinion and U.S. Foreign Policy* (Chicago: Chicago Council on Foreign Relations, 1994 and 1999).
2. Literature arguing the existence of a "democratic peace" may be found in articles by Michael Doyle, John Owen, and Bruce Russett in *Debating the Democratic Peace,* ed. Michael E. Brown, Sean M. Lynn-Jones, and Steven E. Miller (Cambridge, Mass.: MIT Press, 1996).
3. Ivo Daalder, "The United States and Military Intervention in Internal Conflict," in *The International Dimension of Internal Conflict,* ed. Michael E. Brown (Cambridge, Mass.: MIT Press, 1996).

Chapter 3

A Basis for Peace in the Twenty-first Century

Bruce Russett

HENRY LUCE, founder of the *Time, Life,* and *Fortune* publishing empire, characterized the twentieth century as "The American Century." And so it seemed to be, at least after 1941. In the midst of the Cold War struggles, Americans often underestimated the degree to which the United States and its allies dominated international relations during that era. However, the collapse of the Soviet Union made it clear how great that dominance really was. The Soviet Union, which appeared to be a powerful challenger, was outrun in every major dimension of the race. Militarily, it could not match American technology. Soviet weapons were rarely equal to their American counterparts. Economically, it began from too small a productive base, and was unable to keep up in the arms race or match the growth rates of dynamic western economies. For a while it could do some catching up (post–World War II reconstruction, copying western technology, productivity increases from moving rural labor to the cities where they would be more effectively employed), but ultimately the perverse incentive structure of state socialism did it in. Growth rates in the East fell precipitously, and the environmental and human costs of forced industrialization, lacking the constraints of markets and a free flow of information, caught up with it. Ideologically, it lost its legitimacy as citizens of the eastern countries became able to compare their living standards and political fetters with the condition of their western neighbors. In retrospect, it seems obvious that the Soviet Union was destined to lose the struggle; the only thing that could have prevented the American triumph was a nuclear war, which we avoided—with more good luck than we may like to acknowledge.

American hegemony manifested itself in a reduction of international conflict even before the Cold War ended. The years from 1950 to 1980 consistently experienced about nine wars (conflicts resulting in at least a thousand battle deaths) per decade. During the 1980s this rate dropped to four international wars for that entire decade, despite the approximate doubling of the number of states in the international system. Since the demise of the eastern alliance in 1990, we have had but four more international wars. Even civil war—that seeming bane of post–Cold War flux—has not been as common as many would believe. Despite steady growth in the number of countries since the end of World War II, the proportion of states experiencing civil wars in each decade has stayed within a range of 12 to 19 percent and has declined sharply since 1992.[1] While some civil wars arose as a result of the collapse of previously Soviet-supported regimes, many of the conflicts sustained by the chief Cold War adversaries fizzled out after the patrons lost interest or capability. Northern Ireland is the only established democracy to still experience serious civil violence.

I do not mean that war is a phenomenon of the past, or that an era of "perpetual peace" is dawning. There remain so-called rogue states that sponsor terrorists who can make life hazardous for their targets. What I do mean is that the post–Cold War era so far has certainly not been more violent, and probably less so, than the era which preceded it. At the least, the prospect of any war between two great powers in the next couple of decades or so is miniscule. How many other times during past centuries could one have said that? And why can one say it now?

Peace from Hegemony?

One very big reason for this development is, of course, that while the international system may contain several states which can reasonably be characterized as great powers, there is only one really great power: the hegemonic United States. The collapse of the Soviet Union has starkly exposed the absence of any effective current challenger to U.S. dominance. The United States maintains by far the largest and most effective military establishment in the world. Indeed, America spends more for its defense than all the rest of NATO, as well as all the states in the world that are not bound to it by ties of military alliance.[2] At present, no state or combination of states is remotely able to endanger America's existence or sovereignty. The United States may not be able or willing to enforce a condition of peace everywhere in the world. But it can certainly crush anyone who tries to mount a direct challenge to its own security. Memories of the Gulf War live. In that sense, Pax Americana is a reality. It has no precedent since the Pax Romana.

The United States dominates in other ways as well. Its ideological principles of democracy and free enterprise govern much of the global polity and economy. Those—whether Asian authoritarians, religious fundamentalists, or western post-modernists—who reject one or both of those great organizing principles do so in tone more of defensiveness than of confidence. The United States retains great potentially coercive economic leverage. The North American Free Trade Area contains the world's largest market, bigger even than the European Union. Other states must export to that market. America has enormous power to influence trade practices, combat financial and copyright offenses, and compel observance of environmental and safety conditions when it so wishes. The Japanese and German challenges to American productivity and efficiency, so prominent a decade ago, no longer seem very threatening. American economic dominance is not likely to pass away very soon.

The United States does not and will not always get its way. Who does, anywhere? Thanks to self-imposed fiscal restraints the U.S. government is hampered in mobilizing the enormous wealth of its economy for state purposes, especially in peacetime. Its people are understandably reluctant to carry the burdens of policing the world or waging sustained or costly wars. But when it chooses to wave its arms, the United States is a big and compelling gorilla, and will remain so for a long time.

The China Problem

There is, however, a longer-term threat to American global dominance. China has no history of global power ambition, nor do I believe that its present government's intentions are fundamentally more than defensive, to secure a territorial integrity that includes but does not exceed historic Chinese regional claims. Yet whatever its intentions, now or prospectively, China does have the economic and military potential to become a world power at some point in the twenty-first century. Suppose that all of NATO, including the three new candidates, were to continue to grow economically at the rate of 2 percent a year—roughly the experience of the past decade or so. Suppose too that the Chinese economy were to continue to grow at the rate of 8 percent a year— slightly less than it has in the recent past. Using a purchasing power parity measure of gross national product (GNP), China's economy would reach the same size as that of an expanded NATO—and be far bigger than that of the United States alone—around the year 2030.

From the perspective of maintaining American predominance, this growth scenario is not quite as threatening as it may first seem. It depends on a combination of pretty strong assumptions. It requires that China remain politically united and stable—whatever its particular form of government. It also assumes that Chinese industrialization and intensive agriculture do not produce a massive environmental disaster, and that China's growth is not slowed as it loses the great advantage in simply trying to catch up with much western technology. It uses a somewhat controversial and perhaps exaggerated measure of Chinese GNP (rather than exchange rate value). It also represents total GNP rather than per capita wealth, a category in which China would still be not much more than halfway to the average level of the NATO countries. Despite these important caveats, however, great economic capacity, combined with a huge population, could give China more potential leverage in world politics than the Soviet Union possessed at the height of the Cold War.

The unavoidable point is that as China approaches power parity with the West, it will bring a period of risk and instability to the international system. Eras of "power transition," as a potential challenger catches up to and ultimately surpasses the power base of the previously dominant state, carry the threat of cataclysmic war between the great powers.[3] Germany's ambitions earlier in this century illustrate but by no means exhaust the list of challenges. Moreover, danger exists even when the challenger does not espouse a particularly aggressive or expansionist ideology. The uncertainties and potential miscalculations of each other's intentions and capabilities provide dangers enough.

Three strategies offer ways of preventing war from arising out of a power transition. One is simply to try to deter the challenger from adventurism. Deterrence can work, at least for a while. But a purely deterrent strategy, emphasizing counterthreat and military containment, can intensify conflicts and increase the challenger's commitment eventually to achieve its own dominance. Deterrence cannot be relied on indefinitely, and so long as it is practiced can become a self-defeating strategy.

A second strategy—in some respects a variant of the first—is to postpone the power transition as long as possible, allowing alternative means to manage relations to develop and become effective. Here is where we need to be attentive to the size and composition of the American-led coalition, and of any opposing coalition. The greatest potential "loose cannon" in the early twenty-first century is Russia. At the moment, Russia is—politically, demographically, economically, and militarily—but a shadow of the great power represented by the former Soviet Union. It cannot mount an effective challenge to NATO, or even to its neighbors. But it is unlikely to remain so weak forever. It has great natural resources, an educated population, and a military-industrial base of a size and technological sophistication greater than all of Eastern Europe, or even China. Russia is currently selling advanced technology ships, aircraft, and electronics to China. Despite their historical antagonism, an alliance with Russia could offer China real advantages in the form of additional material resources and reassurance on the status of a long and vulnerable border. A new Russian-Chinese alliance, reestablishing what Richard Nixon and Henry Kissinger helped to dismantle, would hasten the power transition period significantly. Russian and Chinese leaders have flirted publicly with each other on this issue, most recently in the April, 1997, discussions and communiqué between Presidents Boris Yeltsin and Jiang Zemin. It is not a near-term danger, but it lurks.

The current policy of limited NATO expansion magnifies the danger. Bringing in the three new Eastern European members surely had its attractions. However, it added little to NATO's basic strength (less than 3 percent to its current GNP) and geographical liabilities at least as great as assets. The strongest argument against it was that it risked creating a condition that does not presently exist: a more authoritarian, militaristic, nationalistic, and paranoid Russia. Such a Russia would not have to remain isolated; it would likely see strong advantages in looking eastward to an alliance with China. A clear-sighted and farseeing western policy must therefore address and prevent that dangerous outcome.

If NATO expansion is still considered to be a pretty good idea (and I have serious doubts about this), a much better idea is to think very seriously about an even bigger NATO expansion. That kind of NATO expansion would include Russia—integrally, not just in some sort of NATO-Russia joint council—and tie a democratic, market-oriented, and maybe prosperous Russia to the West. The current status of Russian democracy and free markets is not as favorable as those of the countries recently admitted to NATO, but surely it is a match for that of Romania, another candidate. Admitting Russia to NATO would encourage and strengthen them. Moreover, admission to the NATO structure, with its internal transparency and integrated command, is the best way to control the Russian military and its threats both to peace and to Russian democracy. NATO guarantees its members' territorial integrity against threats by other members of the alliance as well as outsiders. Russia should be brought into NATO for the same reasons West Germany was in 1955: to encourage the right behavior and prevent it from pursuing an independent hostile foreign policy. It should be admitted not because we entirely trust it, but partly because we don't.[4] Admitting Russia is the best way to insure its behavior as a cooperative, peaceful member of the international system.

A defensively oriented NATO that included Russia need not be an anti-China alliance, nor be perceived as one. The Soviet Union saw substantial advantages in West Germany's secure bond to the West, and Mikhail Gorbachev accepted the continued presence of a united Germany in NATO. Adding Russia would bring resources to the western alliance while at the same time denying those resources to any nascent counteralliance. However, it need not pose an offensive threat to China, whose ample supply of nuclear weapons and the size of its population and territory secure it against attack. If NATO's admissions criteria require a serious commitment to democracy and free markets—but not necessarily the full achievement of those goals on admission—China and many other states can in time reasonably aspire to membership. Russia in NATO, in the next round of expansion, would both postpone the day of the Chinese power transition and provide a model for future relations with China.

The third strategy for managing a power transition is to strengthen shared values and interests with the dominant state or alliance so that the potential challenger lacks incentive to go to war or engage in aggressive behavior. It contrasts with pure deterrence by providing a strong set of positive incentives to maintain peaceful and cooperative international relations. Peaceful power transitions have occurred under these circumstances. The best example is Britain and America roughly a century ago. The British saw the rise of American power but did not feel seriously threatened by it. In turn, the United States did not question the basic organizing principles of international relations at the time, and shared many common economic, political, and security interests with Britain. Deterrence remained in the background for a while, but both sides knew they had powerful incentives to settle their differences peacefully. And they did.

Elements of a Structure for Peace

A model for a peaceful shift of relative power in the future international system model would take its cue from the international system that largely prevailed within the western alliance and economic system during the Cold War. That system depended much less on American hegemony to keep the peace within it than on the demonstrated ability of democracy, economic interdependence, and networks of international organization to manage and reduce violent conflicts among nations. I have already developed this perspective, presented evidence for it, and addressed challenges in a range of writings, so I will not try to justify it in detail here. Let me say simply that some elements of this are solidly established.

First, and most certainly, no two stable democracies have fought each other in full-scale war in this century. Sometimes they have fought limited engagements or come close to war, but even serious military disputes at a level of violence or threat of violence far short of war are very rare, proportionately much less likely than between two dictatorships or a democracy and a dictatorship. The more democratic each state is, the less the likelihood of violence between them. When the governments of long-term military rivals change from dictatorships to democracies—as happened in the last two decades in Argentina, Brazil, and Chile—their hostile relations typically improve dramatically. Furthermore, democracies are peaceful toward each other even when one allows for the known conflict-reducing effects of other influences such as wealth, distance, deterrent power, or ties of military alliance. The situation is short of an absolute law—"democracies never fight each other"—but it is as strong a probabilistic generalization as one can make about international relations. It is not limited only to the established democracies of Europe and European settlement.[5] Democracies also are much less likely than autocracies or transitional regimes to experience civil war.

Second, in addition to the effect of democracy, the more economically interdependent states are, the less likely they are to fight each other. Peaceful trade gives them a strong and continuing stake in maintaining positive political relations and offers lines of communications to help resolve potential problems. The evidence has been less well analyzed than that for the generalization about democracies, but it is pretty clear. Trade wars are not hot wars. Military conflicts between mutually interdependent states are very rare. Not only does a high current level of trade prevent conflict, a trend toward ever-higher levels of trade has similar effects.[6] There are some exceptions, however. For example, many observers regard several of the participants in World War I as exceptions. But even in that instance, none of the other pacifying elements—such as mutual democracy, or international organization ties—operated, and several known aggravating risk factors, such as closely balanced power, geographic contiguity, and opposing alliance systems made the situation much more dangerous. In that case the pacifying effect of trade was overwhelmed.

The third element of a structure of peaceful relations is international organizations. International organizations—for example, the United Nations and its family of agencies—are often derided for their ineffectiveness. Though international organizations cannot by themselves create peace, much of the derision is unjust and ill informed. The vision of an ultimately peaceful relationship between the great powers of Western Europe, made real by the founders of the European Union, was built precisely on ensuring democracy, creating binding ties of trade and investment, and enmeshing both of those in a solid institutional structure of pan-European organizations.

International organizations can offer means of mediation and arbitration, provide institutions to convey information and coordinate action, expand members' perspective on their own self-interest to be more inclusive, and create and strengthen norms of peaceful behavior. Sometimes they can coerce lawbreakers, as did the UN-approved coalition that defeated Iraq. Although not all international organizations work effectively, many do over a wide range of functions and purposes.

Individually, the pacifying effects of mutual democracy, economic interdependence, and international organizations can sometimes fail. But as a coherent and mutually reinforcing system of relationships, they are very powerful. In the post–World War II era, for example, one can look at the frequency of militarized disputes between "average" pairs of states with levels of democracy that were only average by comparison with the entire world, average levels of interdependence, and average ties of shared international organization membership. One can then compare those states' behavior with that of pairs of states that were fully democratic and had relatively high levels of interdependence and organizational ties. The latter group of states had 70 percent fewer militarized disputes—and zero wars. They were almost 85 percent less likely to have disputes than were pairs of states with one at the democratic extreme and the other at the dictatorial end ("cats and dogs") and average on economic and organizational ties.[7]

A number of authors, myself included, have characterized this three-legged structure for peace as Kantian in recognition of Immanuel Kant's vision two hundred years ago as the basis for "perpetual peace." Kant's image of perpetuity sounds naive and utopian to tough-minded analysts of this past century's horrors. There are likely always to be rogue states and leaders who will seek to overturn the status quo by aggression. Not in any of our lifetimes will all states be bound together by deep and enduring ties of democracy, economic interdependence, and strong international institutions. Yet in the 1990s more than half of the countries in the world have been governed more or less democratically—for the first time in history. Much depends on strengthening real democracy, with popular controls over the executive and respect for minority rights. The networks of economic interdependence and international organization are more inclusive than ever. Much of the globe can be enmeshed in a stable zone of peace by widening and strengthening these ties.

Multilateralism and the Legitimacy of Hegemony

Military deterrence will remain an essential tool for preventing and, when necessary, rebuffing some aggressive challenges. However, it cannot be the exclusive tool—nor in most situations even the primary one. A properly expanded

NATO that includes Russia can maintain a favorable military-economic imbalance for the West for decades to come. That imbalance need not threaten China's legitimate interests or security, nor need China ever become an active threat to the West. It is much too premature to consider a policy of "containing" China, but it is not too premature to plan for a wider structure of peaceful international relations that would ultimately include a more democratic China. China's dependence on foreign trade and investment, as well as its increasing willingness to accept and participate in multilateral international organizations that undergird peaceful relations, have already put that country on a path of cooperative relationships that will be strongly resistant to reversal.

Multilateralism—the cooperative exercise of power with states sharing similar though not identical goals—is key to the future of American foreign policy. As any careful student of hegemony knows, the exercise of hegemonic power depends not solely on raw physical power, but also on shared beliefs and perceptions about legitimate action. The less the disparity in physical power between the hegemonic state and other actors, and the weaker the formal institutional structure governing the exercise of power, the more dependent is the hegemonic state on the observation and articulation of accepted principles of legitimacy. Contemporary international relations are characterized by such hegemony. It is a system of states in a hierarchy of power with the United States at the pinnacle, the absence of a formal system of rule substantially limiting states' sovereignty, yet with normative principles (however amorphous) that both encourage and legitimize hegemonic action in the international interest. These principles and their binding power remain unsettled. Nevertheless, they are continually brought to bear, whether as applied to particular interventions (e.g., Iraq, Somalia, Haiti, Bosnia, and Kosovo) or to debates on the proper composition and procedures of the UN Security Council. Hegemony provides opportunity for the hegemonic state, but also feeds fears that it will become an oppressor. It thus requires the hegemonic state to be constrained by perceptions of what actions are legitimate.

Some Americans might like to have it otherwise. Isolationists might prefer not to exercise hegemonic power at all—but they are not always ready to live with the consequences of inaction. Unilateralists are prepared to exercise military power in pursuit of vital national interests without great concern for the niceties of international consent. This strain is evident in those in Congress who would expand the military budget while simultaneously cutting support for international institutions. But a country with only 4 percent of the world's population and only a shrinking fifth of the world's wealth cannot indefinitely rule by unilateral military action. Lacking the power to impose a Pax Romana by dint of total military superiority, its reach will exceed its grasp. It will need not just the approval, but the active support of its allies. President Bush knew this when he set about creating the UN-sanctified coalition that repelled Iraq's aggression.

The international institutions that can provide this approval and support need to be enhanced, not gutted. Other countries must be able to see those institutions as serving their interests as well as those of the United States. American claims of interest have to be bolstered by credible claims to legitimacy. Multilateralists, while fully recognizing and acting on their own interests, understand the necessity for acting within some generally acceptable normative framework. If a Pax Americana is to survive the twentieth century, it cannot be based solely on American power and narrow self-interest.

Notes

1. Frank Wayman, J. David Singer, and Meredith Sarkees, "Inter-State, Intra-State, and Extra-Systemic Wars, 1816–1995" (paper presented to the annual meeting of the International Studies Association, San Diego, Calif., Apr., 1996), updated from Peter Wallensteen and Margareta Sollenberg, "Armed Conflict and Regional Conflict Complexes, 1989–97," *Journal of Peace Research* 35, no. 5 (Sept., 1998): 621–34.
2. U.S. Arms Control and Disarmament Agency, *World Military Expenditures and Arms Transfers, 1996* (Washington, D.C.: GPO, 1997).
3. Jacek Kugler and Douglas Lemke, eds., *Parity and Power: Evaluations and Extensions of "The War Ledger"* (Ann Arbor: University of Michigan Press, 1996).
4. I present the argument for Russia in NATO here in only the most schematic and summary form. For a much deeper discussion of the pros and cons see Bruce Russett and Allan Stam, "Courting Disaster: An Expanded NATO vs. Russia and China," *Political Science Quarterly* 113, no. 3 (fall, 1998): 361–82.
5. Evidence for these statements can be found in books and articles by literally hundreds of scholars. There also exist challenges, as to any scientific generalization, but most observers judge the weight of the evidence to lie with the affirmative side. My own contributions include *Grasping the Democratic Peace: Principles for a Post–Cold War World* (Princeton, N.J.: Princeton University Press, 1993), "Counterfactuals about War and Its Absence," in *Counterfactual Thought Experiments in World Politics,* ed. Philip Tetlock and Aaron Belkin (Princeton, N.J.: Princeton University Press, 1996), and with Harvey Starr, "From Democratic Peace to Kantian Peace: Democracy and Conflict in the International System," in *Handbook of War Studies,* ed. Manus Midlarsky, 2d ed. (Ann Arbor: University of Michigan Press, 2000).
6. This is the clear conclusion of John R. Oneal and Bruce Russett, "The Classical Liberals Were Right: Democracy, Interdependence, and Conflict," *International Studies Quarterly* 40, no. 2 (June, 1997): 267–93; John R. Oneal and Bruce Russett, "The Kantian Peace: The Pacific Benefits of Democracy, Interdependence, and International Organizations, 1885–1992," *World Politics* 52, no. 1 (Oct., 1999).
7. Bruce Russett, John R. Oneal, and David Davis, "The Third Leg of the Kantian

Triangle for Peace: International Organizations and Militarized Disputes, 1950–1985," *International Organization* 52, no. 3 (summer, 1998): 441–67; Bruce Russett, "A Neo-Kantian Perspective: Democracy, Interdependence, and International Organizations in Building Security Communities," in *Security Communities in Historical Perspective,* ed. Emanuel Adler and Michael Barnett (Cambridge: Cambridge University Press, 1998).

Part II

Force and Diplomacy

Chapter 4

The Role of Force in Diplomacy

A Continuing Dilemma for U.S. Foreign Policy

Alexander L. George

> *... when the stakes warrant, where and when force can be effective, where no other policies are likely to be effective, where its application can be limited in scope and time, and where the potential benefits justify the potential costs and sacrifice.*
>
> *There can be no single or simple set of fixed rules for using force . . . . Each and every case is unique.*
>
> —Pres. George Bush, Remarks at the
> United States Military Academy, January 5, 1993

THE PROPOSITION THAT FORCE or threats of force are at times a necessary instrument of diplomacy and have a role to play in foreign policy is part of the conventional wisdom of statecraft. It is also true that both history and recent experience support the view that efforts to deal with interstate conflicts of interest *solely* by means of peaceful diplomacy do not always succeed and may result in substantial damage to one's national interests. On the other hand, one finds in history many cases in which threats of force or the actual use of force were ineffective or seriously aggravated disputes between states.

Given that history supports the necessity of resorting to force or threats of force on occasion and emphasizes the risks of doing so, we are left with a central question: Under what conditions and how can military force or threats of force be used effectively to accomplish different foreign policy objectives at an acceptable level of cost and risk?

Efforts to address this question have sharply divided American strategic thinkers during and ever since the Korean War. As our post–Cold War experiences and frustrations amply demonstrate, this question continues to pose acute dilemmas. Although the geopolitical and strategic context has changed dramatically, the question remains as to what role force or threats of force can be expected to play in a variety of novel settings.

This issue is of central importance in judging whether useful guidelines for the use of force can be formulated and agreed upon. However, consideration of this issue alone does not suffice. We must also consider the efficacy of resorting to threats of force to back up efforts to deter or coerce opponents. Such threats, if effective, would make it unnecessary to resort to the military option. It therefore is important to understand the special conditions under which threatening the use of force is likely to be effective and the reasons why such threats are often *not* a viable tool of diplomacy.

Competing Strategic Lessons of the Korean War

Efforts to address this question have sharply divided American strategic thinkers during and since the Korean War.[1] Recall General of the Army Douglas MacArthur's argument during the war and afterward that "there is no substitute for victory" and that the U.S. military should not be forced to fight with one arm tied behind its back. After the war, many military and civilian strategists argued that the United States should never again fight a similar limited, inconclusive war. Either it should stay out of such conflicts altogether, or, if it intervened, it should use whatever military force might be required to win a decisive military victory. Those who subscribed to this lesson of the Korean War quickly came to be known as the "Never-Again School." The strategic doctrine they advocated regarding American military intervention was appropriately labeled "all or nothing."

Other foreign policy specialists drew a quite different lesson from the Korean War experience. They argued that the United States might well have to fight limited wars again. One had to expect that other regional conflicts would occur in which the United States would feel obliged to intervene because important national interests were at stake. If, as in Korea, there was a risk that such conflicts could escalate to undesirable levels of warfare, then the United

States would most likely have to limit its objectives and the military means it employed. Quite appropriately, adherents of this Korean War lesson came to be known as the "Limited War School."

The disagreement over strategy between adherents of the Never-Again and Limited War viewpoints was not resolved after the Korean War. These contending views had an impact on American policy making in subsequent crises. The Never-Again philosophy played an important role in keeping the Eisenhower administration from intervening in the 1954 Indochina crisis. The leading spokesman of the Never-Again School was Army Chief of Staff Gen. Matthew Ridgway. President Dwight Eisenhower himself held views that echoed the all-or-nothing thinking of the Never-Again view. Aspects of that strategic view were evident in 1958 when a Chinese Communist invasion of the tiny, Nationalist Chinese–held island of Quemoy seemed possible. The Joint Chiefs of Staff (JCS), reflecting the all-or-nothing view, asked President Eisenhower to grant them authority to use tactical nuclear weapons if they judged it necessary. Eisenhower refused.

Several years later, during the 1961–62 Laotian crisis, the JCS displayed all-or-nothing thinking in the sweeping war plans they prepared, which again included the possible use of nuclear weapons. America's military leaders were not really interested in going to war over Laos. They were trying to make the point that if the U.S. intervened on a small scale to begin with, the war might escalate into a direct confrontation with Communist China. Then, in order to avoid losing or fighting another inconclusive war as in Korea, it might be necessary to resort to nuclear weapons.

By the time the United States became involved in Vietnam a few years later, the influence of the Never-Again School had substantially waned and advocates of the Limited War view were in control of U.S. foreign policy. To avoid unwanted escalation, just as Pres. Harry Truman had done in Korea, Pres. Lyndon Johnson imposed significant limits on both the objectives and scope of the U.S. military effort. As a consequence, various strategic options for fighting the war were excluded and the only remaining one was the questionable idea of fighting a prolonged war of attrition to grind down North Vietnam's armed forces and weaken the will of Hanoi's leaders. The strategy failed and the Nixon administration ended U.S. military involvement in a negotiated settlement that led to the eventual North Vietnamese takeover of South Vietnam.

If the Never-Again philosophy had become too impotent to prevent large-scale U.S. military operations in Vietnam, the unsatisfactory outcome of that war triggered a powerful revival of the all-or-nothing approach. The result was an elaboration of the strategic views initially put forward by proponents of the

Never-Again School. The new version of that doctrine soon dominated U.S. strategic thinking and was used to discredit the Limited War School. Those who continued to have misgivings over the all-or-nothing aspect of post-Vietnam doctrine had a hard time gaining a hearing.

The Weinberger-Shultz Debate

Nowhere was this more evident than in the confrontation between Secretary of Defense Caspar Weinberger and Secretary of State George Shultz during Pres. Ronald Reagan's first term. Their debate, at times impassioned if not also acrimonious, was triggered by a number of difficult and controversial decisions the Reagan administration had to make concerning whether American military forces should intervene in some way in Third World conflicts then underway. Weinberger argued that U.S. intervention in such conflicts could once again embroil America, as in Vietnam, in a prolonged, costly, and increasingly unpopular war of attrition that might end inconclusively or in defeat. The first small step of military intervention, he cautioned, would put the United States on a "slippery slope" that would eventually lead to involvement of large-scale U.S. forces and put American prestige on the line. Weinberger, backed by the military chiefs, argued that we should limit ourselves to giving economic aid, military supplies and advice, and make greater use of covert operations. Beyond indirect assistance of this kind, we should rely on diplomacy to protect our interests.

Shultz objected to this, arguing that diplomacy and force could not be completely separated. Diplomatic efforts not backed by credible threats of force and, when necessary, with limited use of force would often prove ineffectual, resulting in damage to U.S. interests. In a speech delivered on April 3, 1984, Schultz insisted that: "Power and diplomacy always go together. . . . Certainly power must always be guided by purpose, but the hard reality is that diplomacy not backed by strength is ineffectual. . . . Power and diplomacy are not distinctive alternatives. They must go together, or we will accomplish very little in the world."[2]

Shultz did not reject the "lessons" of Vietnam, but he observed that situations do arise when a "discrete assertion of power" will be needed to support our limited objectives.

This speech and another one by Shultz several months later provoked Weinberger to rebut the secretary of state publicly. The defense secretary struck back in a speech titled "The Uses of Power" delivered at the National Press Club on November 28, 1984, and in an article published in the spring, 1986, issue of *Foreign Affairs*. He listed "six major tests" that should be made when judging whether the United States should employ its forces in Third World conflicts. These criteria have played an important role in shaping strategic thinking regarding questions of whether, when, and how force should be used or threatened in support of foreign policy objectives. They are briefly summarized here:

1. The United States should use force only when truly vital interests are at stake.
2. If the United States does decide to intervene with combat forces, they should be employed in sufficient numbers to win. Echoing the all-or-nothing maxim, Weinberger added that if the United States was unwilling to commit the forces and resources necessary to win, or if the objective was not important enough that it must be achieved, then America should not intervene.
3. Military forces should not be committed to combat unless they are given "clearly defined political and military objectives," a condition not met in the Vietnam War.
4. Before intervening militarily, the U.S. government should have "reasonable assurance" of the support of the American people and Congress.
5. Use of U.S. forces for combat should be undertaken only as a last resort after exhausting other means for safeguarding America's vital interests.
6. The relationship between objectives and means should be continually reassessed and adjusted as necessary.

Secretary Shultz felt that these conditions were too restrictive. His rebuttal is worth noting not because it was immediately effective in challenging Weinberger's doctrine, but because it foreshadows, as will be noted, subsequent efforts by the Bush and Clinton administrations to amend or bend some of Weinberger's criteria. Shultz emphasized that the United States has many important interests which, though less than "vital," also need to be protected. He argued that "the need to avoid no-win situations cannot mean that we turn away automatically from hard-to-win situations that call for prudent involvement." While not unsympathetic with Weinberger's third condition, Shultz pointed out that there are many murky, complicated crises in which sufficiently important U.S. interests are at stake that military power must be adapted to the situation as best as possible. America's political objectives in such situations, the secretary of state argued, must take priority over the establishment of clear-cut military objectives, and leaders will have to accept political constraints on the employment of military force in such instances.

As for Weinberger's insistence that domestic political support for U.S. military intervention be assured, the importance of which was not lost on Shultz, the secretary of state rejected an extreme and unqualified position on the issue. Decisions to use force in defense of American interests, he argued somewhat acerbically, "cannot be tied to opinion polls." And, in yet another barbed reply to his cabinet colleague, Shultz reminded him that "a president who has the courage to lead will win public support if he acts wisely and effectively."[3]

This revival and important elaboration of Never-Again thinking after Vietnam put on the defensive those who, like Shultz, tried to make the minimalist case for the occasional need to back diplomacy with threats of force or use of force. Indeed, in its extreme form, the post-Vietnam strategic doctrine held that any future contemplated use of force should be rejected unless it adhered to sound military doctrine and gave assurance of effective accomplishment of military objectives. In doing so, the post-Vietnam strategic doctrine in effect called into question Prussian military theorist Carl von Clausewitz's famous maxim that war is a continuation of politics by other means and that political considerations necessarily take precedence over military logic. The new doctrine instead seemed to argue that contemplated uses of force in support of foreign policy must give way if they did not satisfy military requirements for the effective, efficient use of force.

This brief history of U.S. efforts to consider when and how force should be used as an instrument of foreign policy indicates a continuing struggle between the political and military dimensions of the problem. I have concluded that a fundamental conceptual and operational tension exists between the logic of war as a political act, which Clausewitz emphasized, and what he recognized to be the "logic of the instrument" of war itself. The latter downplays political considerations and argues for using sufficient force to destroy or render impotent an adversary's forces. This fundamental tension between political and military considerations permits no easy and certainly no definitive resolution. It has severely complicated efforts to develop useful guidelines for the use of force in the post–Cold War era.

Post–Cold War Complications and Additional Dilemmas

Ever since the Weinberger-Shultz debate, policy makers have continued to struggle with this dilemma. Subsequent efforts to introduce greater flexibility and selectivity in applications of what has come to be called the Weinberger-Powell doctrine were further complicated by the end of the Cold War. This historic development has led to what Richard Haass has aptly called "the central paradox" of the post–Cold War era. On one hand, the United States now faces less awesome risks when contemplating the use of force since military interventions in third areas are now very unlikely to spark the type of superpower confrontation and attendant risks of thermonuclear war. But this new freedom of action is counterbalanced by the fact that the United States is less motivated to take risks. "So far as the use of military force is concerned," Haass observes, "we have gone from a world of high stakes and high risk, to a world of relatively modest stakes and relatively modest risks." Although the United States has emerged as the world's only military superpower, the use of military force in the post–Cold War era is less relevant to the kinds of threats now faced.[4]

The effects of this central paradox have been much accentuated by the shattering of the Cold War consensus that undergirded American foreign policy for many decades concerning the U.S. leadership role in world affairs. Lacking ever since has been anything approximating a national consensus on what the role of the United States should be in the post–Cold War era. In fact, there have been sharp disagreements over this fundamental question. The lack of a new consensus has added new dimensions to the debate as to when and how force or threats of force should be employed in the conduct of foreign policy. Moreover, there is little prospect that a new national consensus can be forged that would provide a fundamental underpinning for U.S. foreign policy.

The problem has been further complicated by the proliferation of intrastate conflicts in the post–Cold War era. The international community has been overburdened by crisis situations that call for peacemaking, peacekeeping, nation building, and humanitarian assistance. The virtues of *preventive diplomacy* to nip such incipient crises in the bud before they get out of hand has been rediscovered and given new emphasis. But the rhetoric of preventive diplomacy has rarely been matched by timely, effective diplomacy or military intervention. The problem in most conflict situations is that governments often ignore an incipient crisis or take a passive stance until the situation explodes into a deadly struggle or catastrophe.

In other words, the problem is not that governments don't know; it's that they don't act! The logic of warning and the logic of policy response often conflict. The logic of early warning is "the sooner one acts in response to warning, the better." Unfortunately, policy makers have a deep-seated penchant for putting off hard choices as long as possible. As a result, the possibility for preventive diplomacy is lost, leaving behind many "missed opportunities."[5]

Related to this is the dilemma created if U.S. policy adheres to Weinberger's fifth criterion—namely that military force should be employed only as "a last resort" after other means for safeguarding American interests are exhausted. A number of observers—including military specialists—have criticized the last-resort criterion on the grounds that waiting until all other means are exhausted will often create a worse situation requiring much more force to deal with it. Such a prospect may well lead to a decision not to intervene and to accept the consequences.[6]

It should be noted that an important reformulation of the criterion of using force only as a last resort is contained in President Bush's statement, quoted at the beginning of this chapter, that force should be considered when "no other policies are likely to be effective."

The perceived need to intervene, however belatedly, to alleviate humanitarian or human rights crises has created additional dilemmas for U.S. policy makers in deciding whether and how to make use of military force for this purpose. The challenge has been whether, and particularly how, to employ military forces for humanitarian purposes without becoming involved in peacemaking, state building, or even peacekeeping missions that might lead to the prolongation or escalation of U.S. military involvement. The Bush administration experienced the fear of "mission creep" and entrapment in a local conflict when it encountered a desperate situation in Somalia in December, 1992. The administration overcame its initial hesitation to send in military forces by strictly limiting the objective to the humanitarian task of providing a secure environment for distributing food and medical supplies, by employing a large enough military force to accomplish the mission, and by establishing in advance the terms and timing of withdrawal of most of the forces. The United Nations was given responsibility for disarming rival Somali clans and reconstructing state structures.

The Bush administration hoped that U.S. forces would quickly accomplish their humanitarian mission and get out, thus avoiding the risk of being drawn into a quagmire. This strategy reflected adherence to key principles of the post-Vietnam doctrine of getting in with ample force, achieving the military mission quickly, and getting out once it was accomplished.

It proved to be a highly successful operation within its self-imposed limits. However, critics of the administration's policy of limited humanitarian intervention warned that withdrawing U.S. forces without first disarming the forces of rival Somali war lords, who could be expected to lie low while U.S. forces were present, would result in the resumption of violence. Among those who voiced such concerns was UN Secretary General Boutros Boutros-Ghali, who failed in his effort to obtain a broadened commitment from the Bush administration to participate with forces in an effort to secure substantial disarmament of the rival Somali clans. The problem was passed on to the Clinton administration, which erred in allowing the insufficient number of U.S. military forces remaining in Somalia to be drawn into an effort to neutralize the forces of Gen. Mohammed Aidid and a botched effort to capture him. The ensuing disaster—

which resulted in a small but politically significant number of American casualties and television coverage of a dead U.S. soldier being dragged through the streets of Mogadishu—led to sharp domestic criticism. The Clinton administration responded by announcing it would withdraw all U.S. forces within six months.

The setback in Somalia reinforced the already strong inhibition against U.S. military involvement in Bosnia and led the Clinton administration to embrace a much more conservative doctrine regarding the future use of American forces, as well to openly question the wisdom of UN intervention in so many unstable situations.

A lesson some observers drew from the disaster in Somalia was that the United States should henceforth not engage in humanitarian interventions unless it was prepared also to participate fully in the tasks of peacemaking and state building. This was certainly one "solution" to the dilemma, and one sees evidence that the Somalia experience contributed to the American and UN reluctance to undertake more timely intervention for humanitarian purposes in Rwanda, as well as the failure to recognize that the atrocities committed there amounted to genocide.

Lest the Somalia "lesson" be overgeneralized to discourage all humanitarian interventions, other observers have urged that a distinction be made between two types of humanitarian crises: those of a nonpolitical character and those stemming from fundamental political causes within a country. Nonpolitical humanitarian crises arise from natural causes. The deadly cyclone in Bangladesh in April, 1991, is an example. Humanitarian crises may also result from or be markedly worsened by internal or external political conflicts. Some humanitarian crises of this kind persist *after* the internal and/or external political factors that caused them are no longer operative. These are relatively safe situations for humanitarian missions. However, when humanitarian problems and the political crises that caused or exacerbate them persist, the humanitarian mission cannot be easily separated and pursued independently of the peacemaking and state-building missions. Furthermore, the requirement that the humanitarian mission be conducted impartially is more difficult to carry out under these circumstances. Thus, for example, some observers would argue that the criterion of impartiality was erroneously applied in Bosnia and actually served the interests of the Bosnian Serbs and disadvantaged the Bosnian Muslims.[7]

The dilemma of whether and how to conduct humanitarian missions without experiencing mission creep is related, of course, to the question of whether U.S. interests are sufficiently engaged in a particular crisis situation to warrant undertaking additional peacekeeping missions, particularly, those of peacemaking and state building. Even when, as eventually in Bosnia, the Clinton administration finally decided to use force and deployed large military units to that country on behalf of peacekeeping and peacemaking, it attempted to differentiate its interests in these two missions. Responsibility for peace*keeping* for a period of time was regarded as more acceptable than a commitment to ensure peace*making* in the long run. In addition to signaling a limited responsibility for both of these missions, the administration has tried to make it clear that it regards its responsibility for state building as even more limited in time and resource expenditures.

These proclaimed constraints on U.S. commitments and responsibilities were clearly influenced by the need to achieve and retain sufficient domestic political support for U.S. military involvement in Bosnia. They were also influenced by the related need to assure the public and Congress that there was a serious commitment for the withdrawal of U.S. military forces from Bosnia by a certain date.

Various justifications have been offered for delimiting (and therefore, not incidentally, also retaining support for) the limited U.S. political-military commitment to Bosnia. Consider, for example, the remarks made by National Security Adviser Anthony Lake on March 6, 1996, in an address titled "Defining Missions, Setting Deadlines: Meeting New Security Challenges in the Post–Cold War World." Setting deadlines for the withdrawal of U.S. forces is very important because "neither we or the international community has either the responsibility or the means to do whatever it takes for as long as it takes to rebuild nations." Such a limitation of commitment is necessary for several reasons. First, "providing a security blanket for an indefinite period" encourages those we are trying to help "to evade their own responsibilities for the future of their societies." Second, assuming too much responsibility for a nation's future undercuts the government you are trying to help: "unless you make clear that your mission is limited in scope and devotion, you risk de-legitimizing a government in the eyes of its own people." Third, "overstaying one's welcome ultimately breeds resentment of our presence and provides an easy target for blame when things go wrong."

Although Lake's observations were ostensibly addressed to listeners who questioned the wisdom of setting deadlines and limiting the U.S. commitment, they also served to reassure listeners who were dubious about the wisdom of U.S. involvement in such situations that its commitment and responsibilities were strictly limited "in scope and duration."

Here, then, is another dilemma experienced in considering whether to commit the United States to participate in peacemaking and peace building. There is an unavoidable tension between limiting responsibility for such missions and avoiding the likelihood that as a result the local government will be unsuccessful in achieving these objectives.

Again, whether intended or not, these reasons for limiting U.S. commitment and responsibility can provide justification for washing one's hands of responsibility in the event that local political leaders fail to achieve these objectives. While much attention has been given to the need for a specific deadline for the withdrawal of military forces, the possible need for a later political exit from such involvement at some point—and the conditions that would warrant it—have been left murky. They were not really clarified by Lake's observations.

Let us look more closely now at some of the dilemmas associated with the requirement for a clear and early date for the exit of U.S. military forces from such critical situations. Articulated early on by Weinberger—and endorsed as a general principle by a number of other civilian and military leaders since then—this requirement became a virtual *prerequisite* for any decision to intervene with U.S. military forces. As a result, the Clinton administration was confronted with a serious paradox: on one hand, a short-term exit date, even a specific one, for the return of U.S. forces was politically essential to gain even minimal domestic support for their use. But the commitment to an early exit itself entailed major political and diplomatic risks insofar as it was not part of a well-considered, realistic strategy for establishing a stable internal peace in that country. Washington was thus caught on the horns of a dilemma. Domestic support for intervention was not possible unless it was accompanied by a specific commitment for an early exit of U.S. forces. However, this risked undermining the efficacy of the intervention and created a serious possibility of paying a large political price later if internal violence resumed and the state collapsed after the withdrawal of U.S troops.

The possible consequences of an early exit are magnified when the forces sent into a conflict area, as in Bosnia, operate under very conservative rules of engagement. This may be deemed essential in order to reduce the possibility of casualties, which, as in Somalia, might well create a domestic political backlash forcing the administration to cut short its commitment. The political-military reasons for an early exit are powerful, but they constitute a major constraint on what Washington will do to cope with the Somalias, the Rwandas, and the Bosnias. The criticism is made that an exit requirement tends to undermine the achievement of the objectives of intervention if it is not part of a well-conceived, overall strategy for achieving those objectives.[8]

The Clinton administration belatedly recognized the disadvantages of announcing a specific exit date at the time of intervention toward the end of 1997 as the deadline for the withdrawal of U.S. military forces from Bosnia approached. On December 18 President Clinton abandoned the June, 1998, deadline he had established and called for an open-ended commitment of troops to the international peacekeeping mission. Admitting his error in having set the exit date, and refusing to set a new one, he said that the mission and its duration should be defined instead by the achievement of "concrete benchmarks," such as the creation of an adequate civilian force.[9]

Decision Rules for Use of Force?

These, then, are dilemmas encountered by the United States in efforts to decide whether, when, and how to use force as an instrument of foreign policy. We turn now to another aspect of the problem: the conclusions drawn by experienced policy makers and analysts as to whether any useful "decision rules" or specific guidelines can be formulated and agreed upon for dealing with the challenges and dilemmas of using force in support of diplomacy.

One cannot fail to be impressed by the general answer to this question provided by President Bush in his farewell address at West Point, which we quoted at the beginning of this paper. It is a wise conclusion that no doubt other U.S. leaders have drawn, would draw, or should draw in addressing this question. Military leaders who have participated in high-level political decisions regarding the use of force come to similar conclusions, as did Gen. Colin Powell, who emphasized that there could be "no fixed set of rules" in answering this question.[10]

If one may resort to academic jargon to elaborate the wisdom contained in their advice, the answers to these questions are heavily "context dependent" and therefore cannot easily be reduced to a simple set of fixed, inflexible "decision rules" applicable to all situations. Rather, the special configuration of each case must be assessed in all of its complexity. Many factors must be taken into account in judging whether some type of military threat or action is appropriate and likely to be feasible at acceptable cost and risk.

This being said, however, it is still useful to pursue the possibility of identifying more specific contingent guidelines or, at least, rejecting or qualifying some of the general ones proposed earlier, as by Caspar Weinberger. Richard Haass has emphasized that the practice of the Bush administration did indeed deviate on occasion from some of the "tests" proposed by the former defense secretary. First, as the Bush administration's intervention in Somalia indicated, U.S. military force was not committed only, as Weinberger had urged, when "vital interests" were at stake. Second, as the Persian Gulf War showed, it is not the case that U.S. forces will be committed only when there is a minimal risk of casualties. Third, again as the Gulf War indicated, it is not the case that

U.S. forces will be committed only when there is strong public support for doing so. However, it is true that the American public must understand and support the objective being pursued and be persuaded that the stakes warrant putting American lives on the line.

Haass concludes that the overall operational "guidelines" or practices of the Bush administration were closer in important respects to the views expressed earlier by Secretary Shultz than to those articulated by Secretary Weinberger.

In reflecting further on the practice of the Bush administration, Haass infers that it followed several important guidelines or rules of thumb articulated in President Bush's West Point speech. First, do not commit U.S. forces unless you believe it will make the critical difference, politically if not militarily. Second, do not commit U.S. military forces unless there is a high probability of success. Third, define, tailor, and circumscribe the mission to enhance the probability of success; "winning" is a function both of the means applied and the ends sought. Fourth, bring overwhelming force to bear in order to enhance the probability of success.[11]

What Contribution Can Scholarly Knowledge Make?

The question arises whether and how scholarly analysis of the problems of using force can be helpful to decision makers. If every case is unique, as President Bush emphasized, can lessons of a general kind be drawn from past experience and, if so, how can they be used by policy makers in dealing with new situations that arise?

Scholars who address this task believe that useful lessons can be drawn from systematic study of each of the many generic problems repeatedly encountered in the conduct of foreign policy. This applies not only to generic problems such as deterrence and coercive diplomacy that are of particular interest here, but also to crisis management, war termination and, indeed, crisis avoidance, mediation, and cooperation. To the extent scholars are successful in doing so, their findings contribute to bridging the gap between theory (another word for "generic knowledge") and the practice of policy makers.

In interviews with policy specialists for one of my projects a few years ago, I quickly discovered that whenever I used the word *theory,* their eyes would glaze. I began substituting "generic knowledge" for theory, and when I did so they nodded approvingly. Why? The answer, quite simply, is that policy specialists know that certain generic problems—such as deterrence and coercive diplomacy—repeatedly arise in the conduct of foreign policy. They thus are favorably disposed to efforts to develop generic knowledge of each of these tasks.

Of what value in policy making is such generic knowledge? How ought it to be used in making decisions? Generic knowledge is most useful when it takes the form of conditional generalizations derived from analysis of past cases. Such generalizations identify the conditions under which, for example, deterrence or coercive diplomacy is likely to be effective and when it is likely to fail.

Such conditional generalizations, it should be emphasized, are *not* prescriptions for action. They do not tell decision makers what to do in a specific situation. Their relevance and value is, rather, that they can help policy makers *diagnose* new situations. The proper analogy here is the relationship of knowledge to practice in clinical medicine. In medicine, before powerful drugs were developed, a doctor attempted to diagnose the patient's problem before prescribing for it. Policy makers, like doctors, must diagnose a new situation as aptly as possible before deciding how to deal with it. Helpful in making such diagnoses is generic knowledge of deterrence and coercive diplomacy that identifies the conditions under which, judging from past experience, deterrence is likely to work or not work. Armed with such conditional generalizations, policy specialists are better able to judge whether such "favoring" conditions are present or can be created in the case at hand.

Generic knowledge should therefore be useful to those intelligence and policy analysts within the government who are responsible for diagnosing emerging situations for the benefit of decision makers. However, I would like to emphasize here, as in previous writings,[12] the fact that a gap exists between even the best generic knowledge (or theory) of deterrence, coercive diplomacy, or other tools of statecraft and practice. The nature of the gap needs to be better understood. Such an understanding leads to a sobering conclusion: The gap between theory and practice cannot be eliminated, it can only be bridged.

One must have a realistic view of the limited, indirect—but still quite important—impact that generic knowledge about such matters can have on policy making. Generic knowledge of strategies such as deterrence or coercive diplomacy, or of activities such as crisis management or war termination, is best viewed as an input to policy analysis of specific situations within the government. Generic knowledge is an *aid* rather than a *substitute* for judgments that decision makers must exercise when choosing a policy.

In other words, it is a mistake to view theory or generic knowledge as capable of providing policy makers with detailed, high-confidence prescriptions for action in each contingency that arises. Such policy-relevant knowledge does not exist and is not feasible. Rather, as noted above, we must think in terms of the analogy with traditional medical practice, which calls for a correct diagnosis of the problem before prescribing a treatment. In accord with this analogy, I have argued that the major function and use of theory and generic knowledge is to contribute to the diagnosis of specific problematic situations with which policy makers must deal, rather than to provide prescriptions or general "decision rules" for action. Like the medical doctor, the policy maker acts as a clinician who strives to make a correct diagnosis of a problem before determining how best to deal with it.

It is in this way that the unique nature of each situation, which President Bush emphasized in his West Point speech, can be diagnosed and better understood in order to decide whether and how force or threats of force may apply.

Deterrence: Lessons of Experience

We now turn to a summary of the lessons of experience that have been drawn from efforts to rely on deterrence and coercive diplomacy as alternatives to resort to warfare.[13] The lessons scholars have drawn from studying a variety of historical cases of deterrence are probably largely consistent with lessons sophisticated policy makers and policy specialists have formulated from their own experience and from their awareness of the historical experience of other practitioners of deterrence. Nonetheless, there may be some value in stating these lessons explicitly to see whether they add anything to the working knowledge of policy makers.

I believe that the lessons of experience with the uses and limitations of deterrence are best captured and formulated by distinguishing the role that this strategy can occupy in the service of an overall foreign policy from observations about operational problems of implementing deterrence.

Deterrence and Foreign Policy
First, then, a discussion of the role of deterrence in foreign policy. The fundamental question here is what type of peace deterrence is intended to help achieve.[14] There are several distinctly different types of peace: "precarious peace," "conditional peace," and "stable peace." Precarious peace refers to an acute conflict relationship between two states when peace means little more than a temporary absence of war. Such peace depends not merely on "general deterrence," to use a term Patrick Morgan introduced into the literature some years ago to describe the kind of deterrence that is ever present in the background of a highly conflictive relationship and serves to contain it. To keep war from breaking out in such a relationship also requires frequent resort to "immediate deterrence"—that is, the timely use of threatening actions and warnings in war-threatening crises. The Arab-Israeli relationship, until recent times, may be regarded as an example of precarious peace.

Conditional peace, on the other hand, describes a less acute, less heated conflict relationship, one in which general deterrence plays the predominant, usually effective role in discouraging policies and actions that might lead to war-threatening crises which, as a result, seldom occur. The parties to the conflict therefore rarely need to resort to immediate deterrence. The U.S.-Soviet relationship during the Cold War qualifies as an example of conditional peace. During the Cold War era there were only a few diplomatic crises in which general deterrence had to be supplemented and augmented with immediate deterrence.

Neither in precarious peace nor conditional peace does either party rule out initiating force as an instrument of policy. In contrast, stable peace is a relationship between two states (or groups of states) in which neither side considers engaging in or even threatening the use of military force. Deterring or compelling actions with military force are simply excluded as instruments of policy. Two states (or more than two as in the European Union) that enjoy a relationship of stable peace may continue to have serious disputes, but they deal with them by nonmilitary means. An example of this is the 1956 Suez crisis in which President Eisenhower made strong, credible threats of economic sanctions to pressure the British government to withdraw its forces from the Suez.

Let us consider now the case in which the long-range objective of deterrence is to move an existing relationship from precarious or conditional peace to one of stable peace. In this context, deterrence is the handmaiden of a policy of containment. Containment, however, is a general concept. John Gaddis, in his study of U.S.-Soviet relations during the Cold War, identified several interestingly different strategies of containment.[15] In the post–Cold War era, the general goal of containment has been applied in U.S. policy toward so-called rogue states such as Iran, Iraq, North Korea, and Libya. However, there is growing criticism of overreliance on containment in dealing with such states, and some have suggested that it be coupled with "engagement." But, like containment, engagement is a general concept that can take the form of significantly different specific strategies.[16]

The long-range goal of containment strategies is to firmly deter expansionist aims of an adversary state in the hope that internal developments will lead its leaders eventually to alter their foreign policy aspirations so that a new relationship of mutual accommodation is possible. For this purpose, containment and deterrence alone are not likely to suffice. Some form of carefully calculated, controlled strategy of engagement will, in all likelihood, be necessary.

These very general observations about the lessons one can draw from past experience provide the framework for the following somewhat more specific lessons regarding the role of deterrence in foreign policy.

- Experience indicates that reliance on deterrence is not a substitute for a well-conceptualized overall foreign policy. Deterrence may be a necessary part of foreign policy, but it is seldom a sufficient basis for dealing with many adversaries. Deterrence cannot compensate for an overall policy that is ill adapted to the nature of a problematic situation.
- Deterrence commitments should be subjected to timely reviews to take into account changes in the situation, in the adversary's intentions, and with regard to the desirability of supplementing deterrence with other means of influencing the adversary.
- The absence of a deterrence commitment—as in U.S. policy in the months prior to North Korea's attack on South Korea—should also be subjected to timely review to ascertain whether deterrence is needed.
- Reassessments of an existing deterrence commitment—or, when it is missing, of the need to add it to overall foreign policy—are difficult to undertake because existing policy usually acquires a momentum that makes it difficult to initiate timely reassessments and changes. Domestic and/or international (including alliance) considerations—as in the Korean and Persian Gulf crises—can severely constrain the need for timely reconsideration of existing or nonexisting deterrence commitments.
- Policy for dealing with an adversary should not rely exclusively on deterrence. It should make use of other instruments for influencing the adversary's behavior.
- Deterrence, which relies on threats, is better conceived as part of a broader influence theory that combines threats with positive inducements and diplomatic efforts to explore the desirability and feasibility of working out a mutually acceptable accommodation of conflicting interests. To do so, however, requires a correct understanding of the adversary's motives, needs, and longer-range goals. This is necessary not only to ascertain how and what kind of an accommodation is possible, but also to assure that the effort to do so will not degenerate into appeasement, which will only whet the adversary's appetite.
- Deterrence is often best viewed and utilized as a time-buying strategy, one that creates an opportunity to explore and possibly achieve an acceptable accommodation of conflicting interests.
- The success achieved by deterrence may turn out to be short-lived. Prudent policy makers will not assume that deterrence will necessarily continue to be effective because it has been effective thus far. A

determined opponent, frustrated by deterrent acts directed against it, may react not by accepting the status quo situation, but rather by working to strengthen its capability to challenge the deterrence and wait for, and attempt to create, new opportunities for challenging it again.

- Deterrence is not simply a matter of announcing a commitment and backing it with threats. Whether or not the adversary will be persuaded by the commitment will be heavily influenced by its judgment—be it correct or incorrect—that the deterrence reflects the opponent's real national and political interests, is not inflated, and does not amount to a bluff. Early deterrence theory was defective in that it placed too much emphasis on various gimmicks for enhancing the credibility of commitment—such as "the threat that leaves something to chance," playing the game of "chicken," etc.—and failed to recognize that credibility is based on the magnitude and nature of the national interests at stake. Rhetorical inflation of a deterrence threat is likely to be perceived by the adversary as being a bluff that warrants being tested and challenged—as the Soviets did in several Berlin crises—by means of either a "limited probe" or a version of "salami tactics."

- The target for deterrence is not necessarily or exclusively an adversary. In "extended deterrence," which is intended to protect allies from attack, the government and people of the allied country are an important target for the deterrence commitment made on their behalf. Thus the primary purpose of a deterrence commitment may be to provide the kind of political and psychological assurance to an ally that will enable it to pursue its domestic and foreign affairs without experiencing the anxiety and destabilizing effect of living under fear of an attack. John Foster Dulles, testifying before a congressional committee in support of the U.S. commitment to defend Western Europe, was asked whether he thought there was danger of a Soviet attack. He replied that he thought it quite improbable, but that a U.S. deterrence commitment was needed nonetheless to provide the political and psychological atmosphere that would permit Western Europe to concentrate on recovery from the devastation of World War II without fear of encroachment and pressures from the Soviet Union. In the case of Japan, the U.S. deterrence commitment has served a similar function, also enabling the Japanese to avoid providing substantial military forces of its own for security against external aggression.

- There are several sobering examples of U.S. failures to assert effective deterrence despite ample warning that an attack might be in the works. Indeed, the America's failure in 1950 to attempt to deter North Korea's attack on South Korea and its inability to mount a strong deterrent effort against Saddam Hussein before he attacked Kuwait in 1990 exemplify a disturbing paradox. The United States responded to aggression with strong military action in both cases. However, what it was willing and able to do *after* the aggression took place, it was not able, for various reasons, to threaten to do *beforehand*. Deterrence is not always a readily available instrument for foreign policy even in situations in which the need for it is paramount.
- Finally, careful consideration should be given to whether one should rely on the strategy of *reassuring* an adversary rather than trying to deter him with threats of a military response.[17] When is a strategy of reassurance preferable to deterrence or a useful accompaniment to it? President Harry Truman placed misguided reliance on reassurances of U.S. friendship and nonhostile intentions toward the People's Republic of China in response to its threats to intervene in the Korean War if UN forces crossed the 38th parallel, instead of attempting to deter such an action. President George Bush attempted to combine reassurance with deterrence when confronted with indications of a possible Iraqi invasion of Kuwait. The administration was able to mount only a weak deterrent action, the efficacy of which was further diluted by an effort to assure Saddam Hussein of a continued desire for friendly relations.

  There is a need for more systematic analysis of the conditions and modalities for choosing between deterrence and reassurance, or for combining them in some way. A hypothesis has been advanced that reassurance of some kind might be more appropriate than deterrence when the adversary's motivation for acting stems from a sense of weakness, vulnerability, or concern over possible hostile actions directed against it. Conversely, deterrence is thought to be more appropriate than reassurance when the adversary's motivation is derived not from its preoccupation with threat and vulnerability but from a belief that an opportunity exists for aggrandizement at acceptable cost and risk.

Operational Problems of Implementing Deterrence

We turn now to lessons that may be drawn regarding some of the problems of implementing deterrence strategy once it is undertaken. (Note, however, that our discussion does not take up important tactics such as the alert and deployment of forces in a crisis.)

- A distinction needs to be made between two types of deterrence strategy. One alternative is to formulate and communicate a broad, generalized deterrent threat that is intended to discourage all options that may be available to the adversary for challenging the deterrent commitment. The U.S. policy of "massive retaliation" was intended at times as a generalized threat that would at least deter the opponent's most serious and troublesome options. John Foster Dulles, for example, appeared to hold the view that the strength and *certainty* of a general U.S. commitment to act against encroachments against allies was more important for preventing the opponent's miscalculation than was specification of the means America would employ in response to different types of encroachments. The alternative deterrence strategy when faced with an opponent who has multiple options for challenging it is to formulate and communicate a number of specific, more discriminating threats, which together, it is hoped, provide comprehensive deterrence coverage. Such a strategy for signaling deterrence corresponds roughly with the political-military doctrine of "flexible response" introduced by the Kennedy administration.[18]

  It does appear that historical experience with these deterrence strategies has not been adequately evaluated as yet.

- A long-familiar distinction in the literature on deterrence focuses on two types of threats that can be utilized in implementing a deterrence commitment. This is the distinction between deterrence that rests on "denial" and that which rests on the threat of "punishment." There are, in turn, two types of denial. One is the threat to defeat the aggressor at whatever level of violence he chooses in making his challenge. The other takes the form of a threat not to limit one's response to the level of violence chosen by the aggressor, but to escalate one's response to a greater level of violence.

- There are also two types of punishment that can be threatened. One is the threat not to limit one's military action to the battlefield, but to strike at highly valued industrial or population targets. The other type of punishment is the threat to force the opponent into a prolonged war of attrition that will bleed the adversary's military forces and his economy. Of course, in practice, some combination of denial and punishment may be threatened and undertaken if deterrence is challenged. The relative utility of these alternatives for purposes of deterrence (as opposed to waging war if deterrence fails) is not easily established, perhaps in part because their effectiveness depends on other variables.

- It is hazardous to base deterrence on the general assumption that the opponent is a rational, unitary actor. The adversary may, in fact, be a small group of individuals who differ from one another in values, beliefs, perceptions, and judgment. To be sure, the calculus of deterrence rests upon the assumption of a rational opponent who can be deterred from a given course of action if made aware that the costs and risks of pursuing it clearly outweigh the benefits to be gained thereby. For the deterring power to act solely on the basis of such a general assumption may lead to grave error in designing and implementing a deterrence strategy. Not all actors in international politics calculate utility in making decisions in the same way. Differences in values, political culture, attitudes toward risk taking, and so on, may vary greatly. There is no substitute for specific knowledge of each adversary's mind-set and behavioral style, and this is often difficult to obtain or to apply correctly in assessing his intentions or predicting his responses.[19]

- Deterrence threats *must be perceived by the adversary* to be credible and potent enough to influence his behavior. Whether they are *sufficiently* credible and potent for this purpose will depend on how strongly motivated the adversary is to challenge deterrence. The strength of his motivation to do so is a variable that may be misjudged by the deterring power. The adversary's motivation will be stronger if he experiences a sense of urgency to change the status quo, and less compelling if believes he can tolerate the status quo for some time in the hope or expectation that prospects for changing it will improve.

- The adversary may deliberately create a crisis that threatens deterrence in order to test the resolution of the deterring power and to find out how firm its commitment is. Such crises are initiated in ways the adversary believes provide him with an opportunity to monitor and control the risks of overreaction by the deterring power. Two strategies for controlled crises of this kind, which represent quite limited challenges to deterrence, are the "limited probe" and "salami tactics."[20] It is important to recognize that even a very strong and credible deterrence commitment may be challenged and tested by relatively safe, low-level controlled actions of this kind.

- Deterrence may fail catastrophically when the adversary resorts to a "fait accompli" strategy for changing the status quo, as did the North Koreans in 1950 and Saddam Hussein in 1990. However, deterrence often fails more slowly, in stages. When this is the case a strategic or tactical warning that deterrence may fail or is in the process of failure provides the deterring power an opportunity to shore up and strengthen deterrence by engaging in military alerts, quick deployments, strong declaratory warnings, et cetera. Such a warning also provides a deterring power the opportunity to reconsider its deterrence commitment or to convey a willingness to engage in diplomatic efforts to see whether it can accommodate the adversary's needs sufficiently to reduce its motivation to use force to challenge the status quo.

Coercive Diplomacy Lessons of Experience

The strategy of coercive diplomacy relies on threats of force or, if necessary, makes exemplary use of quite limited force to persuade an adversary to call off or undo an encroachment—such as halting an invasion, giving up occupied territory, or discontinuing harassment.[21] Whereas deterrence is used to dissuade an adversary from undertaking an action he has not yet initiated, coercive diplomacy attempts to persuade him to stop or reverse an action already undertaken. If force is used in coercive diplomacy, just enough is employed to demonstrate one's resolution and to emphasize the credibility of one's threat to resort to a military strategy. Coercive diplomacy seeks to *persuade* an adversary to cease his encroachment rather than bludgeon him into stopping it.

Coercive Diplomacy and Foreign Policy
What, then, can be said about the role that coercive diplomacy can play as an instrument of foreign policy for dealing with adversaries?

- The attractiveness of coercive diplomacy as a tool of foreign policy is quite clear. It offers the possibility of achieving one's objective economically, with little bloodshed, fewer political and psychological costs, and often with much less risk of escalation than does resort to military action to defeat an adversary's encroachment.
- Coercive diplomacy can be a beguiling strategy for this very reason. Leaders of militarily powerful countries may be tempted to believe that they can, with little risk to themselves, intimidate weaker opponents to give up their gains. However, if the adversary refuses to be

intimidated when subjected to coercive diplomacy and, in effect, calls the coercive power's bluff, the latter must then decide whether to back off or to escalate the use of force.

- A strong power is therefore well advised *not* to engage in coercive diplomacy unless it is prepared to step up military action if the adversary fails to respond. Failure to do so, as on a number of occasions in Bosnia, erodes the strong power's general reputation for resolve. In consequence, the strong power's subsequent efforts to make effective threats are likely to lack credibility and thus be dismissed by weaker adversaries. The result may be a misperception by the adversary of the credibility of the coercive threat, leading to a miscalculation on its part that results in a war that might otherwise have been avoided.

- A strong power may feel it necessary to respond initially to a grave encroachment with coercive diplomacy *even though* it does not expect it to be effective and believes it will be necessary to resort to greater military action to defeat the aggression. It may do so because it believes that alliance partners and other international actors, including the United Nations, as well as domestic opinion will not support an immediate military response to the aggressor unless diplomatic efforts, including coercive diplomacy, are tried first. America's response to Iraq's aggression against Kuwait is an apt example in which first economic sanctions and then coercive diplomacy were tried before international and domestic opinion could be persuaded of the need for and legitimacy of a full military response.

Operational Problems of Implementing Coercive Diplomacy
Let us turn now to some lessons gleaned from experience in efforts to implement a strategy of coercive diplomacy.

- The general concept of coercive diplomacy becomes a strategy only when the policy maker gives specific content to the four components of this tool. The policy maker must answer the following: (1) what to demand of the adversary; (2) whether—and how—to create in the adversary's mind a sense of urgency to comply with the demand; (3) how to create and convey a threat of punishment for noncompliance with the demand that is sufficiently credible and potent enough in the adversary's mind to persuade him that compliance is more in his interest than facing the consequences of noncompliance; and (4) whether to couple the threatened punishment with positive inducements—a "carrot"—to make it easier for the adversary to comply with the demand.

- It should be obvious that the more far-reaching the demand on the opponent, the stronger will be his motivation to resist—and the more difficult the task of coercive diplomacy.
- Depending on the policy maker's answers to these four questions, significantly different variants of the strategy are possible. Three major variants are the following:

1. The ultimatum, either explicit or tacit, in which the demand on the opponent is accompanied by an early deadline or sense of urgency about compliance and is backed by a strong enough and credible enough threat of punishment to follow shortly after the deadline expires.

2. A weaker variant of the strategy is the *gradual turning of the screw*, in which the sense of urgency for compliance is diluted, though not altogether absent, and the threatened punishment is not a single potent action but an incremental progression of increasingly severe actions.

3. Even weaker is the *try-and-see* variant of the strategy, in which the demand is accompanied by neither a sense of urgency for compliance, nor a clear threat of punishment for noncompliance. The try-and-see approach begins with a modest coercive threat or action which, if it proves ineffective, is then followed by a new decision whether to undertake another modest action or threat.

- Study of past cases in which ultimatums have been employed identifies at least four possible risks when using the strongest variant of coercive diplomacy: (1) the adversary may mistakenly believe the ultimatum is a bluff; (2) the opponent may take the ultimatum seriously and decide to initiate war himself rather than accept the demand on him (as did the Japanese government in initiating war against the United States in December, 1941); (3) the opponent may reject the ultimatum because he regards it as humiliating, incompatible with honor, too damaging politically, and the like; (4) the opponent may neither accept nor reject the ultimatum, but instead try to defuse its impact by accepting the demand only partially or with important qualifications.
- Before undertaking to issue an ultimatum, the coercing power must carefully weigh its possible risks, decide which of the four risks is

likely to be operative, and decide whether and how it can reduce that (and the other possible) risks. Inability to satisfy itself that it can avoid the risks of an ultimatum may lead the coercing power either to choose one of the weaker variants of the strategy, attempt to resolve the issue through diplomatic negotiation and bargaining, or initiate war.

- The coercing power may deliberately avoid conveying a very early deadline or may decide to extend it, softening the pressure of its ultimatum, for one reason or another. One example would be to give diplomatic efforts more time to seek a peaceful resolution, to give other international actors an opportunity to persuade the adversary to back off, and to give the adversary more time to make a reasoned response rather than to impulsively overreact. The coercing power may avoid too explicit and harsh an ultimatum for fear it would harden the recipient's resistance. It may signal a willingness to cooperate in some way to enable the adversary to "save face" or even offer some genuine concessions to make it easier for him to accept the most important of its demands.

- The coercing power may change its perception of the risks of an ultimatum as the crisis unfolds. Initially, it may be concerned primarily that the adversary will not regard its threat as credible or very potent. In this event, the coercing power may feel that its primary task, even before delivering an ultimatum, is to make certain that its threat of punishment will be seen as credible and potent. Accordingly, the coercing power may alert or deploy military forces in order to reinforce its verbal signal. Or it may, as the United States did as the deadline for its ultimatum to Saddam Hussein approached, be more concerned with the fourth of these risks: the possibility that the adversary might announce partial or conditional acceptance of the terms of the ultimatum or, avoiding a direct response to it, engage in a limited modification of the action that created the crisis. This possibility was viewed with extreme seriousness by administration leaders during the Persian Gulf crisis, and well-informed journalists referred to it as the administration's "nightmare scenario." Very detailed contingency plans were made to deal with such a ploy by Saddam Hussein and were discussed with coalition partners.

- Systematic study of past cases of coercive diplomacy has shown that this strategy, perhaps even more so than deterrence strategy, is highly context dependent. This means that coercive diplomacy must be tailored in an exacting way to fit the unique configuration of each situation. But the configuration of a crisis in which coercive diplomacy might be employed is seldom clearly visible to policy makers and, as a result, the strategy can easily fail. Success with the strategy rests heavily on skill in improvisation, good intelligence, sophisticated understanding of the opponent's mind-set and behavioral patterns, sensitivity to the requirements of crisis management. The coercing power must choose and time its actions carefully to make it possible for the opponent to appraise the evolving situation and to respond in a constructive manner. And, of great importance in most situations, the coercing power, even while exerting great pressure for compliance with its demands, must leave the opponent with a way out of the crisis that enables him at least to save face and avoid humiliation.

- Experience also indicates that it is risky to rely solely on threats of punishment for noncompliance with one's demands instead of offering incentives as well. Using the "carrot and stick" approach—as President Kennedy did in the Cuban missile crisis—will increase the possibility of a peaceful, mutually acceptable resolution of the crisis. Coercive diplomacy is best conceived as a flexible strategy in which what the stick cannot always achieve by itself can possibly be obtained by adding a carrot. Thus, as already noted, in contrast to reliance solely on military force to achieve one's objective, coercive diplomacy typically requires negotiation, bargaining, and often some measure of compromise.

Analysis of a number of historical cases has led to an identification of at least six variables that help to explain the success or failure of coercive diplomacy. While it is difficult to ascertain whether any of these variables by itself is either necessary or sufficient for success, each may be regarded as "favoring" successful coercion when present in a particular case. At the risk of oversimplifying the explanation for President Kennedy's success with coercive diplomacy in the Cuban missile crisis and coercive diplomacy's failure in the Persian Gulf crisis, I offer the following comparison of the two cases, calling attention to the presence of all six variables in the Cuban missile crisis and their absence in the Gulf crisis.

In the Cuban missile crisis Kennedy and Soviet Premier Nikita Khrushchev could cooperate to avoid war because neither leader believed that their disagreement approximated a zero-sum conflict, and because their image of war— should it occur—was that of a nuclear catastrophe. In contrast, President Bush and Saddam Hussein tended to see their conflict in unconditional terms, a tendency that was reinforced by the highly invidious image each had of the other. Moreover, unlike Kennedy and Khrushchev, who were horrified by the possibility that, if mismanaged, the crisis could lead to thermonuclear war, Bush and Hussein held an image of the outcome, costs, and consequences of war that was not distasteful enough to motivate either to seek a compromise settlement. Incentives for cooperating to avoid war were lacking on both sides. Indeed, it is not far-fetched to characterize the Bush administration's policy as coercive diplomacy without fear of the consequences of its failure: war.

In the Cuban missile crisis, moreover, Kennedy coupled his ultimatum with a substantial carrot: an agreement not to invade Cuba and a secret agreement to remove the U.S. Jupiter missiles from Turkey. In the Persian Gulf crisis, Bush relied solely on the stick and offered no carrot for a compromise settlement, insisting that there be no reward for aggression. However, the possibility of saving face by coupling withdrawal from Kuwait with other means was available to Hussein had he wished to do so. In the Cuban crisis, in contrast to the Persian Gulf crisis, neither side had any significant misperceptions or miscalculations that might have led to war. In the Cuban missile crisis, again unlike the Persian Gulf case, Kennedy operated with an image of Khrushchev as a leader capable of retreating—which he was able to capitalize on in orchestrating an effective carrot-and-stick variant of the ultimatum.

Two other psychological variables that appear to have been important in past cases of successful coercive diplomacy were present in the missile crisis but not in the Persian Gulf crisis. First, Kennedy succeeded in impressing upon Khrushchev that getting the missiles out of Cuba was more important to the United States than keeping the missiles there was to the Soviet Union. Kennedy thus succeeded in convincing Khrushchev that there was an asymmetry of motivation that favored the United States in the dispute. Bush, on the other hand, failed, despite considerable effort, to convince Hussein that getting Iraqi forces out of Kuwait was more important to the United States than refusing to remove them under threat of war was to Iraq. Second, whereas Kennedy created fear of unacceptable escalation of the crisis in Khrushchev's mind, Bush failed to create a fear of unacceptable punishment in Hussein's mind.

In this comparison, all six variables were present in the Cuban missile case but absent in the Persian Gulf crisis. A summary is presented in table 4.1.

Conclusion

The use of force as an instrument of U.S. foreign policy has been a difficult, often highly controversial issue. The problem was severely aggravated during the Vietnam War. Since then, American policy makers have found it difficult to obtain domestic and congressional support for using threats of force to back up diplomacy—and particularly for resorting to force when diplomatic efforts prove to be inadequate or unsuccessful.

Table 4.1. Six Variables that Help Explain Success or Failure of Coercive Diplomacy

	Cuban Missile Crisis	Gulf Crisis
Non-zero-sum view of the conflict	+	−
Overwhelming negative image of war	+	−
Carrot as well as stick	+	−
Asymmetry of motivation favoring state employing coercive diplomacy	+	−
Opponent's fear of unacceptable punishment for noncompliance	+	−
No significant misperceptions or miscalculations	+	−

Note: + = variable present; − = variable absent

Presidents Bush and Clinton have had to confront a striking paradox.[22] With the end of the Cold War, the United States emerged as the only superpower in possession of overwhelmingly superior military capabilities. Nevertheless, it has repeatedly experienced great difficulty in employing deterrence and coercive diplomacy to persuade adversaries from foregoing or stopping actions that impinged on U.S. interests.

Two particularly striking examples will suffice to illustrate this paradox and its unfortunate consequences. First, in the Persian Gulf crisis, as Barry Blechman and Tamara Coffman Wittes put it: "Despite the most amazing demonstration of U.S. military capabilities and willingness to use force—if necessary—to expel the Iraqi military from Kuwait, Saddam refused to comply with U.S. demands and his troops had to be expelled by force of arms."

The second example concerns the efforts of the Reagan and Bush administrations to seek the removal of Panamanian dictator Manuel Noriega from office after he was indicted for drug trafficking and money laundering. After Noriega stole the presidential election in May, 1989, the Bush administration worked through the Organization of American States to negotiate Noriega's resignation and backed that action with an effort at coercive diplomacy that employed a series of military exercises and other actions in the Canal Zone. Noriega refused to comply with the U.S. demand that he step down, and he subsequently survived a coup in which the United States played a minor role. When a U.S. naval officer was murdered in December, 1989, President Bush was forced to send combat forces into Panama to capture Noriega and bring him to the United States for trial.

How can the failure of coercive diplomacy in these cases be understood?

While it is difficult to understand Saddam Hussein's mind-set or his calculations, it would appear that he was insufficiently impressed with the credibility and/or the potency of U.S. threats of force. He may have been influenced more by an image he had formed of U.S. irresolution, one that attributed to the United States a peculiar reluctance and inability to sustain casualties that stemmed from its catastrophic experience in Vietnam.

As for Noriega, it is clear that only a much stronger variant of coercive diplomacy than that employed was necessary to overcome his unwillingness to relinquish power. As noted in our earlier discussion of coercive diplomacy, the stronger and more extreme the demand made on an opponent, the stronger one must expect his resistance to be. Analysis of the Bush administration's efforts to pressure Noriega to comply with its demand to abdicate reveals that it employed a weak version of coercive diplomacy resembling the try-and-see approach. As Blechman and Wittes note, the administration "never stated clearly and definitively that the U.S. would be willing to invade the country and throw Noriega out if he did not comply with the demand to relinquish office . . . a [sufficiently] potent threat was never made. . . . Nor was any deadline set for his compliance with the demand. . . . U.S. verbal demands were not directly supported by tangible military actions. Although reinforcements were sent to the Canal Zone and some exercises were held there, they were all downplayed by U.S. officials and explained by a general concern for the security of the zone in light of deteriorating U.S.-Panamanian relations."

General Colin Powell, former JCS chairman, supported this interpretation in an interview with the authors. Powell observed that the limited military actions taken by the United States in 1988 and 1989 probably reinforced Noriega's preexisting perception that America was irresolute and that he could possibly persevere. When an invasion force was finally assembled, Blechman and Wittes note, "it was done in secrecy, and never displayed publicly or brandished in support of an ultimatum [that was not given] that Noriega surrender or face forceful expulsion."

There are reasons, of course, why a stronger variant of coercive diplomacy was not employed in this case. Administration officials were no doubt operating under strong political and diplomatic constraints. They hoped, if at all possible, to avoid the domestic and international criticism that could be expected if the United States gave the impression that it was returning to a pattern of intervention in Central America associated with its earlier history of relations with nations in that area. This political constraint was a heavy and perhaps unavoidable one. The point that a weak, inadequate version of coercive diplomacy was undertaken is not made in criticism of the administration but rather to emphasize that there are often severe constraints on the ability to engage in the strong type of coercive diplomacy called for by the situation.

Blechman and Wittes, authors of a recent study of these and other cases, observe that "there is a generation of political leaders throughout the world whose basic perception of U.S. military power and political will is one of weakness, [leaders] who enter any situation with a fundamental belief that the United States can be defeated, can be driven away." In support of this observation, Blechman and Wittes cite the explicit, concise expression of the belief conveyed by Mohammed Farah Aidid, leader of a key Somali faction, to Ambassador Robert Oakley, UN special envoy to Somalia during the U.S. involvement there from 1993 to 1995: "I've studied Vietnam and Beirut. I know that all I need to do to send you home is to kill some Americans."[23]

Aidid was proven to be correct. The withdrawal of U.S. forces from Somalia after eighteen U.S. soldiers were killed in a clash with Aidid's forces was not only a humiliating experience, it also confirmed perceptions that America lacked resolve, and further complicated and undermined subsequent Clinton administration efforts to make effective use of threats of force.

It is clear, then, that domestic public and congressional support for threats or use of force is a critical variable. Such support does not guarantee success, but without it, presidents will continue to have great difficulty making threats of sufficient credibility and potency to back their demands on adversaries. The American public's strong aversion to the risk of suffering casualties, a legacy of Vietnam, is all the more constraining when the United States is confronted by the intrastate conflicts that have become so prominent in the post–Cold War era. Ever mindful of this public aversion to casualties, presidents have been reluctant to make threats as clear and potent as required by the situation. They have reacted cautiously or not at all to some challenges to American interests.

The United States has been correct not to intervene in all of the many crises occurring around the globe. American interests do not always clearly require us to do so, and the international community itself is overwhelmed with such crises and cannot respond to all of them. But U.S. interests often *do* merit some response—and that response has tended to be a minimal one taken in the hope of limiting the extent of involvement and costs.

As a result, the United States has often acted in ways that inadvertently support the image of American irresolution. In most cases where firm U.S. military action was finally taken—Panama, Haiti, and Bosnia are examples—it came only after considerable delay. Such belated responses could not be counted upon to erase the image of U.S. hesitation and irresolution held by foreign leaders who thought they could benefit from the pronounced reluctance of the American public, Congress, and administration leaders to accept the risk of casualties. The simple fact is that the inconclusive threats and delayed military action taken in many situations are likely to be perceived by others, as Blechman and Wittes put it, "more as signs of weakness than as potent expressions of America's true military power." As a result, some foreign leaders will likely be willing to withstand American threats—necessitating either recourse to force to achieve American goals, or embarrassing retreats.

At the same time, we should take note of the critical role played by the UN Security Council on two major occasions in helping presidents to overcome strong domestic and congressional resistance to the use of force. Both President Bush (in the preliminaries leading to the use of force against Iraq) and President Clinton (in preparing to use force against Haiti's rulers) were successful in freeing themselves from strong domestic opposition sufficiently to undertake these initiatives. They did so by first securing Security Council resolutions authorizing force. Faced by UN legitimization of the use of force by the United States, a reluctant Congress was not willing to oppose it.

The United States is understandably insistent on retaining the option of unilateral action in defense of U.S. interests, but it will often require strong international legitimization of such actions and, in addition, the participation of multinational forces.[24]

Another option that will have to be employed at times is the carrot-and-stick strategy. Instead, of relying too heavily on economic coercion or threats to use military force, the United States would do well to give more emphasis to offering meaningful positive incentives, as it did in working out the Agreed Framework in 1995 with North Korea.[25]

General Powell was and remains a strong adherent of elements of the Weinberger Doctrine. There is much merit in his observation that "threats of military force will work only when U.S. leaders have decided that they are prepared to use force." The logical and practical implication of this observation is that when presidents are not prepared to use force, threats to do so should not be made.[26] General Powell also pointedly observed that, when resorting to force, "The president must begin the action prepared to see the course through to its end. . . . He can only persuade an opponent of his seriousness when, indeed, he is serious. . . ." He adds to this an injunction the observation that "The use of force must be decisive"[27]—an injunction, however, that cannot be honored in every situation.

The dilemmas regarding use of force and threats of force in American diplomacy will not yield to the imperatives of the Weinberger Doctrine. It is noteworthy that under Secretary of Defense William Perry and JCS chairman Gen. John Shalikashvili, the Clinton administration found it necessary on occasion to introduce some flexibility in applying the Weinberger Doctrine. Force has not always been used, as Weinberger argued, only when truly vital U.S.

interests are at stake. President Clinton resorted to force in Haiti and Bosnia—and, indeed, President Bush waged war against Saddam Hussein—with only marginal domestic political support. Certainly not with the "reasonable assurance" of it that was set down as a prerequisite by Weinberger. The Weinberger injunction that U.S. combat forces should be employed only "as a last resort after exhausting other means" for safeguarding U.S. interests has also been subjected to considerable questioning. As Blechman and Wittes observe, "rightly or wrongly—the press of the world events drives policymaking inevitably toward Secretary Shultz's prescriptions for limited use of force in support of diplomacy."

At the same time, other criteria associated with the Weinberger Doctrine continue to characterize the Clinton administration's approach. These include the requirement for clearly defined political and military objectives and, until recently, the requirement that an exit date for removal of U.S. forces be established when they are committed to a crisis area.

These important emendations of the Weinberger Doctrine in the direction of Shultz's position have been taken uneasily and have occasioned considerable criticism. By no means do we have a synthesis of the two competing points of view. The tensions and dilemmas surrounding the use of force or threats of force remain and can be expected to challenge U.S. presidents into the foreseeable future. This conclusion supports President Bush's observation that: "There can be no single or simple set of fixed rules for using force. . . . Each and every case is unique."

Notes

The author wishes to thank the Carnegie Corporation of New York for its support of this research. This chapter was completed in 1997; it has not been possible for the author to take account of developments since then.

1. This section and the next two draw from the discussion in G. Craig and A. L. George, *Force and Statecraft: Diplomatic Problems of Our Time,* 3d ed. (New York: Oxford University Press, 1995), Chap. 19. For an excellent detailed analysis of the historical development of these competing strategies to the present, see Christopher M. Gacek, *The Logic of Force: the Dilemma of Limited War in American Foreign Policy* (New York: Columbia University Press, 1994).
2. George Shultz, "Address to the Trilateral Commission, Apr. 3, 1984, Department of State Bulletin, May, 1984. Shultz returned to this subject in an address to the New York Synogogue on October 25, 1984, Department of State Bulletin, Dec., 1984.
3. George Shultz, address on "The Ethics of Power" at Yeshiva University, Dec. 9, 1984, Department of State Bulletin, Feb., 1985.
4. Personal communication from Richard Haass to the author.
5. Cf. Alexander L. George and Jane E. Holl, *The Warning-Response Problem and*

Missed Opportunities in Preventive Diplomacy, A Report to the Carnegie Commission on Preventing Deadly Conflict (New York: Carnegie Corporation, May, 1997). See also *Preventing Deadly Conflict, Final Report of the Carnegie Commission on Preventing Deadly Conflict* (New York: Carnegie Corporation, Dec., 1997), and the major comparative study edited by Bruce W. Jentleson, *Opportunities Missed, Opportunities Seized: Preventive Diplomacy in the Post–Cold War World* (New York: Carnegie Corporation, forthcoming).

6. See, for example, Andrew J. Goodpaster, *When Diplomacy Is Not Enough: Managing Multilateral Military Interventions, A Report to the Carnegie Commission on Preventing Deadly Conflict* (New York: Carnegie Corporation, July, 1996), pp. 27–28.

7. The distinction between different types of humanitarian crises is made by Bruce W. Jentleson, "Who, Why, What, and How: Debates Over Post–Cold War Military Interventions," in *Eagle Adrift: American Foreign Policy at the End of the Century,* ed. Robert J. Lieber (New York: Longman, 1997).

8. The problems created by emphasis on an early, fixed date for the withdrawal of U.S. forces recently engaged the interest of the Council of Foreign Relations in New York, which set up a study group to examine the experience thus far in several U.S. interventions. A report summarizing some of the study group's research was published by Gideon Rose, the director of the study group, in *Foreign Affairs* 77, no. 1 (Jan.-Feb., 1998): 56–67.

9. *New York Times,* Dec. 19, 1997.

10. Gen. Colin L. Powell, "U.S. Forces: Challenges Ahead," *Foreign Affairs* 71 (winter, 1992–93): 32–46. In this article General Powell also identified several broad political questions to be addressed in each case in which intervention was contemplated: Are the political objectives important, clearly defined and understood? What are the likely risks and costs?

11. Personal communication from Richard Haass to the author.

12. These ideas are developed in greater detail and illustrated in A. L. George, *Bridging the Gap: Theory and Practice in Foreign Policy* (Washington, D.C.: U.S. Institute of Peace, 1993).

13. The following remarks are distilled from studies by a number of scholars of a variety of deterrence cases. I have drawn for present purposes largely from earlier publications that were undertaken together with other investigators. See A. L. George and R. Smoke, *Deterrence in American Foreign Policy: Theory and Practice* (New York: Columbia University Press, 1974), and G. A. Craig and A. L. George, *Force and Statecraft: Diplomatic Problems of Our Time,* 3d ed. (New York: Oxford University Press, 1995). A selective bibliography of the deterrence literature is provided in Craig and George's bibliographical essay, pp. 194–95.

14. This discussion draws upon the foreword I have written for James E. Goodby, *Europe Undivided: The New Logic of Peace* (Washington, D.C.: U.S. Institute of Peace, 1998). In this book, Goodby addresses the possibility of moving the relationship between the United States and Russia in the years ahead from one of conditional peace to stable peace, and he discusses in some detail both the desirability and feasibility of such a foreign policy goal.

15. John Lewis Gaddis, *Strategies of Containment* (New York: Oxford University Press, 1982).

16. U.S. policy towards so-called rogue states is the subject of a current study by Robert Litwak at the Wilson Center of the Smithsonian Institution.

17. The best discussion of various reassurance strategies that may be adopted instead of or in conjunction with deterrence is Janice Gross Stein, "Deterrence and Reassurance," in Philip E. Tetlock et al., *Behavior, Society, and Nuclear War* (New York: Oxford University Press, 1991), pp. 2:8–72.

18. For a more detailed discussion of these alternative types of deterrence strategy, see George and Smoke, *Deterrence in American Foreign Policy,* Chap. 19, "Commitment Theory."

19. For a more detailed discussion of the need for developing "actor-specific behavioral models" to replace the attribution of general rationality to an adversary, see George, *Bridging the Gap,* pp. 125–31.

20. For a discussion of these strategies employed by the Soviet Union during the Cold War, see George and Smoke, *Deterrence in American Foreign Policy,* Chap. 18, "Patterns of Deterrence Failure: A Typology."

21. This section draws on previous publications: A. L. George, D. K. Hall, and W. E. Simons, *The Limits of Coercive Diplomacy* (Boston: Little, Brown, 1971); a second, much enlarged edition, A. L. George and W. E. Simons, eds., *The Limits of Coercive Diplomacy* (Boulder, Colo.: Westview, 1994); A. L. George, *Forceful Persuasion: Coercive Diplomacy As an Alternative to War* (Washington, D.C.: U.S. Institute of Peace, 1991); and Craig and George, *Force and Statecraft.*

22. This and succeeding paragraphs draw upon the excellent study by Barry M. Blechman and Tamara Coffman Wittes, "Defining Moment: The Threat and Use of Force in American Foreign Policy since 1989," a work in progress prepared for the Committee on International Conflict Resolution of the National Research Council, National Academy of Sciences.

23. Robert Oakley, interview by Blechman and Wittes.

24. Richard Haass has coined the term "reluctant sheriff" to describe the role the United States should play in regulating international conflicts. He emphasizes that it will often have to construct ad hoc coalitions in the service of multilateral operations. Cf. R. N. Haass, *The Reluctant Sheriff: The United States after the Cold War* (New York: Council on Foreign Relations, 1997).

25. During the course of their deliberations, members of the Carnegie Commission on Preventing Deadly Conflicts became aware of an important gap in the scholarly literature having to do with the role of positive incentives as a tool for conflict avoidance and resolution. Accordingly, a major study was commissioned comprising many excellent case studies that demonstrate that positive inducements of an economic, political, or security character can often be helpful in deterring nuclear proliferation, preventing armed conflict, and defending civil and human rights. Cf. David Cortright, ed., *The Price of Peace: Incentives and International Conflict Prevention* (Lanham, Md.: Rowman and Littlefield, 1997).

26. Powell, "U.S. Forces," pp. 32–45; Colin L. Powell, "Why Generals Get Nervous," *New York Times,* Oct. 8, 1992, p. A35, quoted by Blechman and Wittes.

27. Colin L. Powell, interview by Blechman and Wittes.

Chapter 5

Lessons Learned or Not Learned

The Gulf War in Retrospect

Williamson Murray

SEVEN YEARS HAVE NOW PASSED since the Persian Gulf crisis exploded in the summer of 1990. Consequently, we are now in a position to draw some lessons from the conflict and divine possible directions that the U.S. military is taking for better or for worse. Unfortunately, neither the American military nor its critics appear to be looking at the Gulf War from a dispassionate, clear perspective. Rather, what actually happened and what might be suggestive in thinking about military forces in the twenty-first century has been obscured by interservice bickering, special pleading, budget debates, and Monday-morning quarterbacking by "experts" in pursuit of reputations rather than truth. This is not to say that there are no important and useful studies of the war.[1] Unfortunately, much of what might be useful is being lost in noisy and ill-informed partisan pieces such as the recent Government Accounting Office report on the war or William Odom's piece in *Foreign Affairs*. Moreover, peculiar misunderstandings of what happened or did not happen in the Gulf War are driving much of the current defense debate.

Part of the problem in adjusting to the lessons of the war lies in the general disinterest the services displayed in doing a thorough, broad-based, lessons-learned analysis of the conflict. The marines and navy commissioned the Center of Naval Analysis to perform a tactical analysis; the result was useful studies of particular incidents, procedures, and tactical approaches, but there was no larger examination of the war from a maritime perspective. There were a number of army efforts, but these remained at a relatively low level or, because of command influence, dared not walk into the minefield of the conduct of operations at the highest level. The most thorough lessons-learned effort was the Department of the Air Force's *Gulf War Air Power Survey*.[2] Ironically, that study resulted only after the intervention of Secretary of the Air Force Donald Rice, who was appalled that his service had displayed absolutely no interest in conducting such an analysis. More recently, elements within the air force, to include the current chief historian, have mounted an all-too-successful effort to bury the resulting *Gulf War Air Power Survey* volumes even within the air force itself.

It is, of course, impossible to set out the full spread of what has happened and why in the lessons-learned analyses of the war. Consequently, I will focus on the larger trends in defense thinking since the Gulf War as well as some of the peculiar analyses that have appeared and their influence on the services in adjusting to a post–Cold War world of indeterminate enemies and threats. As Thucydides suggested some twenty-five hundred years ago, an analysis of the past can only contribute to thinking about the future by helping those who "want to understand clearly the events which happened in the past and which (human nature being what it is) will, at some time or other and in much the same way, be repeated in the future."[3]

In light of this, I will first examine what might have been learned at the strategic and political levels from the war for thinking about the next century. I will then consider the influence that conflict has had on American thinking about the conduct of war at the operational and tactical levels in the twenty-first century. My purpose is not to provide answers, but rather to suggest potential difficulties that confront American defense policy as the debate about the war and its meaning continues to unfold.

Strategic and Political Lessons Learned or Not Learned

The debate over the Gulf War's conduct on the strategic level has largely degenerated into arguments as to how and why the conflict was halted after a hundred hours—a decision that supposedly allowed a substantial portion of Saddam Hussein's Republican Guard to escape destruction. Admittedly, the survival of the Republican Guard has provided the Iraqi regime with the armed forces needed to put down a substantial revolution within the country. Critics continue to criticize the Bush administration for not completing the Republican Guard's destruction in 1991, citing the facts that Saddam Hussein remains in power, that his minions tried to blow up former president George Bush in Kuwait, and that the movement of Republican Guard forces toward Kuwait forced the United States to begin a major deployment of its own troops to the Middle East as justification for their criticism.

At best, such criticisms represent Monday-morning quarterbacking. They also miss a major point: What might the Middle East look like today had President Bush not acted as strongly as he did? Without Operations Desert Shield and Desert Storm the United States would most probably be looking at a catastrophic situation in the region. Not only would Iraq dominate a substantial portion of the Persian Gulf's oil resources, but Saddam would probably possess nuclear weapons. He still remains a nuisance, to be sure, but one that poses no great strategic threat for the immediate future. To a great extent, the strategic policies of 1990–91 eliminated some dangerous possibilities that might have led the Middle East into a dangerous era, one with negative implications for the world economy. That U.S. strategic policy did not achieve every strategic possibility simply lies in the realm of how the world really works.

President Bush's response to the crisis in the summer of 1990 was a high point in U.S. strategic policy making over the past twenty-five years. It stands in stark contrast to the sorry performance of the U.S. political and military decision makers who landed America in the disastrous Vietnam War.[4] In 1990 the administration identified the threat and prepared the American people to confront casualties on the level of tens of thousands in a war to reverse Iraq's seizure of Kuwait. The administration made clear why it was considering the sternest measures and for the most part pursued a coherent and consistent policy as the mid-January date for Desert Storm approached.[5]

However, governmental processes are open to criticism in the intelligence failures leading up to the Gulf War. In retrospect, it is astonishing that few within—or without, for that matter—the Washington Beltway picked up on the megalomaniacal aims of Iraq's leader. The nature of the Iraqi regime and the aims of its Baathist leadership *should* have been apparent to at least some within the foreign policy and intelligence communities. It was not. Yet it was to those willing to buy Samir al-Khalil's *The Republic of Fear,* a book published only the year before.[6] Still, there is no evidence that the author—one of the few persons who understood Western *and* Middle Eastern politics and history equally well—or his book had any substantive influence on the decision-making process in Washington before the crisis. However, it is worth contrasting what Khalil was able to accomplish, with access only to open source literature but a solid grounding and understanding of Middle Eastern politics and history, with the products of those in the intelligence assessment business.

The crucial intelligence failure was not failing to foresee the Iraqi invasion, it was failing to understand the fundamental nature of the Iraqi regime itself: its ideological bias, the megalomaniacal drives of its leader, the nation's peculiar makeup (the result of its colonial past under both Turkish and British rule), and, finally, the past history of Arab glories stretching back into the ninth century A.D.[7] Moreover, it might have been of some use to possess an understanding of ideological driven tyrannies such as Stalin's Soviet Union. In other words, to understand the dynamics of Iraq one needed a broad understanding of history and culture in the widest sense.

The result of such misunderstanding of the nature of the Iraqi tyranny carried beyond the strategic and political realm. For example, the misestimates of Iraqi military effectiveness—which portrayed a "battle-hardened Iraqi Army"—were a serious impediment to policy making and strategic planning.[8] Similarly, Col. John Warden's August, 1990, initial planning for an air campaign estimated Iraq's military potential far too highly while largely underestimating the political stability of the regime.[9] In the end, President Bush and his advisers were willing to risk war both in the air and on the ground. Yet the length of the air campaign (over five weeks duration) offered Saddam the opportunity to escape a looming strategic disaster before the ground campaign could prove, even to the Palestinians, the worthlessness of Iraq's claims as a great power.[10]

If American strategists got their analysis of Iraq wrong before July, 1990—an Iraq which had launched a murderous war of aggression against one of its neighbors, which had not only used gas on the battlefield but against its own domestic population as well, and which had clearly harbored ambitions of making its own nuclear weapons—what are the chances that American strategists will assess the dangers in the more complex and ambiguous world of the next century? The foremost strategic lesson of the Gulf War suggests that there were fundamental weaknesses in the American understanding of the external world. There is little evidence that things are better—and a good deal that they are worse.

The most obvious explanation for this state of affairs lies in the educational backgrounds of those in the intelligence business as well as among a substantial portion of the U.S. military leadership. The educational backgrounds of U.S. leaders have provided anything but a cultural or historical understanding of the world in the decades of the Cold War. Instead, the emphasis has been and remains on technological knowledge rather than on historical perspective. Supposedly, technical means of collection will be enough. But the Gulf War and events elsewhere have served to underline that they are not. Yet the emphasis in the intelligence community has remained on the products of technical means of collection—satellites, electronic transmission interception, photo reconnaissance—all of which amount to little more than the counting of beans, rather than on estimates of what really matters: capability and intentions. But the latter requires the knowledge of language, literature, and history—items that simply are not quantifiable.

Such a narrow technical Weltanschauung is reinforced by the predilections of the academic world. On one hand, the social sciences seem impervious to a recognition of the complexities of history or of a nonlinear world.[11] On the other, historians have rendered themselves irrelevant as they retreat into social history and eliminate the study of diplomatic and military history from the curricula of major universities.

The largest lesson of the Gulf War thus would seem to be its strategic lesson. In the coming century, which promises to be of vast complexity and where none of the sureties of the Cold War will exist, the United States will have to navigate its course with some larger understanding of the general historical and cultural patterns of those with whom it must deal. Admittedly, history is an ambiguous instructor. As one commentator recently noted: "In this bewildering world, the search for predictive theories to guide strategy has been no more successful than the search for such theories in other areas of human existence. Patterns do emerge from the past, and their study permits educated guesses about the range of potential outcomes. But the future is not an object of knowledge; no increase in processing power will make the owl of history a daytime bird. Similar causes do not always produce similar effects, and causes interact in ways unforeseeable even by the historically unsophisticated."[12]

Nevertheless, the current drift in the strategic and policy-making worlds continues to place an extraordinary emphasis on technological advantages. In 1995 Adm. William A. Owens, the recently retired vice chairman of the Joint Chiefs of Staff, and Joseph S. Nye, Jr., dean of Harvard's John F. Kennedy School of Government, wrote an article for *Foreign Affairs* arguing that "the vast 'American' superiority in information technology could deter or defeat traditional military threats at relatively low cost."[13] According to the authors, this "information edge is equally important as a force multiplier of American diplomacy, including 'soft power,'" which Nye defines as "the ability to achieve desired outcomes in international affairs through attraction rather than coercion."[14] Supposedly, this capacity to gin up huge amounts of data—information—will allow the United States to gain an unparalleled advantage over potential opponents and dominate a peaceful, productive twenty-first century. The Nye-Owens argument is largely driven by the cultural perceptions and biases of English-speaking, middle-class American academics and retired admirals. It is difficult to see how the United States can "control" the flow of information in any meaningful fashion—especially considering the current explosion of information sources—in a world of the ambitious and aggressive, where many, even among the developed nations, harbor deep suspicions—even hatreds—of the United States, and where enormous disparities will remain between the haves and the have nots.

Moreover, data and information do not automatically translate into knowledge, understanding, or insight. Without a background in foreign languages, history, and other cultures, it is difficult to see how American technologists will understand a world in which Saddam Husseins will continue to appear. Saddam got as far as he did because too much of the U.S. government's intelligence process was incapable of analyzing the incalculables of history and culture. Furthermore, American hubris about its national technological and information superiority will only contribute to future foreign policy and military disasters similar to what occurred in Somalia. In the end, Somalia mattered not at all. Nor did misestimates matter in the case of Iraq in the final result. But such mistakes *did* matter in the case of Vietnam. Americans should not forget the strategic and analytical mistakes they made regarding places like Vietnam, Iraq, and Somalia as they look to the future. As Allan Millett and I suggested in an article in the *National Interest* in the late 1980s, nations that get war wrong on the strategic and political levels always lose. Those that get it right on those levels can usually make up for whatever tactical and operational weaknesses their forces may have.[15]

Military Lessons Learned or Not Learned

In most respects, the Gulf War was a considerable success for American arms. The casualty figures reflect the operational and tactical superiority of the U.S. military. There were mistakes, of course, but the quibbling among generals should not mislead us as to the overall superiority and excellence that American forces displayed. However, a substantial portion of the attention within the services in the post Gulf War period has focused on the technological side of the equation—almost to the exclusion of other aspects.

Part of the problem has to do with the extent of the coalition victory in the air and on the ground, especially in light of casualty estimates both within and outside the military before January 17, 1991. The results led many commentators to write about the seemingly frictionless performance of U.S. military forces. Yet those who waged the air and ground wars confronted considerable friction—from the pervasive influence of bad weather on the air campaign to the miscommunication between Generals Norman Schwarzkopf and Fred Franks.[16] This should not minimize the fact that the coalition military forces—capitalizing on their superior training, doctrine, speed, and leadership—imposed a far higher degree of friction on the Iraqis. Because of the tempo and competence of coalition forces, the Iraqis were never in a position to take advantage of the friction the allies encountered while planning and executing military operations.

Too much of the focus in the Gulf War's immediate aftermath was concentrated on technological aspects of victory. Such an emphasis was perhaps inevitable given the pictures of precision-guided munitions and wrecked Iraqi tanks that bombarded American television screens throughout the war. Moreover, the technological biases in analyses of the war have received an additional emphasis from the generational change in the attitudes of the American military occurring in the 1990s. As the Vietnam War generation moved off into retirement, a new generation of officers took over the senior ranks, a generation of officers that missed having the sobering experience of watching technology fail to solve the intractable doctrinal, operational, and tactical issues raised by the Vietnam War.[17]

The result has been increasing interest over the past several years in "the revolution in military affairs." That term has a rather interesting history. In the late 1970s, Soviet military writers picked up on what they described as a military technical revolution occurring in the United States. The Office of Net Assessment in the Pentagon was one of the few organizations in the defense establishment to recognize the significance of what the Soviets were saying. Consequently, it pushed the idea in the late 1980s. The Gulf War gave the idea of a military technical revolution added impetus. However, to their horror, Net Assessment analysts discovered substantial elements within the U.S. military focusing entirely on the technological dimensions of the concept. Even a change in terminology from a "military technical revolution" to a "revolution in military affairs" (RMA) was not sufficient to reverse the tide.[18]

We thus are looking at the makings of a major intellectual debate, the outcome of which will do much to determine the direction of American military policy over the coming decades and will have considerable impact on America's capacity to employ force in the next century. William Owens has led the charge in preaching a technological revolution in military affairs, one that he argues will literally make the fog and friction of the battlefield disappear, at least as far as U.S. commanders are concerned.[19] But Owens is not alone. There have been a number of other enthusiastic proponents and supporters of such ideas inside and outside the services. The claims made by advocates of a current RMA are indeed extraordinary.[20] The air force's *New World Vistas* contends that: "The power of the new information systems will lie in their ability to correlate data automatically and rapidly from many sources to form a complete picture of the operational area, whether it be a battlefield or the site of a mobility operation."[21] Nor is it just a group of analysts in think tanks propagating such views:

Two years ago a senior army general told a group of Marine Corps officers that "the digitization of the battlefield means the end of Clausewitz." And former army chief of staff Gen. Dennis Reimer has argued that if the U.S. military had possessed the information technologies available today, the United States might well have won the Vietnam War.[22]

Recently, some of the enthusiasts have backed away slightly from the more extreme claims of "total battlespace dominance" that were popular several years ago. But their claims still suggest a massive break with twenty-five hundred years of military history: "the system-of-systems promises a new level of battle assessment: the capacity to know, almost immediately, the results of military operations." Future capabilities will supposedly allow "near perfect battle assessment, dominant battlespace knowledge, and near perfect mission assignment."[23]

The result is an argument for U.S. military forces that would be almost entirely based on technology—in other words, doctrine and military concepts would be driven entirely by technology, rather than the other way around. And there are many in the political world who have found these claims attractive.[24] As Admiral Owens's faithful disciple, James Blaker, recently argued: "The important point in all of this is not just the individual advances in the capacity to collect and process information about what is occurring in battle. It's not only the growing capacity to pick out the most important targets in a rapidly changing conflict milieu, nor is it solely the dramatic improvements in the U.S. ability to destroy those targets from ever-greater ranges. It is the interaction of these things—how the ability to see and choose targets better increases the leverage of precision-guided munitions, and how a faster and more accurate capacity to assess the effects of violence makes the subsequent use of violence deadlier."[25]

That argument leads to some attractive conclusions: the United States can have more capability for less money and with a substantial reduction in force structure. Blaker argues that his RMA force structure would be considerably less costly—$210 billion in constant 1996 dollars versus today's approximately $245 billion. But there is, of course, a price. Blaker would give up no less than five active duty army divisions, three carriers, twenty-one surface combatant naval vessels, and nearly fifty attack submarines, with a personnel decrease of more than eight hundred thousand men and women in the active duty and reserve force structures.[26]

All of this will sound most attractive to those interested in making cuts in the military budget. In the coming decade, when federal budget deficits are likely to threaten the nation's economic stability, such cuts will look increasingly attractive to many in the legislative and executive branches, especially if the threats to U.S. national interests appear as vague as at present. But whether such a direction in U.S. defense policy would actually address the strategic and operational problems that the United States will confront in the next century is another matter. Still, there is a major push toward a highly technological vision of the RMA. It is the vision of a group of advocates who believe they understand what that next evolution in military affairs is and how the U.S. military should *now* embark on tailoring its forces and technology to meet the needs of a narrow technological vision. To a great extent that vision is the product of an imaginative and unrealistic reading of what happened in the Gulf War.

The Real Questions

Above all, RMA advocates have cast their vision in a vacuum. They provide no clear context at any level—from the political and strategic to the tactical—in their descriptions of future war. Moreover, their depictions present a vision of war at a distance, one in which U.S. forces do all the acting and killing while their opponents suffer a rain of blows without responding. Such a picture does not draw on any historical experience, nor does it depict any recognizable country or possible opposing military force. In contrast, the successful innovators of the 1920s and 1930s, who pushed blitzkrieg and carrier warfare and who caused *real* revolutions in military affairs, possessed a clear vision of who their opponents might be and how new approaches to war might work in actual combat situations. In fact, the technologists who describe the current RMA largely depict enemy forces that have replicated the high-tech direction they believe the U.S. military should take. Of course, those potential foes have a far less competent version. They clearly dismiss the possibility that U.S. opponents might chart heir own independent course, one that could aim largely at taking advantage of U.S. vulnerabilities. A Chinese general and a senior Indian officer reputedly responded after being asked what lessons they drew from the Gulf War: (1) Possess nuclear weapons, and (2) don't give the Americans six months to get ready.

It is worth underlining that those of us challenging the technological revolutionaries are not Luddites. Technology has significantly enhanced U.S. military capabilities since the early 1940s. The real issue in the emerging defense debate is how the U.S. military will use technology. Will it recast its military with technology as the driving force on the basis of untested and untried promises of visionaries who for the most part possess no combat experience and certainly are willing to draw only from their idealized picture of the Gulf War? Or will the U.S. military adopt a more prudent course in terms of current realities and incorporate technology into innovative, realistic combat doctrine and operational concepts derived from real tests? History at least suggests that doctrine, training, organization, and conceptualization are equally if not more important than state-of-the-art technology. And the process of innovation, the adaptation of technology to the conduct of war, demands enormous testing, challenging, and realistic evaluation.[27]

Those who are presently urging a radical restructuring of the U.S. military along the lines of their conception of a revolution in military affairs have largely ignored four crucial factors:

1. The political context within which U.S. defense policy will and must exist.
2. The strategic environment that will confront the United States for the foreseeable future.
3. The fundamental nature of war, a nature that reflects not only twenty-five hundred years of historical experience, but the nonlinear dynamics of the real world—a world that in scientific terms is dominated by unpredictability, complexity, uncertainty, and change.
4. What history suggests about the actual processes that have guided military institutions in the past in achieving a level of successful innovation in peacetime that resulted in a real revolution in military affairs.[28]

During the Cold War the U.S. military was able to invest in technologies that had no clear payoff. The Pentagon's share of the gross national product allowed a certain leeway for systems to fail.[29] Given America's current political environment it is likely that defense budgets will continue their slow, steady drop for the foreseeable future. The defense budget has *not* bottomed out, especially in view of budget deficits and the problems of financing Medicare as the baby boomers approach retirement. That is the harsh reality, and it is not one the services have paid sufficient attention to, especially in terms of the long-term consequences throughout the past five years of the drawdown. Instead, the services continue to program for high-price items of questionable need. For example, the projected cost for tactical fighter aircraft over the next several decades is somewhere in the neighborhood of $360 to $400 billion. This is quite simply pure insanity.

Consequently, in a time of rapid technological change and low defense budgets, the challenge will be to buy only those items of equipment and technology that U.S. military forces absolutely must have. Unfortunately, technology costs money. The argument that a high-tech military with vast communications capabilities as well as electronic sensors will decrease the defense budget has no basis in the evidence of the past fifty years. In fact, whatever kinds of forces the United States fields in the coming decades will depend to a great extent on the research and development of the past twenty years. The resulting forces, whatever their makeup, will be more effective, but they will also be more costly. And the money is simply not going to be there for massive technological changes in how the U.S. military does business—at least not until a real peer competitor to U.S. interests appears on the horizon.

In many ways, the emerging strategic environment presents an equally great challenge to those who will craft the defense framework in the twenty-first century. What appears likely is that the United States will not confront a peer competitor for most of the first half of the next century. In terms of historical analogy, the United States may be in a position similar to that of Britain after the Congress of Vienna in 1815. For the rest of the nineteenth century, Britain confronted only local and sporadic challenges to its worldwide interests. It was not until the rise of Imperial Germany at the end of the century that the British Empire confronted a real peer competitor, which in turn forced a fundamental reordering of British defense priorities—too late, perhaps, to prevent the catastrophe of World War I.[30]

From 1815 to 1900 the Royal Navy and the British Army engaged in a series of small wars and engagements that were essential to maintaining worldwide stability. The United States will confront similar challenges to its vital interests in the world in coming decades, but those challenges will be on a wholly different order than those of the past fifty years. Peacekeeping, short-term interventions like Haiti, and perhaps even a conflict similar to the Gulf War or Kosovo appear to be the most likely roles for U.S. forces for most of the first half of the next century. That fact raises another critical challenge to the technocratic demands for radical change. The type of military that Owens and his supporters are urging represents forces ideally suited to wage war against a peer competitor of the United States. Their vision of the enemy is of one that possesses highly technological forces, dependent on complex logistics and communications systems supported by an industrialized (or post-industrialized) society. Such forces, they argue, can be defeated or disrupted almost bloodlessly—at least from the U.S. point of view—by precision-guided munitions and viruses fed into enemy computer systems.[31] But is it reasonable to expect that Europe or Japan or South Korea would represent such a threat in our lifetimes?

Given demographic and economic trends it is a most unlikely scenario. And Russia's continuing economic and military woes rule it out as a potential peer competitor. China, of course, represents another problem.[32] It has not yet joined the First World, but its economic explosion suggests that sometime in the next century it will indeed be a major military power, once its military forces receive increased funding and support from a growing economic base. And it may well become a peer competitor. Moreover, China's leaders have on a number of occasions made clear the extent of their goals: no less than the restitution of the Middle Kingdom to its rightful place in the order of things—at least from the Chinese point of view.

But even now China possesses nuclear capabilities, which are likely to grow rather than decrease. Moreover, there is the matter of China's size, population, and the complexities of its society and culture coupled with American ignorance of Chinese culture, history, and language. This combination makes the idea of precision air strikes and information war bringing China to its knees at little cost to the United States so preposterous as to be worthy of a Monty Python skit.

The problems that confronting U.S. military forces in the next century will involve America's vital interests in the Second and Third Worlds.[33] Such challenges will involve peacekeeping operations and nasty little conflicts with military organizations that will not possess the same technological capabilities that American forces have. Nevertheless, as the Somalis proved, seemingly technologically unsophisticated weapons such as rocket-propelled grenades can prove pretty effective against the most modern helicopters. Above all, Americans should not forget the salient lessons of the Vietnam War. There, a technologically unsophisticated opponent successfully adapted his tactics and forces to the American way of war, exacting such a high price on U.S. forces that the United States eventually quit.[34] There are additional problems with dealing with such wars. For one, they demand a substantial ground force structure, one that will not exist under the thinking of those proposing an RMA in the U.S. military. We are already seeing the tension between the demands around the world for U.S. military forces in peacekeeping and deterrence roles and the demands for procurement funding. The lessons of twenty-five hundred years of military history underline the absolute necessity for ground forces to translate air and naval capabilities into victory.[35]

In addition, there will probably be considerable constraints on the use of firepower by U.S. forces given the political and strategic framework under which they will work. Long-distance firepower, no matter how accurate, carries with it the substantial possibility of collateral damage and civilian deaths in the vicinity. It took only one hit on the Al Firdos bunker in February, 1991, and the resulting pictures on the Cable News Network to end the effort to attack the political basis of Saddam Hussein's regime after one night's bombing of selective sites housing the regime's political infrastructure.[36]

But beyond the strategic, political, and financial difficulties with implementing the visionaries' programs for a revolution in military affairs, there is a larger danger in all this technological, mechanistic thinking that has emerged in American planning. *Simply put, it is wrong.* In many ways it reflects the arrogance of Robert McNamara's approach to the U.S. military. It is predicated on a belief that technology will allow America to control the environment in which it operates, even one so complex as the battlefield. The past twenty-five hundred years of military history serve to illustrate that complexity, uncertainty, and ambiguity have always ruled the conduct of war. Nevertheless, the technologists' view is that the past is irrelevant—that the onset of improved technology will allow the American military to do things that were impossible before. But there is now substantial evidence from the scientific world that suggests that the past is a far surer guide to the future than technological hopes for the future. A substantial portion of modern science—to include evolutionary biology, meteorology, and most of modern mathematics—indicates that the historian's traditional suspicion of those who claim the possibility of absolute predictability in human affairs rests on a realistic understanding of how the world really works. Uncertainty, unpredictability, and ambiguity lie at the basis of not just war, but the entire natural functioning of the world. Across the spectrum of research, natural scientists now believe that "nonlinear" phenomena dominate much of the world they study. And in such a world absolute or even general predictability is simply not in the cards.

The implications for understanding war—past, present, and future—are profound. If nonlinearity governs even the apparent regularities of nature, how much more will it rule the conduct of war with its immense complexities?[37] As one commentator on the nature of friction in war has noted: "We will *never* really achieve perfect (or even near perfect) information no matter how much data we collect, how fast we can process and distribute it, or how much artificial intelligence, fusion, etc., we have. The reasons lie in (1) human sensory and cognition limits; (2) the fact that wars ultimately serve political purposes; and (3) the two-sided, interactive nature of combat processes which produces, among other things, fundamental unpredictability in the sense of nonlinear dynamics or 'chaos.'"[38]

The arguments about where technology is going in much of the current commentary on revolutions in military affairs suggest a belief that emerging information technologies will remove most of the "fog of war." The advocates of "information war" indicate a belief that the greater acquisition and display of information will be sufficient to guarantee certainty. But information and data are not knowledge. Military organizations over the course of the past century have not lacked information. The challenge has been to determine, despite the "white noise" of confusion and uncertainty, what really matters.[39] A world in which friction prevails is a world in which the volume of information drowns the users. It is a world where commanders see what they want to see. It is a world where enemy actions, intentional and unintentional, disrupt systems and organizations sufficiently to render prediction impossible.[40]

In war there are simply too many pieces of information inaccessible to sensors and beyond the *understanding* of computers. Indeed, an overreliance on information technology may only serve to increase the risks of deception by opponents. The German experience in World War II is a clear warning as to the price of technological hubris. By trusting so completely in the superiority of their encryption technology, the Germans enabled the British code breakers at Bletchley Park to decrypt most of the Wehrmacht's top secret codes and tip the playing field against the Third Reich for most of World War II.[41]

The richer the information environment, the harder it is to see what really matters. What should have been obvious in retrospect is rarely obvious at the time. Individuals at every level of command possess limits as to what they can absorb *and* what they can pass along. Compounding this problem is the fact that the more they are oppressed by fatigue and danger, the more vulnerable they become to error and miscalculation. Above all, it is the interactive and antagonistic quality that makes war so unpredictable. America's opponents will have options as yet unforeseen, whatever the technological advantages of U.S. forces. Friction is not an artifact of history but rather a condition embedded in the very fabric of war. To suppose that technology can eliminate friction from the battlefield flies in the face of the natural world as it is.

My final point has to do with what we know about the nature of innovation itself. In the 1920s and 1930s, military organizations that approached innovation with a healthy and realistic understanding of the past were able to successfully address the problems raised by war. Such was the case with the German Army and the U.S. Navy in their formulation of armored and carrier warfare concepts, doctrine, and capabilities.[42] On the other hand, organizations that jumped into the technological future without regard for the past came close to foundering. The cases of the Royal Air Force and the U.S. Army Air Forces are particularly useful examples. Both services developed doctrines and concepts that entirely ignored the historical past and instead concentrated on a technological future. In World War II both discovered—at immense cost to their crews and nations—fundamental flaws in their preparations for war. However, they were unwilling to recognize those flaws until late 1943 and early 1944, at which point they had almost lost the war in the air.[43]

The point here is that history suggests that technological innovations are best incorporated into military organizations by a relatively slow but steady process of innovation rather than by a relatively sudden leap into the future that bets on unproven technological capabilities. Only the process of conducting exercises, rethinking doctrine, and engaging in intellectual debate insures the development of capabilities that will prove effective in the next war and which may provide for a true revolution in military affairs.

Conclusion

The Gulf War may yet prove to have been a watershed in the history of conflict. On the other hand, in terms of the history of the coming decades, it may prove only to have been the denouement of the Cold War period—a conflict that had more to do with the past than the future. Consequently, before America's military uses the performance of its forces in that conflict—especially an idealized picture of the performance of those forces—as a benchmark, it would do well to consider the realities of the current political and strategic arena. The likely uses of U.S. forces in the future, the fundamental nature of war, and the parameters of successful innovation in the past all demand careful consideration.

Such an approach would move toward change cautiously. It would demand thorough and rigorous testing. It would display a willingness to challenge the orthodox. Finally, it would demand a real emphasis on professional military education—an emphasis that has not existed since the late 1930s. The U.S. military should also recognize that the world is at present in a period where there are no great challenges to its position as the world's only superpower. Attacks on its interests will be sporadic and largely unexpected. Consequently, what the nation will require will be adaptable, flexible, and innovative military forces. The Vietnam War experience suggests that the American military has not always met such unexpected challenges in an effective fashion.[44]

Notes

1. See in particular Bernard Trainor and Michael Gordon, *The Generals' War: The Inside Story of the Conflict in the Gulf* (Boston: Little, Brown & Co., 1995); and the various volumes of Eliot Cohen, ed., *The Gulf War Air Power Survey* (Washington, D.C.: GPO, 1995).
2. Cohen, ed., *Gulf War Air Power Survey,* classified and unclassified editions.
3. Thucydides, *History of the Peloponnesian War,* trans. by Rex Warner (New York: Penguin Books, 1954), p. 48.
4. In this regard, see particularly H. R. McMaster, *Dereliction of Duty: Lyndon Johnson, Robert McNamara, their Military Advisers and the Lies they Told* (New York: HarperCollins, 1997).
5. The removal of Gen. Michael Dugan as the chief of staff of the air force was not consistent with U.S. policy toward Iraq, whatever the internal political dimensions of that action.
6. Samir al-Khalil, *The Republic of Fear: The Politics of Modern Iraq* (Berkeley: University of California Press, 1989).

7. For a careful critique of the current difficulties of U.S. intelligence agencies and what needs to be done to correct their deficiencies, see particularly Jay Young, "Reengineering U.S. Intelligence," in *Brassey's Mershon American Defense Annual, 1996–1997,* ed. by Williamson Murray and Allan R. Millett (Washington, D.C.: Brassey's, Inc., 1997).

8. Among others in the unclassified literature see the study done at the Army War College's Strategic Studies Institute: Stephen C. Pelletiere, Douglas V. Johnson II, Leif R. Rosenberger, *Iraqi Power and U.S. Security in the Middle East* (Carlisle, Pa.: U.S. Army War College Strategic Studies Institute, 1990).

9. See the discussion in Williamson Murray, *Operations,* report I, vol. II, *Gulf War Air Power Survey* (Washington, D.C.: GPO, 1993), pp. 22–25.

10. In Jan., 1980, shortly after he came to power, Saddam Hussein stated: "we want our country to achieve its proper weight based on our estimation that Iraq is as great as China, as great as the Soviet Union, and as great as the United States." Even allowing for a certain amount of hyperbole, that was an extraordinary claim for the leader of a nation of 17 million people to make. (Ibid., p. 62.)

11. See in particular John Lewis Gaddis, "International Relations Theory and the End of the Cold War," *International Security* 17, no. 3 (winter, 1992–93) for a devastating critique of the predictive capabilities of modern social sciences.

12. MacGregor Knox, "Continuity and Revolution in Strategy," in *The Making of Strategy: Rulers, States, and War,* ed. by Williamson Murray, MacGregor Knox, and Alvin Bernstein (Cambridge: Cambridge University Press, 1994), p. 645.

13. Joseph S. Nye, Jr., and William A. Owens, "America's Information Edge," *Foreign Affairs* 75, no. 2 (Mar.-Apr., 1996): 20.

14. Ibid., p. 21.

15. Allan R. Millett and Williamson Murray, "The Lessons of War," *National Interest,* no. 14 (winter, 1988–89): 83.

16. See in particular Barry D. Watts, "Friction in Future War," in *Brassey's Mershon American Defense Annual, 1996–1997,* ed. by Murray and Millett (Washington, D.C.: Brassey's, Inc., 1996). For friction in the Gulf War, see also Cohen, ed., *Gulf War Air Power Survey,* and Richard M. Swain, *"Lucky War: Third Army in Desert Storm* (Fort Leavenworth, Kans.: U.S. Army Command and General Staff College, 1994), p. 230.

17. For a wider discussion of these issues, see my article "Computers in, Clausewitz Out," *National Interest* (summer, 1997).

18. It is worth noting that outside of the debate about the military revolution in the late sixteenth and early seventeenth centuries, historians have done very little work on the historical parameters of revolutions in military affairs.

19. Among the claims that Owens made while he was still on active duty in print and in interviews were: (1) "technology could enable U.S. military forces in the future to lift 'the fog of war.' . . . Battlefield dominant awareness—the ability to see and understand everything on the battlefield—might be possible." (Thomas Duffy, "Breakthrough Could Give Forces Total Command of Future Battlefield," *Inside the Navy,* Jan. 23, 1995.) Or (2) "when you look at areas such as information warfare, intelligence surveillance, reconnaissance, and command and control, you see a system of systems coming together that will allow us to dominate battlefield awareness for years to come. . . . And while some people say there will always be a 'fog of war,' I know quite a lot about these programs." (Quoted by Peter Grier, "Preparing for 21st-Century Information War," *Government Execu-*

tive 25, no. 8 [Aug., 1995].) And (3) "The emerging system of systems promises the capacity to use military force without the same risks as before—it suggests that we will dissipate the fog of war." (Adm. William Owens, "System of Systems," *Armed Forces Journal International* 133, no. 6 [Jan., 1996]: 47.)

20. The assumptions on which a war game of a possible conflict in the next century on the Korean peninsula were "near-perfect information on all observable phenomena; perfect linkages between sensors and shooters; no need for humans to take time to convert information into intelligence and pass it on to shooters; near-perfect battle damage assessment and follow-up strikes (should they be required); flawless, instantaneous human and technical performance in battle management and command and control; flawless, frictionless overall execution (we have repealed Clausewitz.)" (Off-the-record conversation with Department of Defense official, Jan., 1995.)

21. Department of the Air Force, "New World Vistas, Air and Space Power for the 21st Century," Summary Volume, USAF Scientific Board, Dec. 15, 1995, p. 11.

22. Gen. Dennis Reimer, quoted in *Inside the Pentagon*, Oct. 17, 1996, p. 11.

23. James R. Blaker, "Understanding the Revolution in Military Affairs: A Guide to America's 21st Century Defense," Progressive Policy Institute Defense Working Paper No. 3, Jan., 1997, p. 10, and fig. "The RMA System-of-Systems Argument," p. 10.

24. As the new secretary of defense recently commented after a visit to the army's National Training Center at Fort Irwin, Calif.: "I think that what you are seeing here is a revolution in military warfare. We've had the age-old expression that knowledge is power, and absolute knowledge is absolute power. What we're witnessing now is the transformation of the level of information through as broad and as absolute as one can conceive of it today. So the actual domination of the information world will put us in a position to maintain superiority over any other force for the foreseeable future. . . . So we look to the future. The future is as Toeffler says, 'Unless you tame technology, you will encounter future shock.' We're not only taming technology, we are turning technology into not future shock, but future security." (Marine Corps internal message, Mar. 24, 1997.)

25. Blaker, "Understanding the Revolution," p. 10.

26. Ibid., p. 20.

27. Ibid., especially Alan Beyerchen, "Radar and Innovation."

28. For a discussion of the problems involved in successful as well as unsuccessful innovation during the interwar period see Williamson Murray and Allan R. Millett, *Military Innovation in the Interwar Period* (Cambridge: Cambridge University Press, 1996).

29. Edward Luttwak, "We Need More Waste, Fraud, and Mismanagement in the Pentagon," *Commentary* 73, no. 2 (Feb., 1982).

30. It is worth noting that the near century of peace until 1914 allowed Britain's military institutions to slip into a mechanistic and unrealistic view that their commanders would be able to control combat from the top down without allowing any individual initiative. The results were the disasters of Loos, the Somme, and Paschendaele for the army, and the less than satisfactory outcomes at Dogger Bank and Jutland for the navy. In regards to the ill effect of the long decades of peace on the Royal Navy and its preparations for the coming war, see in particular Andrew Gordon, *The Rules of the Game: Jutland and British Naval Command* (London: Naval Institute Press, 1997).

31. Something along the lines, one supposes, of the 1996 Hollywood film *Independence Day.*

32. For the nature of the short- and long-term threats that China represents see Arthur Waldron, "China," in *Brassey's Mershon American Defense Annual, 1996–1997,* ed. by Murray and Millett, chap. 6.

33. See the perceptive essay on the demands for ground forces in the next century by Lt. Gen. Paul Van Riper, USMC, and Maj. Gen. Robert Scales, USA, "Preparing for War in the 21st Century," *Strategic Review* 25, no. 3 (summer, 1997): 14–20.

34. See in particular the sections dealing with Vietnam in Robert H. Scales, Jr., *Firepower in Limited War,* rev. ed. (Novato, Calif.: Presidio Press, 1995).

35. Van Riper and Scales, "Preparing for War."

36. Murray, *Operations,* pp. 206–208.

37. As one historian has recently suggested, one of the principal reasons that Clausewitz has remained relevant through the end of the twentieth century lies in the fact that "*On War* is suffused with the understanding that every war is inherently a nonlinear phenomena, the conduct of which changes its character in ways that cannot be analytically predicted." (Alan Beyerchen, "Clausewitz, Nonlinearity, and the Unpredictability of War," *International Security* 17, no. 3 (winter, 1992–93): 61.

38. Barry D. Watts, "Some Observations on Dominant Awareness," unpublished paper in the possession of the author.

39. Neither Japan's attack on Pearl Harbor nor Nazi Germany's launching of Operation Barbarossa came out of the blue. In both cases, warning failed not from a dearth of information, but rather from the failure of policy makers and military leaders to understand the mind-set of their potential opponents.

40. Hence the extraordinary nature of the claims recently made in a conference held recently by one of the larger consulting firms in the Washington, D.C., area: What the [revolution in military affairs] promises, more than precision attacks and laser beams, is . . . to imbue the information loop with near-perfect clarity and accuracy, to reduce its operation to a matter of minutes or seconds, and — perhaps most important of all — to deny it in its entirety to the enemy." (Michael I. Mazarr et al., "The Military Technical Revolution: A Structural Framework," Center for Strategic and International Studies, Mar., 1993, p. 38.)

41. See in particular F. H. Hinsley, et al., *British Intelligence in the Second World War,* 5 vols. (London: H.M.S.O., 1979–90).

42. See Murray and Millett, *Military Innovation,* chap. 1.

43. See John Terraine, *The Right of the Line: The Royal Air Force, 1939–45* (London: Hodder and Stoughton, 1985); Williamson Murray, *The Luftwaffe, 1933–45: Strategy of Defeat* (Baltimore, Md.: Nautical & Aviation Publishing Company of America, 1996); and Barry D. Watts, *The Foundations of U.S. Air Doctrine: The Problem of Friction in War* (Maxwell Air Force Base, Ala.: Air University Press, 1984).

44. See in particular Andrew F. Krepinevich, Jr., *The Army in Vietnam* (Baltimore: Johns Hopkins University Press, 1988).

Chapter 6

Upside-Down Policy

*The U.S. Debate on the Use of Force
and the Case of Bosnia*

Susan L. Woodward

THE FIRST USE OF FORCE by NATO in its fifty-year history occurred in the Federal Republic of Yugoslavia in March–June, 1999. The reason, according to U.S. Secretary of State Madeleine Albright and her colleagues
such as NATO Secretary General Javier Solana and British Foreign Secretary
Robin Cook, was the lesson of Bosnia. Without a willingness to use military
force in support of human rights and humanitarian principles, the world was
not safe for Western values and diplomacy was ineffective. But the massive
bombing campaign unleashed on March 24 took eleven weeks to succeed in
obtaining the consent of Yugoslav President Slobodan Milošević to NATO's
terms: a withdrawal of Yugoslav security forces—armed forces and police—
from its province of Kosovo and their unopposed replacement with an international security force under United Nations (UN) authority and NATO
command. Although America's NATO allies had determined by the previous
October, 1998, that ground troops were needed to halt the Kosovo crisis—
particularly the refugee and humanitarian emergency provoked by the war
between the Kosovo Liberation Army and Yugoslav forces over the province's
political status—the United States was unwilling to commit ground troops.

The only choice—given the lesson drawn from the war in Bosnia and Herzegovina—was to bomb.

The following analysis, written in September, 1997, forecast the June, 1998, NATO decision to issue a threat of force, through aerial bombing, and the inadequate response to the Kosovo conflict, where one year later, almost to the day, 60,000 NATO troops were deployed for the foreseeable future. A fundamental principle of political science is that decision outcomes are determined by the way the agenda of choices gets defined. The debate on U.S. foreign policy toward the Yugoslav crisis, beginning no later than the fall of 1991 when the secession of Slovenia and Croatia had led to war, became defined as a question of whether to use military force. Eventually, if these are the only alternatives—whether or not to use military force—force will be used. But to use military force has consequences, including long delays while the interagency tug of war works its way toward the president. The lesson of Bosnia, and later of Kosovo, is that these consequences do not necessarily make for an effective response or lead to global stability.

To its critics, U.S. policy toward Bosnia can be represented by two, now classic, quotations. One is the exchange at a 1993 cabinet meeting early in the first Clinton administration when the U.S. representative to the United Nations, later secretary of state, Madeleine Albright, asked the chairman of the Joint Chiefs of Staff, General Colin Powell, a Bush appointee, "What's the point of having this superb military that you're always talking about if we can't use it?"[1] The other is attributed to Colin Powell the year before, during the Bush administration. When challenged to justify why the United States was not intervening militarily in Bosnia, particularly after the recent success of Operation Desert Storm in the Persian Gulf, he is reported to have said, "We don't do mountains."

The war in Bosnia and Herzegovina, 1992–95, was the bloodiest, thus far, of the wars of Yugoslav succession that began in 1991 with the secession of two federal units, Slovenia and Croatia. Thanks to the spin of the Bush administration, the war came to symbolize European failure. But neither the Bush nor the Clinton administrations could brush off public outrage at the carnage or the demands for action from highly mobilized lobbying groups on behalf of Bosnian Muslims, making the Bosnian war the most persistent emblem of presidential failure in foreign policy in the new world emerging after the Cold War. Why then was the failure to prevent and act in Bosnia blamed on the U.S. military?

The war in Croatia in summer–fall, 1991, could have been stopped in its earliest stages, critics insist, by sending in interposition forces, but the United States refused to play. At first arguing that no European force could deploy unless it were NATO, it then refused American participation. Without American military participation at the time (only months after Operation Desert Storm)—the British continued to argue in the West European Union (WEU) as late as September, 1991—Europeans did not have the resources to go it alone. The peace plan for Bosnia and Herzegovina, ready in January, 1993, failed, it is said, because the Americans were unwilling to contribute ground troops to its implementation. Only in July–October, 1995, did that war end, the conventional wisdom now holds, when the United States reversed course: leading a bombing raid on Bosnian Serbs, committing American soldiers and commanding officers to an implementation force for a peace settlement, and restoring badly damaged international credibility with military power.[2] (So strongly implanted did this conventional wisdom become that it led directly to the decision to threaten Slobodan Milošević with bombing over Kosovo, and then to follow through on the mistaken interpretation of the role that bombing played in Bosnia in 1995.)

From 1992 to the summer of 1995, the fear of a Vietnam-like quagmire among the senior officer corps of the United States military was said to be driving policy.[3] Honor restored in the Persian Gulf permitted consideration of air power and its far lower vulnerability to casualties.[4] Transferring its experience in dealing with the internal aftermath in Iraq ("ethnic" or "religious" conflicts) to Bosnia, beginning in the fall of 1992, the United States then led the United Nations Security Council in imposing a no-fly zone over Bosnia, helped enforce six safe areas (repeating the safe havens for Kurds in northern Iraq) with air power, and air-dropped humanitarian relief. But the experience in Somalia in the spring of 1993 reinforced the U.S. military's allergy to ground commitment in such conflicts. Until U.S. troops could be sent under conditions of consent by the parties to implement a peace, they would not go. Even then the model of success became Haiti: in and out quickly and emphasizing police, not soldiers.

The policy reversal on Bosnia in 1995 did not end the struggle, however. Despite military success in the Dayton implementation, the same issues were raised again in regard to Kosovo, the province of Serbia that became the next war of Yugoslav succession, in 1998, and the next battleground over American willingness to commit military force in the post–Cold War era. Between late 1997 and spring, 1999, policy debate over Kosovo focused almost entirely over what were called the lessons of Bosnia. These were said to be: force should not be the last resort but be used early in a conflict, and diplomacy must be backed by the threat of force. And just as in the debate over Bosnia and Herzegovina, critics of American policy aimed their fire at the president's weakness and the Pentagon's obstruction. This time, however, the critics won. So powerful was the conventional wisdom on Bosnia, in fact, that the NATO powers, under British and American leadership, issued a threat of bombing many months before diplomatic negotiations even began. At the same time, the reluctance to use force remained and those who opposed its use remained sufficiently strong to delay its use for another nine months when the issue of NATO credibility, not the diplomatic process, forced their hand.

The experience of Bosnia and Herzegovina, of Croatia before it and Kosovo after, does raise the most difficult questions for the United States about the use of military force by the president in the post–Cold War era. These questions cannot be answered, however, by starting with the instrument of military power. This analysis of the Bosnian case suggests a different lesson for future conflicts: the debate on the use of force has been a trap preventing effective policy.

The Trap

Throughout the decade of the Yugoslav crisis, 1990–99, American policy toward the Balkans was characterized by interagency and interbranch conflict over the use of force. Players and agencies changed positions, but at the core of this conflict on the executive side has been a confrontation between State and Defense, with the National Security Council changing sides depending on the advisor's position on the use of military force. To the extent that the president was drawn into this fight at all, and it is notable how protected both Presidents Bush and Clinton were from this battle, criticism of the president for lack of leadership focused on the use of military force—to stop the Yugoslav army at Vukovar or Dubrovnik in Croatia in 1991, to halt and even reverse ethnic cleansing and gross violations of international humanitarian law in the atrocities, concentration camps, and rapes in Bosnia in 1992, to protect the six Bosnian safe areas in 1993–95, to force relief through to Sarajevo and endangered enclaves, to bomb the Serbs all the way to Belgrade, and in 1995–98, to arrest indicted war criminals and protect returning refugees. Even the long series of hearings on the use of force in the post–Cold War period held by the House Armed Services Committee in late winter–spring of 1993 was motivated by and focused almost entirely on the case of Bosnia.

The military's defense against these criticisms, made by commanders on the ground as well as by military analysts, forms one of two sets of lessons in the accumulating conventional wisdom on Bosnia. Military force is an instrument of political leadership; without sufficient political will and clarity of purpose, the use of military force will fail. Tell us what to do, they say, and we'll do it, but give us a clear political objective. The problem of international action toward violence in Bosnia was a lack of political, not military, will. This call for clarity of purpose came not only from the American military but also from commanders in the United Nations mission in 1992–95 and analysts of its failures.[5]

The other set of lessons was voiced by the diplomatic community and the critics of military inaction in Bosnia. They argued that there is no effective diplomacy without the threat of force. Without the threat of enforcement, international law and principles are worthless. Without the willingness to use force, "rogue states" and "rogue leaders" will be undeterred and will proliferate as the primary threat to international peace and security in the post–Cold War era. Only bombing the Bosnian Serbs brought them to the bargaining table to sign a peace,[6] and without American leadership, war would still be raging in the Balkans.

These two camps are in fact talking past each other, with the role of the president apparently reduced to mediator. But taken together these two lessons have terrifying implications for the United States and for global peace. There are two reasons why, one having to do with the end of the Cold War, and the other with the characteristics of ethnonationalist conflicts that Bosnia exemplifies.

The end of the Cold War meant the end of restrictions on the use of American military power. As the sole remaining superpower, all eyes looked to the United States for leadership and resources. The restraint or excuse not to act that came from the threat of Soviet response was gone. Even the vilified Soviet veto had been useful as a limiting device, as contrasted with the willingness of Russia to cooperate with U.S. aims—in exchange, of course, for payoffs in aid and recognition as a major power. The international role of the United States also changed, from defender of the free world and its principles to an unlimited guardian of global order and morality. As has been all too commonly recognized, this leaves the United States with no criteria for intervention, no ideology to define national interest, no clear basis for making choices among the many occasions calling for external action. The task of the president in defining when and why the United States should contemplate the use of force and commit its troops is infinitely more difficult. The military's demand for political leadership is far more important, and the task of the president in selling policy—to explain to the "mother in Peoria" and to persuade the Congress— is far greater because nothing can be taken for granted. New arguments must be devised and precedents calculated.

The experience of conflicts like Bosnia since 1989 suggests that the end of the Cold War should have made this task of presidential leadership easier. Huge areas of the globe, particularly in Africa and in areas bordering spheres of Soviet or American interests, such as Central America, the Horn of Africa, the

Balkans, or Central Asia, are no longer of strategic significance to the United States. In former Secretary of State James Baker's famous remark on Bosnia, "we have no dog in that fight." But in fact, the consequences of American abandonment in 1989–91 of states that had been its Cold War clients, such as Liberia or Yugoslavia, were to make matters much worse and to bring opprobrium on the United States or require its action when the costs and risks, including the necessity of using force, were much greater than they would have been had action occurred early in these conflicts. Abandonment turns out not to have been the best policy, and its consequences have strengthened the assessment that the United States does not yet know how to calculate its national interests effectively and, further, may therefore be unreliable.

This new category of post–Cold War conflict—cases of no strategic interest to the United States that begin domestically—have generally earned the label of ethnic conflict. Their primary characteristics, however, are that they begin as domestic conflicts, receive little attention in prevention stages because they are not strategically important, and evolve toward conflict over persons and territory (ethnonationalist, if you will) that have international consequences. In other words, it is only when they become violent and threaten to spill over borders, create humanitarian and refugee crises, or violate international humanitarian law that action is contemplated. Although the parties at conflict may be differentiated ethnically or religiously, the essence of the conflict is state collapse. Following the two criteria of Weber's classic definition of the state, the government is no longer able to enforce its will over all of its defined territory and people, and it has lost its monopoly over the legitimate use of violence. Proliferating arms, paramilitary gangs, and armies; rebellious or secessionist regions; efforts to expel or eradicate some social groups with force; and criminal and gang warfare are the consequence and the conditions facing the international community when it must decide whether to act. Even if it chooses to intervene on humanitarian grounds alone, such as in Somalia and in Bosnia, the problem it faces is not the delivery of relief but violence and the security needs of international relief workers. The question of intervention—at the point when action is contemplated—cannot be separated from the need to use force, but the very clarity of purpose and political direction that the military require are unlikely to be forthcoming in such cases. As former secretary of defense in the Bush administration, Richard Cheney, revealingly said about Bosnia in a TV interview in October, 1993, nine months after leaving office, "No one could ever define a clear-cut mission."[7]

As was revealed so clearly in the case of Kosovo, the lessons being drawn from Bosnia are terrifying, in other words, because they say that there are no obvious reasons why the United States should not act but also no developed justifications for why it should; that when such action is permissible and thus likely to occur, it will almost inevitably require the use of force; and that therefore, if action is to occur, American leadership and military participation are likely to be necessary.

Is there any way out of this trap other than the growing cynicism toward the coming era? For some the only solution is triage, choosing to limit America's battles and admitting that many will not be helped, but for others this cynicism (which is likely to grow under a policy of triage) is bound to eat away at the moral basis of American global leadership as it is currently defined. Because legitimacy reduces the need to use force, the second possibility would be truly counterproductive.

Strategic Calculation

The experience of Bosnia suggests that this trap comes from how we define the question of intervention and American leadership. American policy towards Bosnia begins with its policy toward the disintegration of Yugoslavia, which was the necessary (though not sufficient) precondition of war in Bosnia. Although a serious analysis of the Yugoslav crisis cannot ignore the role of the United States in 1981–89, the critical moment for the discussion here came in 1989. Then the disintegration of Yugoslavia began to loom as likely unless outsiders weighed in to support the federal government and non-nationalist forces or to engage actively in preventing the process of dissolution from turning terribly violent, as diplomats in the field and intelligence agencies began to warn was likely.

As the Cold War patron of Yugoslavia, its independence of Moscow, and its military role in NATO's containment policy, the United States was the critical actor. European reintegration, the fear of being left out in the cold that motivated all of eastern and central European political events in the late 1980s, and above all Slovene moves toward independence gave Europe substantial independent leverage over the Yugoslav conflict, but the determining influence was the decision of the United States that it had no national interest in the outcome in Yugoslavia, that because of developments in the Soviet Union, Yugoslavia was no longer strategically important to the United States and its postwar alliances. Communicated to the Yugoslav federal government as early as 1987, and repeated when a new ambassador, Warren Zimmermann, presented his credentials in March, 1989, this policy change took on significance in 1990 after the ruling communist party fell apart irretrievably and the Slovene republic headed for independence. If Yugoslavia were no longer strategically significant, then it was not worth risking American lives to save it. In February, 1990,

Deputy Secretary of State Lawrence Eagleburger said publicly in Belgrade that if Slovenia chose to leave, "the United States . . . would have no choice except to live with it,"[8] and in November, 1990, at a NATO summit, the Bush administration vetoed NATO action on the grounds that Yugoslavia was "out of area."

In principle, this decision could simply have opened up opportunities for other countries and organizations to act in Yugoslavia. A dominant theme in Washington beginning in 1991, heard loudest in Congress but shared by the executive branch under Bush, was that Yugoslavia was a European problem. In fact, however, the decision reflected the Bush administration policy to retain NATO, and American dominance, as the preeminent European security organization after the Cold War, and thus to prevent others from acting in Yugoslavia who might challenge NATO's role. Not only did the United States, together with the Soviet Union, veto action by the Conference on Security and Cooperation in Europe (CSCE) at its summit in November, 1990, on the grounds that the Yugoslav conflict was an internal affair. It also prevented the Western European Union (WEU) from acting on a plan to deploy a WEU interposition force in the event of violence that its secretary general, Willem van Eeklen, ordered drawn up in December, 1990. And it made sure that a French proposal to deploy the EuroCorps—to fill the vacuum of a United States retreating from Europe built on a core of French and German troops—as interposition forces in Croatia in July, 1991, got nowhere, despite a declaration in support of this idea at the G-7 summit in July.

Critics of the view that the United States was influential at this stage in blocking active European efforts to stem the mounting violence in Yugoslavia cite the fact that Germany was still constitutionally prohibited from deploying troops, including in such a EuroCorps, and that Britain actively opposed military intervention, including at a decisive debate over the matter at a WEU summit in September, 1991. But Franco-German discussions about a European defense identity in the lead up to the Maastricht Treaty that would commit the EU to a common foreign and security policy (Title 5), as well as growing Franco-British defense cooperation and the interest of many smaller European states such as the Dutch and the Belgians in such proposals, were only delayed by the American wet blanket, to the detriment of Yugoslavs. The overriding reason that Britain opposed WEU action is that it did not then have the necessary military assets to act without American military participation.[9]

The American decision that the fate of Yugoslavia was not strategically significant did not prevent the administration from attempting to influence the path of the crisis. In December, 1990, the U.S. ambassador began a series of warnings to the Yugoslav federal army not to follow through on its threats to act in the domestic crisis when the minister of defense was attempting to use his constitutional authority, in the vacuum created by a nine-month-long election process to install a new collective presidency, to stop the covert actions of Slovene and Croatian leaderships to form and equip independent armies in preparation for leaving. American warnings were repeated in January, 1991, when the new Yugoslav collective presidency (chosen after republican elections held during 1990) added its legitimacy to the army's warnings and attempted to regain control over the proliferating paramilitary organizations in Croatia because of the violence growing in that republic since August, 1990. While acting on the view that the federal prime minister, his government, and his reform policies were too weak to support,[10] the United States supported the European faction that would not entertain negotiation of Yugoslavia's dissolution and new borders because it still opposed the country's breakup (even after Slovenia and Croatia announced their independence and the Dutch presidency of the EU explicitly proposed such negotiations in July). And yet by the end of June, 1991, Deputy Secretary of State Eagleburger and Secretary of State Baker were publicly defining the moves by the Yugoslav army to preserve the country's territorial integrity against the Slovene assertion of independence by taking over customs posts and border crossings as Serbian aggression. Even while insisting that the country not break apart, that this was an internal matter and that Slovene and Croat independence should not be recognized, they accused the army of cross-border aggression against Slovenia and then Croatia, as if the two were already independent states, the federal government did not exist, and the army were overnight a Serbian army.

From then on, western policy toward Yugoslavia was trapped in a vicious circle: outsiders, led by the United States, defined the conflict in terms of the (illegitimate) use of force by the Yugoslav army, but they would not themselves use force to stop it. The strategic calculation had been turned on its head: because the United States would not contribute troops, would not allow NATO to act without it, and obstructed others from acting militarily outside of NATO, the Yugoslav conflict could not be easily viewed in terms of *European* security. The United States reversed its position on CSCE engagement, but only after war had begun, when CSCE crisis instruments were of no avail. Intervention became framed in terms of what the United States and its European allies would *not* do, ironically reinforcing a tendency to see the conflict in military terms. Means, not ends, drove calculation of strategic interest and appropriate policy.

Having prevented transatlantic or European military action early on in the Yugoslav dissolution, the United States then retreated and left the field to organizations unsuited to war—the European Union, the CSCE, and a United Nations still bound by the American (and Soviet) judgment that this was an internal affair governed by rules of sovereignty. Moreover, the decision of several Western allies—Austria, Canada, Britain, and France—to take the case to the UN Security Council in August, 1991, had the unintended consequence of reinforcing this American policy, for the Yugoslav federal army in late August was reassessing its goal of defending a country that had clearly collapsed. In deciding instead to draw and defend the borders of a new, rump Yugoslavia, the general staff apparently relied on its internal appraisal of American post–Cold War behavior: viewing the Persian Gulf intervention as an "instrumentalization" of the United Nations for American strategic interests, they assessed a very low probability that the United States would then intervene militarily in Yugoslavia.[11]

Does Diplomacy Need the Threat of Force?

The decision not to commit military assets left the field to diplomacy, without force. Contrary to the view that European Community (EC) efforts to negotiate a peace settlement in Yugoslavia (they opened a peace conference at The Hague on September 7, 1991, under the chairmanship of Lord Peter Carrington) were fated to fail because there was no will to impose a settlement, the conference actually failed because its peace proposal treated the conflict in isolation from the separate actions of EU member states toward the main parties at war. For the federal army, the Serbian government, and those Croatian Serbs living in border areas, the peace proposal refused even to consider the one issue that mattered: where the border between an independent Croatia and an independent Serbia (or rump Yugoslavia) would be drawn. The borders of the new states had to remain as they were, and all those who now found themselves to be a national minority in a foreign state had no choice but to adjust to their new status. For the Slovene and Croatian governments, the European Community members were in disagreement, and both republics had gained enough powerful supporters for their positions (led by Germany and Austria but soon gaining Italy as well) that they did not have to compromise. The Slovenes successfully refused any common links among the successor states, such as the proposed customs union, and the Croats refused any special status for Serbs or reconsideration of the border. In other words, the EU conference wanted to impose a settlement against the will of those who held predominant military power without using military force because of a prior American decision. At the same time, they could not obtain concessions from those who were at a disadvantage in the military balance because they had skillfully exploited this disadvantage to obtain the decisive EU diplomatic support. The hope for a negotiated settlement of the conflict as an alternative to force was kept alive only through the success of former U.S. Secretary of State Cyrus Vance, as special envoy for UN Secretary-General Pérez de Cuellar. Vance negotiated a cease-fire between Croatia and the federal army that met the conditions for deploying foreign troops in Croatia under a United Nations mandate, with a fairly standard peacekeeping mission, and permitted negotiations over the future of this contested territory to continue.[12]

This lesson of the complex relationship between political negotiations and a credible threat of force was lost on the United States, which repeated the same mistakes within months in Bosnia and Herzegovina.

With the collapse of the communist party in Yugoslavia in January, 1990, the vacuum was filled in Bosnia and Herzegovina by ethnonationally defined political parties. By November, they had captured voter loyalty in the first multiparty elections. There is no way to know whether that loyalty would have become stable or been replaced in time by parties based on economic interest and social status, as are common throughout the rest of Europe, east and west, if Yugoslavia itself had not collapsed as a result of nationalist rhetoric and claims for separate statehood on the basis of national self-determination by politicians in its republics (primarily in Slovenia, Croatia, and Serbia, the three wealthier northern republics). The creation of two nation-states, Slovenia and Croatia, out of this dissolving Yugoslavia, and the efforts of Serbia to do the same left tri-national Bosnia in an untenable position. Negotiations in the months prior to Slovene and Croatian secession on June 25, 1991, between the presidents of its neighboring republics, Croatia and Serbia, had aimed at preventing war between them over Bosnia—where Croats and Serbs were two of the three constitutionally recognized nations (meaning, with legal rights to self-determination)—by partitioning the republic between them. Like the Sikhs in Punjab after the partition of India and Pakistan, this would leave people from the third constituent nation—Muslims—who comprised 44 percent of the population of Bosnia in 1991, to seek minority rights in an independent Croatia or Serbia (or, as became a more likely option in the first months after the breakup, in a rump Yugoslavia of Serbia, Montenegro, Macedonia, and Bosnia, without Croats).

The European Community conference at The Hague aimed to prevent these scenarios (and precedent elsewhere) by insisting that the borders of the republics of former Yugoslavia were the sovereign borders of independent states and could not be changed.[13] The EC solution for Bosnia and Herzegovina, therefore, was to get the three ruling parties, each representing one of the three nations of Bosnia (but note that more than 18 percent voted for non-national parties, giving them 31 seats in the parliament), to agree to Bosnian independence by negotiating a constitutional pact in which the three would share power. Two events preempted these talks, begun at Lisbon in February, 1992. First, on the recommendation of an arbitration commission set up for the Yugoslav case, the European Community also obliged the Bosnian leadership to hold a voters' referendum on independence and then accepted a majoritarian result. Ninety percent of those voting said yes, but over 90 percent of one of the three nations (Serbs) refused to vote, because they opposed independence but knew their votes (maximum 33 percent) would lose under majoritarian voting rules. Three days after the referendum polls closed, on March 4, the president of the Muslim party who held the rotating chair of a seven-person collective presidency announced Bosnian independence and gave the Serbs a casus belli. Nonetheless, EC negotiations continued on an internal agreement until the second event. Angered at German leadership in the Croatian case, U.S. Secretary of State Baker began in March to pressure its European allies to recognize Bosnian independence immediately—so as to retake American leadership. His success, on April 6–7, removed any leverage over the parties to continue negotiations.

Although the Bush administration gave the argument that Germany had made for Croatia, that recognition would prevent war, it had not been true for the Croatian war; German support had, in fact, encouraged Croatia to fight, and recognition came after Vance's cease-fire had been agreed. The argument would not hold for Bosnia, either. This act repeated the mistakes of the EC conference. It attempted to impose an outcome that one of the three political parties in Bosnia (the Serbs) had publicly threatened would lead to war and that by April was publicly opposed by two of the three parties (Croats as well as Serbs), without being willing, in advance, to commit the military means to impose. The decision also did not have, any more than did Carrington, the power of a united external front against attempts by any one of the three Bosnian parties to veto the plan. But now the unwillingness to use force mattered, for unlike the recognition of Croatia, which occurred after Cyrus Vance had negotiated a cessation of hostilities and consent for peacekeeping troops, neither the United States alone nor the United Nations Security Council was willing to deploy troops to protect Bosnian territorial integrity.

The war in Bosnia and Herzegovina thus erupted over the political future of its three national communities, while ignoring the hundreds of thousands of Bosnians who did not fit, or want to fit, into one of these three categories. Would Bosnia become an independent state, multinational as had been Yugoslavia but with an emerging Muslim majority in a region of new nation-states? Would it be divided between Croatia and Serbia/Montenegro? Or would it divide three ways to carve out a Muslim nation-state and separate areas for Croats and Serbs that would likely join, respectively, Croatia and Serbia/

Montenegro? Moreover, when the EU and the UN joined forces in August, 1992, to initiate a second peace conference for Yugoslavia and produced a peace plan for Bosnia and Herzegovina the next January (1993) that attempted to achieve this first, American-initiated, objective of an independent, multinational Bosnia and Herzegovina, the problem once again was not the absence of force to coerce the parties, but the defection from the united position of the major power with the greatest leverage over the parties—in this case the United States instead of Germany. The reason for the refusal of the Clinton administration to support the Vance/Owen Peace Plan was its unwillingness to commit troops to a multinational operation for its implementation. In his failed effort to maintain the unity of support from European countries for their plan that Cyrus Vance and David Owen had worked so hard to win and to reverse the damaging position taken by the Clinton administration, Owen reports deciding to "go for the jugular vein of US policy, namely their refusal to put troops on the ground in Bosnia. I would simply urge the Clinton administration to do so in every interview, with the implicit message that only then would they have the right to veto or subvert the VOPP [Vance-Owen Peace Plan]."[14]

The Use of Troops as the Driving Criterion

American policy toward Bosnia in the first year of the war developed directly as a consequence of framing the question in terms of national interest, as defined by the willingness to commit ground troops—and then of answering in the negative. Without ground troops, there is no compulsion to define a policy and particularly for the president to articulate its purpose. With no prior White House direction, policy becomes the product of pressures on it from domestic lobbies and resources (such as the mass media and public opinion) and from other foreign interests that impinge. The recognition of Bosnia itself had been largely in response to the domestic lobby of Croatian emigrés who demanded recognition for Croatia (just as the refusal to recognize Macedonia, which met the EC arbitration commission conditions for recognition when Bosnia did not, was a response to the Greek lobby). Even before the outbreak of violence, the Bush administration was under pressure from moderate Islamic allies in the Middle East, above all Turkey and secondly Saudi Arabia, to support the Bosnian Muslims and also from the direct lobbying of Bosnian Muslim politicians, most notably foreign minister Haris Silajdžić (and later, UN representative Mohamed Sacirbey). Relations with Middle Eastern allies, particularly in the wake of the Persian Gulf operation and dual containment of Iraq, became and remained priorities for U.S. policy. At the same time, the pressure from these allies and from leaders of the ruling Bosnian Muslim party, the Party of Democratic Action, for U.S. military intervention on their side, was not sufficient to overcome the primary decision not to send troops.

Combined with the American public's growing horror at television pictures featuring the siege of Sarajevo and at journalists' accounts of concentration camps, mass rape, and other atrocities committed by Bosnian Serbs, which provoked congressional hearings on administration policy in August in the midst of the presidential election campaign, this pressure did move the Bush administration to act. In the spring of 1992, it had already helped to mobilize economic sanctions on Serbia and Montenegro as an alternative to military force; in June, it had voted in the UN Security Council to extend the mandate of UN peacekeeping troops in Croatia so as to provide humanitarian assistance to Bosnian civilians when Europeans, who were also opposed to sending combat troops (the French, British, and for other reasons, the Germans) but who faced a growing refugee influx, sought to provide relief to civilians *in Bosnia*. Now, in the autumn of 1992, the Bush administration agreed to sponsor UN security council resolutions that would permit troop-contributing countries (not the United States) to "take all necessary measures" to protect the delivery of this humanitarian relief to Bosnian civilians while negotiations occurred. At the same time it began to explore, perhaps under pressure from candidate Clinton's campaign rhetoric, the option of lifting the arms embargo on the Bosnian government and supporting it militarily from the air with selective bombing against the Bosnian Serbs.

Not only did policy reflect decisions on the use of force but so did the factional alignments on Bosnia policy. On the one hand were those who opposed intervention because they saw no vital national interest in Bosnia or those who believed that the war could only be stopped when its political causes were addressed, making the question of force subordinate to political negotiations. On the other hand were those who defined the conflict as Serbian aggression, made possible by a military imbalance between Bosnian Serbs—assisted by the former Yugoslav army—and Bosnian Muslims—unjustly hamstrung by the arms embargo. They promoted "lift and strike" (lift the arms embargo and assist Bosnian ground troops with aerial bombing) to change the military balance in favor of Muslim victims to defeat the Serbs. Although the first approach was increasingly labelled the path of appeasement by the second camp, the apparent militarism of this second camp was also aimed at avoiding an American troop deployment by giving the Bosnian Muslims the means to defend themselves, aided in the early stages by NATO airpower. Thus, those whose views were that the United States had no interests in Bosnia were, in fact, votes for either camp and, indeed, as Cyrus Vance and David Owen discovered, this group did shift to a "lift and strike" policy when the success of diplomacy implied a commitment of ground troops to help implement a peace. The possibility, already slim, of any American debate about what the political objective in Bosnia should be and what was appropriate policy also grew dimmer as these positions converged.

The tension between these two positions and their advocates crystallized not in Washington, however, but over the United Nations operation (the United Nations Protection Forces, UNPROFOR), and thus in Sarajevo, Zagreb, and New York, and its *rules on the use of force*. Although the Bush administration first explored the policy of "lift and strike," its policies had supported the actual deployment of a humanitarian operation under United Nations auspices and joint EU-UN diplomacy. What debates over the use of force in the UN operation glaringly failed to respect (out of ignorance or political tactics) was that there are very well-developed and clear rules governing humanitarian operations and UN peacekeepers. These rules are essential to mobilizing necessary troops—that countries contributing troops are assured that the risk of casualties will be acceptably low because the authorities in the target area have given their consent to the deployment, including the signing of official memorandums of understanding (MOUs) on their terms; because consent is given for passage of convoys; and because the rules of engagement (ROE) on the use of force by these troops are appropriate to their mission—in self-defense, proportionate, impartial, and transparent (publicly warned). The rules are also essential to the *understanding* of force—including military doctrine in a general sense—that underlies peacekeeping practice: the purpose of peacekeepers is to contain violence while diplomats do their job, and they do so by interrupting incidents of force that could escalate and spiral out of control. This *dynamic of force* could as easily be generated by the actions of foreign soldiers as by warring factions, if force were not used to dampen the spiral but instead inflamed it.

To the faction of lobbyists and government officials who viewed the war in Bosnia as a case of external aggression, these rules on the use of force were immoral, treating the parties as if they were morally equal and the aggressor Serbs as only one of the warring parties in a civil war.[15] Moreover, the rules appeared to prevent UN soldiers from doing anything to stop the violence, atrocities, rape, camps, and, eventually, the war. There was an echo of Madeleine Albright's question to Colin Powell in the growing public outrage over Bosnia—what was the use of sending soldiers if they did not fight? Lost from view was what the soldiers and their commanding officers felt they were doing and were doing well—saving lives and laying the conditions for local cease-fires and a diplomatic end to the war. Lost also was an appreciation of the difference between peacekeeping and war making—that the role of the peacekeeping soldier includes accepting and sustaining humiliation, without response if response would fuel further violence, whereas the American doctrine of overwhelming force, in particular, was its antithesis. And lost was any recognition that peace-keeping had been chosen instead of war because Americans would not go.

Torn between the deep reluctance of the president and the Pentagon to send troops to Bosnia and a moral view of the war as aggression and gross violations of humanitarian law, including genocide against Muslims, the Clinton administration increasingly favored "lift and strike" rhetorically, while seeking a practical compromise through UN Security Council resolutions to oblige the troops that *were* on the ground to fight Serb aggression and enforce international principles. But as resolutions mounted, the UNPROFOR mandate ballooned, and where it had originally defined a clear objective, it became increasingly complex, muddied, unimplementable, and contradictory. While unfairly raising expectations that the "protection" in UNPROFOR's title was not for humanitarian aid workers, as its mandate defined, but for the civilian population of Bosnia and for Bosnian Muslim political goals, the new tasks were also unenforceable without the troops to do them. From an original deployment of one thousand, UNPROFOR rose toward twenty-four thousand in Bosnia (and about forty-three thousand in its three mission areas of Croatia, Bosnia and Herzegovina, and a Macedonian preventive deployment not discussed here). Yet the troops required for each new task—supervising and controlling heavy weapons, defending six safe areas, stopping ethnic cleansing, opening "blue routes" for humanitarian convoys or forcing them through, and so on—were always far above those that the Security Council was willing to authorize, and that number, in turn, was also far above those that countries were willing (and even able) to contribute. In addition to the irreconcilable contradictions between a peacekeeping mandate and its rules for using force, on the one hand, and the enforcement and indirect war-fighting mandate of the new tasks being assigned, under the initiative of the United States and nonaligned states, on the other, the military aspects of the operation were bound to unravel under the increasing complexity of the mandate, its slippage away from impartiality and growing risk to troops, and the growing size of the force and number of troop-contributing countries to be coordinated.

Yet the declining credibility of UNPROFOR, and the dire consequences for UN peacekeeping in the long run of the propaganda campaign waged (above all by the United States) against it, tended to be associated solely with the use of force—the troops' ROE, light weaponry, and alleged reluctance to use force against the Serbs. Even many UNPROFOR commanders drew the lesson that in the future they wanted heavy weaponry—tanks and artillery, in addition to the close air support (air strikes that could be called in for self-defense of their troops) that Bosnia added to peacekeeping experience—even though this violates peacekeeping doctrine and the conviction that if you have a weapon, you will eventually use it.[16] In fact, the lessons of UNPROFOR's failed credibility point instead to the issue of political direction. Without the space to provide a full analysis of the use of force in UNPROFOR, four lessons will illustrate.[17]

First, while any use of military power must be tied to a clear political objective if it is to succeed, the use of force in humanitarian and peacekeeping operations (UNPROFOR was not the latter but the rules of its mission were) is preeminently political, not military. The exercise of force is a last resort, and the psychological instruments wielded by military commanders are far more robust than robust ROE and weapons alone. Although these are always multinational operations, composed of national units, the value placed on low casualties by national capitals leads them to insist on retaining national influence (and in some cases final control) over their ground deployments and activities. Thus, the less unified the purpose, less clear the objective, or more risky the task, the more the unity of command essential to mission effectiveness and managing risks to soldiers' lives tends to break down.

Second, the particular instruments of coercion available—in the Bosnian case, the no-fly zone, enforcement of sanctions and embargoes, close air support, and air strikes—can be applied to different policy objectives. At the same time that the Clinton administration was calling for their use to punish Serbs, the peace negotiators were trying to use these same instruments (largely against the Serbs but not solely) to get a settlement: first, to improve their bargaining position with the parties, second, to obtain eventual military compliance with the provisions of the peace plan without having to resort to combat, and third, to persuade the reluctant party, the Bosnian Muslims, that they were better off negotiating sincerely than waiting for the American army to arrive as combatants on their behalf. The two uses were at cross purposes.

Third, the use of air power also has rules and conditions that must be respected.[18] To hit identified targets, they must be available, not just imagined; they must be visible, and not hidden under a hill, hospital, fog, or low cloud cover; and they require forward air controllers on the ground as spotters, thus requiring certain skills from countries willing to risk casualties after they have contributed soldiers under other terms. To engage in air strikes, as the "lift and strike" policy entailed, is to risk the loss of impartiality and even greater casualties on the ground, somewhere in theater. The use of air power also introduced into the field a second military organization—NATO—whose criteria, culture, doctrine, and political guidance were vastly different from the United Nations and from peacekeeping operations.

And fourth, many of these problems in the case of UNPROFOR originated in American policy. Although President Clinton protected his primary goal of not sending U.S. troops to Bosnia by altering the UNPROFOR mandate, his view of the use of air power and his administration's growing shift in favor of "lift and strike" (particularly its covert operation to ignore the arms embargo, then its open refusal not to enforce the embargo or share further intelligence with the UN, and finally its policy to alter the strategic picture entirely with Croatian troops and three military operations in Croatia and western Bosnia in 1995[19]) were UNPROFOR's undoing. The lesson drawn by U.S. allies who did have troops in UNPROFOR is that one cannot lead without troops on the ground and, conversely: do not keep troops on the ground if a power without troops on the ground is defining policy. Unity of policy is even more important than unity of command.[20] As David Owen concludes, "if the US is to assert leadership in the post–Cold War world they have to bear the military consequences of their political decisions."[21]

American Leadership

No negotiated peace settlement will succeed without an external implementation force in its first years.[22] Just as with the unity critical to successful diplomatic negotiations discussed earlier, therefore, that settlement must have as large a base of external support as possible so that countries will contribute troops and those who do will feel that their troops will not be undermined by spoilers (among the parties to an agreement or external powers) once on the ground. The Pentagon plan for a force to implement the Vance-Owen Peace Plan of January–May, 1993, called for fifty to seventy thousand troops, in contrast to the fifteen thousand that Vance and Owen thought they could get and resigned to work with. General Powell, according to David Owen, "was arguing seriously for going in with even larger forces initially to get the situation under control, with a view to winding down after six months."[23] Laying out conditions for the use of American force in the spring of 1993, Secretary of State Warren Christopher identified four tests to operationalize his prior insistence that they not be engaged in "imposing" a settlement.[24] In fact, the European insistence that the United States be involved in implementing the Vance-Owen Peace Plan was what killed it, for above the caution of a new administration, days old, a president who had not begun to overcome military distrust of his lack of military service and his running start with a policy on homosexuality and the military, and a foreign policy team who thought a better plan could be written for the Bosnian Muslims, the bottom line was that the United States was not ready to send troops. Even Pentagon objections to a policy of lifting the arms embargo and using air strikes, on grounds that it would not work and would eventually require troops, began to soften when faced with the alternative of sending American soldiers.

As late as August, 1995, U.S. policy toward Bosnia was to avoid at all costs sending troops. What happened to change this policy by November? To explain this paradox, that a policy that defined national interest in these terms led to the opposite, is to confront (if not to answer) the fundamental issue of the president and the use of force in the post–Cold War period.

Just as the fighting in Bosnia followed a seasonal cycle—a season for fighting and a season for talking—so the policy of the major powers followed an electoral cycle. The slow shift in American policy beginning in 1993 was the result of the election campaign rhetoric in 1992, and a new presidential campaign was looming in 1996. That shift in American policy, moreover, had led the diplomatic negotiations and the UN operation into crisis. The instrumentalization of air power had turned this crisis into a growing crisis between NATO and the UN, and between the United States and its NATO allies who had troops on the ground in Bosnia and Herzegovina. Britain and France (also under new leadership as a result of elections) reacted to the resulting stalemate and increasing risk with growing impatience. They determined by 1995 to retake the initiative and force a choice. Although more analysis needs to be done on why President Clinton first made a commitment to NATO allies to assist in the withdrawal of UNPROFOR, he faced a looming crisis of his own making with Congress over the deployment of troops. Would that commitment to NATO require him to send American soldiers into conditions where casualties were likely, risking not only soldiers' lives and Pentagon objections but also Congressional defiance, or could it be kept by taking the lead in finding a political settlement under which American soldiers could enter Bosnia under conditions of consent and a cease-fire so that the risk of casualties was minimized?

The NATO-led and American-commanded Implementation Force (IFOR) that replaced UNPROFOR after the Dayton accords were signed was assigned robust rules of engagement and heavy weaponry to avoid the lessons drawn from UNPROFOR. Somewhat in contradiction to those lessons, American officials also insisted on priority to force protection. The size of IFOR at just under sixty thousand; their mandate to implement the military Annex 1A of the Dayton peace framework over six months; and their exit strategy of twelve months to win congressional support replicated the Pentagon plan for implementing the Vance-Owen Peace Plan in 1993. The issues surrounding the use of force in UNPROFOR also faced IFOR (and its successor, the Stabilization Force [SFOR]): impartiality, consent, cooperation of the parties with an agreement the United States would not impose, an unclear political objective for the troops, and unity of purpose and alliance cohesion.

With American troops in Bosnia, the Congressional division between those who favored the "lift and strike" option and those who supported a diplomatic solution transferred to Bosnia, in a conflict between an American "train and equip" program for a Bosnian federation army (to create a "military balance" as the road to peace and a reunified Bosnia), which the Dayton negotiators promised Congressional critics to win support for the troop deployment, on the one hand, and the European preference for arms control, impartiality, and political reconciliation, on the other. Congressional opposition to the troop deployment, or its prolongation, remains, however, over questions of national interest and whether the United States should be involved in Bosnia at all. As the twelve-month time limit on the deployment of troops, which the president proposed to gain congressional support, ran up against delays (and in some cases even stalemate) in the Dayton peace process during 1997, the State department began to chafe at the reluctance of the Pentagon and NATO troops to use force to impose some elements of the peace settlement. American policy once again had to face the question of objectives. Was it in Bosnia for containment, to prevent the resumption of violence; to help restore a multiethnic Bosnia and a modicum of justice for Bosnian Muslim victims; or to establish stability in the Balkan region and restore the credibility of NATO as the Clinton administration sought to fulfill the Bush administration objective of ensuring that NATO remains the core of European security? The uncanny repetition of previous policy toward the next conflict of the Yugoslav succession, that over the Serbian province of Kosovo, made it clear that none of the issues on the use of force had been resolved.

Conclusion

The theme of this discussion is that if questions of U.S. national interest and its use of force abroad begin with the means—defining national interest *in terms of the use of force*—rather than the ends for which that force is used, the question about the use of military force can never be answered. Worse, if intervention is defined in terms of military force, in the post–Cold War era the United States will be pressured eventually to intervene far more often than might be prudent because of the particular assets it alone has and the military superiority on which its superpower status rests. Waiting for the United States to decide, moreover, builds in a response delay during which the conflict itself is likely to move more intractably onto a path of violence and logic of war. And if the United States refuses to use soldiers, there are direct and serious consequences for other states' willingness or even ability to use force. When it does agree to use military force, whether air power or ground troops, that use cannot occur unilaterally in the post–Cold War era. American primacy places a far greater burden on alliance-building and -maintaining and the necessary constraints that implies. All these lessons, written in September, 1997, were fully demonstrated one and a half years later over Kosovo.

Ethnonationalist conflicts are particularly susceptible to this problem because they do not, by their very definition as ethnic or nationalist conflicts, contain an intrinsic or obvious strategic significance to the United States. Secondly, the intractability mentioned above is even more likely because they rarely even come to the attention of policy makers until they are violent and threaten others (borders, neighbors, refugees, international norms). This violence is not a characteristic of ethnonationalist conflict but of the conditions in which such conflict emerges—the decline in state capacity and its legitimate control over means of force in the society leading to contest over and disintegration of the security apparatus (army, police, courts, executive power), and secondly, economic collapse in societies where access to jobs and welfare were in part linked to membership in an ethnic group or where regional inequality has ethnic elements.

In fact, ethnonationalist conflicts have a dynamic that is amenable to different approaches depending on the stage at which one intervenes. Where this contest becomes nationalist—legitimating a separate state on the basis of national rights (to the potential exclusion of all others in that territory)—it is characterized by security dilemmas and spiraling behavior. But this makes it least amenable to the theories of deterrence that U.S. policy makers favor when they view a conflict in military terms. In Bosnia, for example, the enemy became the proliferation of arms—paramilitary gangs, arms merchants hawking fear, the local stocks of the country's territorial defense system, arms industries located in Bosnia, separate armies for each political party and locality, the federal army as one of many contestants—but in place of demilitarization, the U.S. policy was to infuse more arms to create an illusory military balance and deter the Bosnian Serbs. Taking sides in a substate ethnic conflict that has become nationalist, when one is not willing to defend the state-in-the-making of that chosen side, reinforces this spiraling and may be a recipe for long-term military involvement.

The lesson of Bosnia is one of caution: there is insufficient evidence for either of the lessons currently being drawn from the case. As UNPROFOR commanders liked to suggest, only when the United States has its own soldiers on the ground will it be able to draw proper lessons. The lesson of American policy toward other cases of state collapse, such as elements of the former Soviet

Union—the Baltics, the four nuclear successor states, and the retreat of the Soviet army and protection of minority rights from the western parts—is that there are alternatives to the use of military force in conflicts that are very similar. The difference, tellingly, was the greater level of U.S. interest. The lesson of Dayton implementation, as with UNPROFOR, is that military force is an instrument of policy—only one of many instruments—and cannot be separated from it. Taken alone, it can separate combatants, threaten punishment, and at best build confidence among military officers. To overcome the violence and security dilemmas of nationalist conflict, it must be integrated with other instruments—diplomatic, economic, psychological—that reward cooperation, facilitate reconciliation, and build stable states.

Notes

1. Cited by Colin Powell in his autobiography, written with Joseph E. Persico, *My American Journey* (New York: Random House, 1995), p. 576, he then adds, "I thought I would have an aneurysm. American GIs were not toy soldiers to be moved around on some sort of global game board."
2. Richard Holbrooke's memoir of his role in negotiating an end to the war in Bosnia and Herzegovina is written largely to implant this view. See *To End a War* (New York: Random House, 1998).
3. For decision makers like Colin Powell, in fact, the fear of Beirut was more immediate, but the "quagmire" of Vietnam remains a live apprehension and can still be heard even from junior officers who have actually been stationed at some time in Bosnia after 1992.
4. This was more a political than a military judgment, and see Eliot A. Cohen, "The Mystique of US Air Power," *Foreign Affairs* 73, no. 1 (Jan.-Feb., 1994).
5. For an example of the burgeoning literature analyzing the use of force in Bosnia, which draws these lessons, see Chantal de Jonge Oudraat, "The Use of Military Force in Bosnia," typescript, September, 1996, draft chapter from a forthcoming book.
6. This is not factually true, although most accounts wrongly assert that it is, because the Bosnian Serbs had already agreed (in the presence of U.S. negotiators and publicly announced) to be represented by Slobodan Milošević and to accept the outlines of the American plan five days *before* the air campaign, Operation Deliberate Force, began.
7. October 22, on the CNN program, "Crossfire."
8. Cited in Warren Zimmermann, *Origins of a Catastrophe: Yugoslavia and Its Destroyers—America's Last Ambassador Tells What Happened and Why* (New York: Times Books, 1996), p. 62, who calls this extraordinary statement, perhaps sufficient to explain everything that followed, "unexceptionable," although he also admits that it "set off shock waves in Slovenia." They knew they could go, that "the United States and NATO would not use force to keep Yugoslavia together."
9. This was a strictly military assessment within the Ministry of Defense, which they maintained privately and publicly under bitter public criticism. According

to David Owen, this view was also shared at the Foreign Office by Foreign Secretary Douglas Hurd: "His attitude to the use of force was inextricably linked to whether the US would participate with troops on the ground" (*Balkan Odyssey* [London: Victor Gollancz, 1995], p. 103).

10. David Gompert, special assistant to President Bush for national security affairs at the time, writes, "the prime minister wanted debt relief and a public signal of unreserved American political backing—commitments that seemed unwarranted in view of his government's apparent terminal condition. . . . the Marković government was beyond help. . . . the Bush administration could not justify putting the dying Yugoslav federal authority on life-support systems." See his "The United States and Yugoslavia's Wars," in *The World and Yugoslavia's Wars,* ed. Richard H. Ullman (New York: Council on Foreign Relations, 1996), p. 123. He adds, "Because Washington did not view even a violent breakup of Yugoslavia as likely to lead to a Europe-wide war or to threaten the democratic revolutions elsewhere in eastern Europe, a major program to shore up Belgrade's last federal government was no more seriously contemplated than was preemptive military action" (p. 124).

11. James Gow, writing in "The Role of the Military in the Yugoslav War of Dissolution," in proceedings of a conference, *Armed Conflict in the Balkans and European Security,* held April 20–22, 1993 (Ljubljana, Slovenia: Ministry of Defense-Center for Strategic Studies, June, 1993), draws this conclusion from analyses in the army's primary journal, *Vojno Delo* (Military Affairs).

12. This was not, in the end, the fate of this territory, because German success in persuading other EC member states to recognize Croatian independence, in its republican borders, on December 16, 1991, preempted the Carrington negotiations, and the admission of Croatia to the United Nations, in these borders, in May, 1992, together with a combination of diplomatic and military actions to take full control of the area under United Nations protection, created a fait accompli in Croatia's favor that no outsider cared to reverse.

13. This position was later said to be "not changed by force," but there was no willingness to entertain negotiated changes in the borders—the change by mutual agreement later said to be acceptable—in the crucial year of March, 1991, to March, 1992.

14. Owen, *Balkan Odyssey,* p. 109.

15. Particularly eloquent on this view, however much it misunderstood peacekeeping doctrine and rules, is David Rieff's attack on UNPROFOR, *Slaughterhouse: Bosnia and the Failure of the West* (New York: Touchstone, 1995). See also the work by a collective of journalists gathered in London to monitor the Yugoslav crisis in a periodical, *Warreport,* and the book by some of them, *With No Peace to Keep . . . : United Nations Peacekeeping and the War in the Former Yugoslavia,* ed. Ben Cohen and George Stamkoski (London: Institute for War and Peace Reporting, 1996).

16. The extreme to which commanders on the ground felt these failed credibility arguments can be illustrated by the fact that I first heard this lesson from a commanding general in the Macedonian preventive deployment, where there was no war and where the Nordic contingent, to which he belonged, still represented commitment to the purest form of peacekeeping doctrine.

17. One good source of analyses on UNPROFOR are the series of UN Commanders' Workshops in 1995–96 on "Lessons Learned from former Yugoslavia," of the

Danish-Norwegian Research Project on UN Peacekeeping (Danorp) of NUPI, Oslo, and COPRI, Copenhagen, under the direction of Wolfgang Biermann and Martin Vadset.

18. See Carsten F. Ronnefeldt and Per Erik Solli, *Use of Air Power in Peace Operations* Peacekeeping and Multinational Operations, no. 7 (Oslo: The Norwegian Institute of International Affairs, 1997).

19. The role of Congress in motivating the covert operations (initiated by officials in the NSC, State Department, and U.S. Embassy in Zagreb) to deliver arms to the Bosnian Muslims (and therefore the Bosnian Croats, who controlled the supply routes), the role of congressional pressure to lift the arms embargo, and the role of Military Professional Resources, Inc. (MPRI), the Pentagon, and American diplomats in Germany, Croatia, and the Contact Group in this American policy are essential elements of this story, but beyond the scope of this discussion.

20. The acrid conflict between the United States and the United Nations over the dual key arrangement between NATO and UNPROFOR for deciding on the use of air power (as close air support for troops or as air strikes to enforce agreements such as the heavy weapons exclusion zone around each safe area), an arrangement in fact insisted on by Britain, is one of the saddest commentaries on this principle.

21. Owen, *Balkan Odyssey,* p. 366.

22. This is a necessary but not sufficient condition for success. See Owen, *Balkan Odyssey,* p. 129, and for an empirical demonstration, see Barbara Walter, "The Critical Barrier to Civil War Settlement," *International Organization* 51, no. 3 (summer, 1997).

23. Owen, *Balkan Odyssey,* p. 134.

24. The four rigorous tests were "the goal must be stated clearly; there must be a strong likelihood of success; there must be 'an exit strategy'; and the action must win substantial public support." See Owen, *Balkan Odyssey,* p. 146; also, Elaine Sciolino, "Christopher Explains Conditions for Use of U.S. Force in Bosnia: He Says Success and Quick Exit Must Be Likely," *New York Times,* April 28, 1993, p. A1. The list was longer for American participation in peacekeeping operations, as enunciated in Presidential Decision Directive 25, *The Clinton Administration's Policy on Reforming Multilateral Peace Operations* (U.S. Department of State, Bureau of International Organization Affairs, State Department Publication 10161 [Washington, D.C.: GPO, 1994]).

Part III

Force, Politics, and Society

Chapter 7

Cowards, Beliefs, and Structures

Congress and the Use of Force

James M. Lindsay

> *"You put your finger on a very difficult question. People say to me,
> How many lives? How many lives can you expend? Each one is pre-
> cious. I don't want to reminisce, but I've been there. I know what it's
> like to have fallen comrades and see young kids die in battle. It's only
> the President that should be asked to make the decision: Is it worth it?"*
>   —Pres. George Bush, November 30, 1990

> *"I would welcome the support of the Congress [for an invasion of
> Haiti], and I hope that I will have that. Like my predecessors, I have
> not agreed that I was constitutionally mandated to get it."*
>   —Pres. Bill Clinton, August 3, 1994

THE BELIEF THAT PRESIDENTS have an inherent authority to initiate the use of force would have struck the delegates to the Constitutional Convention as heresy. George Mason argued in Philadelphia that he was "against giving the power of war to the executive" because the president "is not safely to be trusted with it."[1] James Wilson held that he and his fellow delegates had created a political system that "will not hurry us into war; it is calculated to guard against it. It will not be in the power of a single man, or a single body of men, to involve us in such distress."[2] James Madison wrote that the Constitution has, "with studied care, vested the question of war in the Legisl[ature]."[3] Even Alexander Hamilton, the patron saint of those who applaud presidential initiative in foreign affairs, believed that "it belongs to Congress only, to go to War."[4]

The huge gap between what modern presidents claim as their war powers and what the founders originally intended has provoked a rich and vigorous debate among legal scholars. On one hand, presidentialists argue that presidents have broad powers to initiate the use of force without congressional authorization. The source of this authority is variously attributed to the president's role as commander in chief, his possession of the executive power, international treaty obligations, and customary practice over the past two hundred years. On the other hand, congressionalists argue that the president's authority to initiate the use of force is severely restricted in the absence of congressional authorization. In their view, the original design of the founders remains binding on presidents.

The merits of these competing constitutional visions are likely to be debated for some time. The Constitution is, as Charles Evans Hughes once remarked, "what the judges say it is." In the case of war powers issues, the courts have preferred to remain silent. Thus, rather than analyze the constitutional issues, my focus here is on two different questions. First, why have presidents come to eclipse Congress when it comes to the war power? Second, why, despite the passing of the Cold War and the urgings of a wide range of academics and political commentators, has Congress failed to claim the role the founders envisioned for it?

Most discussions of these questions contend that the root problem is that members of Congress fear making politically risky decisions on war and peace. While political cowardice can never be discounted as a motivating force on Capitol Hill, the obstacles to congressional action go far beyond political will. They are instead rooted in political beliefs and structures that give any president a decided advantage over Congress when it comes to the decision to use force. The hopes of congressionalists notwithstanding, legislative reform is not likely to nullify this advantage.

From Washington to McKinley

The founders made clear which branch of government should control the war power: Congress.[5] Article I, Section 8 of the Constitution states that Congress shall have the power "to declare War." In recognition that not all hostilities reach the level of full-scale war, the Constitution further assigns to Congress the power to "grant Letters of Marque and Reprisal."[6] In assigning the war power to Congress, the founders explicitly rejected a proposal to lodge the authority to use force (outside of the narrow case of a sudden attack on the United States) in the executive branch. When Pierce Butler moved to vest the war power in the president, none of the other delegates to the Constitutional Convention seconded his motion. The founders also made explicit their limited conception of presidential authority in their battle to win ratification of the Constitution. Alexander Hamilton wrote that the president's power as commander in chief "would amount to nothing more than the supreme command and direction of the military and naval forces . . . while that of the British king extends to the *declaring* of war and to the *raising* and *regulating* of fleets and armies: all of which by the Constitution under consideration would appertain to the Legislature."[7]

The founders' conception of the war power to a large extent guided political practice over the next hundred years.[8] In 1798, at the start of the undeclared naval war with France, John Adams called Congress into special session "to consult and determine on such measure as in their wisdom shall be deemed meet for the safety and welfare of the said United States." Congress subsequently passed more than a dozen laws authorizing hostilities.[9] When Andrew Jackson sought to force France to pay damage claims that dated back to the Napoleonic wars, he asked Congress to pass a law "authorizing reprisals upon French property."[10] Congress declined the request. And when the Chilean government refused to apologize in 1891 after a mob killed two American sailors, Benjamin Harrison asked Congress to take "such action as may be deemed appropriate."[11] Harrison deferred to congressional action even though he and all the members of his cabinet favored war.[12]

In the relatively few nineteenth century cases that raised war powers issues, the courts generally supported an expansive view of congressional authority and restricted the range of presidential authority. In a series of cases arising out of the undeclared naval war with France, the Supreme Court held that Congress had authorized hostilities and that the limitations it placed on American conduct were binding on the president.[13] In one case, Chief Justice John Marshall went so far as to write: "The whole powers of war being, by the Constitution of the United States, vested in Congress, the acts of that body alone can be resorted to as our guide."[14]

In the Civil War's famed *Prize* cases, the Court ruled that "by the Constitution, Congress alone has the power to declare a national or foreign war. . . . [The president] has no power to initiate or declare a war either against a foreign nation or a domestic state."[15] And where the courts did recognize a presidential authority to act without benefit of explicit congressional sanction, as in an 1860 finding that the president had a duty to protect American citizens in danger overseas, the exceptions were small and limited.[16]

None of this is to say that original intent was always followed during the nineteenth century. The U.S military on occasion—the exact number of times is a matter of some dispute—used force without specific congressional sanction.[17] Most of these incidents involved relatively inconsequential attacks on nonstate actors such as brigands and pirates. Furthermore, they often were pursuant to broad statutes that Congress had passed over the years authorizing the navy to punish piracy and protect American citizens in danger abroad.[18] Still others occurred without the benefit of either congressional or presidential authorization.

The success of congressional control of the war power during the nineteenth century rested on two key factors. One was the country's relative disengagement from world affairs. Blessed with weak neighbors and focused on continental interests rather than global ones, presidents were largely free of the pressures and temptations to use force without congressional approval. The paucity of perceived external threats also meant that there was no need for a large standing peacetime army, thereby limiting the means available to any president seeking to start a war on his own initiative.

A second, and more important, factor in the success of congressional control over the war power was that most nineteenth century presidents believed that the war power resided in Congress and not the White House (a position the courts reinforced). Presidents as diverse as Jefferson, Madison, Monroe, Jackson, Buchanan, Lincoln, Grant, and McKinley explicitly recognized that they were severely limited in their ability to use force overseas without benefit of congressional authorization. And these expressions were more than polite fictions. Nineteenth century presidents generally were cautious in exercising their power to initiate foreign policy to establish what Alexander Hamilton called "an antecedent state of things" that would bind Congress politically and morally if not legally to using force.[19]

Just how politically vulnerable the congressional war power was in the nineteenth century to presidential initiative was made clear with the Mexican-American War. When Pres. James Polk provoked fighting by sending U.S. troops into territory claimed by Mexico, many members of Congress denounced him for having maneuvered the country into war. But in testimony to the political (if not constitutional) import of such "an antecedent state of things," Congress voted overwhelmingly to recognize that a state of war existed. By the time the House passed legislation declaring that the fighting had been "unnecessarily and unconstitutionally begun by the President of the United States," the war was over.[20] Yet even in this case, no claim was made that the president possessed an independent war-making authority. Indeed, immediately after learning of the initial fighting, Polk asked Congress to issue a declaration of war, a clear sign that he believed he could not conduct the war under his own authority.

From Roosevelt to Roosevelt

With the dawn of the twentieth century the United States began to look beyond its borders and see itself as a global power. American "ownership of distant possessions and [the] many sharp struggles for foreign trade" in turn created, in the words of Woodrow Wilson, the need for a president who "must stand always at the front of our affairs."[21] Suddenly turned on its head was the nineteenth century view that presidents could exercise only powers explicitly granted to them by the Constitution or statutory law, or that could be clearly implied from those sources. The new view, as its initial and most ardent proponent, Theodore Roosevelt, put it, was that it is not only the president's right "but his duty to do anything that the needs of the Nation demanded unless such action was forbidden by the Constitution or by the laws."[22]

Emboldened by this more expansive view of executive authority, Roosevelt and his immediate successors encroached on the congressional war power. In the first three decades of the twentieth century the United States intervened repeatedly in the Caribbean without congressional consent. In 1917, Woodrow Wilson responded to a Senate filibuster of his proposal to arm U.S. merchant ships by ordering that the ships be armed anyway. Citing "the plain implication of my constitutional duties and power," Wilson took the step even though he knew the action was "practically certain" to draw the country into war.[23] Later, in the months preceding America's entry into World War II, Franklin Roosevelt unilaterally dispatched U.S. troops to first Greenland and then Iceland, and issued a "shoot-at-sight" order against German submarines operating in the North Atlantic. In undertaking these initiatives, presidents put the burden on Congress to rein them in. Congress seldom did.

The actions of presidents from Roosevelt to Roosevelt eroded congressional control over the war power and broadened the zone of presidential authority. But in many respects presidential uses of force in the first half of the twentieth century had much in common with nineteenth century practice. Few of the U.S. interventions abroad looked like war or involved much (if any) fighting. For example, U.S. support for Panama's secession from Colombia merely involved sending U.S warships into Panamanian waters. There were no casualties, and no shots were fired.[24] Even the extended U.S. occupations of Haiti, the Dominican Republic, and Nicaragua were, from a purely military point of view, relatively minor affairs that typically involved fewer than a thousand U.S. Marines and little or no sustained combat.[25]

Even more notable than the small scale of any fighting that did occur is that in none of these cases did presidents claim any inherent authority as commander in chief to initiate war. For example, in defending President Taft's decision to intervene in Nicaragua in 1912, the State Department solicitor general made no reference to the commander-in-chief clause.[26] The commander-in-chief theory was hardly any more developed by the time of Franklin Roosevelt. In more than eighty press conferences in 1941, Roosevelt "never once alleged special powers in foreign affairs as commander in chief."[27] Instead, U.S. military interventions abroad typically were justified on the grounds that they were limited military actions designed to preserve order and protect American lives. Presidents continued to acknowledge that congressional authorization was required before the United States could initiate force in major conflicts.

From Truman to Bush

The presidential view of executive war-making authority changed fundamentally with the Korean War. Harry Truman became the first president to claim that the commander-in-chief clause empowered him to commit U.S. forces to a major conflict without congressional authorization when he ordered U.S. forces into South Korea.[28] With the exception of Dwight Eisenhower—who declared that there would be "no involvement of America in war unless it is a result of the constitutional process that is placed upon Congress to declare it"— Truman's successors all have embraced his expansive view of presidential prerogative.[29] Perhaps none did so more colorfully than George Bush, who boasted he "didn't have to get permission from some old goat in the United States Congress to kick Saddam Hussein out of Kuwait."[30]

Truman's claim of an inherent presidential authority to initiate the use of force was widely accepted on Capitol Hill in the 1950s and 1960s. However, as U.S. casualties in Vietnam mounted, many members of Congress began to doubt the wisdom of deferring to presidential leadership and to recognize how much power they had ceded to the White House. Their answer was to enact, over Richard Nixon's veto, the War Powers Resolution. Ironically, the Tonkin Gulf Resolution almost certainly met the constitutional requirement for congressional authorization of the use of U.S. forces in Vietnam.[31]

Despite the intentions of its authors, the War Powers Resolution has had at best a slim effect in achieving its stated goal: to "insure that the collective judgment of both the Congress and the President will apply to the introduction of United States Armed Forces into hostilities, or into situations where imminent involvement in hostilities is clearly indicated by the circumstances."[32]

Events leading up to the Gulf War illustrate the ineffectiveness of the War Powers Resolution as a tool for injecting congressional preferences into decisions involving war and peace.[33] President Bush did not consult with congressional leaders during the five days between the Iraqi invasion of Kuwait and his decision to dispatch U.S. troops to Saudi Arabia. Nor did he consult with them before doubling the number of troops in November, 1990, and changing U.S. strategy from defending Saudi Arabia to liberating Kuwait by force. Bush submitted reports to Congress in August and again in November "consistent with" but not "pursuant to" the War Powers Resolution—a legal device to avoid acknowledging the legitimacy of the law. Both reports denied that hostilities were imminent, which effectively put the onus on Congress to start the sixty-day clock. (The War Powers Resolution stipulates that the use of U.S. armed forces must be terminated if Congress fails to authorize the operation within sixty days of the time troops are introduced into imminent or actual hostilities.) Throughout 1990 no consensus formed in Congress on starting the clock. Congress finally passed legislation in January, 1991, authorizing U.S. forces to participate in the Gulf War, but it was legislation that ratified a policy that had been developed by the president alone and not one developed jointly by the two branches.

The ineffectiveness of the War Powers Resolution owes in part to poor legislative drafting. Terms such as "hostilities" and "imminent hostilities" are nowhere defined, and no mechanism exists to automatically start the sixty-day clock.[34] The Gulf War illustrates the fundamental flaw in the War Powers Resolution: presidents have not accepted its central premise, that presidential authority to commit U.S. troops to combat is limited and that congressional authorization is required when the United States initiates the use of force. Moreover, when members of Congress have turned to the courts for judicial enforcement of the War Powers Resolution, they have been disappointed.[35]

After the Cold War

Although Congress ratified rather than helped determine President Bush's Gulf War policy, the January, 1991, congressional vote nonetheless remains remarkable. Unlike the Tonkin Gulf Resolution twenty-seven years earlier, when all but two members of Congress rallied behind President Johnson, the Iraq Resolution saw forty-seven senators and 183 representatives vote no. Does the end of the Cold War mark a new era of congressional assertiveness on war power issues?

A definitive answer to this question is impossible. Of the three major U.S.

military operations in the six years after the liberation of Kuwait, only the events leading up to the intervention in Haiti raised the same core war powers issues that the Gulf War raised and that the War Powers Resolution was designed to address. Rather than being instances of the use of military *force,* U.S. military deployments to Somalia and Bosnia were both instances of the use of military *forces,* in the former case to deliver humanitarian relief and in the latter case to help implement a peace agreement. In neither case was combat intended or anticipated (as the Pentagon's term for such actions—"operations other than war"— suggests). Although the Constitution says nothing about which branch of government has the authority to order troop deployments overseas during peacetime, presidents have for more than a century ordered such deployments, and Congress has generally acquiesced in the practice.[36] Moreover, under the terms of the War Powers Resolution, troop deployments where hostilities are not indicated neither trigger the sixty-day clock nor require any congressional action.

Looking at the broader issue of presidential decisions to deploy troops overseas—which also raise unsettled constitutional issues—the congressional record is mixed in the first six years after the Gulf War. On one hand, congressional activism increased, at least when compared to the record of the 1950s and 1960s. The decisions to deploy troops to Somalia, Haiti, and Bosnia, and the Clinton administration's reliance on multilateral peacekeeping more generally, all prompted congressional efforts to rewrite presidential policy. On the other hand, this activism frequently failed to translate into influence, particularly with respect to decisions to send troops overseas.

Somalia

When President Bush ordered more than twenty thousand U.S. troops to Somalia in December, 1992, he did not request congressional authorization for the mission, nor was congressional authorization necessarily required.[37] Nonetheless, the Senate passed a resolution in February, 1993, authorizing the U.S. mission in Somalia. Rather than invoking the War Powers Resolution, the Senate measure stated it was "consistent with" the 1973 law.[38] The House did not take up the Senate bill for three months. During that time responsibility for the Somalia mission was handed over to the United Nations and the goals of the operation were expanded to include disarming Somali factions and restoring the country's political institutions. The House passed a revised resolution in May that retroactively authorized the initial troop deployment and authorized U.S. participation in the UN mission for an additional twelve months. In light of sporadic fighting in which four U.S. soldiers died, the House resolution provided specific statutory authorization under the War Powers Resolution should U.S. troops become involved in combat.[39] However, this assertion of congressional prerogative never became law. The Senate put the House bill aside after forces loyal to Somali warlord Mohammed Farah Aidid killed twenty-four Pakistani peacekeepers in June.

In response to the escalating violence, the Senate in early September attached a nonbinding resolution to the defense authorization bill asking the president to report to Congress by October 15 on the goals of U.S. forces in Somalia and to win specific congressional authorization for the mission by November 15. The resolution, which was sponsored by Senate Majority Leader George J. Mitchell (D-Maine) and Senate Minority Leader Robert Dole (R-Kansas), was designed as a substitute for a more restrictive amendment offered by Sen. Robert Byrd (D–West Virginia), chairman of the Senate Appropriations Committee. Byrd's resolution would have terminated funding for the Somalia mission if Congress did not authorize it within one month.[40] The House followed the Senate's lead two weeks later and passed the nonbinding resolution.

The September resolution initially looked as if it would satisfy congressional concerns over Somalia. However, just one week after the House vote, eighteen Army Rangers were killed during a raid on a suspected Aidid stronghold. The deaths, the highest suffered by any army unit in combat since the Vietnam War, led to a firestorm of criticism. During debate over the annual defense appropriations bill, Clinton's supporters turned back an amendment sponsored by Sen. John McCain (R-Arizona) that would have repudiated the administration's policy and required the prompt withdrawal of U.S. troops. Instead, the Senate passed an amendment sponsored by Senator Byrd endorsing the administration's policy. But the victory was a hollow one for the White House. It came only after Clinton agreed to narrow the goals of the U.S. mission in Somalia and to withdraw all U.S. troops from Somalia by March 31, 1994.[41] Subsequent efforts by House Republicans to move the withdrawal date up to January 31 were rebuffed.[42]

Haiti

Unlike Somalia, the Haiti case clearly raised war powers issues from the start.[43] When armed Haitians prevented two hundred American and Canadian engineers aboard the USS *Harlan County* from landing in Port-au-Prince in October, 1994, to work on development projects in Haiti, there was speculation that the Clinton administration would restore Jean Bertrand Aristide to power by force. Senator Dole responded to the speculation by announcing he would introduce binding legislation requiring the administration to obtain congressional authorization before using force in Haiti unless the president certified that American lives or national security interests were imperiled.

Dole's proposal generated a firestorm of criticism. The criticism was fueled at least in part by his longstanding record of opposing Democratic attempts to fetter Republican presidents and by his admission that if he were president he would oppose the amendment he was offering.[44] Faced with criticism by even his staunchest Republican allies, Dole withdrew his proposal. However, Sen. Jesse Helms (R–North Carolina) stepped in to offer a similar amendment. The Senate rejected the Helms amendment by a vote of 81-19. Senators then overwhelmingly adopted two separate nonbinding amendments urging the administration to obtain congressional authorization before using force in either Haiti or Bosnia.

The Senate revisited the Haiti issue in the summer of 1994. In June, Sen. Judd Gregg (R–New Hampshire) sponsored an amendment similar to the one Senator Helms proposed eight months earlier. Several Clinton supporters criticized the administration's policy during the floor debate, but the senators again refused to mandate that the White House obtain congressional authorization before using force.[45]

Less than a month later, amid renewed speculation of a U.S. invasion, senators turned back another proposal, offered by Senator Dole, to postpone military action until a bipartisan commission had time to study the Haitian crisis. Although a majority of senators once again refused to tie the president's hands, the Clinton administration's margin of support slipped. Whereas the Helms amendment had garnered only nineteen votes, the Gregg amendment received thirty-four, and the Dole amendment forty-two.[46]

At the end of July, after the UN Security Council voted to authorize the use of force to depose the Haitian military junta, the Senate unanimously passed a resolution declaring that the UN vote "does not constitute authorization for the deployment of United States Armed Forces in Haiti under the Constitution of the United States or pursuant to the War Powers Resolution."[47]

The issue of Haiti moved to the top of the foreign policy agenda in September, 1994, when it became clear that the Clinton administration planned to make good on its threat to use force to restore Aristide to power. Members of Congress from both sides of the aisle denounced the proposed invasion, and many argued that Clinton could not act without congressional authorization. As pressure mounted for a vote on the issue, Democratic leaders in Congress blocked floor consideration of any legislation on Clinton's policy.[48] On September 15, the Thursday before Congress was finally to vote on Haiti, Clinton told the nation that the time for negotiations had ended. Immediately after the speech, however, in an apparent bid to derail congressional opposition by showing that he was willing to "go the extra mile," Clinton asked former president Jimmy Carter to lead a high-level delegation to Haiti to persuade that nation's military leaders to step down voluntarily.

The success of the Carter delegation derailed a potential constitutional crisis over the war power, but it did not stop congressional criticism of the Clinton administration. A Republican-led proposal to recall U.S. troops from Haiti immediately was narrowly defeated in the House, while a provision requiring that all troops be withdrawn by March 1, 1995, was defeated overwhelmingly. Instead, the House and Senate passed identical resolutions calling for "prompt and orderly withdrawal" of U.S. forces in Haiti and stating that 'the president should have sought and welcomed" the support of Congress before sending troops to Haiti.[49]

Bosnia

Bosnia was a source of executive-legislative tension even before Bill Clinton entered the White House.[50] In 1992, the Senate passed a nonbinding resolution urging President Bush not to send U.S. troops into the former Yugoslavia unless U.S. policy had clearly defined objectives. Over the next year the U.S. role in Bosnia increased as U.S. forces airlifted humanitarian relief and enforced an embargo against Serbia and a "no-fly zone" over Bosnia. As expectations rose that the United States might send troops to participate in the UN peace-keeping mission in Bosnia, members of Congress sought assurances that the Clinton administration would obtain congressional authorization before making such a commitment. It was a point that senior administration officials seemed to concede.[51] In November, 1993, Congress passed a resolution, initially drafted by Senators Mitchell and Dole, urging the president to seek congressional authorization before sending troops to Bosnia.[52]

In February, 1994, U.S. planes enforcing the no-fly zone shot down four Serbian aircraft, marking the first time NATO forces had engaged in combat.[53] Four times over the next ten months U.S. planes attacked Serbian and Bosnian Serb targets.[54] In May, Majority Leader Mitchell introduced an amendment authorizing U.S. forces to support the UN peacekeeping mission in Bosnia.[55] The House did not act on the Mitchell proposal. In September, Congress passed another nonbinding resolution stating that none of the funds appropriated for the Defense Department for fiscal year (FY) 1995 should be used to send U.S. troops on a peacekeeping mission in Bosnia unless Congress authorized it.[56]

Congress and the White House struggled throughout 1995 over whether the United States should lift its arms embargo against Bosnia. In midsummer Congress finally passed legislation directing that the embargo be lifted.[57] Although Clinton vetoed the bill, the fact that the legislation had passed by more than the two-thirds margin needed to override the veto—coupled with the dramatic defeats Serbian forces suffered during a Croatian military offensive—pushed the administration to invigorate its Bosnia diplomacy. That effort ultimately culminated in November with the announcement of the Dayton Peace

Agreement, which called for sending twenty thousand U.S. troops to Bosnia as part of a NATO peacekeeping force. Since the troops would be overseeing the implementation of a negotiated peace settlement rather than imposing peace by force of arms, President Clinton probably did not need congressional authorization to order the deployment.[58]

In the weeks preceding the Dayton announcement, Congress as a whole and the two houses individually passed a variety of measures stating that U.S. troops should not be deployed to Bosnia without congressional authorization. All but one of the measures were nonbinding.[59] Once the deployment was announced, the House and Senate each considered and rejected proposals to prohibit the deployment. The House did, however, approve a nonbinding measure stating its "serious concerns and opposition" to the peacekeeping force and expressing "pride and admiration" for the U.S. troops deployed there. For its part, the Senate passed a nonbinding resolution stating that it unequivocally supports" the U.S. troops, "recognizes that preserving United States credibility is a strategic interest," and urged the president to fulfill his commitment "for approximately one year."[60] The conflicting House and Senate versions were never reconciled as the congressional leadership concluded that the formal signing of the Dayton Accords in Paris in mid-December had rendered the issue moot.[61]

UN Peacekeeping

If Congress failed to claim a formal role in the decisions to send troops to Somalia, Haiti, and Bosnia, it did pass legislation designed to curb U.S. involvement in UN peacekeeping operations. One of the first steps it took was to use its power of the purse to cut administration funding requests for UN peacekeeping operations. Congress also enacted legislation in 1994 that unilaterally cut the U.S. share of UN peacekeeping costs from 31.7 percent to 25 percent. As a result of these actions, U.S. peacekeeping arrears in 1997 exceeded $650 million according to U.S. government accounting and $1 billion according to UN accounting.

Congress also took steps to ensure that the administration kept it fully informed about UN operations and to prevent the executive from circumventing its funding restrictions. In April, 1994, Congress required the administration to report monthly on, among other things, "any changes in the duration, mandate, and command and control arrangements" of ongoing UN operations as well as the "duration, mandate, and command and control arrangements" of any new operation."[62] In 1995 and 1996 Congress passed legislation denying funding for the U.S. share of new UN peacekeeping operations unless Congress is notified fifteen days in advance and the administration identifies how it will pay for such operations.[63] The intent of this legislation is to curtail new operations (and American participation in them) by making it more difficult to fund them. Finally, in 1997, the Clinton administration reluctantly agreed— as a price for Senate support for its plan to pay U.S. arrears to the UN—to legislation that would have severely restricted the president's ability to provide military support to UN peacekeeping operations on a nonreimbursable basis. Senate Republicans insisted on this provision after the General Accounting Office reported that the Defense Department had spent more than $3 billion in unreimbursed funds to support UN peacekeeping operations between FY 1992 and FY 1995.[64] A dispute over an unrelated provision in the same bill authorizing support for family planning overseas ultimately derailed passage of the peacekeeping legislation.

In addition to cutting funding for UN peacekeeping efforts, imposing detailed reporting requirements on the administration, and seeking to restrict support for UN peacekeeping operations, Congress also sought to limit the president's ability to contribute U.S. troops to UN peacekeeping operations if they would be under the command or operational control of foreign commanders. The House first passed such legislation in February, 1995, as part of the National Security Revitalization Act, one of ten planks in the "Contract With America."[65] The Senate declined to take up the House bill but a nearly identical provision was inserted in the FY 1996 defense authorization bill. President Clinton vetoed the bill in December, 1995, in part because of the UN peacekeeping provisions.[66] In April, 1996, Congress passed a measure barring payments for any UN peacekeeping operation in which U.S. troops served under foreign command unless the president reported to Congress that the deployment served U.S. national security interests.[67] In September the House resurrected the ban on placing U.S. peacekeeping troops under foreign command.[68] However, faced with a clear veto threat, the Senate did not take up the House measure.

As this brief review indicates, congressional activism on U.S. military deployments overseas has been substantial in recent years. Although the end of the Cold War made possible military involvement that previously had been impossible, no consensus has developed on Capitol Hill regarding the wisdom of these operations. At the same time, however, no consensus has developed on directly overruling presidential decisions to send U.S. forces overseas. Instead, the general pattern has been for members to carp and complain, but for Congress as an institution to act to curtail presidential discretion only after an operation has soured.

Yet if Congress has not directly blocked a presidential decision to send troops overseas, its activism has influenced what presidents decide to do. Fearful of the consequences of another Somalia, the Clinton administration sharply curbed its enthusiasm for multilateral peacekeeping and humanitarian intervention. In May, 1994, President Clinton signed off on a revised peacekeeping policy that incorporated many of the changes that his critics had demanded. When genocide in Rwanda burst onto the world stage, the administration delayed acting for several months and finally chose a short-term humanitarian relief operation rather than a Somali-style intervention. The administration became equally reluctant and financially constrained in its ability to endorse new UN peacekeeping operations in other hot spots around the world. And in Haiti and Bosnia, the administration deliberately kept its policy objectives narrow for fear of antagonizing both Congress and the U.S. military.[69]

Cowards, Beliefs, and Structures

Why has Congress failed to reclaim the war power from the president as many on Capitol Hill and in the academic world have hoped? The answer most commonly offered is political cowardice—members of Congress believe that decisions over war and peace are fraught with political risk and thus avoid responsibility. Arthur Schlesinger writes that "in foreign policy the inclination is to let the Presidency have the responsibility—and the power."[70] Louis Fisher argues that Congress needs to gain "the institutional courage and constitutional understanding to share with the president the momentous decision to send U.S. forces into combat."[71] John Hart Ely goes so far as to claim that since World War II "a tacit deal has existed between the executive and legislative branches, not just with respect to foreign policy but more generally, to the effect that the president will take the responsibility (well, most of it) so long as he can make the decisions, and Congress will forego actual policy-making authority so long as it doesn't have to be held accountable (and can scold the president when things go wrong)."[72]

The temptation to embrace congressional cowardice as an explanation for presidential predominance is powerful. After all, complaints about the lack of political courage on Capitol Hill are deeply ingrained in American culture, as even the briefest exposure to talk radio makes clear.

Yet on closer inspection, the adequacy of the political cowardice explanation is suspect. One problem is that it fails to explain why members of Congress were more assertive on war powers issues before 1945 than they are today. Presumably, decisions on war and peace were tough and politically risky before Harry Truman's presidency. Another problem is that political cowardice fails to explain why presidents eagerly embrace the responsibility and accountability that members of Congress supposedly dread. Given that voters typically know more about where the president stands on the issues than where their elected representatives do, the high political risks ascribed to decisions to use force would seem more likely to encourage political cowardice in the White House than on Capitol Hill.

A third problem is that discussions of political cowardice usually treat Congress as a monolithic institution with its own preferences and wants. But Congress is a *they,* not an *it.* On any war powers vote there are typically a hundred members on each end of the political spectrum who put aside their supposed electoral fears to vote for or against the president's policy. Why members at the extremes should find war powers issues less risky than their colleagues in the middle do is not clear. Moreover, because Congress is a *they,* it is worth remembering a point that economists frequently make and that is just as frequently ignored: micromotives cannot be inferred from macrobehavior. One of the oddities (and frustrations) of collective decision making is that it can produce decisions that no one intends.

A fourth problem with the political cowardice explanation is that it does not explain why Congress fails to act even when public sentiment runs counter to presidential policy. In the case of Haiti and Bosnia, for example, public opinion polls repeatedly found that a majority of Americans opposed the deployment of U.S. troops.[73] Yet despite what appeared to be an ideal opportunity to gain political profit—especially in the case of Bosnia, where the Republican congressional majority did not feel the countervailing tug of party loyalty—Congress failed to vote in advance to authorize (or block) the deployments. Nor is it clear that votes on war and peace issues are as politically risky as contended.[74] Little evidence exists, for example, to suggest that members of Congress who voted against authorizing Operation Desert Storm suffered politically for their opposition. Finally, political cowardice fails to explain the behavior of legislators like Senator McCain. Despite being a leading critic of the Clinton administration's Bosnia policy and despite the fact that constituent calls to his office were "running 100-to-1 against" the troop deployment, McCain ultimately supported the president.[75]

So while political cowardice may explain part of the puzzle—an institution with 535 members will always have those who prefer to dodge responsibility—it falls short of supplying a complete explanation. The reasons for Congress's inability to reclaim the war power from the president instead lie elsewhere, in beliefs about America's proper role in the world and in the structural rules of American government.

Since the end of World War II, most members of Congress, like most Americans, have accepted as a basic premise of American foreign policy that the United States should play a leading role in world affairs. The corollary to this internationalist worldview, forged from the bitter lessons of the 1930s, is the belief that successful foreign policy requires a high degree of presidential discretion. For some members this belief has risen to the level of constitutional principle. For most others it has been a matter of prudence because the presidency, as Alexander Hamilton pointed out more than two hundred years ago, has the advantages of "decision, activity, secrecy, and dispatch."[76] And while Vietnam, Iran-Contra, and the end of the Cold War have made some members of Congress skeptical about the need for presidential discretion, it continues to exert a powerful hold over many others.

The belief in the need for presidential discretion creates problems for Congress's ability to control the war power. These problems are aggravated by the structural rules governing the organization, procedures, and powers of the American government.[77] One such structural rule is the war-making authority claimed by presidents and implicitly ratified by the courts.[78] The default assumption underlying the founders' conception of the war power was that presidents would voluntarily defer to superior congressional authority. So long as they did so, Congress's tendency toward inertia reinforced rather than undermined its prerogatives. However, once presidents began to act and dared Congress to say no, the burden of proof shifted dramatically. The tendency toward inertia now works to Congress's disadvantage. Whereas the founders had intended for Congress to be able to put its imprint on decisions to use force through inaction—a point often lost on today's commentators—it now has to pass legislation to affect policy.

Presidential claims to inherent war-making authority would not prove fatal to congressional authority if the structural rules of American government made it easier for members of Congress to rein in presidents. But they don't. The institutional divisions the founders created are compounded by ideological, partisan, and regional ones. The result is that unless widespread agreement exists within the institution on what policy should be—something that is missing from most war power debates—Congress finds it difficult to act. Even when agreement to hold a vote does exist, well-placed opponents may still prevent the institution from acting. This is precisely what happened with Somalia in 1993 and Haiti in 1994. In each case, Democratic congressional leaders loyal to a Democratic president blocked efforts to reverse administration policy.[79] And should Congress overcome its own institutional hurdles, it confronts the specter of a veto and the difficult task of overriding the president.

Another structural rule that puts members of Congress at a disadvantage is that their sole formal tool for influencing war power decisions is legislation authorizing or prohibiting the use of force. Although some members might prefer it to be otherwise, Congress has no constitutional role in the conduct of diplomacy. Nor does it control the management of ongoing military operations. Once Congress votes to authorize the president to use force, his plenary powers of command as commander in chief come into operation.

Whatever the merits of authorizing legislation in theory, in practice it is a far more difficult tool to wield than most observers realize. The question facing members of Congress is not whether to hand the president a victory or a defeat. The question is what course of action is most likely to advance one's conception of the national interest. The rapid pace with which events can change in the international arena and Congress's inability to control how foreign governments respond to its actions work to create voting dilemmas for members.

On one hand, even the best-intentioned vote against a president's preferred policy can have perverse consequences. Members opposed to a particular use of force may still recognize the virtues of coercive diplomacy. Indeed, the recent case of Haiti shows that coercive diplomacy can work. But a vote to deny a president the authority to act will destroy any attempt at coercive diplomacy and, as a result, may make combat more rather than less likely. Such a vote may also encourage an adversary to become more belligerent since U.S. forces would by law be forbidden to respond. A presidential decision to present Congress with a fait accompli presents a similar problem. Members opposed to the deployment must confront the compelling argument, which former presidents and former top national security officials invariably will make, that whatever the wisdom of a president's decision, the costs to American credibility of undercutting presidential commitment will outweigh the costs of supporting the White House.[80]

On the other hand, because Congress cedes control over policy once it passes authorization legislation, a vote to authorize the use of force is a "use it and lose it" decision. Although members may hope that a president will use such authority wisely, as the Gulf of Tonkin Resolution demonstrates, a president who has been given the authority to use force is not bound by congressional expectations regarding the conditions under which he will use it.[81] House Republicans raised just this objection during the 1993 debate over legislation seeking to authorize a U.S. combat role in Somalia.[82] Although it is possible in theory to write legislation that limits what the president can do, such conditions may well backfire and endanger the troops they are designed to protect. For example, time limits encourage an adversary to hold out while geographical limits may encourage an adversary to use areas that are off limits as sanctuaries.

The dilemma members of Congress face between not wanting to undercut a sincere president or empower a rogue one has two consequences for congressional behavior. One is that it makes many members reluctant to vote on decisions to use force until events have made armed conflict likely. It makes sense, after all, to delay making a decision until an issue ceases to be hypothetical and becomes real. By doing so, however, members virtually guarantee, as Sen. Arthur Vandenberg (R-Michigan) once put it, that crises will "never reach Congress until they have developed to a point where Congressional discretion is pathetically restricted."[83]

The second consequence of the deficiencies of legislation is that it encourages members to pursue nonlegislative courses of action. Preeminent among these is "framing." This technique involves packaging an issue in a way that attracts media attention and puts pressure on the administration to mold policy to a member's liking.[84] Members have many different vehicles through which to frame issues. These include hearings, floor speeches, and appearances on television or radio, to name some of the most prominent. Although congressional critics typically dismiss such efforts as political posturing, framing is an important tool in the congressional arsenal. Not only does it help level the playing field with the White House by mobilizing other political actors, it communicates congressional sentiment to presidents who might not be inclined to consult with Congress. But framing has one decided shortcoming: While it can raise the political costs for the White House, it cannot compel the president to adopt a policy.

In sum, beliefs about the need for presidential discretion and the structure of American government put Congress at a distinct disadvantage relative to a president who wishes to use force, a disadvantage that political will in and of itself cannot overcome. Indeed, an ideologically diverse Congress composed entirely of political brave hearts would likely behave in much the same way as the one we have now.

What would dramatically change congressional behavior would be a change in the intellectual underpinnings of U.S. foreign policy or in how presidents conceive their constitutional powers. Congress's role in war powers decisions would grow measurably if either it or the country were to embrace isolationism. Such a political orientation would erase the deficiencies of legislation simply by defining most foreign entanglements as unacceptable. Yet the sometimes-overheated rhetoric directed against conservative Republicans notwithstanding, internationalism rather than isolationism continues to characterize U.S. foreign policy. (A disastrous military deployment overseas might well change this.) By the same token, if presidents were to return to a nineteenth century conception of their office, then Congress by definition would play a greater role. However, presidents do not appear likely to embrace such a norm, and the courts do not appear ready to force it on them.

Reforms

The U.S. deployments in Somalia, Haiti, and Bosnia have stirred considerable debate over the merits of the War Powers Resolution. So far the debate has produced no consensus over whether to fix the law or repeal it. Democrats have generally been more sympathetic to the resolution, but efforts to strengthen it made no headway when they controlled Congress. Because Republicans have generally been critical of the resolution, many predicted its demise following the 1994 elections.[85] Yet when a motion to repeal it reached the House floor in June, 1995, it went down to defeat.[86]

Even if a consensus existed on what to do with the War Powers Resolution, no legislative fix is likely to produce the outcome that either congressionalists or presidentialists anticipate. Take first proposals designed to strengthen the congressional role in decisions of war and peace.[87] No revision of the War Powers Resolution will ensure that decisions to use force reflect the collective judgment of Congress and the president because legislation cannot solve the disadvantages under which Congress labors. No law, no matter how thoughtful or precisely crafted, can prevent presidents from sending troops abroad without notice, thereby presenting Congress with a fait accompli. If the deployment turns out to be for a short duration, as happened in Grenada, Libya, and Panama (among other instances), members have no practical recourse against the president for acting without congressional authorization.

Of course, what presidents intend as a short-lived military venture may lead to protracted combat and the opportunity for members of Congress to become involved in policy making. In theory, Congress would wield a much stronger hand if a strengthened version of the War Powers Resolution were in effect. In this case, congressional inaction by itself would compel the withdrawal of troops (assuming, of course, the president obeys the law and the Supreme Court does not dodge the issue or find the law unconstitutional). In practice, however, this leverage may well be illusory since members would be in the politically and morally difficult position of allowing funds for troops who may be fighting for their lives to be cut off. Moreover, a president facing a strengthened version of the War Powers Resolution might well respond by seeking congressional approval early rather than late, thus taking advantage of the rally 'round the flag phenomenon that often (but not always) follows military operations.[88] As a result, a strengthened version of the War Powers Resolution is likely to work only in a limited number of situations where presidents have misjudged both the likely success of military operations and the sentiment on Capitol Hill and in the country.

Presidential attempts to present Congress with a fait accompli are one matter. What about situations such as the Gulf War and Haiti in which the decision to use force is made over the course of several weeks or months? Some proposals for reform seek to specify both what constitutes consultation and who should be consulted in an effort to force a dialogue between the White House and Congress.[89] Even assuming that such legislation could be written without loopholes that presidents could exploit, the dialogue required by a consultative mechanism may not affect policy. The problem is that the ability of members of Congress to advise the White House depends on a president's willingness to listen. As the gap between executive and legislative preferences grows—hence, the more important consultation becomes to members of Congress—the less likely presidents are to follow congressional advice. In the cases of both Haiti and Bosnia, the problem wasn't a lack of executive-legislative dialogue but that President Clinton fundamentally disagreed with what congressional leaders were telling him.

What about a strengthened sixty-day clock and a slow build up to war? In theory, this reform has the most potential to increase congressional influence over decisions to send U.S. troops into combat. (This influence would not extend to humanitarian relief efforts like Somalia or peacekeeping missions like Bosnia because they are not covered by the clock and because presidents can claim a constitutional authority over the peacetime deployment of troops.) In practice, however, it may lead to consequences quite different from what its proponents anticipate. The reason is that a fixed clock undercuts presidential attempts at coercive diplomacy by undermining the credibility of the threat upon which coercive diplomacy rests. (It is for precisely this reason that a strengthened sixty-day clock is the war powers reform that is least likely to be adopted.) As a result, if a strengthened time limit were in place, Congress would face considerable pressure to hold an early vote authorizing the deployment of U.S. troops and thereby strengthen the president's bargaining leverage.

The prospect of an early congressional vote on a build up to war will please congressionalists. However, as mentioned earlier, congressional authorization is a use-it-and-lose-it power. If Congress gives its approval, it loses control of policy. Members might try to make their authorization conditional, but anything other than the most simple condition (for example, "Unless Iraq withdraws from Kuwait by January 15, 1991") would greatly complicate presidential diplomacy and encourage executive branch sleight of hand. Efforts to narrow the scope of the authorization run the same risks. As a result, if a president enjoys a modest amount of public support when he orders troops overseas—as President Bush did when he dispatched U.S. troops to Saudi Arabia—members of Congress may well find it impossible for political and policy reasons to avoid authorizing the operation at the start, even if they doubt its wisdom.

Presidentialists are likely to be equally disappointed should the War Powers Resolution be repealed.[90] While repeal would end the recurrent debates about the resolution's constitutionality, it is not likely to materially improve the president's diplomatic leverage. Members of Congress would still be free to introduce legislation, hold hearings, give interviews, and write opinion pieces criticizing White House policy, either because they have legitimate policy differences with the White House or because they hope to curry favor with key constituents. Moreover, Congress still would retain its constitutional powers to declare war and regulate the common defense. Thus, with the same two-thirds majority needed in both houses that Congress currently needs to start the sixty-day clock ticking under the War Powers Resolution, it could limit or end any presidential use of force.

Conclusion

Most essays on the war power conclude by bemoaning the current state of affairs. Presidentialists fear that congressional activism threatens to "convert the strong, autonomous president which is one of the great achievements of the Constitution into a mere lackey of an omnipotent Congress."[91] Conversely, congressionalists worry that Congress has "been laying back, neither disapproving presidential military adventures nor forthrightly approving them, instead letting the president use troops wherever and whenever he wanted and waiting to see how the war in question played politically."[92]

My own view is that both schools of thought have it wrong. Presidentialists offer a vision of unlimited foreign policy success as unfettered presidents boldly advance the national interest. Yet the Bay of Pigs, Vietnam, and Iran-Contra cast doubt on presidential omnipotence. They also remind us why Alexander Hamilton wrote, "the history of human conduct does not warrant that exalted opinion of human virtue which would make it wise in a nation to commit interests of so delicate and momentous a kind as those which concern its intercourse with the rest of the world to the sole disposal of a magistrate created and circumstanced, as would be a president of the United States."[93]

For their part, congressionalists offer a vision of an accountable Congress that claims a coequal role with the president by passing legislation. But such a vision romanticizes the virtues of legislation while ignoring its pitfalls. Because legislation is a clumsy tool for managing crisis diplomacy, accountability (especially early in a crisis) can work at cross-purposes with responsibility. Nor does initial congressional approval guarantee that congressional support will continue when a policy falters. On this point one need only recall Lyndon Johnson's famous lament: "I said early in my presidency that if I wanted Congress with me on the landing of Vietnam, I'd have to have them with me on the takeoff. And I did just that. But I failed to reckon with one thing: the parachute. I got them on the takeoff, but a lot of them bailed out before the end of the flight."[94]

Our current pattern of an assertive president and a second-guessing Congress works reasonably well because it balances, however uncomfortably and however messily, the competing values that presidentialists and congressionalists emphasize. Presidentialists rightly warn us that an effective foreign policy demands a president who has flexibility and discretion; Congress simply cannot manage foreign affairs from the back seat. Congressionalists correctly remind us of the lessons of the 1960s: that leaving presidential discretion unchecked risks another Bay of Pigs or Vietnam.

Thus, we have today a system of governance in which the two branches compete and conflict. Presidents have considerable freedom to initiate the use of force. Yet their discretion has distinct limits. Even if members of Congress don't act in the Mr.-Smith-goes-to-Washington fashion that congressionalists envision, the very fact that they are poised to pile on in defeat exerts an important constraining and shaping effect on any administration, both before and after it commits troops abroad. To paraphrase Samuel Johnson, knowing that Congress might hang you in two weeks has a way of concentrating the minds of presidents and their advisers.

Notes

1. Quoted in Leon Friedman and Burt Neuborne, "The Framers, On War Powers," *New York Times,* Nov. 27, 1990.
2. Jonathon Elliot, ed., *Debates in the Several State Conventions on the Adoption of the Federal Constitution,* 2d ed. (Philadelphia: J. B. Lippincott & Co., 1881), p. 528.
3. James Madison, *The Writings of James Madison,* vol. 6, ed. Gaillard Hunt (New York: G. P. Putnam's Sons, 1906), p. 312.
4. Alexander Hamilton, *The Papers of Alexander Hamilton,* vol. 25, ed. Harold C. Syrett and Jacob E. Cooke (New York: Columbia University Press, 1997), pp. 455–56. (Emphasis in the original.)
5. For arguments that the founders intended to lodge the war power with Congress, see David Gray Adler, "The Constitution and Presidential Warmaking: The Enduring Debate," *Political Science Quarterly* 103 (spring, 1988): 1–36; Raoul Berger, "War-Making by the President," *University of Pennsylvania Law Review* 121 (Nov., 1972): 29–86; Arthur Bestor, "Separation of Powers in the Domain of Foreign Affairs: The Intent of the Constitution Historically Examined" *Seton Hall Law Review* 5 (spring, 1974): 529–665; Charles A. Lofgren, "On War-Making, Original Intent, and Ultra-Whiggery," *Valparaiso University Law Review* 21 (fall, 1986): 53–68; Charles A. Lofgren, 'War-Making Under the Constitution:

The Original Understanding," *Yale Law Review* 81 (Mar., 1972): 672–702; Abraham D. Sofaer, *War, Foreign Affairs, and Constitutional Power: The Origins* (Cambridge, Mass.: Ballinger, 1976), pp. 1–129; W. Taylor Reveley III, *War Powers of the President and Congress: Who Holds the Arrows and Olive Branch?* (Charlottesville: University Press of Virginia, 1981), pp. 29–115; and William Van Alstyne, "Congress, the President, and the Power to Declare War A Requiem for Vietnam," *University of Pennsylvania Law Review* 121 (Nov., 1972): 1–28. For dissents, see Philip Bobbit, "War Powers: An Essay on John Hart Ely's *War and Responsibility,*" *Michigan Law Review 92* (May, 1994): 1354–1400; Eugene V. Rostow, "'Once More into the Breach:' The War Powers Resolution Revisited," *Valparaiso University Law Review* 21 (fall, 1986): 1–52; Robert F. Turner, "War and the Forgotten Executive Power Clause of the Constitution: A Review Essay of John Hart Ely's *War and Responsibility,*" *Virginia Journal of International Law* 34 (summer, 1994): 903–79; and John C Yoo, "The Continuation of Politics by Other Means: The Original Understanding of War Powers," *California Law Review* 84 (Mar., 1996): 167–305.

6. See Jules Lobel, "Covert War and Congressional Authority: Hidden War and Forgotten Power," *University of Pennsylvania Law Review* 134 (June, 1986): 1035–1110, and Jules Lobel, "'Little Wars' and the Constitution," *University of Miami Law Review* 50 (Oct., 1995): 61–79.

7. Alexander Hamilton, "Federalist No. 69." in Alexander Hamilton, James Madison, and John Jay, *The Federalist Papers,* ed. Garry Wills (New York: Bantam, 1982), p. 350. (Emphasis in the original.)

8. On the exercise of the war power in the nineteenth century, see Henry Bartholomew Cox, *War, Foreign Affairs, and Constitutional Power: 1829–1901* (Cambridge, Mass.: Ballinger, 1984); Louis Fisher, *Presidential War Power* (Lawrence: University Press of Kansas, 1995): 13–44; Arthur M. Schlesinger, Jr., *The Imperial Presidency* (Boston: Houghton Mifflin, 1989), pp. 35–126; Sofaer, *War, Foreign Affairs, and Constitutional Power,* pp. 131–379; and Francis D. Wormuth and Edwin B. Firmage, *To Chain the Dog of War: The War Powers of Congress in History and Law* (Dallas, Tex.: Southern Methodist University Press, 1986).

9. Quoted in Schlesinger, *Imperial Presidency,* p. 21.

10. Quoted ibid., p. 28.

11. *The Public Papers and Addresses of Benjamin Harrison: March 4, 1889 to March 4, 1893* (Reprint, New York: Kraus, 1969), p. 185.

12. See Joyce S. Goldberg, *The Baltimore Affair* (Lincoln: University of Nebraska Press, 1986), p. 108.

13. *Bas v. Tingy,* 4 Dallas (4 U.S.) 37 (1800); *Talbot v. Seeman,* 5 U.S. (1 Cranch) 1, 28 (1801); and *Little v. Barreme,* 6 U.S. (2 Cranch) 170, 179 (1804).

14. *Talbot v. Seeman,* 5 U.S. (1 Cranch) 1, 28 (1801).

15. *The Prize Cases,* 2 Black (67 U.S.) 635 (1862).

16. Fed. Case 111 (No.4186) (CCSDNY 1860).

17. In 1967 the State Department listed 137 cases of unilateral presidential action. (Department of State, Historical Studies Division, *Armed Actions Taken by the United States Without a Declaration of War, 1789–1967* [Washington, D.C.: GPO, 1967].) A study subsequently prepared for Sen. Barry M. Goldwater placed the number at "at least 197 foreign military hostilities." (Barry M. Goldwater, "The President's Ability to Protect America's Freedoms—The Warmaking Power," *Law and the Social Order: Arizona State University Law Journal* 3 (1971): 423–24.

18. Schlesinger, *Imperial Presidency,* pp. 50–51.
19. Alexander Hamilton and James Madison, "Letters of Pacificus and Helvidius on the Proclamation of Neutrality of 1793," in Jean E. Smith, *The Constitution and American Foreign Policy* (St. Paul, Minn.: West, 1989), p. 52.
20. *Congressional Globe,* 30th Cong., 1st sess., 1848, p. 95.
21. Woodrow Wilson, *Constitutional Government in the United States* (New York: Columbia University Press, 1908), pp. 76–77. For extended discussions of this theme, see Walter LaFeber, "Congress, the Executive and Foreign Policy,' in *Encyclopedia of the American Legislative System,* ed. Joel H. Silbey (New York: Scribners, 1994); and Walter LaFeber, *The Cambridge History of American Foreign Relations,* vol. 2, *The American Search for Opportunity, 1865–1913* (New York: Cambridge University Press, 1993).
22. Theodore Roosevelt, *An Autobiography* (New York: Macmillan, 1914), p. 372.
23. Quoted in "Congress, the President, and the Power to Commit Forces to Combat," *Harvard Law Review* 81 (June, 1968): 1785.
24. Thomas Paterson, *Major Problems in American Foreign Policy,* vol. I (Lexington, Mass.: D. C. Heath, 1984), p. 484.
25. See Robert H. Ferrell, *American Diplomacy: A History,* 3d ed. (New York: Norton, 1975), pp. 405–16; Fritz Grob, *The Relativity of War and Peace* (New Haven, Conn.: Yale University Press, 1949), pp. 230–31; and Thomas G. Paterson, J. Garry Clifford, and Kenneth J. Hagan, *American Foreign Relations: A History, Since 1895,* 4th ed. (Lexington, Mass.: D. C. Heath, 1995), pp. 51–56.
26. Francis D. Wormuth, "The Nixon Theory of the War Power: A Critique," *California Law Review* 60 (May, 1972): 663.
27. Schlesinger, *Imperial Presidency,* p. 113.
28. Department of State Memorandum of July 3, 1950, "Authority of the President to Repel the Attack in Korea," in *Department of State Bulletin,* July 31, 1950, pp. 173–78.
29. *Public Papers of the Presidents of the United States: Dwight D. Eisenhower, 1954* (Washington, D.C.: GPO, 1954), p. 306.
30. *Public Papers of the Presidents of the United States: George Bush, 1992–1993,* vol. I (Washington, D.C.: U.S. GPO, 1993), p. 995.
31. See John Hart Ely, *War and Responsibility* (Princeton, N.J.: Princeton University Press, 1993), chap. 2.
32. PL 93-148, 87 Stat. 555 (1973). The literature assessing the efficacy of the War Powers Resolution is large. Among others, see Ellen C Collier, "Statutory Constraints: The War Powers Resolution," in *The U.S. Constitution and the Power to Go to War: Historical and Current Perspectives,* ed. Gary M. Stern and Morton H. Halperin (Westport, Conn.: Greenwood, 1994); Christopher Ford, "War Powers as We Live Them: Congressional-Executive Bargaining Under the Shadow of the War Powers Resolution," *Journal of Law & Politics* 11, no. 4 (1995): 609–708; Richard F. Grimmett, "The War Powers Resolution: Twenty-Two Years of Experience," Congressional Research Service, May 24, 1996; Robert A. Katzmann, "War Powers: Toward A New Accommodation," in *A Question of Balance: The President, the Congress, and Foreign Policy,* ed. Thomas E. Mann (Washington, D.C.: Brookings, 1990); and Marc E. Smyrl, *Conflict or Codetermination? Congress, the President, and the Power to Make War* (Cambridge, Mass: Ballinger, 1988).
33. See Eileen Burgin, "Rethinking the Role of the War Powers Resolution: Congress and the Persian Gulf War," *Journal of Legislation* 21, no. 1 (1995): 23–47.

34. Among other discussions of the failings of the War Powers Resolution, see Joseph R. Biden and John B. Ritch III, "The War Power at a Constitutional Impasse: A 'Joint Decision' Solution," *Georgetown Law Journal* 77 (Dec., 1988): 367–412; John Hart Ely, "Suppose Congress Wanted a War Powers Act That Worked," *Columbia Law Review* 88 (Nov., 1988): 1379–1431; and Michael J. Glennon, "The War Powers Resolution Ten Years Later: More Politics than Law," *American Journal of International Law* 78 (July, 1984): 571–81.

35. See John Hart Ely, "Kuwait, the Constitution, and the Courts: Two Cheers for Judge Greene," *Constitutional Commentary* 8 (winter, 1991): 1–8; Harold Hongju Koh, "Presidential War and Congressional Consent: The Law Professors' Memorandum in Dellums v. Bush," *Stanford Journal of International Law* 27 (spring, 1991): 247–64; Michael J. Glennon, *Constitutional Diplomacy* (Princeton, N.J.: Princeton University Press, 1990), chap. 8; and Michael Ratner and David Cole, "The Force of Law: Judicial Enforcement of the War Powers Resolution," *Loyola LA Law Review* 17, no. 3 (1984): 715–66.

36. See Jane E. Stromseth, "Collective Force and Constitutional Responsibility: War Powers in the Post–Cold War Era," *University of Miami Law Review* 50 (Oct., 1995): 161–62.

37. For discussions of the Somalia case, see Fisher, *Presidential War Power,* pp. 153–54; Grimmett, *War Powers Resolution,* pp. 31–34; and Stromseth, "Collective Force and Constitutional Responsibility," 168–72.

38. "Senate Gives Belated Blessing to Somalia Intervention," *Congressional Quarterly Weekly Report,* Feb. 6, 1993, p. 277.

39. See Gregory J. Bowens, "House Backs Measure Allowing U.S. Role in U.N. Operation," *Congressional Quarterly Weekly Report,* May 29, 1993, p. 1373.

40. See Elizabeth A. Palmer, "Senate Demands Voice in Policy But Shies From Confrontation," *Congressional Quarterly Weekly Report,* Sept. 11, 1993, p. 2399.

41. See Carroll J. Doherty, "Clinton Calms Rebellion on Hill by Retooling Somalia Mission," *Congressional Quarterly Weekly Report,* Oct. 9, 1993, pp. 2750–51; Pat Towell, "Behind Solid Vote on Somalia: A Hollow Victory for Clinton," *Congressional Quarterly Weekly Report,* Oct. 16, 1993, pp. 2823–27; and Pat Towell, "Clinton's Policy Is Battered, But His Powers Are Intact," *Congressional Quarterly Weekly Report,* Oct. 23, 1993, pp. 2896–2901.

42. See Carroll J. Doherty, "House Sends Mixed Message Over Somalia Mission," *Congressional Quarterly Weekly Report,* Nov. 13, 1993, p. 3139.

43. For discussions of the Haiti case, see Fisher, *Presidential War Power,* pp. 154–55; Grimmett, *War Powers Resolution,* pp. 40–43; Stromseth, "Collective Force and Constitutional Responsibility," pp. 172–79; and Jane E. Stromseth, "Understanding Constitutional War Powers Today: Why Methodology Matters," *Yale Law Journal* 106 (Dec., 1996): 899–902.

44. See Janet Hook, "Dole: Trying to Find 'Some Balance,'" *Congressional Quarterly Weekly Report,* Oct. 23, 1993, p. 2899.

45. See Carroll J. Doherty, "Senate Defeats GOP Proposal to Limit Clinton on Haiti," *Congressional Quarterly Weekly Report,* July 2, 1994, p. 1814.

46. See Carroll J. Doherty, "Senate Declines to Restrict Clinton's Options on Haiti," *Congressional Quarterly Weekly Report,* July 16, 1994, p. 1943.

47. *Congressional Record,* Aug. 3, 1994, p. S10433.

48. See Jeffrey H. Birnbaum and John Harwood, "Clinton Sets Haiti TV Talk To-

morrow; Invasion Idea Has Only Faint Support," *Wall Street Journal,* Sept. 14, 1994; Carroll J. Doherty, "President, Rebuffing Congress, Prepares to Launch Invasion," *Congressional Quarterly Weekly Report,* Sept. 17, 1994, pp. 2578–83; and Katharine Q. Seelye, "Congress Weighs the Political Profit and Loss," *New York Times,* Sept. 17, 1994.

49. See Carroll J. Doherty, "Congress, After Sharp Debate, Gives Clinton a Free Hand," *Congressional Quarterly Weekly Report,* Oct. 8, 1994, pp. 2895–96.

50. For discussions of the Haiti case, see Grimmett, *War Powers Resolution,* pp. 34–40; and Stromseth, "Understanding Constitutional War Powers Today," pp. 902–905.

51. See Grimmett, *War Powers Resolution,* pp. 35–36.

52. "Issue: Bosnia-Herzegovina," *Congressional Quarterly Weekly Report,* Dec. 11, 1993, p. 3405.

53. Fisher, *Presidential War Power,* p. 160.

54. Grimmett, *War Powers Resolution,* p. 36.

55. See Carroll J. Doherty, "Senate Hands President a Muddled Mandate," *Congressional Quarterly Weekly Report,* May 14, 1994, pp. 1233–35.

56. Grimmett, *War Powers Resolution,* p. 36.

57. See Carroll J. Doherty, "Congress' Foreign Policy Role at Issue in Veto Override," *Congressional Quarterly Weekly Report,* Aug. 5, 1995, p. 2386.

58. Stromseth, "Understanding Constitutional War Powers Today," p. 904. For an argument that congressional authorization was needed, see Louis Fisher, "What Power to Send Troops?" *New York Times,* Dec. 2, 1995.

59. See Donna Cassata, "House Flouts Clinton Policies on B-2 Production, Abortion," *Congressional Quarterly Weekly Report,* Sept. 9, 1995, pp. 2728–30; Carroll J. Doherty, "Lawmakers Wary of Bosnia Role," *Congressional Quarterly Weekly Report,* Sept. 30, 1995, p. 3018; Pat Towell, "House Opposes Peacekeeping Role, Delays Vote on Cutoff of Funds," *Congressional Quarterly Weekly Report,* Nov. 4, 1995, pp. 3390–91; Pat Towell and Donna Cassata, "House Votes to Block Clinton From Sending Peacekeepers," *Congressional Quarterly Weekly Report,* Nov. 18, 1995, p. 3549

60. See Pat Towell and Donna Cassata, "Congress Takes Symbolic Stand on Troop Deployment," *Congressional Quarterly Weekly Report,* Dec. 16, 1995, pp. 3817–18.

61. See Grimmett, *War Powers Resolution,* p. 40.

62. *Legislation on Foreign Relations through 1996,* vol. II (Washington, D.C.: GPO, 1997), p. 119.

63. See U.S. Congress, House, *Making Appropriations for Fiscal Year 1996 to Make a Further Downpayment Toward a Balanced Budget and for Other Purposes,* 104th Cong., 2d sess., 1996, H. Rept. 537, pp. 41–42; and U.S. Congress, House, *Making Omnibus Consolidated Appropriations for Fiscal Year 1997,* 104th Cong., 2d sess., 1996, H. Rept. 863, p.52.

64. See U.S. General Accounting Office, *Peace Operations U S Costs in Support of Haiti, Former Yugoslavia, Somalia, and Rwanda,* Mar., 1996, GAO/NSIAD-96-38.

65. See Pat Towell, "House Votes to Sharply Rein in U.S. Peacekeeping Expenses," *Congressional Quarterly Weekly Report,* Feb. 18, 1995, pp. 535–38.

66. *Public Papers of the Presidents of the United States, William J. Clinton,* bk. II, *July 1 to December 31, 1995* (Washington, D.C.: GPO, 1991), p. 1929.

67. See *Congressional Record,* Apr. 25, 1996, p. H3859.

68. Carroll J. Doherty, "U.N. Command of U.S. Troops Restricted by House Again," *Congressional Quarterly Weekly Report,* Sept. 7, 1996, p. 2537.

69. For a similar assessment, see Stromseth, "Collective Force and Constitutional Responsibility," p. 179.

70. Schlesinger, *Imperial Presidency,* p. 420.

71. Louis Fisher, "War Powers: The Need for Collective Judgment," in *Divided Democracy,* ed. James Thurber (Washington, D.C.: CQ, 1990), p. 215.

72. Ely, *War and Responsibility,* p. 54.

73. For public attitudes toward Haiti, see "'Close Consultations' on Invasion of Haiti," *USA Today,* July 18, 1994; Carroll J. Doherty, "President, Rebuffing Congress, Prepares to Launch Invasion," *Congressional Quarterly Weekly Report,* Sept. 17, 1994, p. 2582; "Opinion Outlook," *National Journal,* July 30, 1994, p. 1822; "Opinion Outlook," *National Journal,* Sept. 3, 1994, p. 2050; and Elaine Sciolino, "Clinton Aides Say Invasion of Haiti Would Be Limited," *New York Times,* Sept. 13, 1994. For public attitudes toward Bosnia, see R. W. Apple, Jr., "Flimsy Bosnia Mandate," *New York Times,* Dec. 14, 1995; "Opinion Outlook," *National Journal,* Nov. 25, 1995, p. 2945; and "Opinion Outlook," *National Journal,* Dec. 23, 1995, p. 3174.

74. For example, see George S. Swan, "Presidential Undeclared Warmaking and Functionalist Theory: *Dellums v. Bush* and Operations Desert Shield and Desert Storm," *California Western International Law Journal* 22 (1991–92): 116.

75. See Elaine Sciolino, "Dole Backs Plan to Send U.S. Force on Bosnia Mission," *New York Times,* Dec. 1, 1995.

76. Alexander Hamilton, "Federalist No. 70," p. 356.

77. See Peverill Squire, James M. Lindsay, Cary R. Covington, and Eric R. A. N. Smith, *Dynamics of Democracy,* 2d ed. (Madison, Wis.: Brown and Benchmark, 1997), pp. 11–12.

78. See Gordon Silverstein, *Imbalance of Powers: Constitutional Interpretation and the Making of American Foreign Policy* (New York: Oxford University Press, 1997).

79. See Doherty, "President, Rebuffing Congress, Prepares to Launch Invasion," p. 2580; and James M. Lindsay, "Congress and the Use of Force in the Post–Cold War Era," in *The United States and the Use of Force in the Post–Cold War Era* (Queenstown, Md.: Aspen Institute, 1995), pp. 79–80.

80. The reaction of the Republican foreign policy establishment to President Clinton's decision to send U.S. troops to Bosnia is a classic example. See Frances X. Clines, "Balkan History Lesson: Not With a 10-Foot Pole," *New York Times,* Nov. 29, 1995; Katharine Q. Seelye, "Legislators Get Plea By Clinton on Bosnia Force," *New York Times,* Nov. 29, 1995, Pat Towell, "Congress Reluctantly Acquiesces in Peacekeeping Mission," *Congressional Quarterly Weekly Report,* Dec. 2, 1995, p. 3668; and Pat Towell, "Congress Torn Over Response as Deployment Begins," *Congressional Quarterly Weekly Report,* Dec. 9, 1995, p. 3752.

81. See Ely, *War and Responsibility,* pp. 17–18.

82. See U.S. Congress, House, *Resolution Authorizing the Use of United States Forces in Somalia,* 103d Cong., 1st sess., 1993, H. Rept. 89, pp. 16–17.

83. Quoted in Walter LaFeber, *America, Russia, and the Cold War, 1945–71,* 2d ed. (New York: John Wiley, 1972), p. 60.

84. See James M. Lindsay, *Congress and the Politics of U.S. Foreign Policy* (Baltimore: Johns Hopkins University Press, 1994), pp. 132–38.

85. See, for example, Gabriel Kahn, "With No Fanfare, Taps for Hill War Powers," *Roll Call,* May 29, 1995, p. 2.

86. Carroll J. Doherty, "House Approves Overhaul of Agencies, Policies," *Congressional Quarterly Weekly Report,* June 10, 1995, pp. 1655–56.

87. See, for example, Biden and Ritch, "The War Powers Resolution at a Constitutional Impasse," pp. 367–412; Ely, "Suppose Congress Wanted a War Powers Act That Worked," pp. 1379–1431; Ely, *War and Responsibility,* pp. 115–38; Fisher, *Presidential War Power,* pp. 191–94; Glennon, *Constitutional Diplomacy,* pp. 111–22; and Glennon, "The War Powers Resolution Ten Years Later," pp. 571–81.

88. The classic study of the "rally 'round the flag phenomenon" is John E. Mueller, *War, Presidents and Public Opinion* (New York: John Wiley and Sons, 1973).

89. See, for example, *Congressional Record,* 101st Cong., 1st sess., 1989, 135, pt. 1:465–66; Katzmann, "War Powers," pp. 67–68; and James A. Nathan, "Revising the War Powers Act," *Armed Forces & Society* 17 (summer, 1991): 513–43.

90. Among other proponents of repeal, see Dick Cheney, "Congressional Overreaching in Foreign Policy," in *Foreign Policy and the Constitution,* ed. Robert A. Goldwin and Robert A. Licht (Washington, D.C.: American Enterprise Institute, 1990); Rostow, "'Once More into the Breach,'" 1–52; and Robert F. Turner, "Separation of Powers in Foreign Policy: The Theoretical Underpinnings," *George Mason University Law Review* 11 (fall, 1988): 97–117. For an argument for repeal by a proponent of a greater congressional role in decisions to use force, see Michael J. Glennon, "Too Far Apart: Repeal the War Powers Resolution," *University of Miami Law Review* 50: 17–31.

91. Rostow, "'Once More Unto the Breach,'" p. 2.

92. Ely, *War and Responsibility,* p. 48.

93. Alexander Hamilton, "Federalist No. 75," *The Federalist Papers,* pp. 380–81.

94. Quoted in Rostow, "'Once More into the Breach,'" p. 15.

Chapter 8

Post–Cold War Attitudes toward the Use of Force

Andrew Kohut

BY THE SUMMER of 1941, the Germans had defeated the French, driven the British army into the sea and were attempting to bomb London into submission. The Gallup Poll took the extraordinary effort of conducting a poll in each of the then forty-eight states asking: "If you were asked to vote today on the question of the United States entering the war against Germany and Italy, how would you vote—to go into the war or to stay out of the war?" The war option was rejected in every state of the union. The most support for engagement was found in Florida and Arizona, where the "going in" sentiment was as high as 35 percent and 33 percent, respectively. In the more isolationist upper Midwest states of Wisconsin, Minnesota, and Iowa, as few as 15 percent favored war.

Clearly, America has a long history of wariness regarding the use of force. Despite the conventional wisdom that it is more difficult today to obtain public support for committing troops to the field, our historical studies of opinion polling data show little change in the dynamics of public opinion over a very long time. However, changing public priorities and conceptions of the national interest in the post–Cold War era have created new considerations for policy makers attempting to galvanize support for military involvement.

Continuities In Public Opinion

Before exploring what is different today, it is useful to examine what remains unchanged in the way Americans think about such things. A mid-1990s Pew Center analysis of public attitudes toward recent military interventions identified a number of discernible patterns in thinking that underpin a disposition to commit to or reject the use of force.[1] Three of the most important of these were as apparent in 1941 as they are today:

- Early on in a crisis, the public reveals a basic disposition to accept or reject the use of force based on whether significant U.S. national interests seem to be at stake, or based on feelings that the United States has a moral responsibility to act. This basic disposition or judgment colors response to specific proposals to use force.
- Even when the public feels the U.S. has a responsibility to act, large percentages of Americans (sometimes majorities) will favor no action, unless the disposition to act is stimulated by presidential leadership.
- Even when the public feels the United States has a responsibility to act, it will always gravitate to diplomatic or economic options over military force if these are in play as options.[2]

The prewar public (1939–41) recognized that its national interest was at stake and was inclined to act, if all other alternatives failed. However, it steadfastly held on to a "stay out" position as long as it seemed possible to do so. In the summer of 1941, for example, a majority of Americans (62 percent) believed that if Germany and Italy defeated Britain, Hitler would then attack the United States.[3] Accordingly, majorities expressed opinions that indicated a clear recognition that it would probably be necessary to fight. As many as 62 percent of respondents in a May, 1941, poll said they would rather have the United States go into the war than see Britain surrender to Germany. And two-thirds of the public said that if it "appeared certain" that the only way to beat the Axis was for the United States to become involved, they would favor joining in combat.

Nonetheless, throughout the first two years of World War II Gallup never found significantly more than one in five Americans supporting U.S. entry into the war at any given time.

Roosevelt recognized the necessity to go slowly and prepare the American public for war. Gradual public acceptance of Lend Lease and other measures to aid Britain were testimony to his ability to sell involvement to a public that seemed to understand the risks of inaction but required dragging into harms

Table 8.1. Some Opinions about War, 1941

January: Which of these two things do you think it is more important for the United States to try to do—to keep out of the war ourselves, or to help England win, even at the risk of getting into the war?

Keep out	40%
Help England	60%

If you were asked to vote on the question of the United States entering the war against Germany and Italy, how would you vote—to go into the war, or stay out of the war?

Go in	12%
Stay out	88%

March: Would you approve or disapprove of the United States leasing about 40 additional destroyers to England?

Approve	52%
Disapprove	26%
No opinion	22%

May: If Germany and Italy should defeat Britain in the present war, do you think Germany and Italy would start a war against the United States within the next 10 years?

Yes	62%
No	29%
No opinion	9%

October: In general, do you approve or disapprove of having the United States navy shoot at German submarines or warships on sight?

Approve	62%
Disapprove	28%
No opinion	10%

November: It has been suggested that Congress pass a resolution declaring that a state of war exists between the United States and Germany. Would you favor or oppose such a resolution at this time?

Favor	26%
Oppose	63%
No opinion	11%

Source: Gallup Poll, 1941.

way. In the end, Roosevelt did not have to overcome this American ambivalence, as the attack on Pearl Harbor immediately put an end to America's two-mindedness.

More recently, George Bush faced a comparably ambivalent state of public opinion. In the months leading up to the Persian Gulf War there was majority support for the *general* idea that the United States should take necessary steps to liberate Kuwait from the Iraqis, including even the use of force, as the public recognized that its vital interests were at stake. But substantial majorities opposed an assault in Kuwait throughout much of 1990.

The Bush administration skillfully gained public acceptance by taking a number of steps that put public opinion on a war footing. First and foremost, it effectively communicated the American interest in the Gulf during the fall of 1990. In August, only half the public said that the President had explained clearly his decision to send troops to Saudi Arabia (*NYT*/CBS), but one month later 77 percent said they had a clear idea on the matter (*WP*/ABC).[4]

Multilateral participation in the form of a UN resolution and congressional debate were also both crucial in convincing the American public of need for intervention, polls at the time found. Before those events, in mid-November, 1990, only 37 percent of the public favored United States going to war to drive the Iraqis out of Kuwait, according to Gallup. By January, 1991, a 55 percent majority favored taking such steps.

These data suggest that two conditions have not changed since the 1940s. First, the public is by instinct averse to the use of force. Second, it is necessary for the president to sell war as the only alternative that can protect the national interest. However, the public's definition of the "national interest" in the post–Cold War era and the role the modern media plays in shaping public response *have* changed substantially.

A U.S. Centric Mood

While on balance the American public continues to be internationalist in outlook, an isolationist minority has grown substantially over the past 15 years. In 1980, only 30 percent of respondents polled by Gallup agreed that the "U.S. should mind its own business internationally, and let other countries get along as best as they can on their own." By 1995, the percentage expressing this sentiment had increased to 41 percent. At the high point of internationalism in 1964, only 18 percent of Americans held this opinion.[5]

An isolationist drift is being accelerated by the increasingly partisan tone of foreign policy debate, particularly debate over the United States' role in the world. The 1992 election highlighted the popularity of protectionist views across

Table 8.2. Gallup Trend on Forces in Gulf

View of United States Going to War with Iraq to Drive the Iraqis Out of Kuwait

	Favor (%)	Oppose (%)	No opinion (%)
Jan. 11–13, 1991	55	38	7
Jan. 3–6, 1991	52	39	9
Jan. 4, 1991	One day of Senate debate		
Dec. 13–16, 1990	48	43	9
Dec. 6–9, 1990	53	40	7
Nov. 29–Dec. 2, 1990	53	40	7
Nov. 29, 1990	U.N. Security Council adopts resolution setting Jan. deadline		
Nov. 15–18, 1990	37	51	12

the political spectrum—from Republican presidential candidate Pat Buchanan on the right to the labor movement on the left. More recently, the media has made much of the often bitter disputes between Senate Foreign Relations Committee Chairman Jesse Helms and the Clinton administration over foreign aid and UN financial support. And the xenophobia of the far right militia movement is an extreme indicator of a broader isolationist minority.

Where's That?

The fact that the hearts and minds of the *majority* of the public are at home, not overseas, is even more important than the growth of the isolationist minority. With the end of the Cold War, American interest in news of international events has plummeted. A recent summit meeting drew an attentive news audience of 26 percent of the public—one-half to one-third the level of interest shown in Cold War Summits (PRC). Despite having more years of education and more news media sources than citizens of most other nations, Americans know less about what is going on in the world. A multinational study that included the major democracies of Western Europe and North America found that only the Spanish knew less than Americans about world events such as the latest news from the Middle East and problems with North Korea.[6]

What is true of Americans in general is even more true of younger Americans. Historical studies indicate that younger generations are paying much less attention to news about the larger world today, particularly when compared to prewar generations of younger people. An analysis of the Pew Research

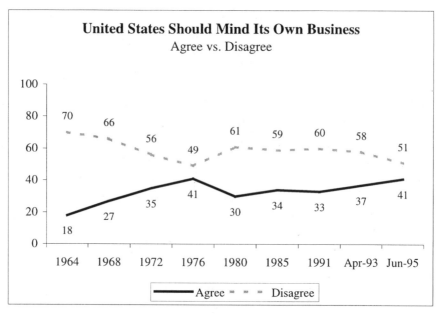

Fig. 8.1. United States should mind its own business, agree vs. disagree. Data from the Gallup Organization and the Pew Research Center.

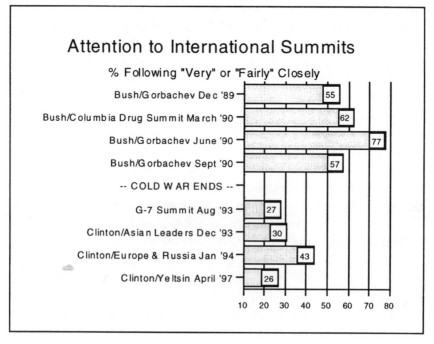

Fig. 8.2. Attention to international summits. Data from the Pew Research Center and the Times-Mirror Center for the People and the Press.

Center's news interest index database shows that on average, 25 percent of those over age fifty pay very close attention to stories about international politics (already not an impressive number), compared to only 15 percent among Generation Xers.[7] Throughout the 1960s, however, young Americans were as interested as their parents in the major news stories of the day.[8] A similar gap currently exists in *knowledge* about international events (on average, 40 percent of those over fifty answered the Center's international news quiz questions correctly compared to 28 percent of those under thirty).[9]

Poll after poll finds Americans saying loud and clear they want a foreign policy that serves the domestic agenda. In both 1993 and 1995, the public's top foreign policy priority was to stop international drug trafficking (PRC). Improving America's economic competitiveness and stopping illegal immigration also ranked near the top. Traditional geopolitical objectives, such as ending warfare in Bosnia and insuring the success of democracy in Russia, received the lowest ratings.

In such an environment there is little consensus as to the nature of the national interest in matters of *international* affairs. A major 1993 study of policy elites and the general public found that only two interests were shared by both groups: protecting U.S. oil supplies and preventing the spread of nuclear weapons.[10] The Gulf War was a clear instance of intervention in support of the former. Polls in 1993 showing majority support for using force to prevent or eliminate North Korea's nuclear capabilities reflect the latter (Gallup/*LAT*).

If there are few issues that Americans see as affecting their vital interests, there are even fewer situations where the public is disposed to act in what Joseph Nye has termed "interventions on behalf of important but not vital interests and interventions on behalf of humanitarian or moral causes."[11]

The response to American interventions in Haiti and Bosnia reflects this climate of opinion. In both instances, Americans uncharacteristically failed to support a presidential decision even when troops took to the field. Approval of the policies was not achieved, despite apparent success and extremely low casualties.

Hesitant about Haiti

The decision to send American troops to Haiti was met with the lowest degree of support of any U.S. military intervention since the 1950s. In September, 1994, only 41 percent of Americans had a positive response to intervention, compared to 74 percent for intervention in Somalia in December, 1992, and equivalent percentages at the start of the Gulf War conflict. Early in the crisis, a majority of the public (63 percent) approved of the oil embargo of Haiti, but support for sending troops varied depending on the scope of their stated mission (*WP*/ABC). Fully 77 percent of the public favored the use of force to evacuate U.S. citizens (*NYT*/CBS), and slightly fewer to prevent illegal immigration (69 percent [*WP*/ABC]). But majorities almost as large opposed the use of U.S. troops to restore President Aristide to power (69 percent in October, 1993 [*WP*/ABC], 68 percent in May, 1994 [*Time*/CNN]).

In the eyes of most foreign policy analysts, the international intervention in Haiti was a success. Yet neither during the actual operation, nor in retrospect, did a strong majority of the American public approve of President Clinton's handling of the situation. In September, the month U.S. troops began moving into Haiti, the public was evenly split in its approval of Clinton's actions: 46 for and 47 against *(Newsweek)*. This approval rating moved up to a 54–39 percent margin in October (PRC). However, by February and June of 1995, with the advantage of hindsight, the public was again evenly divided on Clinton's decision to use force (PRC). Given the low level of support when confronted with a *successful* operation, it is clear that Haiti could have been a political disaster for Bill Clinton if it had resulted in a significant loss of American lives.

Not Our War

Since the beginning of the recent war in Bosnia, there have been two constants in American opinion toward the conflict: At no time has a majority thought the United States had a responsibility to do something about the fighting, and there has never been significant interest in the tragic events of this Balkan state.

Throughout the conflict, even when reports of so-called ethnic cleansing were receiving significant attention in the media, American attention to Bosnia has been low. At the start of the country's breakup in 1991, fewer than one in ten said they were paying "very close" attention to news of Yugoslavia. Indifference remained high and steady over the next four years, with the percent paying very close attention topping 20 percent only twice: in May, 1993 (23 percent), when U.S. military action appeared possible, and in June, 1995 (22 percent), with the coverage of downed air force Capt. Scott O'Grady and the taking of UN peacekeepers as hostages. It took the January, 1996, deployment of twenty thousand U.S. troops to Bosnia for the public to become attentive to news from that part of the world.

Americans have been remarkably consistent in declaring that Bosnia is not our war. In January, 1993, when U.S. air drops of food were just beginning, fully 67 percent of the public said that the United States had no responsibility to "do something about the fighting between Serbs and Bosnians." Only 24

Table 8.3. First Responses to Decision to Send Troops

	Positive Response	Negative Response	Don't Know
Korea			
Aug., 1950	65	20	15
Vietnam			
Jan., 1965	50	28	22
May, 1965	52	26	22
Nov., 1965	64	21	15
Grenada			
Nov., 1983	63	29	8
Panama			
Jan., 1990	72	18	10
Iraq/Kuwait			
Aug., 1990	75	17	8
Jan., 1991	77	15	8
Somalia			
Dec., 1992	74	21	5
Haiti			
Sept., 1994	41	52	7
Bosnia			
Jan., 1996	48	49	3

Note: Positive response refers to "should be involved," "not a mistake," "a good idea," "approve," and "right decision"; negative response refers to the opposite.
Sources: Gallup Poll (through 1983 and Aug., 1990); NBC/WSJ (Panama and Somalia); TMC (Jan., 1991 poll on Iraq); NYT (Haiti); and PRC (Bosnia).

percent saw an American role. Although the percentage acknowledging a U.S. role has gone up and down slightly over the past four years, it never exceeded 41 percent—a high reached in April, 1994. One year later, in June, 1995, by a two-to-one margin Americans once again said the United States had no responsibility to get involved.[12]

Absent a sense of responsibility, it is not surprising that polls have shown consistent opposition to the involvement of U.S. forces in the area. In January, 1993, 55 percent of the public said it opposed the *idea* of using U.S. military forces in Bosnia to help end the fighting there (TMC). In January, 1996, when the forces were first sent to the former Yugoslavia, the public was divided about the decision: 48 percent approved and 49 percent disapproved (PRC). Four months later, the margin had shifted to opposition (43 percent in favor, 52 percent opposed [PRC]). As was true in Haiti, even in the face of seeming success—a peace achieved and held—the American public today continues to remain wary of the use of troops in Bosnia. However, more recently, despite a broadly popular air war, only a narrow majority of the public (56 percent

Table 8.4. Interest in News about Bosnia
(percentage following stories)

Date	Very closely	Fairly closely	Not at all closely/ don't know
July, 1996	16	37	47
Mar., 1996	18	43	39
Jan., 1996	37	45	18
Aug., 1995	16	36	48
June, 1995	22	42	36
Mar., 1995	11	27	62
Dec., 1994	13	37	50
Sept., 1994	9	29	62
May, 1994	18	37	45
Jan., 1994	15	38	47
Oct., 1993	16	36	48
Sept., 1993	17	38	45
May, 1993	23	34	43
Jan., 1993	15	33	52
Sept., 1992	10	27	63
Dec., 1991	5	21	74

Note: Wording of questions varied.
Source: PRC News Interest Index.

favored, 37 percent opposed) supported deployment of seven thousand U.S. troops as part of a NATO peacekeeping force in Kosovo.

Haiti, Bosnia, and Somalia give clear indication that the American public rejects a sheriff of the planet role for the United States. There is very little support for police or nation-building missions, even in this hemisphere. Public opinion about U.S. participation in *peacekeeping* operations is less clear-cut. Most believe that the United States has a responsibility along with other leading nations to help maintain world order. But the public rejects assertive multilateralism or a first-among-equals leadership role because it believes it will result in the United States bearing a disproportionate share of the costs and the burden.

The News Media Prism

The news media plays an important role in the public's willingness to support military interventions in the post-Vietnam, real time news era. However, its power is overstated and the nature of its influence misunderstood. In each of the post–Cold War interventions examined here, media coverage *modulated* the climate of opinion rather than *dictated* it.

Dramatic, real-time coverage of events in the Persian Gulf connected the public to a crisis already believed to involve a national interest. In Bosnia and Kosovo, on the other hand, equally graphic images have not convinced an inward-looking public that America has a responsibility to intervene. In fact, the public's lack of emotional involvement with events in Yugoslavia is a clear example of the limited power of news coverage to influence public opinion. No matter how many minutes of coverage or inches of copy, no matter how graphic the pictures or gripping the stories, until the percent of Americans following the war in Bosnia has never risen above 20 percent. Just 11 percent were paying very close attention to events in Kosovo prior to NATO military action. However, once the United States became engaged in an air war against Serbian targets, news interest climbed to 43 percent.

In Somalia, media coverage shone brightly on initial hunger relief missions and then brought graphic illustrations of the human costs of peacekeeping missions directly into American homes. Public opinion did dovetail with the coverage, but the pictures merely played to preexisting American opinion—from the outset, the public supported a limited humanitarian role for the United States but did not want to risk American lives.

Clearly, the media's ability to provide instant, graphic images of American casualties does have an effect on the public's opinion on the use of force. Some suggest that this "CNN effect" is at the root of the public's low tolerance for casualties. The truth is that none of the recent interventions—neither Somalia,

Table 8.5. Responsibility in Bosnia

Question: Do you think the United States has a responsibility to do something about fighting between Serbs and Bosnians in what used to be Yugoslavia, or doesn't the United States have this responsibility?

	U.S. Has Responsibility (%)	U.S. Doesn't Have Responsibility (%)	Don't Know(%)
June, 1995	30	64	6
Apr., 1994	41	49	10
Feb., 1994	36	53	11
Dec., 1993	26	65	9
June, 1993	37	51	12
May, 1993	37	52	11
Jan., 1993	24	67	9

Sources: Data from 1993 and 1994 are from NYT/CBS and CBS News. Data from 1995 are from TMC.

nor the Gulf, nor Haiti, nor Bosnia, nor Kosovo—provide final proof of this proposition. A true test case of television's power would necessarily involve factors that do not coincide in any of the above-mentioned crises: a strong sentiment that America has a responsibility or a national interest in the conflict, combined with heavy, persisting American casualties.

The media is often given credit for shifts in public opinion stemming from the average American's personal judgments about responsibilities and risks. Edward Luttwak points out that although residents of the former Soviet Union did not see American-style television coverage of the war in Afghanistan, "the reaction of Soviet society to the casualties of the Afghan war was essentially identical to the American reaction to the Vietnam War."[13]

On the other hand, drumming up public support for humanitarian interventions or peacekeeping operations is further hampered by dwindling media coverage of international events. A recent study by the Center for Media and Public Affairs shows that international news represents a declining share of what the public sees on the three major network television news shows. In 1990, international coverage made up nearly a third (32 percent) of the news agenda. In 1996 that proportion had dropped to 20 percent.[14]

Conclusions

Clearly, America's national interest will evolve as we move into the next century. The end of ideology as an organizing element in public thinking about foreign affairs, and declining public concerns about and interest in traditional geopolitical issues, may mean that global issues such as the environment, population control, crime, and trade increase in importance. Public wariness about the use of force in peacekeeping operations is likely to continue in this scenario. However, support for the use of force to deal with international crime and drugs or to better control U.S. borders may grow. Interestingly, a mid-1993 Roper poll found high approval ratings for military interventions related to top priority domestic issues: 82 percent favored the use of force to stop the flow of illegal drugs into the country, and 70 percent to police the flow of illegal immigration. At the bottom end of the scale, fewer than half favored using force to overthrow a foreign government that practices genocide, to stop an invasion of one foreign country by another, or to intervene in a civil war to protect innocent lives.

More immediately, the continued presence of U.S. troops in the former Yugoslavia may well test the public's equivocal views about participation in multilateral peacekeeping operations. Our analysis suggests that Americans have almost zero tolerance for casualties there. If NATO forces increasingly become objects of Serb frustration, or a terrorist attack is carried out comparable to the bombing of the U.S. air base in Saudi Arabia, calls for U.S. disengagement may soon follow.

Notes

1. Portions of this research were previously presented by Andrew Kohut and Robert C. Toth in "The People, the Press and the Use of Force" (prepared for the Aspen Strategy Group, Aug., 1994); "Arms and the People," *Foreign Affairs* (Nov.-Dec., 1994): 47–61; and "Managing Conflict in the Post–Cold War World: A Public Perspective" (prepared for the Aspen Institute Conference on Managing Conflict in the Post–Cold War World, Aspen, Colo., Aug., 1995).
2. Kohut and Toth, "The People, the Press and the Use of Force."
3. All 1941 polling numbers are from the Gallup Poll.
4. For brevity, most polls are identified by the initials of the polling organizations. Abbreviations include: *WP*/ABC for *Washington Post*/ABC, *NYT*/CBS for *New York Times*/CBS, TMC for the Times Mirror Center for the People and the Press, PRC for the Pew Research Center for the People and the Press, and *LAT* for *Los Angeles Times*.
5. Trend data from 1964 to 1991 are from public opinion surveys conducted by Potomac Associates, The Gallup Organization, and the Institute for International Social Research. The 1993 and 1995 data are from TMC.
6. "Mixed Message about Press Freedom on Both Sides of the Atlantic," Times Mirror Center for the People and the Press, Mar. 16, 1994. Cooperating were *El Pais* in Spain, *La Republica* in Italy, *Liberation* in France, and *El Norte* in Mexico.
7. "Ten Years of the Pew News Interest Index," by Kimberly Parker and Claudia Deane, The Pew Research Center for the People and the Press, prepared for the 1997 meeting of the American Association for Public Opinion Research. The Center's *News Interest Index* periodically asks the public how closely it follows major news stories current at the time of the poll. Responses are categorized as follows: very closely, fairly closely, not too closely, not at all closely, and don't know/refused. Only "very closely" responses are tabulated in the *Index,* whose data extends back to 1986.
8. "The Age of Indifference: A Study of Young Americans and How They View the News," Times Mirror Center for the People & the Press," June 28, 1990.
9. "Ten Years of the Pew News Interest Index," 1997.
10. "America's Place in the World," Times Mirror Center for the People and the Press, Nov., 1993.
11. Quote from presentation at Aspen Institute Conference, Aug., 1995.
12. Trend data from 1993 and 1994 are from *NYT*/CBS and CBS News. The 1995 data is from TMC. In contrast to the public's feelings about the U.S. role in Bosnia, a majority of Americans (58 percent) feel that the UN *does* have a responsibility to take action to end the Balkans fighting (CBS News, June, 1995).
13. Edward N. Luttwak, "Where Are the Great Powers? At Home with the Kids," *Foreign Affairs* 73, no. 4 (July-Aug., 1994): 25.
14. "Media Monitor," July-Aug., 1997, Center for Media and Public Affairs, Washington, D.C. The 1990 figure does not include news about the Persian Gulf.

Chapter 9

The New Cold War

Confronting Social Issues in the Military

Charles Moskos

THAT THE END OF THE COLD WAR has ushered in a new era in international relations and with it changes in the composition and culture of the armed forces is incontestable. Although many of these changes can be traced back prior to the end of the Cold War, they have become more prominent since the tearing down of the Berlin Wall in November of 1989 and the end of the Soviet Union two years later.

At one level, the very missions of the military shift from primarily war-fighting or war deterrence to military deployments for peace and humanitarian purposes. Since the end of the Persian Gulf War in 1991, American forces have taken part in more than thirty overseas deployments, not to mention border patrol, disaster relief, and riot control missions in the United States. Virtually all of these missions were of a peacekeeping or humanitarian nature.

All this is happening at the same time that the armed forces are going through a massive personnel reduction. During the Cold War years of the 1950s, the active-duty force stood at 2.6 million people. During the Cold War years of the all-volunteer force in the 1980s, the figure was 2.1 million. By 1999, the number had dropped to 1.4 million, with the likelihood of a further "drawdown" in the offing. The realities of a smaller military force and the increasing deployment of military personnel in overseas operations dramatically heightens the "operation tempo," causing command concern over the deterioration of morale.

America's armed forces rapidly created new training exercises and manuals to incorporate lessons learned from deployments since the end of the Cold War. New buzzwords entered the Pentagon lexicon: "operations other than war," "other military operations," or "sustainment and stability operations." Whatever these kinds of missions are called, they reflect a fundamental shift in the U.S. military's emphasis from defense of the homeland, or alliance partners, to multinational peace and humanitarian missions.[1]

The Military and the Media

The post–Cold War and post–Gulf War era initiated a new phase in military-media relations. During World War II, the American news media were basically incorporated into the armed forces. Not only were journalists subject to censorship, they also had formal status in the armed forces including the wearing of military uniforms. In essence, both the media and the military were on the same team. This state of affairs changed during the Vietnam War. The media were subjected to an extraordinary degree of control during the American operations in Grenada, Panama, and the Gulf War. The defense establishment effectively controlled the media through the use of press "pools" in which only small, select groups of journalists were given access to the troops. The media saw itself, correctly, as being manipulated by the military, even though there was no formal censorship.[2]

The post–Cold War era, as represented by the operations in Somalia, Haiti, and Bosnia, presents an entirely different situation.[3] The media are frequently "in country" before the military arrives and take care of their own logistical needs. More important, the media are essentially autonomous entities as technological advances allow for direct transmission of news to the outside world. Whereas the media were manipulated by the armed forces in the Cold War era, they are being courted by the military in the post–Gulf War era. The ultimate in Marshall McLuhan's global village may well be the "CNN factor": field commanders watching commercial television to see what is happening in their areas of operation.

Civilians and the Military

One of the least noted but most significant changes in the post–Cold War era is the growth of the defense establishment's civilian component.[4] The increased demand for civilian employees is due to the military's increasing reliance on complex weapons systems, which has resulted in a corresponding need for contract and direct-hire maintenance experts to work in the field and at sea. At least since the 1950s, the capabilities of American warships would be severely handicapped without the civilian technicians—"tech reps"—who maintain their weapon systems. In the buildup leading to the Gulf War, some ten thousand "Emergency Essential Civilians" working for the U.S. military were sent to Saudi Arabia to help operate logistics systems. Interestingly enough, these civilian personnel had a lower rate of being returned back to the United States for physical and disciplinary reasons than regular military personnel.[5]

In the post–Gulf War era, civilians have become even more intimately involved in military functions. Without the contractors—who were responsible for many of the logistics and housekeeping duties—it would be hard to conceive of the American missions to Somalia, Rwanda, Haiti, and Bosnia taking place.[6] It is more than just a historical footnote that the first American casualty in Operation Provide Comfort in Somalia was an Army civilian employee who died when the vehicle in which he was traveling hit a mine.[7] When the 1994 military relief mission to Rwanda ended, the task was turned over to civilian contractors.[8]

Yet another contemporary sign of the permeability between armed forces and civilian spheres is the closer cooperation between armed forces and non-governmental organizations (NGOs) in humanitarian operations. Although we are accustomed to thinking of the military and the NGOs as contrasting types of organizations, even contrasting character types—the tough-minded and the high-minded—this is becoming increasingly wrong. At the same time the military is becoming more sensitive in its dealings with local populaces in peace and humanitarian missions, NGOs are becoming more reliant on and even more supportive of the military. A more martial attitude begins to characterize hitherto pacifist inclined NGOs. The secretary general of Doctors Without Borders argues for an international force to break the grip of Hutu gangs in refugee camps in Zaire.[9] Similarly, the humanitarian agency Oxfam wants UN troops to secure refugee areas in Rwanda.[10]

Yet when all these profound changes are taken into account, the fact remains that public understanding of the armed forces is more focused on social issues confronting the military than anything else. Let us start with two military examples that have received widespread publicity in recent years: homosexuals and adultery.

Homosexuals in the Military

As homosexuals have become increasingly accepted in society at large, pressure has mounted to allow open homosexuals to serve in the armed forces.[11]

For years, America's higher education establishment has urged the Defense Department to remove the ban on homosexuals entering the military as a condition for maintaining Reserve Officer Training Corps (ROTC) detachments on campus. Efforts to remove ROTC from several prestigious campuses stalled when Congress passed legislation prohibiting government contracts to universities that disestablished ROTC.

On another front, shortly after taking office, Pres. Bill Clinton announced he would lift the ban on homosexuals in the military. The controversy surrounding President Clinton's effort to lift the gay ban in 1993 dominated much of the news coverage of the new administration. After much negotiation between the service chiefs, the Congress, and the administration, the new policy announced in 1994 forbade the military to inquire as to a service member's sexual orientation, but service members who declared their homosexuality would be discharged. This "Don't Ask, Don't Tell" policy thus makes it possible for a discreet homosexual to remain in the service. (Full disclosure: the author is the architect of this policy.)

In point of fact, the number of homosexuals discharged increased slightly after the "Don't Ask, Don't Tell" policy was introduced. However, more than 80 percent of those discharges were a result of service members "telling." Noteworthy was that the number of discharges was disproportionately high for women, especially white women. This was probably in some part due to the lesser stigma homosexuality has among women than men, as well as among whites. Only time and the Supreme Court will tell whether "Don't Ask, Don't Tell" will hold firm or serve only as a way station to the full integration of open homosexuals into the U.S. armed forces.

Adultery

In May, 1997, the nation was transfixed by the case of an air force officer, 1st Lt. Kelly Flinn, the first female B-52 pilot. Her adulterous affair with a civilian married to an airwoman led to her removal from the air force. The military's antiadultery regulations came under heavy attack from the establishment press. Shortly after the Flinn affair, the nation's second highest-ranking officer, Gen. Joseph Ralston, was removed from consideration to be the chairman of the Joint Chiefs of Staff because he had had an adulterous affair with a civilian woman over a decade earlier. This apparent double standard led the *New York Times* to castigate the armed forces' "antiquated adultery rules."[12] The very idea that the military's moral codes and those of civilian society should be different was itself the subject of criticism.

Do the armed forces follow an outdated mode of sexual morality by enforcing an antiadultery code? Contrary to popular understanding, adultery in the military is not a "stand-alone" offense. Under Article 134 of the *Manual for Courts-Martial,* adultery is punishable only when "directly prejudicial to good order and discipline and not to acts which are prejudicial only in a remote or indirect sense. . . . It is confined to cases in which the prejudice is reasonably direct and palpable."[13]

What distinguishes the armed forces from the rest of society is the necessity for good order and discipline. To see the military's moral code as antiquated is to lose sight of the reason behind it. Only the armed forces have as a main purpose the responsibility, as it is so aptly put, "to kill people and break things." A military unchecked by a moral code is asking for chaos that unnecessarily risks the lives of our young men and women in uniform. Indeed, the pragmatic understanding of adultery in the armed forces might well be one that civilian organizations should consider emulating.

General Ralston being allowed to remain the vice chairman of the Joint Chiefs of Staff was contrasted with the summary dismissal from the service of Lieutenant Flinn. The double standard accusation does not hold up, however. It is a reach to ascribe a "palpable" effect on good order and discipline to the known facts of Ralston's indiscretions. This differs from the case against Flinn, whose charges included fraternization with an enlisted man, disobeying a direct order, and lying to her commander. That these acts would be deemed prejudicial to good order and discipline should surprise no one.

The substance of the adultery code in the military and the differences in adultery cases are not always easy to communicate to the general public, the news media, or even Capitol Hill. Nevertheless, the issues at stake are not really all that complex. The heart of the matter is always good order and discipline. Also germane to this argument is the sexual behavior of President Clinton, the commander in chief. His indiscretions added other ingredients to both the military and public cognizance of adultery regulations in the armed forces.

The salience of the social issues facing the commander in chief is best exemplified by looking at the two most pressing issues: race relations and gender relations. We will also look at why the first of these, relatively speaking, has generally been successful, and why the second has been the cause of much discord.

Race

Black failure is the dominant paradigm in the way race is talked about in America. That commentators attribute this failure to a diverse array of causes—

white racism, black family breakdown, macroeconomic changes, cultural differences, public policy, and so on—does not change the relentlessly negative picture of black America that is the premise for most racial discussion as we enter the twenty-first century.

The U.S. Army contradicts the prevailing racial paradigm.[14] The army enjoys a level of racial integration that is unmatched elsewhere. It is an institution with a broad record of black achievement that is equally unmatched. It is a world in which the African American heritage is part and parcel of the institutional culture. It is the only place in American life where whites are routinely bossed around by blacks.

In noting the success of race relations in the army, we do not intend to turn a blind eye to real and serious problems that continue to exist. Certainly, the army is not a racial utopia. Black and white soldiers are susceptible to the same kinds of interracial suspicion and resentment that exist outside the service. Although it stands in sharp and favorable contrast to nonmilitary institutions, the army is not immune to the demons that haunt race relations in America.[15]

We focus on the army because it is the largest of the armed services and the one with by far the highest proportion of blacks. In 1999, the 130,000 blacks in the army constituted about half of all blacks in military uniform. African Americans make up close to 27 percent of all army personnel on active duty. By rank, the number of blacks in the army breaks down as 24 percent of the lower enlisted levels, 35 percent of noncommissioned officers (NCOs), 11 percent of commissioned officers, and 9 percent of all generals.

Even if we grant that racial integration and black achievement have gone farther in the army than in any other institution, can any lessons be drawn for civilian life? Certainly the army is not a democracy—but the same is true of most other organizations. Let us also not forget that racist norms and behavior can prevail in large-scale organizations including those with quasi-military structures such as law enforcement agencies. We must remember and stress that the same authority structure existed in the army of the 1970s when racial turbulence was endemic. What allowed the army to move from a racially tense situation to the relative harmony of the present period?

We suggest a broad principle. Race relations can best be transformed by an absolute commitment to nondiscrimination, coupled with uncompromising standards of performance. To maintain standards, however, paths of opportunity must be created—through education, training, and mentoring—for those who otherwise would be at a disadvantage. Comprehension of how race relations work in the army does suggest some concrete lessons.

Lesson One. Blacks and Whites Will Not View Opportunities
and Race Relations the Same

Even in the army, the most successfully racially integrated institution in American society, blacks and whites still have disparate views of equal opportunity. Blacks consistently view racial matters in a less favorable light than do whites. This cuts across gender and rank. There is no foreseeable situation in any American institution, much less society as a whole, where this is likely to change. What the army does show, however, is that black and white social attitudes can become significantly closer in egalitarian settings with shared experiences. It also shows that blacks and whites do not have to hold identical views of the racial situation in order to succeed together.

Lesson Two: Focus on Black Opportunity Channels
Rather than Eradicating Racism

Better to have blacks in substantial numbers in leadership positions in an organization with some white racists than to have an organization with few blacks and fewer black leaders where racial bigots are absent (or, more likely, invisible). The proclivity in civilian organizations, most notably academia, is to foster a better racial climate through eradication of racist statements and symbols. Such efforts are meaningful only when accompanied by concrete steps to expand the pool of qualified students and faculty. The focus first and foremost should always be on avenues that promote black achievement rather than on the rhetoric of nonracism.

Lamentable as the presence of white racists may be, it is not the core issue. Indeed, African American history offers eloquent testimony of how black accomplishment can occur despite pervasive white racism. In no way should the absence of white racists be considered a precondition for African American achievement. This is one of the most significant morals of the army experience.

Lesson Three: Be Ruthless against Discrimination

Although formal efforts to prohibit racist expressions can be a way to avoid a genuine opening up of channels for black advancement, this does not imply a retreat from antidiscrimination. Racist behavior cannot be tolerated within the leadership of an organization. Individuals who display such tendencies must not be promoted to positions of responsibility. Racist behavior in the army effectively terminates one's career. That one rarely hears racial remarks among army NCOs and officers, even in all-white groups, reflects how much this norm is adhered to. Whether formal or informal, the promotion criteria must include sensitivity on racial matters.

*Lesson Four: Affirmative Action Must Be Linked to
Standards and the Qualified Pool*

The army eschews promotion quotas, but it does set goals. These goals are based on the relevant pool of qualified candidates, not on the proportion of blacks in the entire organization, and much less on general population figures. Failure to meet goals must be explained, but "timetables" do not exist. This "soft" affirmative action contrasts with the quota-driven programs that have characterized other federal agencies.[16] Indeed, the promotion lag of blacks compared to whites at certain levels, especially from captain to major, indicates that army promotions are not bound to goals.

The army's minority promotion goals are based on the number of minority candidates in the promotion pool for each rank rather than on the overall number of minority soldiers. This criterion cuts through much of the thicket that surrounds affirmative action in civilian life and allows for some picking and choosing among numerous minority candidates. Maintenance of common standards for promotion may cause short-term turmoil, as it did in the army of the 1970s, but it also means that those who attain senior positions are fully qualified. That the army contained few putative liberals willing to rationalize an initial drop in standards allowed those blacks who were promoted in the early days to become the strongest defenders of standards for their own black subordinates. An organization that promotes the less qualified to buy temporary peace only invites long-term disaffection.

Lesson Five: A Level Playing Field Is Not Always Enough

The army's success in producing black leaders occurs because it recognizes that a level playing field is not always enough. This in turn points to another army lesson for civilian society. Rather than compromise standards, soldiers are trained to meet competitive standards. Toward this end, the army has established far-reaching educational programs that emphasize mathematics, reading, and writing. The army has successfully introduced internal programs to bring young people up to enlistment standards, to raise enlisted soldiers to noncommissioned officer standards, to bring undergraduates up to officer commissioning standards, and to prepare high school graduates to meet West Point admission standards. These programs are not designed exclusively for minority soldiers, but the participants are disproportionately African American.[17]

If liberals must learn white racism is not the central point, conservatives have something to learn, too. The skill-boosting programs that produce so many black leaders in the army are costly. These programs require a big commitment of money and resources. Sometimes, as in the army's remedial programs, "throwing money" at a social problem *does* solve it.

Lesson Six: Recognize Afro-Anglo Culture as the Core American Culture

An unquantifiable component in the army's success in race relations is that the organization is multiracial, but unicultural—and the uniculture is Afro-Anglo. Our central argument here is that something similar must occur in American society as a whole. One of the most striking effects of racial integration in the army is that enlisted life has become somewhat African Americanized. White Americans become attuned to African American cultural patterns as fully as black soldiers adapt to "white" culture. An invocation of our black heritage that has deepened and enhanced the American dream is as important as our economic and military might. Our own civil rights struggle has become part of the world movement toward freedom. John Hope Franklin, the dean of black historians, puts it succinctly: "The role of the Negro in America is not only significant in itself but central in the task of fulfilling the nation's true destiny."[18]

We must abandon the mind-set that being "black" and being "American" are somehow mutually exclusive. This is a false dichotomy even though it is accepted by many black nationalists and most whites. The relationship between being black and being American is not "either-or" but "both-and." The titles of the autobiographies of two black generals are informative: *Benjamin O. Davis, Jr., American,* and *My American Journey* by Colin Powell.[19]

Gender

Space precludes a full review of the changing status of women in the military.[20] It is sufficient to note that women make up 15 percent of the force and can be assigned to virtually any duty except positions in ground combat units. Except for basic training in the Marine Corps and the army's combat arms, all training is gender integrated. Starting in 1995, navy women were allowed to serve aboard warships (excluding submarines) and as combat pilots aboard aircraft carriers. Similarly, women pilots (albeit a small number) were assigned to bombers and fighter planes in the air force. Although still excluded from ground combat assignments, the role of women in the American military has expanded dramatically since the end of the Cold War.

If race relations in the military are relatively good in comparison with civilian society, the ongoing difficulties of the services in gender relations has been the cause of much embarrassment and scandal. The sexual shenanigans of navy fighter pilots in the 1991 Tailhook Association convention in Las Vegas, Nevada, became a national news story.[21] In 1996, incidents of sexual harassment at training camps—especially at the Aberdeen Proving Ground, Maryland, training center—rocked the army. Shortly thereafter, charges of sexual abuse were brought against the sergeant major of the army.

Yet even these scandals could serve as an impetus for opening up the remaining proscribed roles for women. It has become an article of faith for feminist spokespersons to hold that sexual harassment will be controlled only when women are no longer regarded as second-class members of the military, that is, no longer excluded from the combat arms. Certainly the Tailhook scandal facilitated the opening up of combat aircraft and warships to women. However, survey data clearly show that few enlisted women (and not that many female officers either) want to be assigned to the combat arms. In other words, there is a disconnect between the agendas of some feminists and the concerns of the vast majority of military women.[22]

Any approach to gender relations in the military must begin with a fundamental principle. Consensual sex among equal ranks (allowed in the military) may have as much of an effect on good order and discipline as does adultery or fraternization between ranks (not allowed). The prevalence of consensual sex among equals sets a tone in which superior-subordinate sex becomes a minor, rather than a major, step. There is a contradiction to tell commanders to be vigilant regarding superior-subordinate sex, but to look the other way when sex occurs between those of the same rank.

On sexual harassment, the overriding goal must be to get more reporting of true harassment cases and reduce the number of false accusations. False accusations undermine the credibility of true victims who are now second-guessed. In point of fact, enlisted women report that false accusations of sexual harassment are as much of a problem as genuine sexual harassment.[23] Male superiors are worried that their authority is undermined because of potential sexual harassment charges. We must be wary of those who view the sexual harassment scandals simply as being the result of a "few bad apples." The focus must be on organizational changes that directly address both sexual harassment and false accusations of the same.

The following is a list of recommendations addressing gender issues:

1. Minimally, a female in each Inspector General's (IG) office must be readily available so that an aggrieved woman can be assured of seeing one if she wants. Other options: (a) a female-male "team" within each IG office to screen all sex abuse cases or (b) an all-female "chain of complaint" within the IG system (as exists in Israel).[24]

2. Rethink allowing consensual sex among equals. Prohibitions might be appropriate in training and deployment situations. A precedent exists in the ban on sexual relations on ships. To make the point clearer, consideration should be given to prohibit sex even among married couples during operational overseas deployments. At the

same time, rethink the fraternization ban in office or other routine work settings (not that the civilian workplace has resolved this issue).

3.   Consider unit punishment as a way to punish those who know of sexual abuse but do not take action against malefactors.

4.   Have lawyers rethink "constructive force" as always being rape in a superior-subordinate setting.

5.   Punishment of some sort should be meted out to female subordinates who misbehave sexually. Presently, we have a gender-normed standard of morality that demeans women. Item: No female officer who misbehaved at the Tailhook convention was reprimanded. Item: Regulations current in 1997 at Fort Jackson, South Carolina, exempt female trainees from prosecution for soliciting sex with male drill sergeants.[25]

6.   Abolish the term "zero tolerance" as no consensus on what constitutes petty harassment in either sex.

7.   Establish a statute of limitations for reporting sexual harassment cases (unless they are truly criminal).

There are also blind alleys in dealing with sexual harassment in the armed forces. One is to confound power relations with sex. If power relations are the chief cause of sexual abuse in the military, then there are only two realistic options: either reduce the authority of superiors, or separate men from women. Also, what are we to make of survey data that show enlisted women prefer male superiors?[26]

The other dead end is to blame the prevailing culture within the military. In a bizarre appointment, the secretary of the army in 1997 hired as a temporary consultant an advocate of replacing the service's "masculinist" culture with an "ungendered vision" of military culture.[27] For those who want to abolish the prevailing culture, what is the preferred culture? Men don't tell dirty jokes in front of women. Men don't tell dirty jokes at all. Women laugh at dirty jokes when men tell them. Women tell dirty jokes to men.

Gender relations in the military confront a fundamental dilemma. Do we want more female generals or less sexual harassment? Enlisted women state that harassment will increase if females are put into the combat arms. But without women in the combat arms there will never be many female generals. Acknowledging this dilemma should help clear the air.

Then there is the matter of race and gender. The sexual harassment scandals at Aberdeen Proving Ground and other locales were marked by a stark sociological reality. The large majority of the accused sergeants were black and the large majority of accusers were white women. Yet black women are the plurality among army women. In 1997, blacks accounted for 48 percent of all army enlisted women and whites 40 percent, with other ethnic groups making up the rest.

Here is an examination question. What best explains the inverse racial ratios in the sexual harassment scandals?: (a) black superiors are hitting on white trainees; (b) white female trainees are flirting with black superiors; (c) black women know how to fend off harassment better than white women; (d) cross-race sexual harassment is more likely to be reported than same-race harassment. The correct answer is: (e) all of the above.

It may be relevant to note that the attrition rate (that is, those who fail to complete their initial enlistment for one cause or another) in the contemporary army is about 34 percent for males of any race and black females. For white women, however, the attrition rate is an astoundingly high 54 percent. (The attrition rate for males in the all-volunteer force is three times greater than it was for draftees in the Cold War era!)

A commonplace observation is to find parallels between race and gender integration. This is a false analogy. The differences between the races and the sexes are of a qualitative nature. For blacks in the military, officer and enlisted agendas are similar, and civil rights organizations align themselves with blacks regardless of rank. For females in the military, officers and enlisted persons have different agendas, and feminist organizations align themselves with officers. Between the races, there are no privacy needs based on modesty. Between the sexes, there are privacy needs based on modesty. Between the races, there are no differences in physical standards. Between the sexes, physical standards are gender normed. The key issue for successful racial integration is black opportunity channels. The key issue between the sexes is to enhance cross-gender cohesion without sexuality.

One other avenue must be explored with regard to race and gender. Why does racial integration work relatively well in the army but not so well on the university campus? Why does gender integration work relatively well on campus but encounter major difficulties in the armed forces? This is a topic that deserves greater examination than can be brought to bear here, but two hypotheses can be suggested. Jane Jacobs has posited two basic types of authority systems.[28] One, the "guardianship" model, has the qualities—vertical structure, emphasis on cohesion, loyalty as a core value—that typically characterize a military organization. The other, the "commercial" model—horizontal structure, emphasis on individualism, honesty as a core value—more closely approximates that of the university. Could it be that the former makes for better race relations and the latter for better gender relations? The implications of this hypothesis are troubling. We cannot expect to have successful race relations and gender relations in the same organization.

The intersection of race and gender in the U.S. armed forces does have an important positive side, however. Revelations of killings and torture of local civilians by their soldiers in the 1993 Somalia mission led to a wave of soul-searching in Canada, Belgium, and Italy. It should be quickly noted that the atrocities committed by the soldiers of those three countries were almost certainly less than those of countries that have not even looked into the behavior of their soldiers in Somalia. The U.S. military was a striking exception to the general pattern of harsh treatment of Somalis (not that the behavior of American soldiers was perfect).

The exceptionally good behavior of the Americans in Operation Restore Hope derived in large part from the fact that they were part of the only contingent in Somalia mixed in both race and gender. All the other nations contributing to the Somalia operation dispatched forces that were all male and all of one race (whether white, brown, or black). A field study of American troops in Somalia showed that blacks and women were more empathetic with the locals than white males.[29] It appears, moreover, that the emotional fervor required for atrocities does not gain momentum as easily when a military unit is diverse in terms of race and gender.

When Elite Youth No Longer Serve

Volumes have been written on race and gender in the armed forces. Yet what is perhaps the most significant social change in the armed forces is the one least likely to be commented upon: namely, the near absence of service members coming from the ranks of America's social elite. The likelihood of volunteer recruitment drawing upon future political leaders and opinion shapers becomes increasingly remote.

During World War II virtually every able-bodied young man served in the military, including those coming from families in the highest social strata. This state of affairs lasted, more or less, through the Korean and Cold War years that followed. The end of military service for young men coming from America's elites began to erode during the early years of the Vietnam War, and by the late 1960s such young men were, for all practical purposes, not being drafted.

What are the consequences, if any, of not having elite youth serve in the armed forces? On one level, the end of conscription makes military service less salient to the general populace as a whole. It is of some note that since conscription's end in the United States in 1973 not one novel of note has been written about the all-volunteer force. Military cinema, however, continues to be a major genre, although the military is portrayed with a sinister edge. In the 1996 movie *Broken Arrow,* an air force major plots to steal two nuclear bombs for which he plans to hold Denver in ransom. In *The Rock* (1996), a maverick marine general holds San Francisco hostage by threatening to use poison gas. In *The Siege* (1998), an army general oversees martial law in New York City and tortures prisoners.

On the other hand, two recent box-office hits—*Independence Day* (1996) and *Air Force One* (1997)—portrayed a contemporary president as a former war hero (the Persian Gulf War and the Vietnam War, respectively). Still, the two biggest box office and hits in the military genre—*Saving Private Ryan* (1998) and *The Thin Red Line* (1998)—were both set in World War II.

There is, however, a more serious consequence to the end of privileged youth: the country's unwillingness to accept casualties in combat operations. The threshold of casualty acceptance by a society is one of the most crucial factors affecting the deployment of troops, whether for conventional warfare or peace and humanitarian missions.

Many observers are acutely aware of America's greater reluctance to accept casualties than in times past. We need only remember the abrupt evacuation from Beirut following the 1983 bombing of the marine barracks or the quick turn-around in Somalia following the October, 1993, deaths of eighteen U.S. soldiers. The American force that went to Bosnia in 1996 has seen its original goals transformed in what has become, in effect, a force protection mission.

Why has the threshold of casualty acceptance changed? Certainly the small number of combat losses in recent military operations contributes to the lower tolerance for casualties. The invasions of Grenada and Panama were over with in a matter of days and incurred just 18 and 23 American deaths, respectively. Even with more than a half-million troops in place during the Gulf War, America almost miraculously suffered only 183 combat dead. In Haiti, only one American soldier has been killed by hostile fire.

The increasing reluctance to accept casualties, however, also suggests that something deeper has changed in society. One school of thought holds that a declining birthrate and the resultant smaller families makes the loss of children in war much more traumatic than in an era of large families.[30] While this explanation has a certain surface plausibility, what are we to make of the fact that the U.S. birthrate is higher than in the former Yugoslavia, where the ethnic willingness to suffer—as well as cause—casualties has become legendary?

The most frequently voiced explanation of casualty acceptance is that the public will not accept combat deaths unless the national interest—sometimes the adjective "vital" is interjected—is clearly at stake. Commentators are virtually unanimous on this point.[31] Intervening in a civil war in Lebanon or in clan warfare in Somalia did not meet the criterion of national interest. Hence America's quick departure once the going got tough. From economic and strategic viewpoints, the Gulf War more easily fit, though not perfectly, into the framework of American national interest. But the Gulf War was not a true test of the national-interest theory because we have little idea how Americans would have reacted had the combat deaths been in the thousands rather than in the low hundreds.

All of this is wide of the mark, however. The answer to the question of what America's national interests are is found not in the cause itself but rather in who is willing to die for that cause. Only when the privileged classes perform military service does the country define the cause as worth young people's blood. Only when elite youth are on the firing line do war losses become more acceptable. This explains the seeming paradox of why we have a lower acceptance of combat casualties with a volunteer military than we had with a draft army.

History in this century supports the argument that casualty acceptance correlates with a force that drafts privileged youth. In World War II, battle deaths approached 300,000. Yet casualty acceptance was high because virtually every able-bodied male served in the military. A slightly less draconian draft occurred in World War I when 53,000 American soldiers died. Although never popular, the Korean War, with its 33,000 deaths and fought mainly by draftees, lasted four years. Support for the Vietnam War, where 47,000 Americans died in battle, waned as more and more elite youth evaded the draft.

The advent of the all-volunteer force in 1973 insured that the children of our national elites would not be found in the military, especially in the enlisted ranks. This social reality more than any other factor has, for better or worse, lowered our country's willingness to accept casualties. Citizens accept hardships only when their leadership is viewed as self-sacrificing.

We finish this discussion with a caveat, a speculation, and a conclusion. The caveat is not to take for granted that the movement toward greater permissiveness in the larger society will continue into the future. The speculation is that we are moving into an era in which the military will grow increasingly isolated from the society it defends.[32] The conclusion is that, for now at least, social issues will occupy the commander in chief's attention as much, if not more, than the traditional concerns of weapons development and force structure.

Table 9.1. Post–Gulf War Military Roles of United States through 1998 (partial listing)

Location	Date	Mission	Participants
1. U.S. borders: "Joint Task Six"	1990–	assist in drug interdiction	100–1,500 military, plus law enforcement agencies
2. Turkey: "Operation Provide Comfort"	1991	Kurdish refugee relief and enforce no-fly zone	U.S. forces and coalition partners (23,000 peak)
3. Bangladesh: "Operation Sea Angel"	1991	flood relief	8,000 U.S. Marines and Navy
4. Phillippines: "Operation Fiery Vigil"	July, 1991	Mt. Inatubo volcano rescue	5,000 U.S. Navy and Marines
5. Cuba (Guantanamo): "Operation Safe Passage"	Nov, 1991– May, 1992	Haitian refugee relief	U.S. military and Coast Guard (2,000 peak)
6. Italy: "Operation Volcano Buster"	Dec., 1991	Mt. Etna volcano rescue	small U.S. Marines/ Navy force
7. California: "Joint Task Force Los Angeles"	May, 1992	restore domestic order	8,000 U.S. Army Marine Corps, 12,000 National Guard
8. Florida	Aug.–Sept., 1992	disaster relief following Hurricane Andrew	21,000 U.S. Air Force, Marines, 6,000 National Guard
9. Iraq: "Operation Southern Watch" and "Northern Watch"	Aug., 1992–	surveillance	U.S. Air Force, Navy
10. Hawaii	Sept., 1992	disaster relief following eruption of Iniki	National Guard, small U.S. Marines/Air Force
11. Somalia: "Operation Restore Hope"	Dec., 1992– May, 1993	famine relief and restore order	Large U.S. and UN force (35,000 peak)

Table 9.1. Post–Gulf War Military Roles of United States through 1998 (continued)

12. Former Yugoslavia and Macedonia: "Able Sentry"	Dec., 1992	monitor border	1,000 UN force: Nordic contingent USA Bn
13. Kuwait: "Operation Iris Gold"	Jan., 1993–	Kuwait defense coalition forces	4,000 U.S. Army
14. Somalia (UNOSOM II)	May, 1993– Dec., 1994	establish order and humanitarian aid	15,000 UN force(peak); esp. U.S., Belgium, Italy, France, Nigeria
15. Iraq	June, 1993	Baghdad bombing	U.S. air forces
16. Puerto Rico	July, 1993	anti-drug law enforcement	300 National Guard troops with local police
17. Colombia	Jan.–Feb., 1994	civic works	150 U.S. Army engineers
18. Bosnia	Feb., 1994	downing of Serb fighter planes	United States (first NATO military action)
19. Rwanda	Apr., 1994	rescue foreign nationals	Belgium and French troops; also U.S. Marines in Burundi
20. Bosnia	Apr., 1994	bombing of Serb positions	U.S. planes under NATO
21. Washington state	July, 1994	forest fire fighting	600 active-duty; 7,000 reserves
22. Haiti: "Operation Uphold Democracy"	Sept., 1994– Mar., 1995	secure change of government	20,000 U.S. military at peak, token force from 24 other nations
23. Kuwait: "Operation Vigilant Warrior"	Oct.–Dec., 1994	protect Kuwait from Iraq	13,000 force at peak, mainly U.S. forces
24. Bosnia	Nov., 1994	air strikes against Serbs in Croatia	U.S., British, and French planes (largest NATO military action)

25. Kazakhstan: "Operation Sapphire"	Nov., 1994	removal of uranium	U.S. civilian-military team
26. Panama: "Operation Safe Haven"	Sept., 1994–Mar., 1995	guarding Cuban refugees	3,000 U.S. military at peak (240 hurt Dec., 7–8)
27. Somalia: "Operation United Shield"	Dec., 1994–Mar., 1995	aid evacuation of UN troops	1,800 U.S. Marines, 400 Italians
28. Bosnia: Implementation Force unit (IFOR); "Operation Joint Endeavor"	Dec., 1995–Dec., 1996	enforce peace agreement	60,000 NATO force (20,000 U.S. including those in Hungary)
29. Liberia: "Operation Quick Response"	May–Aug., 1996	evacuate U.S. nationals	U.S. Marines and Special Forces
30. Atlanta, Ga.: "Joint Task Force Olympics"	July–Aug., 1996	security and transportation	8,000 U.S. Army (mainly reserve components)
31. Bosnia: Stabilization Force (SFOR)	Dec., 1996–	enforce peace agreement	20,000 NATO force (6,000 U.S.)
32. Zaire	Apr., 1997	evacuate foreign nationals	1,200 troops from U.S., Belgium, France, Britain
33. Sierra Leone	June, 1997	evacuate foreign nationals	U.S. Marines
34. Haiti: "Operation New Horizon"	Dec., 1997	civil works	500 U.S. military
35. Persian Gulf: "Operation Desert Thunder"	Feb., 1998	bombing of Iraq	large U.S. military force with some allies
36. Sudan and Afghanistan	Aug., 1998	attack terrorist sites	U.S. cruise missiles

Notes

1. As this was being written in April, 1999, NATO forces were conducting a major air campaign in Yugoslavia and there was discussion of sending in ground troops to bring about an end to the Kosovo crisis. Noteworthy was that this major military action was defended in terms of humanitarian goals.

   On the changing nature of the American military, see Morris Janowitz, ed., *The New Military: Changing Patterns of Organization* (New York: Russell Sage Foundation, 1964); David R. Segal, *Organizational Designs for the Future Army* (Alexandria, Va.: U.S. Army Research Institute for the Behavioral and Social Sciences, 1993); Mark J. Eitelberg and Stephen L. Mehay, eds., *Marching Toward the 21st Century* (Westport, Conn.: Greenwood, 1994); Sam C. Sarkesian, John Allen Williams and Fred B. Bryant, eds., *Society and National Security* (Boulder, Colo.: Lynne Reinner, 1995); and James Burk, ed., *The Adaptive Military* (New Brunswick, N.J.: Transaction, 1998).

2. A caustic account of how journalists covered the Persian Gulf War is John J. Fialka, *Hotel Warriors* (Washington, D.C.: Woodrow Wilson Center, 1992).

3. See Peter R. Young, ed., *Defence and the Media in Time of Limited War* (London: Frank Cass, 1992); Larry Minear, Colin Scott, and Thomas G. Weiss, *The News Media, Civil War, and Humanitarian Action* (Boulder, Colo.: Lynne Rienner, 1994); and Charles Moskos with Thomas E. Ricks, *Reporting War When There Is No War: The Media and the Military in Peace and Humanitarian Operations* (Chicago, Ill.: McCormick Tribune Foundation, 1996).

4. There is little research on the subject of civilians who work for the military. For one of the few analytical treatments, see Martin Binkin, *Shaping the Defense Civilian Work Force* (Washington, D.C.: Brookings Institution, 1978).

5. Of the 2,297 Department of the Army civilians assigned to Operations Desert Shield/Storm, five would not go and four were sent back after arrival in Saudi Arabia. Personal communication to author by a Department of the Army official, 1994.

6. Thomas E. Ricks, "U.S. Military Turns to Civilian Workers for Support Services," *Wall Street Journal,* May 1, 1995, p. 1.

7. *New York Times,* Dec. 24, 1992, p. 1.

8. "Successful Rwandan Mission Phasing Out," *Army Times,* Sept. 12, 1994, p. 8.

9. Alain Desxthe, "We Can't be a Party to Slaughter in Rwanda," *New York Times,* Feb. 9, 1995, p. A15. See also, Thomas G. Weiss and Kurt M. Campbell, "Military Humanitarianism," *Survival* 33, no. 5 (Sept.-Oct., 1991): 451–65; and Larry Minear and Thomas G. Weiss, *Mercy Under Fire* (Boulder, Colo.: Westview, 1995).

10. Reuters, Apr. 24, 1995.

11. A balanced compendium on homosexuals in the armed forces is Wilbur J. Scott and Sandra Carson Stanley, eds., *Gays and Lesbians in the Military* (New York: Aldine de Gruyter, 1994).

12. "The Discharge of Kelly Flinn," *New York Times,* May 23, 1997, p. A18.

13. Article 134, *Manual for Courts-Martial* (Washington, D.C.: GPO, 1995), p. IV-93.

14. For a fuller discussion of race relations in the military, see Charles C. Moskos and John Sibley Butler, *All That We Can Be: Black Leadership and Racial Integration the Army* (New York: Basic Books, 1996).

15. A 1994 report of the House Armed Services Committee reiterated the disparate

readings blacks and whites have on race relations, and, although reporting an absence of overt racism in the military, found continuing "subtle forms of racism" that affected minority career advancement and disciplinary actions as well as perception of reverse discrimination by whites.

16. See the story on the Office of Federal Contract Compliance programs by Steven A. Holmes, "Once-Tough Chief of Affirmative-Action Agency Is Forced to Change Tack," *New York Times,* Aug. 6, 1995, p. A13.

17. One example may suffice. The U.S. Military Academy at West Point remains the most prestigious source of commissions in the army. Almost half of the black cadets who enter West Point are products of one of the most unusual secondary schools in America: the U.S. Military Academy Preparatory School (USMAPS). The ten-month program, in effect a thirteenth year of high school, has a sole academic emphasis on reading, writing, and mathematics. Without the Prep School, as it is known in army circles, the number of black cadets would be perilously low. Remarkably, black "prepsters" are just as likely (74 percent) to graduate from West Point as white cadets admitted directly (75 percent). But the costs of the Prep School are steep: $40,000 to $60,000 per student per year, depending on who does the figuring. (General Accounting Office, *DOD Service Academies* [Washington, D.C.: GPO, 1992].)

18. John Hope Franklin, "The New Negro History," in *Race and History: Selected Essays 1938–1988* (Baton Rouge: Louisiana State University Press, 1989), p. 47.

19. Benjamin O. Davis, Jr., *Benjamin O. Davis, Jr., American: An Autobiography* (Washington, D.C.: Smithsonian Institution, 1991); Colin L. Powell, *My American Journey* (New York: Random House, 1995).

20. The literature on women in the armed forces is vast. See, especially, Jeanne Holm, *Women in the Military: An Unfinished Revolution,* rev. ed. (Novato, Calif.: Presidio, 1992); Sandra Carson Stanley, *Women in the Military* (New York: Julian Messner, 1993); Judith Hick Stiehm, ed., *It's Our Military, Too* (Philadelphia: Temple University Press, 1996); Laura L. Miller, "Not Just Weapons of the Weak: Gender Harassment as a Form of Protest for Army Men," *Social Psychological Quarterly* 60, no. 1 (Mar., 1997): 32–51; and Linda Bird Francke, *Ground Zero: The Gender Wars in the Military* (New York: Simon and Schuster, 1997).

21. William H. McMichael, *The Mother of All Hooks: The Story of the U.S. Navy's Tailhook Scandal* (New Brunswick, N.J.: Transaction, 1997).

22. Laura Miller, "Feminism and the Exclusion of Army Women from Combat," *Gender Issues,* summer, 1998, pp. 33–64.

23. Survey data collected by the Congressional Commission on Military Training and Gender-Related Issues, 1999.

24. On women in the Israeli military, see Reuven Gal, *A Portrait of the Israeli Soldier* (Westport, Conn.: Greenwood, 1986).

25. *Army Times,* Aug. 4, 1997, p. 31.

26. Laura L. Miller, "Gender Détente" (Ph.D. diss., Northwestern University, 1995).

27. See Madeline Morris, "By Force of Arms: Rape, War and Military Culture," *Duke Law Journal* 45, no. 4 (1996): 651–781.

28. The dichotomy between commercial systems of authority with heavy reliance on honesty as a core value and guardianship systems of authority with heavy reliance on loyalty has been made Jane Jacobs, *Systems of Survival* (New York: Random House, 1991). Seven core values were identified by the U.S. Army chief of staff in a 1997 memorandum. These were duty, honor, courage, integrity, loy-

alty, respect, selfless service. Except for integrity, these values would seem to be located on the "loyalty" side of the honesty-loyalty dichotomy. (U.S. Army Chief of Staff, "Memo for Army Leaders," July 27, 1997.)

29. Laura L. Miller and Charles Moskos, "Humanitarians or Warriors? Race, Gender, and Combat Status in Operation Restore Hope," *Armed Forces and Society* 21, no. 4 (summer, 1995): 615–37.

30. The argument that acceptance of combat casualties relates to family size is made in Edward N. Luttwak, "Where are the Great Powers?" *Foreign Affairs* 73, no. 4 (July-Aug., 1994): 23–29.

31. See, especially, E.V. Larson, *Ends and Means in the Democratic Conversation: Understanding the Role of Casualties in Support for U.S. Military Operations* (Santa Monica, Calif.: Rand Corporation, 1996). Also relevant is John E. Mueller, *War, Presidents and Public Opinion* (New York: John Wiley and Sons, 1973); and Mueller, *Policy and Opinion in the Gulf War* (Chicago: University of Chicago Press, 1994).

32. Thomas E. Ricks, in *Making the Corps* (New York: Scribner, 1997), documents a growing gap between young marines and the prevailing youth culture in American society. For broader discussions of the growing gap in civil-military relations, see Don M. Snider, ed., *U.S. Civil-Military Relations: In Crisis or Transition?* (Washington, D.C.: Center for Strategic and International Studies, 1995); and Michael Desch, *Soldiers, States, and Structure* (Baltimore: Johns Hopkins University Press, 1998).

Part IV

A Revolution in Force?

Chapter 10

Transforming the American Military

Andrew Krepinevich

THE UNITED STATES TODAY FACES a challenge that is unprecedented in the nation's history. It must transform its armed forces into a very different kind of military from that which now exists while sustaining the military's ability to play a very active role in supporting U.S. near-term efforts to preserve global stability within a national security strategy of engagement and enlargement.

The Defense Department's recently completed Quadrennial Defense Review (QDR) continues to accord primary emphasis in the defense program on preparing to fight, nearly simultaneously, two regional conflicts of the scale and nature of the Persian Gulf War.[1] This emphasis seems misplaced. So too, in many respects, is the current debate over "How much is enough?" to sustain such a defense posture. Indeed, in a period of major geopolitical and military technology changes, the defense debate seems dominated by consideration over how best to wage the last war more efficiently, as opposed to preparing to meet new challenges both efficiently and effectively. In this respect, the situation is akin to observing France's deliberations in the late 1920s over how much it would cost to construct and maintain the Maginot Line—a system of fortifications designed to deflect a World War I–style German assault. The French ignored the strong incentives for the German military to exploit rapidly emerging technologies and thus to avoid a repetition of that war's outcome.[2]

A U.S. military oriented toward meeting the challenges encountered in

Operation Desert Storm is likely to depreciate rapidly over the next two decades, while its principal value will be realized during a period of relatively low risk to the national security. Thus the defense "train wreck" that some Cassandras speak of is not, at its core, budgetary in nature, it is *strategic*.[3]

Why the need for a military transformation? After all, the strategic environment in which the United States finds itself today is far more favorable than that which existed during the Cold War. It could be argued that America's military superiority over any prospective near-term challenger is so great that it is unlikely to confront a major threat to its vital interests over the next ten years, and perhaps even longer. The Defense Department describes this period of relatively low danger as one of "strategic pause." However, the United States should not take that as an invitation to become complacent in its current relative advantage.

Indeed, historical patterns over the last three hundred years strongly suggest that competition among the great powers is the rule, rather than the exception.[4] Today's strategic environment is characterized by far greater uncertainty than existed during the Cold War. Simply stated, the United States does not know when it will face another major challenge to its security, what nations might pose such a challenge, or how a challenger would choose to compete.

Moreover, technology eventually diffuses. America's seeming military monopolies (for example, in such weaponry as precision-guided munitions [PGMs], stealth technology, and in the exploitation of space for military purposes) will most likely not endure much beyond the next decade. Technology diffusion will allow future U.S. adversaries to present the U.S. military with new, and far more difficult, military problems to solve than those encountered during the Gulf War. The principal challenge before the U.S. military is not to be found in its ability to fight and win two nearly simultaneous major regional conflicts of the magnitude and type of Desert Storm. Rather, it is in the military's ability to extend its current advantage in military effectiveness in a world of rapidly changing—and far more formidable—challenges. This would contribute to an overall U.S. national security strategy, where the principal goal should be to avoid yet another cycle of great power military competition and conflict such as that which has dominated this century.

The need for a transformation strategy is also stimulated by a growing awareness that the world is likely entering into a period of military revolution.[5] Such transitions are characterized by discontinuous leaps in military effectiveness and dramatic shifts in the military "tools" available to commanders, in the ways in which armed forces fight, and in how they organize for combat.[6] This century has witnessed two such periods. The most recent is the nuclear weapon-ballistic missile revolution of the 1940s and 1950s. An earlier revolution occurred in the 1920s and 1930s. It was characterized by the transformation of warfare on land, which culminated in the blitzkrieg; at sea, with the rise of naval aviation and carrier battle groups; and in the air, with the emergence of strategic aerial bombardment.[7] The emerging military revolution may offer the U.S. military an opportunity to better prepare for new challenges.

The Defense Department confronts this era of transformational change, both geopolitical and military technological, within an environment of declining resources for defense. Consequently, there is the risk that if the wrong transformation path is chosen (or if no attempt is made to transform), it will prove difficult, if not impossible, for the Pentagon to buy its way out of mistakes. It also is important to begin the transformation process soon. It is no exaggeration to say that, given the time it takes to field new military systems, develop new doctrine, and field test new combat organizations, the U.S. military twenty years hence is already being formed (and *limited*) by decisions being made today.

Recognizing this, Congress passed legislation in August, 1996, requiring the Defense Department to undertake "a comprehensive examination of defense strategy, force structure, force modernization plans, infrastructure, budget plan, and other elements of the defense program and policies with a view toward determining and expressing the defense strategy of the United States and establishing a revised defense program."[8] The Defense Department has dubbed this examination its Quadrennial Defense Review, and asserts that, given the resources available, the defense program it has produced offers an optimal blueprint for the first two decades of the next century.[9]

The Emerging Military Regime

What new challenges will the U.S. military confront early in the next century? While no one can say for certain, the broad outlines of a post-transformation conflict environment are beginning to emerge. General John Shalikashvili, former chairman of the Joint Chiefs of Staff, observed that "Accelerating rates of change will make the future environment more unpredictable and less stable, presenting our armed forces with a wide range of plausible futures."[10] Much of this change is being stimulated by rapid advances in information and information-related technologies, which are transforming societies and economies, and which seem likely to effect major changes in warfare. General Shalikashvili noted that "the emerging importance of information superiority will dramatically impact how well our armed forces can perform its duties in 2010."[11]

Indeed, this emerging military revolution is characterized, in part, by a rapidly growing potential to detect, identify, and track a far greater number of targets, over a far larger area, for a much longer period of time than ever before. Moreover, there also is the rapidly growing potential to order and move this information much more quickly and effectively than ever before. This seems likely to produce a very different kind of competition between military "finders" and "hiders" than we have seen in the past.

Finders operating a reconnaissance system composed of a network of satellites, unmanned aerial vehicles, remote sensors, and "networked" individual soldiers, among other elements, would be able to create a condition of information superiority in which most of an adversary's forces and infrastructure are clearly identified. At the same time, the bulk of friendly forces would remain shrouded from the enemy. Such a reconnaissance system could dissipate much of the fog of war and substantially reduce the friction that dilutes military effectiveness.

On the other hand, the hiders will seek to frustrate the finders' efforts through a variety of means, including strikes against the reconnaissance system and passive measures such as stealth, electronic countermeasures, and the dispersion, cover, and concealment of forces. Thus, while it will be important to seek information superiority to realize the enormous boost it could provide to military force effectiveness, it is not at all clear that this condition will be easily achieved. What does seem clear is that those military organizations that are not prepared for such a competition will likely find themselves at a great disadvantage.

The importance of creating a favorable information gap between friendly and enemy forces is highlighted by the rapidly growing potential of advanced military organizations (the U.S. military in particular) to engage a far greater number of targets, over a far greater area, in far less time, and with much greater lethality, precision, and discrimination than ever before. Combined with information superiority, such a capability could be an instrument of decisive advantage for the force that possesses it. As this new military regime emerges and matures, it will present the U.S. military with challenges and opportunities that are dramatically different from those of today.

New Challenges

The Defense Department's depiction of the future conflict environment is summarized in *Joint Vision 2010*. It declares that "power projection, enabled by overseas presence, will likely remain *the fundamental strategic concept* of our future force."[12] Yet *Joint Vision 2010* also recognizes that power-projection operations may have to be executed far differently in the future than they were in the Gulf War, declaring: "Our most vexing future adversary may be one who can use military technology to make rapid improvements in its military capabilities that provide *asymmetrical counters* to U.S. military strengths."[13]

Recently retired U.S. Air Force chief of staff Gen. Ronald Fogleman voiced concerns over a particularly vexing asymmetric challenge when he spoke of the consequences of facing a competitor that has chosen to invest primarily in a missile force, as opposed to an air force. The general observed: "Saturation ballistic missile attacks against littoral forces, ports, airfields, storage facilities, and staging areas could make it extremely costly to project U.S. forces into a disputed [region], much less carry out operations to defeat a well-armed aggressor. Simply the threat of such enemy missile attacks might deter the U.S. and coalition partners from responding to aggression in the first instance."[14]

According to a recent study by the Defense Science Board, a regional power's development of this kind of "anti-access" capability by 2010 is certainly plausible, even given relatively severe resource constraints.[15] Iran, for example, seems far more interested in fielding anti-access systems, such as ballistic and cruise missiles, anti-ship cruise missiles, submarines, and advanced anti-ship mines, than in military systems such as the tanks and combat aircraft that proved largely ineffective for the Iraqis during the Gulf War.[16] Indeed, what Third World regime today is looking to create its own version of the Republican Guard? A major power like China may not choose to increase its military leverage in East Asia by aping the U.S. Navy's affinity for carrier battle groups and the U.S. Air Force's emphasis on manned tactical combat aircraft. Rather, Beijing might follow an asymmetric competitive path, developing an ability to isolate Taiwan through long-range blockade forces composed of precision-guided ballistic and cruise missiles, and close-range blockade forces centered around submarines and advanced anti-ship mines.[17]

These types of forces, employed as described, could hold Taiwan's major ports and airfields at risk, posing a very different kind of blockade from that imposed, for example, on Iraq during the Gulf War. As one retired Indian general observed, the issue of access to forward bases is "by far the trickiest part of the American operational problem. This is the proverbial 'Achilles heel.' India needs to study the vulnerabilities and . . . develop plans and execute operations to degrade these facilities in the run up to and after commencement of hostilities. Scope exists for low-cost options to significantly reduce the combat potential of forces operating from these [forward base] facilities."[18]

Anti-access forces will almost certainly benefit from commercial space-based systems capable of providing imagery, communications, and position location. In 1996, commercial investment in space exceeded military investment for the first time, and the trend is almost certain to continue in the coming years. Over the next decade, between twelve hundred and fifteen hundred commercial satellite launches are planned.[19] This will increase the number of commercial satellites in orbit by an order of magnitude. States seeking to boost their anti-access forces will tap into the growing number of countries and multinational consortia operating satellite constellations that are willing to sell their services to anyone able to pay for them. The U.S. military, which anticipates employing commercial satellites for well over half of its space-based communications, also will be a principal customer of these space consortia, which include firms such as Globalstar, Iridium, and Teledesic.[20]

The economic value of space assets will also grow. Associated investment in space will reach roughly $500 billion for the period 1996–2000, and annual growth rates will approach 20 percent.[21] Thus, by the end of the next decade, the U.S. military will likely be confronted with the responsibility for protecting sizable economic assets in space (some of which will also support military functions) as well as its own space platforms. It will also have the task of denying an enemy the use of space for military purposes during periods of crisis and war.[22]

The new challenges facing the U.S. military—establishing information superiority, defeating anti-access capabilities, and establishing control of space—will be formidable. But they should not come as a surprise. Capabilities such as long-range precision strikes and the use of space to support terrestrial military operations are not monopolies that have been awarded to the U.S. military in perpetuity. Indeed, previous periods of military revolution have found a technological leader's advantage to be fleeting.[23]

Nor are these the only major new challenges that will likely appear over the next decade or two. Other relatively new challenges may emerge out of political and economic imperatives or from demographic trends. For example, the United States and its NATO allies have recently moved to admit three central European nations—Poland, the Czech Republic, and Hungary—with the possibility of more new eastern members to follow. This has pushed NATO's borders and military commitments farther east and farther inland. The Pentagon, which now focuses principally on developing forces for conflicts in the world's littoral regions, may, early in the next century, find itself having to project military power far inland against an opponent with an anti-access capability.

This condition may also obtain as a consequence of an emerging oil rush to tap the enormous oil reserves of Central Asia, a region that is remote from the world's littoral and politically unstable as well. The United States has demonstrated its willingness to wage war, if necessary, to preserve its access to oil. Consequently, if this region emerges as a major supplier of oil, the U.S. military may also be required to project power into Central Asia. Not only would such operations be remote from the littoral (thereby greatly limiting the ability of maritime forces to support such operations), they would also suffer from the absence of the relatively extensive forward-basing structure that the United States has established in Europe, the Far East and, to a lesser extent, the Persian Gulf.

Another emerging challenge for the U.S. military is exercising control over urban areas as a mission in peacekeeping operations, and evicting enemy forces from urban areas. Simply put, more and more of the world population resides in urban areas. The trend toward urbanization is particularly pronounced in Third World states, where the U.S. military also sees significant potential for engaging in major theater wars (MTWs).

In future conflicts, be they MTWs or peacekeeping operations, the U.S. military may find itself confronted with the "eviction" problem that faced the German Army at Stalingrad in 1942, U.S. forces in Hue in 1968, and the Israeli Army in Beirut in 1982, or possibly the "control" problem that recently confronted U.S. forces in Port-au-Prince and Mogadishu, and which British forces face in Belfast and Russian forces encountered in Grozny. The Marine Corps commandant, Gen. Charles Krulak, recently observed, "If the regional players (state actors and nonstate actors alike) become embroiled in crises, we will likely find urbanized terrain our future battlescape."[24]

Urban warfare is substantially unique from other forms of land combat, requiring drastically different operational concepts and force structures than does warfare in open terrain.[25] Urban warfare also tends to be manpower intensive and typically dilutes the effectiveness of advanced military systems. Both of these characteristics work against the U.S. military's preference to minimize the risk of casualties and to emphasize its comparative advantage in sophisticated military equipment.

Uninvited Guests

In developing a transformation strategy, the U.S. military will also need to consider some unwelcome, uninvited guests in the form of weapons of mass destruction and unconventional warfare, which may well become interrelated problems over the next decade or two.

While earlier military revolutions typically displaced many of the central forms of military power that preceded them (for example, cannons making castles obsolete and carriers supplanting battleships), the emerging military revolution will not likely produce the same kind of result with respect to nuclear weapons. Nuclear weapons, and other weapons of mass destruction (WMD) — chemical and biological — are almost certain to cast a long shadow over the emerging military regime. These weapons may, in fact, represent a key element in a regional power's anti-access capability.

At the other end of the conflict spectrum, unconventional warfare may no longer be synonymous with low-intensity, or low-technology, conflict. Ever greater destructive power, especially in the form of chemical and biological weapons, seems likely to be available to small groups involved in terrorism, subversion, insurgency, and ethnic conflict. Moreover, the information revolution—represented by fax broadcasts, cellular phones, the Internet, and the global positioning system—promises to enhance such groups' effectiveness by improving dramatically their ability to coordinate their activities and to influence the media and the public directly.[26]

The United States will likely be confronted with the growing challenge of defending against nontraditional homeland attacks by chemical and biological WMD. The use of sarin gas on the Tokyo subway system in 1995 and the confiscation of biotoxins in the possession of criminal elements within the United States indicate that the barriers to acquiring these weapons are eroding rapidly.[27] The ability of small groups to execute these kinds of attacks may make them instruments of both terrorism and state conflict. Regional rogue states might view the threat of WMD attacks by nontraditional means as both a deterrent to future Desert Storm–like U.S. air campaigns on their homeland, or perhaps as a means of executing covert strikes against the U.S. homeland that leave no means of identifying the perpetrator. Finally, as the United States continues its shift from an industrial-based economy to the world's first information-based economy, it also may be confronted with the challenge of defending against electronic attacks on its economic and social infrastructure.

The QDR: Talking the Talk

The QDR, which was released in May, 1997, represents an improvement over its predecessor, the so-called Bottom-Up Review (BUR), which was completed in September, 1993. However, it also suffers from major shortcomings.[28] Despite its declarations to the contrary, the QDR actually places the U.S. defense program's principal emphasis on meeting near-term requirements, such as MTWs and smaller-scale contingencies.

To its credit, the QDR acknowledges that the U.S. military will likely face very different long-term challenges from what it does today. The QDR also subscribes to the contention that, for the U.S. military to "meet the demands of a dangerous world . . . throughout the period from 1997 to 2015," it must not only "meet our requirements . . . in the near term, [but] *at the same time* we must transform U.S. combat capabilities and support structures to be able to shape and respond effectively in the face of future challenges."[29]

Yet the resulting QDR program differs little in form from that of the 1993

BUR, which offered a smaller but similar defense program to that established by the Bush administration's 1991 Base Force, which was formulated before the Soviet Union passed into history. The QDR's recommended changes in force structure and modernization programs are incremental. They appear to be driven less by the strategic imperative to effect a transformation of the American military than by a fiscal imperative to reduce an overly ambitious Bottom-Up Review that could not be sustained by the resources projected to be made available to the Defense Department.

This view is seconded by the National Defense Panel (NDP), an independent group mandated by the same congressional legislation that established the QDR to evaluate the report's results. The NDP concluded that the QDR suffers from "insufficient connectivity between the [call for a transformation] strategy on the one hand, and force structure, operational requirements, and procurement decisions on the other."[30]

To be sure, the QDR emphasizes exploiting this revolution in military affairs (RMA) as a means for helping the U.S. military prepare to meet the very different challenges of the future.[31] However, it is difficult to identify the QDR's strategy for doing so. While the military services are independently (and unevenly) engaged in some very interesting initiatives to develop a better understanding of the post-RMA military regime's opportunities and challenges, and to identify the systems, operational concepts, and organizational changes that will be required if the U.S. military is to sustain its competitive advantages, one strains in vain to find a "guiding hand" at work fashioning an overall transformation strategy.[32]

Tight Shoes: The Long-Term Budget Challenge

The QDR should be given credit for its efforts to bring the defense program into balance with the resources projected to be available for sustaining it. The report clearly recognizes that the migration of funding out of modernization programs and into operations and support (O&S) accounts has become both a clear trend and a potential serious long-term problem.[33]

However, the QDR offers what will likely prove only a temporary fix to this problem. The reason is that, relative to the BUR, the QDR expands the range of challenges for which U.S. forces must prepare. It does so, however, with no corresponding increase in resources, no apparent increase in risk, and no elaboration of priorities. This happy state of affairs (static budgets and increased commitments, with no corresponding increase in risk) could be effected if the Pentagon were either to field far more effective forces (for example, by vigorously exploiting the emerging military revolution) or become far more efficient in its management of existing resources. Yet neither condition seems likely to obtain.

As with previous defense plans, the QDR assumes that major efficiency savings will be realized in the future, allowing the Defense Department to avoid more tough choices today (for example, with respect to force structure and modernization cuts).[34] Moreover, although much is made of exploiting the military revolution, no transformation wedges have been programmed into the budget to facilitate it. Vigorous experimentation and innovation characterize periods of military revolution. As new systems, operational concepts, and military formations are identified, funding will be needed to transform the existing force. Not only is the QDR unclear as to where this funding will come from, it also risks another episode of O&S migration from the research and development, test and evaluation, and procurement accounts by failing to explicitly decrease near-term commitments (for example, the two-MTW posture, forward presence levels, and peacekeeping operations tempo) — that is to say, by failing to accept increased near-term risk.

Over the long-term, the QDR's recommended cuts in force structure and modernization plans, if coupled with its proposed two new rounds of base closures, could yield annual savings of $7–8 billion. However, achieving these savings will be difficult given Congress's reluctance to support some of these measures, including further base closures and reductions in the National Guard. In any case, such savings would not be sufficient to eliminate the gap between the cost of the Defense Department's long-term plans and projected funding levels, which likely amounts to some $25 billion a year over the long run. Given the QDR's emphasis on near-term challenges, such as the two MTW capability and engagement in smaller-scale contingencies, budget shortfalls could crowd out investment in preparing for future challenges, further hobbling efforts to effect a transformation of the American military.

Military Transformation: Why Now?

Given the magnitude of the transformation involved, the natural tendency of senior defense officials to worry about today's problems, and what seems likely to be substantial annual shortfalls between the QDR defense program and the resources available to sustain it, the temptation to defer the development and execution of a transformation strategy is likely to remain strong. Yielding to such a temptation, however, would be a grievous error, for the reasons elaborated upon below.

Military transformations typically take a considerable amount of time, at least a decade and often closer to a score of years, to play out. Indeed, military systems that today are given priority for development and fielding often take ten years or more to reach forces in the field. Considerable additional time is required to determine how best to employ new military systems and to make the appropriate force structure adjustments.

Periods of military revolution also are characterized by an increased risk of strategic surprise, such as that which occurred with submarine warfare early in this century. Such a surprise might occur again with the onset of anti-access capabilities and competition in space. Given these considerations, senior Defense Department leaders must begin now to develop and execute a transformation strategy if the U.S. armed forces are to be prepared for the very different kinds of challenges they may confront over the long term.

Moreover, as noted above, military revolutions typically find the effectiveness of certain military systems in rapid decline. The displacement of the horse cavalry by mechanized forces is but one example. However, it is far from clear in advance which military systems, operational concepts, or new force structures will prove effective, and which will not. Put another way, not only should a transformation strategy be initiated soon, it should take into account the uncertainty of military technology. But how?

For a start, the military services will have to tap into rapidly advancing technologies to develop new military systems that can be applied within the framework of new operational concepts (for example, the long-range precision strike capability), and executed by new kinds of military organizations. It is this combination of technology, emerging military systems, new operational concepts, and force restructuring that often produces the discontinuous leap in military effectiveness characteristic of military revolutions. Greater emphasis should be placed on experimenting with a variety of military systems, operational concepts, and force structures, with the goal of identifying those that are capable of solving emerging strategic and operational problems, or exploiting opportunities, and of eliminating those that are not.

The result would provide the Defense Department with strategic options on a range of military capabilities. These options could be retained to dissuade prospective competitors from resuming a high level of military competition. In the event dissuasion or deterrence fails, these options could be exercised to support U.S. forces' efforts to prevail in war. Furthermore, the creation of strategic options does not necessarily involve a massive increase in defense budgets. Recall, for example, that the U.S. military developed the foundation for strategic aerial bombardment, the carrier navy, modern amphibious warfare, and mechanized air-land operations during the relatively lean budget years of the 1920s and 1930s. What it does imply is a different set of budget priorities, and a different apportioning of security risk.[35]

While the defense budget need not be a major barrier to transformation, such barriers can appear in the form of budget politics, old ways of doing business, and misplaced notions of efficiency. Supporting experimentation and innovation in a period of great change and uncertainty implies a heightened tolerance of honest failure. There should be some wildcatting involved in trying to identify the solutions to new military problems and opportunities. By contrast, if a "zero defects" approach to transformation is adopted, the result will likely be a smaller but similar U.S. military, as strong incentives will exist to deviate as little as possible from what has proven to be effective in today's military. In effect, the desire for efficiency may well crowd out the innovation that will enable the transformation to a far more *effective* military.

In some instances, effecting a military transformation will mean greater competition among the military services, not less. Congress and many military reformers have—in many cases, quite rightly—decried the amount of overlap and redundancy that exists among the four military services. However, competition among the services can also assist in determining how best to exploit new capabilities or how to solve emerging challenges. This kind of competition should be encouraged. Allocating a new mission to one military service runs the risk of falling into the trap of false efficiencies. In the case of the anti-access challenge, for example, it is not yet clear whether the solution is to be found in air force long-range precision strikes; strikes from a navy task force composed of "distributed" capital ships (for example, carriers and arsenal ships or Trident "stealth battleships" fitted with hundreds of vertical launch systems for long-range PGMs, all linked by an expanded version of the navy's Cooperative Engagement Capability battle-management network, and marine "infestation" forces); army forces employing long-range missiles and armed unmanned aerial vehicles (UAVs); a combination of these capabilities; or perhaps something quite different.[36]

America's military leaders seem divided as to how best to proceed. Some see a future that is indeed very different from today, one that will require major changes in the U.S. armed forces. Yet for many there is also the temptation to emphasize today's threats and challenges, even if they seem small relative to those encountered during the Cold War, or those that might be confronted over the longer term. This is natural; no commander wants something to go wrong on his watch. There is also a fear among some senior military officials that if they volunteer to accept increased risk in the near term (say, by reducing the size of their force structure or by adopting a staggered or tiered readiness posture) while the danger to U.S. security is relatively low, they risk having the funds thus saved for transformation siphoned off to pay for other priorities.[37] This "volunteer's dilemma" thus serves as a strong incentive for the military services to support the QDR defense program, even if it seems increasingly inappropriate for the future.

Conclusion

The United States military today has a commanding advantage in military capability. But in a period of great geopolitical and military technological change and uncertainty, it is far from clear that this advantage will be sustained over the long term. If, as seems likely, we are in the early stages of a military revolution, it will yield both new challenges and new opportunities for the U.S. military. These will ultimately require some major changes in existing operational concepts, and perhaps the emergence of altogether new operational concepts—such as information superiority, long-range precision strikes, and space control.

The U.S. military will almost certainly have to undertake a major transformation if it is to meet emerging challenges and exploit new opportunities in a way that will preserve its current relative advantages and support what should be the principal U.S. national security objective: ensuring that the next century is not scarred by the global conflicts and cold wars that have characterized the past hundred years. Finally, because military transformation will likely require a decade or more to complete, it is important that the Defense Department develop a transformation strategy that can be initiated in the near future.

Notes

1. William S. Cohen, *Report of the Quadrennial Defense Review* (Washington, D.C.: Department of Defense, May, 1997), pp. 12–13. (Hereafter cited as *QDR*.) The *QDR* goes so far as to declare: "If the United States were to forego its ability to defeat aggression in more than one theater at a time, our standing as a global power, as the security partner of choice, and as the leader of the international community would be called into question."
2. The Maginot Line was the subject of nearly a decade of study by the French military, and its major fortifications took five years to construct. Its construction led to an unwillingness on the part of the French government and military to consider how the enemy or the French military might conduct military operations differently from those that dominated the western front in World War I. As General Maurin, France's minister of war, declared, "How can anyone believe that we are still thinking of the offensive when we have spent so many billions to establish a fortified frontier!" William L. Shirer, *The Collapse of the Third Republic* (New York: Simon and Schuster, 1969), pp. 164–68.
3. See Don M. Snider, "The Coming Defense Train Wreck . . . ," *The Washington Quarterly* (winter, 1996): 89–101; Don M. Snider, Daniel Goure, and Stephen Cambone, *Defense in the Late 1990s: Avoiding the Train Wreck* (Washington, CSIS, 1995); Andrew F. Krepinevich, Jr., " . . . And What to Do About It," *The Wash-*

ington Quarterly (winter, 1996): 106–109; and Andrew F. Krepinevich, Jr., "Train Wreck Coming?" *National Review,* July 31, 1995.

4. See, for example, Paul Kennedy, *The Rise and Fall of the Great Powers* (New York: Random House, 1987); Henry Kissinger, *Diplomacy* (New York: Simon and Schuster, 1994); and Donald Kagan, *On the Origins of War* (Garden City, N.Y.: Doubleday, 1995).

5. This phenomenon has been referred to by various names, including the "military-technical revolution" (MTR) and "revolution in military affairs" (RMA). The latter term is currently in vogue in the Department of Defense. The author uses the term "military revolution," which is associated with scholarly efforts to examine the historical incidents and consequences of these phenomena. See, for example, Geoffrey Parker, *The Military Revolution: Military innovation and the rise of the West, 1500–1800* (Cambridge: Cambridge University Press, 1988).

6. Andrew F. Krepinevich, "The Military-Technical Revolution: A Preliminary Assessment" (Unpublished Paper, Office of Net Assessment, Office of the Secretary of Defense, July, 1993); Andrew F. Krepinevich, "Cavalry to Computer: The Pattern of Military Revolutions," *The National Interest* (fall, 1994); Andrew F. Krepinevich, "Keeping Pace With the Military-Technological Revolution," *Issues in Science and Technology* (summer, 1994); and Michael G. Vickers, *Warfare in 2020: A Primer* (Washington, D.C.: Center for Strategic and Budgetary Assessments, 1996).

7. See, for example, Geoffrey Till, "Adopting the Aircraft Carrier: The British, American, and Japanese Case Studies," in *Military Innovation in the Interwar Period,* ed. Williamson Murray and Allan R. Millett (Cambridge: Cambridge University Press, 1996), pp. 191–226; Williamson Murray, "Strategic Bombing: The British, American, and German Experiences," in *Military Innovation,* ed. Murray and Millett, pp. 96–143; Richard R. Muller, "Close Air Support: The German, British, and American Experiences," in *Military Innovation,* ed. Murray and Millett, pp. 144–90; and Williamson Murray, "Armored Warfare: The British, French, and German Experiences, in *Military Innovation,* ed. Murray and Millett, pp. 6–49.

8. U.S. Congress, PL 104-201, div. A, title IX, subtitle B (sec. 921–26), "Military Force Structure Review Act of 1996," Sept. 23, 1996.

9. Cohen, *QDR,* p. 68.

10. Gen. John M. Shalikashvili, *Joint Vision 2010* (Washington, D.C.: Department of Defense, 1996), p. 8.

11. Ibid.

12. Ibid., p. 4. Author's emphasis.

13. Ibid., pp. 10–11. Author's emphasis.

14. Bill Gertz, "The Air Force and Missile Defense," *Air Force,* Feb., 1996, p. 72.

15. See, for example, Dr. John S. Foster, *Defense Science Board Summer Study: Investments for 21st Century Military Superiority,* Briefing Papers, Nov., 1995. Enemy mobile missile forces also would be supplemented by use of commercial satellites for a range of military activities, to include reconnaissance, targeting, and positioning. The enemy might also invest in weapons of mass destruction and, if in a littoral region, substantial quantities of anti-ship mines and cruise missiles, and perhaps some submarines as well.

16. Andrew F. Krepinevich, Jr., *A New Navy for A New Era* (Washington, D.C.: Center for Strategic and Budgetary Assessments, 1996), pp. 7–13.

17. See, for example, Andrew F. Krepinevich, Jr., *The Conflict Environment of 2016: A Scenario-Based Approach* (Washington, D.C.: Center for Strategic and Budgetary Assessments, 1996), pp. 1–10.

18. Brigadier V. K. Nair, *War in the Gulf: Lessons for the Third World* (New Delhi: Lancer International, n.d.), p. 230.

19. U.S. Commander in Chief, Space, "Briefing to the National Defense Panel," Aug. 18, 1997.

20. Gen. Thomas Moorman, interview by author, Nov. 14, 1996.

21. Gen. Howell M. Estes III, interview by author, Aug. 18, 1997.

22. Department of Defense, *Space Program: An Executive Overview for FY 1998–2003* (Washington, D.C.: Department of Defense, Mar., 1997), p. 4. The four space missions are: space support, force enhancement, space control, and force application.

23. For example, the Royal Navy's monopoly on dreadnought battleships lasted but a few years, as did U.S. dominance of the nuclear weapon regime and Germany's mastery of mechanized air-land operations (i.e., *blitzkrieg*). Other military transformations, such as the rise of naval (carrier) aviation and the development of strategic aerial bombardment and integrated air defenses were effected concurrently by multiple powers.

24. Gen. Charles C. Krulak, "A Matter of Strategic Focus," *Air Power Journal* (spring, 1997): 60.

25. Ibid., 60–61. The marines are undertaking field experiments dubbed "Urban Warrior" with an eye toward developing capabilities to meet the growing challenge of urban control and eviction operations.

26. See Michael G. Vickers and Robert Martinage, *The Military Revolution and Intrastate Conflict* (Washington, D.C.: Center for Strategic and Budgetary Assessments, 1997), pp. 10–13, 18–24.

27. Richard Danzig and Pamela Berkowsky, "Why Should We Be Concerned About Biological Warfare?" *The Journal of the American Medical Association* (Aug. 6, 1997); Memorandum. Stephen Rosen to Richard Danzig, Subject: Ricin-A, Mar. 21, 1994; and Raymond A. Zilinskas, Iraq's Biological Weapons: The Past As Future?" *The Journal of the American Medical Association* (Aug. 6, 1997).

28. For a more detailed assessment of the QDR, see Michael G. Vickers, "The Quadrennial Defense Review: A Strategic Assessment," *Center for Strategic and Budgetary Assessments,* June 18, 1997.

29. Cohen, *QDR,* pp. 13–14. Emphasis in the original.

30. National Defense Panel, letter to Secretary of Defense William S. Cohen, *Assessment of the May 1997 Quadrennial Defense Review,* May 15, 1997, p. 2.

31. Cohen, *QDR,* pp. 14–15.

32. The army is engaged in several transformation initiatives, to include a series of "Force XXI" exercises and studies and war-gaming on "The Army After Next." See Department of the Army, *Knowledge and Speed: The Annual Report on the Army after Next Project of the Chief of Staff of the Army* (n.p., July, 1997); and Gen. William W. Hartzog and Lt. Col. (Ret.) Keith E. Bonn, *Back to the Future* (n.p., n.d.). The air force has fashioned its own transformation plan that will see it become, over time, a "space and air force." See Gen. Ronald R. Fogleman and Sheila E. Widnall, *Global Engagement: A Vision for the 21st Century Air Force* (Washington, D.C.: U.S. Air Force, 1996). The navy is conducting, and has planned, a series of fleet exercises to determine future force structures and opera-

tional concepts. See Vadm. Arthur K. Cebrowski, *Advanced Warfighting Experiments,* Briefing Papers, Aug. 25, 1997. Finally, the Marine Corps is engaged in a series of initiatives under the rubric "Sea Dragon," which comprises staff studies, war games, and field exercises such as "Hunter Warrior" and "Urban Warrior," all designed to prepare it for future challenges. See Marine Corps Warfighting Laboratory, *Sea Dragon: Forward From the Sea,* Briefing Papers, Aug. 26, 1997.

33. Cohen, *QDR,* pp. 19–21, 59–61.

34. Ibid., pp. 53–57, 62–63.

35. For a more detailed discussion of the elements relating to transformation, see Andrew F. Krepinevich, Jr., *Restructuring for A New Era: Framing the Roles and Missions Debate* (Washington, D.C.: Defense Budget Project, 1995), pp. 53–67.

36. A notional operational concept for defeating the anti-access challenge can be found in Krepinevich, *New Navy,* pp. 27–34.

37. See, for example, Adm. J. G. Prout III, Memorandum for the Commander in Chief, U.S. Pacific Fleet, *CNO Comments at Surface Warfare Flag Officer Conference,* Sept. 23, 1994.

Chapter 11

Assessing Theories of Future Warfare

Stephen Biddle

IN LESS THAN SIX YEARS, orthodox opinion on the future of warfare has been transformed. As recently as 1991, most observers still assumed that armored breakthrough battles would determine the results of major wars, with air and missile forces playing mostly a supporting role.[1] Today, this traditional view has almost disappeared. The end of the Cold War played a part in this, but the proximate cause was the 1991 Persian Gulf conflict. The performance of a new generation of high-tech weapons in this war gave rise to a widespread assumption that we now face a revolution in military affairs (RMA). This has led some to conclude that the United States, thanks to its technological leadership and the Soviet Union's demise, now enjoys an unassailable military advantage for the foreseeable future.[2] Others say that American supremacy in mechanized warfare will be the end of such wars, with opponents turning to terrorism, low-intensity conflict, or the use of weapons of mass destruction in the face of such overpowering U.S. strength.[3]

However, many argue that the revolution is only beginning—its realization, they hold, will require sweeping changes in American defense policy. Without these changes, the United States could well lose its current advantage in major warfare. The RMA thus holds both promise and danger, they argue. It will make possible a new form of warfare in which long-range precision air and missile strikes will dominate the fighting, where ground forces will be reduced mostly to the role of scouts, and where the struggle for information supremacy will replace the breakthrough battle as the decisive issue for success. It may even mean that the collection and destruction of information per se will become the sole focus of hostilities, leading to "strategic information warfare" where no physical objects are destroyed. Such radically new forms of warfare could offer enormous military power to states that master them. America's lead in key technologies gives it a head start in the race to do so, but no more than a head start. Ultimate success, it is argued, will require sweeping organizational and doctrinal changes to realize the new technology's potential—yet the complacency that often accompanies leadership, combined with the military's inherent conservatism, could easily block such radical change. Other powers who see the opportunity and accept radical change sooner or more completely could thus leapfrog the United States, leaving it to follow nineteenth century France and Imperial Britain into military decline.[4]

These views have become highly influential among U.S. defense planners.[5] Each, however, has serious analytical shortcomings.

The first view—that U.S. weapon technology now affords it dominance in high-intensity warfare—rests on a misunderstanding of the Gulf War. I have argued elsewhere that new technology was not sufficient to account for the war's unprecedentedly low U.S. casualty rate.[6] In 1991, technology enabled the United States to punish Iraqi errors with radical severity, but the same technology would have been far less effective against opponents able to operate competently. In the past, Americans have fought enemies much more skilled than the Iraqis; only if this never happens again can we assume a pattern of 1991-like U.S. supremacy in future conflicts.

My purpose here is to assess the second view: that 1991 was merely a harbinger of an RMA that will come only to states that adopt sweeping changes in military doctrine and organization.[7] I believe that this view is also based on much weaker evidence than commonly supposed. By contrast, a non-RMA projection calling for a future of only incremental change is more consistent with the available facts.

Continuous technological improvement since at least 1900 has made war progressively more complex. Military forces unable to cope with this ever-increasing complexity have been fully exposed to the increasing lethality of modern weapons, and have suffered increasingly severe consequences. Others, however, have found ways to manage this complexity, and have been much less exposed to the growing power of their opponents' weapons. The result has been a progressively widening gap in the real military power of organizations that can and those that cannot cope with complexity, but little change in the outcomes of wars fought between equally skilled opponents—and no revolutionary discontinuities in the nature of warfare itself.[8]

In this process of continuous change, radical innovation of the sort advocated by most RMA theorists has neither been necessary nor even conducive to success. Even in eras of unusual technological change, as many RMA advocates describe the 1920s and 30s, the most radically innovative military forces have often been among the least successful on the battlefield. In fact, the pace or speed of innovation has been mostly beside the point—the ability to cope with an increasingly complex battlefield has been a more important determinant of success and failure, and incrementalism can be perfectly consistent with this. Nor is this likely to change any time soon. The long-standing relationship between technology, complexity, and battlefield success has not been significantly altered by recent developments, and is unlikely to be changed by technologies now on the drawing boards.

This new projection has very different implications for policy and scholarship than the RMA view. Advocates of the coming-RMA thesis have argued for radical shifts in service roles and missions, with a major reduction in ground and surface naval forces and a major increase in reliance on air and missile forces. They hold that the demands of the new environment imply major changes in defense spending, such as protecting modernization at the expense of readiness and force structure, or shifting modernization away from "sunset systems" like tanks or aircraft carriers, and toward "sunrise systems" like deep precision strike weapons or information infrastructure. They further contend that an RMA requires radical changes in the organization and doctrine of the current U.S. military. Among the changes proposed are replacing divisions, corps, and air wings with wholly new entities of less hierarchical, more interconnected nature, and replacing current, close-combat-oriented operational concepts with new ideas less dependent on closing with the enemy or occupying territory.[9]

For scholars, the RMA thesis holds important implications for realist theories of great power emergence, offense-defense theory, and the salience of research on the sources of organizational innovation. Many RMA advocates, for example, hold that new technology will permit faster transitions to great power status while systematically altering the sources of the power that underwrites that status.[10] For offense-defense theory, RMA advocates often argue that postrevolutionary warfare will shift the offense-defense balance toward offense and provide stronger incentives for preemption.[11] If the coming-RMA thesis is correct, the key distinction between victory and defeat will be a state's ability to induce conservative military forces to accept an extranormal pace and depth of change. And if that is the case, understanding the determinants of organizational change is of paramount importance.[12]

By contrast, if there is no coming revolution, then radical changes in service roles and missions, defense spending, military organization, or doctrine would be unnecessary and probably counterproductive. The scholarly implications for international system structure and offense-defense theory would likewise be very different, and the key issue for innovation theory would be to identify the proper content of incremental change, rather than to find ways to increase the scope or speed of change per se.

To substantiate these conclusions, I first review the main arguments for a coming RMA. I then describe my alternative projection. As this alternative theory has not previously been fully described, I provide a detailed deductive causal mechanism to show why it takes the form it does, to establish a degree of prima facie plausibility, and to facilitate the empirical work to come.[13] While this detailed deductive argument is an important element of the analysis, readers interested mainly in the competing theories' relative empirical performance may wish to skip to the following section, where I infer testable propositions from each school, compare these with the available evidence, and determine which is most consistent with the observed facts. Finally, I sketch the implications of the results for policy and scholarship.

Arguments for Military Revolution

So how does the coming-RMA literature arrive at the conclusion that the times demand radical change? Two main arguments can be identified: the economic determinist thesis, and the contingent innovation view.[14]

The Economic Determinist School
Economic determinists see military revolution as the inevitable outgrowth of basic changes in the mode of civil economic production. The industrial revolution, for example, is often cited as the driving force behind a mid–nineteenth century transformation of warfare induced by the substitution of machine for animal power, the introduction of mass production to war, and associated changes in the balance of power among states that varied in their rate of industrialization. Similarly, the agricultural revolution brought great increases in human population, more complex social organization, and changing sources of wealth—all of which are held to have radically altered the nature of warfare beginning about ten thousand years ago.

Economic transformations of this magnitude are very rare, however. Economies are constantly changing, but few such changes produce military revolutions. In fact, agriculture and industrialization are the *only* two historical examples that appear in this literature. This is because the scale of the underlying economic change needed to transform war as well as business is held to be truly profound. Only radical expansions in the productive potential of an economy (a basic shift in the mode of production, or as Alvin and Heidi Toffler refer to it, "the system for creating wealth") are enough to spur such sweeping change. Mere shifts in the composition of inputs or outputs are insufficient, as are changes limited to the style of work performed or the organization of businesses per se. Only when these things induce major expansions in real output do the results spur an RMA, and such expansions are very unusual things.[15]

For this economic determinist school, the crucial evidence for a coming RMA is the civil information revolution now widely held to be transforming the U.S. economy. New microelectronics, data processing, and communications technologies, they argue, are creating a "third wave" society in which information processing replaces mass manufacturing as the main source of wealth and the chief engine of economic growth. In this new third wave economy, services will predominate; large, hierarchically organized corporations will be replaced by smaller, more numerous, more agile competitors. Marketing, broadcasting, and manufacturing will all be "de-massified," with small scale, custom-tailored products replacing large production runs intended for mass consumption. Such a transformation is held to rival that of the industrial or agricultural revolutions in its economic impact—and since shifts of this magnitude have induced military transformation in the past, we should thus expect a comparable military revolution now.[16]

The Contingent Innovation School

The second school holds that revolutions result not from broad economic forces but from the actions of specific innovators who see novel possibilities in new technologies and create new organizations and military doctrines to exploit them. The defining example of this process is often held to be the German development of blitzkrieg prior to World War II. The tank, the airplane, and the radio, proponents of this view argue, were available to all the great powers, but only the Germans saw their true potential and accepted the radical changes in military practice needed to make the most of them. By contrast, the French and British bought the new equipment in quantity but, failing to perceive its potential, merely grafted the new technologies onto traditional doctrines and organizations. German innovation thus created a military revolution in the form of a powerful new style of war only they possessed. This enabled them to destroy the less innovative French army and British Expeditionary Force in less than two months in 1940, knocking France out of the war and leaving Germany the preeminent power on the continent.[17]

The critical issue here is the scale and pace of innovation. All organizations change over time, including both the agents and the victims of military revolutions.[18] Change per se is not enough—the literature emphasizes that revolutions demand innovation of extraordinary scope and speed. Incrementalist, business-as-usual updating of a traditional concept, or so the argument goes, is unacceptable in a time of revolutionary transition:

> What is revolutionary . . . is *the recognition, over some relatively brief period, that the character of conflict has changed dramatically, requiring equally dramatic—if not radical—changes in military doctrine and organizations.* . . . When this occurs, military organizations will either move to adapt rapidly or find themselves at a severe competitive disadvantage.[19] (Emphasis in original.)

> Preparing U.S. forces to fight in the twenty-first century will require a more radical approach to doctrine than traditional service methods. . . . The U.S. military is scarcely realizing the full potential of revolutionary weapons with mere modifications of years-old doctrines for conventional warfare on land, sea, and in the air.[20]

This view is reinforced by the literature's emphasis on the dangers of conservatism. Among this school's more common themes are the need to induce hidebound organizations to accept changes they would otherwise reject, and the concern that merely grafting new technologies onto old doctrines must be avoided.[21] In a time of revolutionary transition, incrementalism born of inertia is the central danger—RMAs demand a radical boldness that we could not get, and probably would not want, in more ordinary times.

An Alternative Theory: Essential Continuity

A future of revolutionary change is not the only possibility. At least one incrementalist alternative can be identified.[22] This alternative implies that twenty-first century warfare will be mainly a continuation of a century-long increase in the importance of skill in managing complexity—not a revolutionary break with the past.

What follows is a deductive argument for this "essential continuity" thesis. I will first argue that the effectiveness of military technology depends heavily on human behavior, and especially, on the countermeasures adopted by its targets to reduce their exposure. To illustrate this point, I will describe the responses of twentieth century armies to increases in the range and speed of major weapon systems.[23] Second, while effective countermeasures are usually available, they are often very difficult to implement properly. As technology has become more sophisticated, proper implementation of such counters has grown increasingly complex. Third, military organizations vary widely in their ability to cope with the growing complexity of the measures needed to limit exposure to increasingly potent weapons. Some have fared reasonably well, but others have failed systematically. Fourth, the result of this has been a widening gap in the real military capability of organizations that can and those that cannot cope with this complexity. The latter have suffered large increases in vulnerability over time as the nominal effectiveness of weapons has improved; the former have been much less exposed to changes in their enemies' nominal weapon effectiveness, and thus their vulnerability has changed only slowly even as technology has improved dramatically. Fifth, this relationship is unlikely to change fundamentally any time soon. Twentieth century weapon technology's sensitivity to behavioral variation is the result of underlying properties that have changed little even as specific weapons have changed form and increased in performance. To illustrate, I will describe two such properties: susceptibility to cover and concealment, and the problem of trade-offs in weapon design.

As this argument has not previously been developed, I discuss each of these steps in some detail. This both helps establish the argument's plausibility a priori, and facilitates later testing by providing a richer array of possible observable implications. I will later turn to a comparison of the three available theories against the relevant evidence.

The Effects of Behavior on Weapon Performance
To illustrate the general relationship between military behavior and the effectiveness of technology, I will focus on two representative changes in twentieth century technology: increasing weapon lethality, and increasing platform speed.[24]

Both speed and apparent lethality have increased dramatically since 1900, and are continuing to do so as the century ends. Figure 11.1, for example, plots maximum tank speeds for designs fielded between 1916 and 1991, and shows an average increase of about 0.5 miles per hour per year, or a more than tenfold improvement across the interval as a whole, With the increasing use of helicopters on the battlefield after the 1960s, the effective increase in the speed of the most mobile ground forces is arguably at least 50-fold since 1916. Figures 11.2 to 11.4 plot the maximum range of a representative array of twentieth century weapons. Both within and across weapon types, range has increased dramatically: from a maximum of less than a hundred meters for 200 mm armor penetration by direct-fire antitank weapons in the 1930s to more than six thousand meters by 1980; from less than ten kilometers for tube artillery in 1900 to more than 250 kilometers for missile artillery in the 1990s; and from an unrefueled combat radius of under five hundred kilo-

Tank Speed

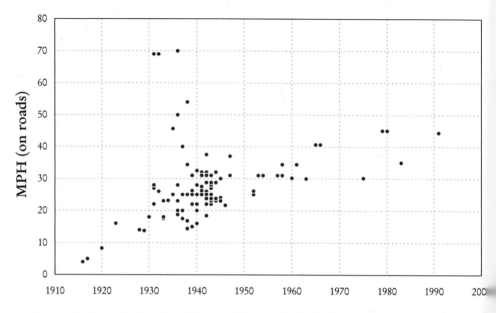

Fig. 11.1. Tank speed. Data from Kenneth Macksey, *Tank Warfare: A History of Tanks in Battle* (New York: Stein and Day, 1972), pp. 271–73; Milsom, *Russian Tanks,* pp. 20–38, 82–125, 160–81; Von Senger und Etterlin, *German Tanks of World War II,* pp. 21–28, 34–74, 194–210; and R. T. Pretty, ed., *Jane's Weapon Systems, 1985–6* (Coulsden, Surrey: Jane's, 1985).

meters for ground-attack aircraft in the 1920s to more than two thousand kilometers today.

Of course, as the nominal range of weapons has increased, so too has the weight of armor deployed to protect their targets. While the net balance between penetration and protection has fluctuated, the aggregate trend is strongly toward increased lethality over time. Figure 11.5, for example, plots a weighted mean lethal range for the armor-penetrating weapons in a U.S. armored division when fired against the tanks in a representative opposing division between 1945 and 2005.[25] This range increases from under five hundred meters in 1945 to almost seven thousand in 2005, an improvement of more than a factor of ten.

Such tremendous growth in speed and lethality creates a powerful incentive to find ways of limiting one's vulnerability to such weapons. The result has been a series of operational adaptations that have proven highly effective in limiting exposure to hostile firepower and speed—but only at the cost of increased complexity.

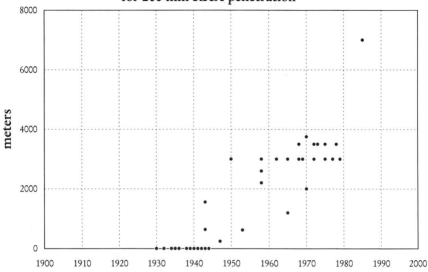

Fig. 11.2. Maximum range for 200 mm armor penetration by antitank weapons. Data from Von Senger und Etterlin, *German Tanks of World War II*, pp. 21–28, 34–74, 194–210; Ellis, *Brute Force*, table 62; Nicholas and Rossi, *U.S. Missile Data Book, 1996*; and Ogorkiewicz, *Technology of Tanks*, p. 111.

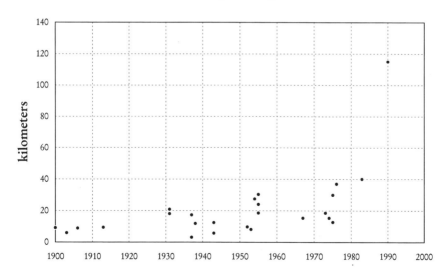

Fig. 11.3. Artillery range. Data from I. V. Hogg, *The Guns, 1914–18* (New York: Ballantine, 1971); David Isby, *Weapons and Tactics of the Soviet Army* (New York: Jane's, 1988); and Nicholas and Rossi, *U.S. Missile Data Book, 1996*.

Tactical Ground Attack Aircraft Combat Radius

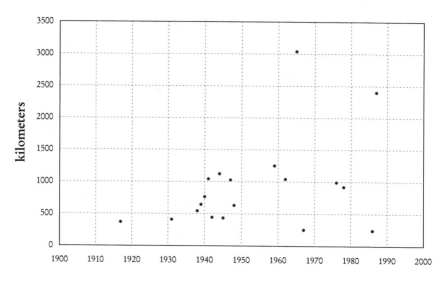

Fig. 11.4. Tactial Ground attack aircraft combat radius. Data from Gordon Swanborough and Peter Bowers, *United States Military Aircraft since 1909* (London: Putnam, 1989).

Mean Penetration Range of U.S. Heavy Antitank Systems

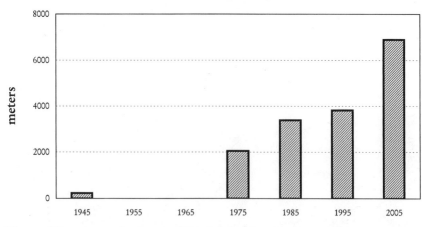

Fig. 11.5. Mean penetration range of U.S. heavy antitank systems. Data from House, *Toward Combined Arms Warfare,* p. 109; Ogorkiewicz, *Technology of Tanks,* p. 111; Nicholas and Rossi, *U.S. Missile Data Book, 1996;* Milsom, *Russian Tanks,* pp. 20–38, 82–125, 160–81; Von Senger und Etterlin, *German Tanks of World War II,* pp. 21–28, 34–74, 194–210; and Pretty, ed., *Jane's Weapon Systems.*

Exposure to hostile firepower, for example, can be limited by the coordinated use of cover, concealment, suppressive fire, dispersion, combined arms integration, and small-unit independent maneuver. The increased weapon range in figures 11.2 to 11.4 shows the physical ability to project ordnance. However, for this to be meaningful requires that targets be found, and that intervening obstacles not block the projectiles' flight to those targets. Concealment thwarts the former, whereas cover thwarts the latter.[26] In principle, both are usually available, even when the terrain is apparently flat and open. On the North German plain, for example, only about 35 percent of the ground within a thousand meters is visible, on average, from a typical weapon position.[27] Cover can thus have a major effect on weapon performance. A guided antitank missile nominally able to penetrate a tank's armor at five thousand meters is little better than an older weapon with one-fifth the range if its targets can remain under cover until closing to less than a thousand meters.

Suppressive fire can reduce an attacker's exposure by forcing hostile observers to take cover. Suppression can take many forms—from the use of tanks or machine guns in overwatch positions to drive defenders away from the best firing positions; to the use of artillery to spoil defenders' aim, obscure their vision, or dissuade them from exposing themselves to fire; or the use of deep fires to force defending artillery to cease firing and move to a new location, thus reducing its net firing rate by compelling it to spend much of its time moving rather than shooting. Such fires can greatly reduce the effectiveness of targets that they do not necessarily kill. By forcing hostile artillery to "shoot and scoot," for example, counterbattery fire can reduce its targets' net firing rate by a factor of ten or more even if it kills none of them.[28] Unhindered by suppression, a single tube-launched, optically sighted, wire-guided (TOW) missile crew can kill as many as seven targets in five minutes at ranges of up to three kilometers. If the crew is forced to take cover by suppressive fire and reposition between shots, their kill rate can be cut to one or less even if they are unharmed.[29]

Dispersion and independent small-unit maneuver enable better use of scattered cover by breaking up large formations. They also facilitate suppressive fire by enabling small units to split alternately into stationary overwatch elements and moving subunits that sprint to the next covered position then switch roles. In addition, such methods degrade the effectiveness of hostile artillery or submunition antitank weapons by reducing the number of targets in any given weapon footprint. A one-hundred-soldier infantry company advancing in a skirmish line on a 200-meter front, for example, can be wiped out by a single battalion volley from hostile artillery; dispersed over a 1,000-meter front and a 200-meter depth. However, the same unit might suffer less than 10 percent losses.[30]

Combined arms integration reduces net vulnerability by teaming together weapon types with contrasting strengths and weaknesses. Tanks, for example, offer armor protection and firepower—but suffer poor visibility (especially when buttoned up), and are easy for the enemy to see and hear. Operating alone, tanks are thus extremely vulnerable to concealed, dug-in antitank weapons. Dismounted infantry, by contrast, are much better observers, and can be much harder for the enemy to detect if advancing stealthily and making maximum use of cover and concealment—but infantry lacks armor protection and is restricted to light weapons in the attack. Operating alone, it is readily pinned down by hostile fires, enabling defending artillery to take a heavy toll on immobilized targets. When infantry and armor are combined, however, they mask one another's weaknesses. Infantry in the attack can detect concealed antitank defenses, whereas tanks can destroy hardened positions that would otherwise force the infantry to ground, enabling momentum to be maintained and thus reducing the infantry's vulnerability.[31]

COUNTERMEASURES TO HOSTILE SPEED

Like lethality, the practical speed of weapon platforms can be radically reduced by hostile counteractions. Two illustrative examples of such countermeasures are depth and reserves.

Defensive depth exploits the sharp trade-off between speed and exposure in the attack. Vehicles moving at maximum speed are extremely vulnerable.[32] Tanks, if they are to maintain the top speeds shown in figure 11.1, must drive in columns, on roads, without halting to scout out changing terrain, and without delaying for preliminary artillery barrages, calling for air strikes, clearing minefields, or dismounting infantry to deal with concealed defenders. Helicopters operating at maximum speed cannot make full use of terrain for concealment (or "nap-of-the-earth" flying), but must straighten out flight paths to avoid flying into the ground or other obstacles. Nor can they await scouting or suppressive artillery fire against suspected air defense sites, or employ evasive maneuvering to elude observed enemy fire. Should an attacker attempt to advance at such high speeds, even a handful of well-concealed defenders can take a very heavy toll. As a result, most attackers reduce their net forward speed dramatically when in the presence of the enemy. High speeds are reserved for movements out of contact (e.g., exploitation of breakthroughs or redeployments in the rear), or sprints between cover in forward areas.[33]

This enables defenders to slow an attacker's advance by distributing defensive positions in depth—prolonging the period of slow attacker movement by covering a larger area with less-dense defensive positions. These less-dense positions are typically not strong enough to halt an attack outright, but they pose enough of a threat to high-speed movement to force an attacker to slow down, buying time for defenders to assemble a stronger force by moving reserves from elsewhere on the battlefield. If the defended zone is deep enough, and sufficient reserves are withheld from forward positions, then defenders can usually halt even numerically superior attackers short of a clean breakthrough.[34] Alternatively, as deep-strike weaponry has become more effective, defenders have increasingly sought to extend the depth of the battlefield in the opposite direction—by creating an imminent threat of fire against units located far behind enemy lines.[35] In either case, the opponents' potential speed is constrained by the need to adopt protective measures to reduce vulnerability. The result can be a major reduction in hostile rates of advance: attackers in the 1970s, for example, were equipped with tanks able to reach speeds of thirty to forty kilometers per hour yet managed advance rates of less than eleven kilometers per *day* when confronted with even light opposition.[36]

Countermeasures and Complexity

Technology's nominal or proving-ground performance can thus often be dramatically reduced by evasive action on the part of its targets. Evasive action is inherently difficult to implement, however, and is becoming increasingly more so as technology advances.

To make the most of cover and concealment requires each of the hundreds to thousands of local commanders in a mass army to fashion his or her own unique plans for movement and disposition based on the vagaries of local conditions. Most terrain types offer cover, but useable dead ground (i.e., areas masked to hostile fire or observation) is often irregularly shaped, irregularly distributed, and widely varying in size. To make the most of it requires careful scouting, custom tailoring of movement orders, and individual siting of fighting positions to fit the peculiarities of a unit's immediate surroundings. Troops cannot simply be laid out in standard, textbook formations and marched toward the objective, or deployed in formulaic cookie-cutter defensive layouts.

Proper use of suppressive fire requires very tight coordination between widely separated, moving units and multiple commanding officers. To protect moving assault units, suppression must be maintained until the last possible minute, but lifted in time to allow the assault to overrun the objective without taking casualties from friendly fire. Sightings of enemy weapons must be communicated to distant supporting units, and suppressive fire redirected as intelligence is developed. As units move forward, artillery must eventually cease firing and advance to maintain coverage. If support is not to be lost in the meantime, these moves must be coordinated with both neighboring batteries and forward maneuver elements. Since the pace of an assault varies unpredictably with local terrain or unanticipated enemy action (the discovery of minefields, for example), maintaining continuous suppression thus requires a complex combination of planning, adaptation, and efficient communications between harried commanders at many different echelons.[37]

Dispersion and independent small-unit maneuver increase the number of independent decision makers in any given organization. They also demand greater initiative and tactical judgment from junior leaders, make it harder for those leaders to see and communicate with their troops, and challenge morale and combat motivation by putting more distance between soldiers, reducing the power of group reinforcement to motivate individual behavior.[38]

Combined arms tactics impose very high orders of complexity. Commanders must be knowledgeable in the respective pros and cons, conditions for effective employment, maintenance needs, training procedures, and resupply requirements of a whole range of unique (and individually very complex) weapons. Furthermore, the closer the integration is to be, the more junior is the rank of the officers that must possess this knowledge. Great care must be exercised in the field to keep weapons of such different mobility within mutual supporting distance as they move over changing terrain and encounter unexpected obstacles or hostile resistance, and to prevent fratricide (especially when combining rapid maneuver with remote firepower sources like artillery or aircraft). Finally, the troops themselves often require special training in methods for cooperative operations.[39]

Defensive depth obtained by dispersion requires heavy reliance on independent small-unit combat action, which, as noted above, places heavy demands on junior leadership and enlisted training and morale.[40] Alternatively, to obtain depth by "extending the battlefield" behind the enemy's lines poses complications of its own. Chief among these is the need for accurate, timely intelligence on the location and activities of the intended targets, and rapid communication of this intelligence to delivery systems capable of reaching such targets with appropriate weapons. To obtain targeting information in the necessary detail typically requires the integration of data from many, diverse sources. It means integrating a patchwork of partial data into an accurate picture, deducing its meaning, transmitting the results to firing units, and delivering the ordnance before the target has moved away. This is a daunting technical and managerial task.

Effective operations in the face of twentieth century weapons thus require an ability to cope with complexity. Although this has been the case since at least 1900, the magnitude of the problem has grown progressively over time.

When mean nominal weapon range was limited to 2–5 kilometers, then only frontline units needed to be covered, concealed, dispersed, and integrated. Units to their immediate rear could be massed in assembly areas and moved safely in the open. Effective ranges of 5–10 kilometers extended the zone of maximum complexity to frontline units and their immediate supporting elements. Today's ranges of 50–200 kilometers can place entire theaters at risk. While this is an important change, it is reflects only an increase in the scale and not the nature of the problem: The increase in operational complexity created by increasing firepower and speed has characterized warfare throughout the twentieth century, and in continuously increasing degree.

Variations in Organizations' Ability to Cope with Complexity
Some argue that in war, complexity is inherently inconsistent with victory, and that military forces faced with a complex operating environment will usually fail as a result.[41] In fact, some do. Others, however, have proven able to manage extremely complex campaigns without collapsing under the strain. More generally, military forces vary widely in their ability to manage complexity. While none do so perfectly, many have done so well enough to mitigate substantially their exposure to increasingly lethal weapons.

Two recent cases illustrate this point: the U.S. and Iraqi forces that engaged in the Gulf War.[42] The Iraqis made a wide variety of serious mistakes from the grand strategic to the tactical levels. The following are a few representative examples keyed to the operational issues described above. Iraqi ground commanders made poor use of cover and concealment in preparing combat vehicle fighting positions. Minefields or barriers to Coalition movement were haphazard or absent from much of the battlefield. Combined arms integration was almost wholly absent, as was suppressive fire in support of Iraqi counterattacks or artillery support of Iraqi defenders. (Iraqi artillery proved incapable either of adjusting fire to hit moving Coalition units, a difficult task, or massing fire against fixed points as Coalition units moved past them, a much easier job.) Iraqi pilots and air defense system crews were poorly trained and motivated, while ground weapon maintenance was systematically poor.[43]

The U.S. military, by contrast, while certainly not perfect, nevertheless handled an extraordinarily complicated undertaking with a high degree of professionalism and considerable skill. Daily missions were planned for thousands of aircraft requiring coordination of bomber, fighter, jamming, midair refueling, and surveillance platforms; deconfliction of flight paths; coordination of ingress points, egress routes, and time over targets; and the incorporation of changing information on target status, air defense threats, and friendly mission priorities.[44] Thousands of ground vehicles were maneuvered over hundreds of kilometers of trackless desert without significant logistical failures.[45] Individual weapon crews performed at consistently high levels in what was, for most, their first combat experience. At the Battle of 73 Easting, for example, the first three shots by the lead U.S. tank destroyed three Iraqi armored vehicles in less than ten seconds in the midst of a raging sandstorm. Overall, 182 of 215 shots fired by U.S. participants in the battle hit their targets, a performance corresponding to a hit probability of 85 percent, at ranges of up to two thousand meters, in foul weather under combat conditions.[46]

Of course, the U.S., too, made mistakes. Perhaps the most widely publicized were the incidents of friendly fire among U.S. forces and between U.S. and British troops. But, as a whole, an extremely complex campaign was handled with neither systematic collapse nor the failure of any significant number of individual organizational components, under conditions that many had predicted would overwhelm a military force equipped with such complicated technologies in such large numbers. While many organizations are incapable of doing so, at least some have thus been able to cope fairly effectively with even very complex operations.

Consequences of Skill Variations

The net effect of variations in the ability to cope with complexity has been to winnow organizations according to their skills as technology has advanced. Of course, mistakes are always damaging, and errors like the Iraqis's poor position preparation, weak combined arms coordination, or failure to maintain weapons and equipment would have hurt any twentieth century defender. As technology has become more sophisticated, however, the consequences of such errors have consistently risen.

For example, against an attacker approaching on foot armed with light machine guns of under 100 meters' effective range and supported only by artillery with little capability to adjust fire quickly, such defensive errors would be harmful but not necessarily catastrophic.[47] Against an armored attacker with an effective range of 500–1,000 meters in daylight, and supported by aircraft dropping unguided bombs, the cost would be higher.[48] But against an attacker with all-weather, day/night tank thermal sights, stabilized 120 mm guns armed with depleted uranium ammunition effective on the first shot at 3,000 meters, aircraft armed with precision-guided missiles (PGMs) and complete command of the sky, or attack helicopters with 5,000-meter-range missiles capable of responding in minutes to a radio call from a forward observer, such slip-ups can be very quickly lethal to a very large number of defenders. Armies prone to such mistakes have thus seen their vulnerability grow rapidly with improvements in technology.

By contrast, military forces that can cope with battlefield complexity have been able to reduce substantially the effects of their opponents' weapons by such means as cover and concealment, suppressive fire, dispersion, combined arms integration, small-unit independent maneuver, depth, and reserves. As a result, the vulnerability of such organizations has risen only slowly over time.

Prospects for Change

This pattern is unlikely to change any time soon. This is because even in a time of great technological change, some things change faster than others—and the roots of the effects described above lie in qualities that are changing only slowly if at all. To illustrate the general problem, I will describe two examples of important causes of the dynamics described above that are changing only very slowly: modern weapons' susceptibility to cover and concealment, and the persistence of trade-offs in weapon design.

SUSCEPTIBILITY TO COVER AND CONCEALMENT

Cover and concealment are two of the most important of the countermeasures discussed above, and they are likely to remain so for a long time to come. This is because weapon performance against covered or concealed targets has grown very slowly relative to performance against targets in the open.

Rifles, machine guns, tanks, and at least the first three generations of PGMs, for example, are all direct-fire weapons requiring a clear line of sight between shooter and target. However accurate or whatever their range, such weapons have thus been of limited effectiveness against targets they cannot see.[49]

Artillery, aircraft, or long-range missiles are capable of firing over a terrain mask, but still require accurate target locations to be effective. This has traditionally been very hard to obtain for targets in wooded or urban areas.[50] Foliage and buildings block the view of aerial or ground-based forward observers, and heavily degrade current surveillance radars and infrared (IR) sensors.[51] Counterprojectile radars can detect hostile artillery under cover, but only after it has fired. Gun crews able to displace rapidly after firing can often leave the area before return fire directed by such means can arrive.[52] Communications intelligence (COMINT) or signal intelligence (SIGINT) may reveal the location of active emitters in forests or towns, but this is rarely sufficient for targeting more than the emitter itself.[53]

Nor are cover and concealment going to lose all their value any time soon. Programmed improvements in U.S. deep-strike systems are oriented overwhelmingly toward enhancing our ability to destroy massed armor in the open.[54] An initial effort is underway to explore the feasibility of low frequency wideband radar for penetrating foliage, but this program is in its early stages. If the technology proves both feasible and suitably resistant to countermeasures (which cannot yet be determined), a fielded military system could still be a generation away.[55] Remotely delivered, unattended ground sensors using seismic, acoustic, or infrared signatures might provide some capability against targets in forests or in the lee of hills (and thus obscured from distant airborne radars). But such systems have limited effective sensor ranges and would thus have to be used in quantity to provide extensive coverage. For the foreseeable future, cost considerations are likely to restrict such systems to use in relatively limited areas.[56]

Moreover, a workable target acquisition system would have to be teamed with effective munitions to threaten targets in wooded areas. Foliage-penetrating terminal guidance for such munitions could well prove more challenging than development of an appropriate surveillance system. Low-frequency radars require large apertures to provide the needed resolution. For a terminal guidance system, whose physical aperture is limited to the diameter of the weapon itself, this would require synthetic aperture techniques. These are extremely expensive for use in an expendable munition, and would also be impractical for the terminal descent phase of the engagement.[57] The effectiveness of other sensor regimes in a forested environment has not been studied even as extensively as radar. The availability of a suitable guidance system is thus far from established, even in principle.[58] Finally, a feasible weapon would need to penetrate the forest canopy without suffering significant deflection en route.

This is not to say that progress will not be made. Improvement is likely, but will probably come slowly and may well be partial. Surveillance, for example, may prove easier than weapon guidance, and either will probably remain more effective against massed armor in the open than against dispersed targets under cover.

Perhaps most important, better sensors encourage research in technical countermeasures. While countermeasures are unlikely to offset completely the ongoing, century-long increase in the ability to see and kill distant targets in the open, they *are* likely to slow its pace—but only for armies capable of making the most of them, that is, for those that can cope with complexity.

Countermeasures increase complexity in at least four ways. First, the equipment itself can be complex. Whereas twenty years ago the most complicated piece of electronics in a tank was an FM radio, future tanks are likely to receive radar and infrared warning receivers, active sensor systems to detect the approach of incoming munitions, active defenses to engage and defeat these munitions, and active electronic spoofing systems like those already found on ships and aircraft.[59] And keep in mind that this more complex equipment must be maintained and operated properly by tired, frightened soldiers under combat conditions.

Second, to use modern countermeasures in the field requires both efficient staff planning and very disciplined execution at the small-unit and vehicle crew levels. Expendable countermeasures like chaff or smoke can only be carried in small quantities by moving armored vehicles. Timely resupply is thus needed for survival under intense attack, aggravating logistical burdens and creating additional administrative challenges. Decoys must be available at the proper times and places to protect frequently moving units. Camouflage discipline must be maintained in the face of fatigue and constant movement. Nets and coverings must be maintained, deployed carefully, and stowed properly.

Third, countermeasures are likely to pose increasing demands for high-level system integration. Tactical missile and air defense systems, for example, are an important element of U.S. plans for countering hostile deep-strike threats.[60] Such systems demand very high interconnectivity between warning, interceptor, and command decision-making systems for several different altitude and range bands. The high speed and tight coupling such architectures require creates tremendous technical and organizational complexity.[61]

Finally, countermeasure effectiveness will be substantially enhanced by integration with traditional means of avoiding exposure: cover, concealment, and dispersion.[62] Massed, moving tank columns in the open are susceptible to the whole range of modern sensor and PGM types. The sheer variety of these will make effective countermeasure use very difficult. However, by restricting the variety and degrading the effectiveness of hostile sensors, cover, concealment, and dispersion greatly ease the countermeasures' task. In fact, it is entirely possible that cover and concealment will be *required* for plausible technical countermeasures to succeed against the growing variety of information gathering technologies. Rather than negating their importance, technological change at the end of the twentieth century is thus probably *increasing* the significance of both the traditional means of limiting exposure in particular, and the ability to cope with operational complexity in general.

DESIGN TRADEOFFS ON WEAPON PERFORMANCE

A second relative constant in twentieth century technology is the persistence of trade-offs in weapon effectiveness. Whether in 1916 or 1996, all desirable properties cannot simultaneously be maximized. While improving technology may allow many properties to be *increased* simultaneously, *maximum* performance in one respect can typically be obtained only by accepting less than maximum attainable performance elsewhere. This means that to maximize any one aspect of weapon performance is to accept relative weaknesses in others, which opponents who have chosen differently can typically exploit. Only by combining different weapons with differing design strengths (and thus, differing weaknesses) can one shield oneself from such exploitation, whatever the predominant level of technological sophistication. This in turn implies that combined arms techniques will remain both powerful, and necessary, for the foreseeable future.

To maximize armor protection, for example, means accepting less than the maximum attainable sensory acuity and stealthiness. Armor is opaque to all major battlefield sensors and adds weight. Maximum sensory acuity requires large apertures, whether the sensor is eyesight (requiring peripheral vision) or radar (whose performance is, ceteris paribus, proportional to antenna size). But a large window, or a TV camera or radar antenna outside the armor envelope, represents a vulnerability that reduces net armor protection to the system as a whole. Maximum stealthiness, on the other hand, requires minimum energy consumption, since larger powerplants produce, ceteris paribus, greater noise and/or heat, either of which can be sensed by an opponent. However, a less energetic platform is less capable of carrying a heavy armor suite for a constant speed or range.

This means that weapons designed to emphasize armor protection must trade reduced sensory acuity and stealthiness relative to the available state of the art. In 1944 this meant that moving tanks with narrow glass periscopes could be seen and heard by concealed infantry that were often invisible to the tank's crew. In 1999 this means that moving tanks with magnified, stabilized thermal sights can be detected by concealed, camouflaged observers (whether human scouts, unattended sensors, or reconnaissance drones) using their own thermal imagers, seismic sensors, or moving target indicator (MTI) radars well before the tank's crew can see them. While a 1999 tank is a better sensor (under some conditions) than a 1944 dismounted observer with binoculars, tanks are always inferior to other sensor systems of comparable vintage *because* they have superior armor protection. The dismounted infantry of 1944 and the high-tech scouts of 1999 obtain their superior sensory acuity by sacrificing the armor protection of contemporary tanks.

Because no one weapon can ever outperform all contenders in one respect without accepting inferiority in others, the result is a powerful incentive to integrate multiple weapon types with different, complementary design strengths. One consequence is that traditional combined arms techniques will remain essential for the foreseeable future. While armored vehicles, for example, are becoming better sensor platforms all the time, they will never be the equals of other devices designed to maximize sensory acuity, and thus will always need to be teamed with other weapons to cover their weaknesses. Similarly, though, it is unlikely that something resembling a tank will ever be completely unnecessary. Other weapons' advantages over the tank are bought at the price of weaker armor, or smaller payloads, or lighter weapons, each of which can be a major disadvantage under some important conditions—such as offensive operations in broken terrain against opponents with significant deep surveillance and indirect-fire capabilities. To establish control of territory under such conditions is likely to require an ability to destroy defenses located under cover. This in turn is likely to demand a significant direct-fire, close-combat capability and the capacity to cross limited stretches of open ground in order to reach the effective direct-fire range of such positions. Some kind of armored vehicle is likely to prove the best weapon for such a mission, given its relative hardness to indirect fire, its ability to carry significant countermeasure payloads (relative to pure infantry, for example), and its effectiveness against covered, concealed targets (relative to missile or tube artillery or aircraft, for example).[63]

Another important consequence is that *untraditional* combined arms methods will also be necessary. While the discussion above has emphasized weapon technologies per se, the integration of diverse sensors, long-range missiles, and high-speed communications and data processing links is another example of the need to combine dissimilar devices to exploit the varying strengths and weaknesses that emerge from inherent design trade-offs. This "system of systems" approach is thus a novel, but fundamentally similar, form of combined arms integration—and it can thus be expected to extend and reinforce the long-standing twentieth century pattern of payoff at the price of complexity.[64]

IMPLICATIONS FOR FUTURE WARFARE IF TRUE

If true, this implies a future of smaller, and different, change than that projected by either current RMA school. Rather than a new era of great opportunity (if we innovate radically to exploit new technologies) and great peril (if we do not but others do)—or a new age of pure deep strike or third wave information warfare—this hypothesis suggests that future warfare will look much like an incremental extension of ongoing, and very long-standing, trends. This means that continuing technological improvements will provide increasingly one-sided outcomes in major theater wars against unskilled opponents.[65] However, as the Gulf War indicates, such wars are already very one-sided, and it is not clear that a continuation of this trend would provide any meaningful difference.

Against skilled opponents, however, ongoing improvements in deep-strike capabilities are unlikely to provide nearly so much real combat power. Operations on a future battlefield would be different by degree from those of today—and even more complex, requiring extreme care to limit exposure throughout the depth of the theater, and to integrate increasingly complicated systems of systems for maximum offensive and defensive effect. But for those capable of coping with such complexity, the *results* would likely bear a closer resemblance to the events of 1944 than those of 1991: superior forces slowly imposing their will on their opponents by a combination of close combat and supporting deep fires. Close combat would still be necessary to deal with forces inaccessible to deep-strike systems by virtue of cover, dispersion, and countermeasures. In fact, skilled combatants may provide few lucrative targets for deep attack. The need to limit exposure will restrict the scope for grand, sweeping maneuver (as it often has in the past), and the majority of the actual fighting would tend to occur (as it has in the past), on the margins of exposure, where the tight interaction of direct and indirect fires determines the outcome in a series of methodical local engagements.

Testing the Theories

We have identified three plausible theories with very different implications for future warfare: economic determinist RMA, contingent innovation RMA, and essential continuity. Which of these provides a better basis for defense planning and scholarship? To answer this I will consider each school in turn, first specifying key testable propositions, then assessing their consistency with available evidence.[66]

Economic Determinist RMA: Observable Propositions
The economic determinist RMA thesis is based on two premises. The first is that economic revolutions cause military revolutions. The second is that a new economic revolution is now underway, hence we should expect a coming military revolution as well. Both are testable. If either were false, the policy implications would change significantly even if the other were true. Given this, I will focus here on the argument that information technology (IT) is now revolutionizing the U.S. economy.

The key evidence for assessing this contention is economic productivity, for two reasons. First, economists view productivity as the key to technology's effects on economic performance.[67] It is the underlying force that motivates a whole range of secondary outcomes, from economic growth to changes in labor allocation, shifts in input composition, or the development of new forms of business organization.

Second, it is the key indicator for the specific arguments advanced by the economic determinists. According to Alvin and Heidi Toffler, the most influential exponents of this theory, every revolution in the system for creating wealth since the creation of agriculture has triggered a corresponding revolution in the system for making war.[68]

It is this emergence of a new, superior "system of creating wealth" (or means of producing goods and services) that triggers revolution, not mere shifts in the composition of inputs or style of work performed. The reason that agriculture and industrialization are held to have revolutionized war and society is that they produced valuable goods and services that could not be produced under the old system. This powerful advantage caused other changes in society to exploit the new potential (such as shifting population from farms to industrial cities), but these societal changes themselves are epiphenomenal— it is the underlying shift in productive potential that is truly causal.

This implies that if the economic determinist thesis is correct, then productivity should be positively, and strongly, correlated with IT, and that productivity growth data should show strong ongoing acceleration effects attributable to IT.[69]

Economic Determinist RMA: Evidence

Study of the relationship between IT and productivity has generated a large body of literature.[70] Very little of it, however, supports the economic determinist RMA school's implications. On the contrary, its central finding to date is that there is little evidence of any significant productivity acceleration attributable to IT. While counterintuitive, this finding has been quite robust.

THE PRODUCTIVITY EVIDENCE

Aggregate productivity statistics show consistently declining growth rates throughout the postwar era—both before and during the alleged information revolution of the 1980s or 1990s. Figure 11.6, for example, plots U.S. business sector annual productivity growth between 1948 and 1994.[71] The data shows considerable year-to-year and business cycle fluctuations, but no systematic upturn at any point in the interval. In the same period, the ratio of information workers to production workers in the U.S. economy almost tripled (see figure 11.7).

Efforts to disaggregate these results have failed to resolve this "productivity paradox" or the apparent failure of IT investments to arrest declining productivity. Econometric analyses conducted over a period of ten years have assessed the IT-productivity relationship at the level of firms, industries, and major sectors of the economy. The results provide little evidence for any major productivity benefit from IT.

Prior to 1993, for example, direct analyses consistently found negligible or negative IT productivity effects.[72] Gary Loveman of the Harvard Business School observed that "IT capital [has] had little, if any, marginal impact on output or labor productivity. . . . [P]rofit maximizing firms in this sample would best have invested their marginal dollar in non-IT factors of production."[73]

U.S. Business Sector Annual Productivity Growth

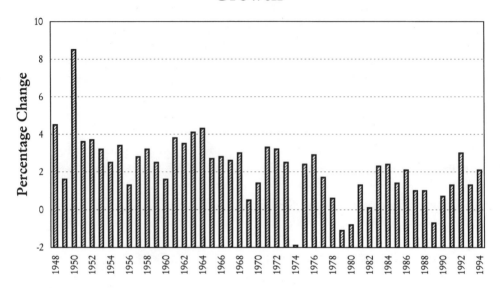

Fig. 11.6. U.S. business sector annual productivity growth. Data from U.S. Department of Commerce.

Ratio of Information to Production Work Force

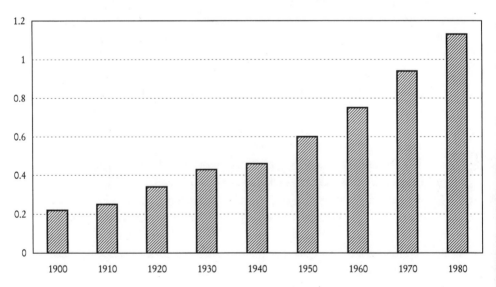

Fig. 11.7. Ratio of information to production work force. Data from U.S. Bureau of the Census and U.S. Bureau of Labor Statistics Data, as reproduced in Jonscher, "An Economic Study of the Information Technology Revolution," p. 10.

Northwestern University's Catherine Morrison and the National Bureau of Economic Research's Ernst Berndt similarly note: "There is little evidence to suggest that increases in office and information technology equipment have a substantial acceleration impact on technical progress in U.S. manufacturing industries; what impact there is appears to be rather small."[74]

Perhaps the most systematic national-level analysis, William J. Baumol et al.'s *Productivity and American Leadership,* concluded that America is not becoming an "information economy." While there had been significant growth in information industry employment as a fraction of the total U.S. labor force, this had not produced a meaningful increase in productivity, or in the fraction of U.S. output attributable to information activities. On the contrary, information employment growth was attributable chiefly to this industry's relatively low productivity growth by comparison. In the case of manufacturing, for example, as productivity growth in other industries outstrips that of the information sector, employment will gravitate toward the more labor-intensive information industry and away from activities such as manufacturing where production is increasingly automated.[75]

Since 1993, continued negative findings[76] have been accompanied by two, more positive assessments. An analysis of survey data from 367 Fortune 500 firms between 1987 and 1991 found a large, statistically significant excess return to IT investments.[77] The study's authors attribute this mainly to more recent data and conclude that IT should show larger benefits in the future than prior studies would suggest. However, as the authors were careful to point out, there are significant problems with the data used.[78]

Moreover, subsequent analysis of the same data to control for firms' differing managerial efficiency reduced the magnitude of the original study's results by about half.[79] Critics point to a variety of other potential problems in the analysis. These range from computer price deflators that are held to underestimate the equipment's cost (thus overstating its productivity, possibly by another factor of two), to the exclusion of costs from software, maintenance, operation, or user training (thus overstating the equipment's productivity benefit by possibly another factor of two to three), to the possibility of an unrepresentative sample of firms in the original study.[80]

The majority of the literature thus shows very limited productivity effects from IT. Some very recent but disputed evidence is more optimistic, but most results are much less so, and few economists are ready to declare the productivity paradox resolved on the basis of information available to date. Overall, these findings pose a serious challenge to the economic determinist RMA thesis.

The persistent difficulty of demonstrating a large economic return to IT investment in spite of continued large expenditures by industry has led some to question the validity of the underlying measurements. Critics contend that traditional gross productivity data understate IT's benefits because they do not account for improved quality of output, only its quantity. Especially in such hard to measure sectors as finance, insurance, trade, or government services, the argue, IT has actually made major improvements in the timeliness, accuracy, visual appeal, or convenience of products in ways that have been poorly captured by official productivity statistics.[81]

IT clearly poses measurement problems. These problems may even account for some of the paradox of declining productivity in spite of increasing IT investment (although economists are divided on this point). However, they are very unlikely to account for the difference between IT's measured productivity performance and the scale of effect claimed for such technologies by the economic determinists for three reasons.

First, even if better accounting were to close the IT productivity gap altogether, this would hardly justify claims of a revolution in civil production. It is one thing to conclude that, properly measured, IT would be competitive with (or even superior to) other capital—it is another altogether to show that IT so outperforms prior technologies as to cause a fundamental shift in the way the economy produces wealth.[82]

Second, for measurement error to account for even the productivity decline—much less a revolutionary increase—requires error on a truly massive scale: "By 1995, the cumulative shortfall in output—the total amount by which measured annual GNP in the United States would have been larger if productivity growth had continued at precomputer rates—is, conservatively, about $1 trillion per year. That's roughly $4,000 per year for each man, woman, and child, about half the average family's disposable income."[83]

It is far from clear that a majority of consumers attach this much value to the convenience, visual appeal, or product variety improvements provided by IT but unmeasured by traditional productivity data.[84] And if they do not, then the real magnitude of IT measurement error would be insufficient to explain even the productivity decline, which itself would fall short of the Economic determinist RMA thesis' requirements.

Third, analyses of such easy to measure sectors as manufacturing, mining, and transportation have shown poor IT performance.[85] In these industries, IT is typically an intermediate good rather than a final product. As such, its quality-enhancing properties would be captured by improved sales of the final goods, or increased profitability for the investing firms. If IT is to show an important effect anywhere, for example, it should be in manufacturing: not only is this a sector enjoying high productivity gains, it is one where IT is primarily an intermediate good, and where productivity measurement is easy. Yet Morrison and Berndt's results show that in 1986, IT investments' marginal cost exceeded marginal benefit for eight of the fourteen manufacturing industries studied (as well as for the average results across all fourteen together).[86]

Finally, IT is hardly the only recent technology to improve quality or consumer welfare in ways not captured by gross productivity data—but it is the only one where such effects are held to have induced an RMA. This implies that IT's unmeasured quality effects must radically outstrip those of, say, electric lighting, or antibiotics, or the telephone. Each of these improved consumers' lives in important ways that were not fully reflected by productivity data, yet none by enough to induce an RMA. Quality is hard to measure, but it is not obvious that IT's quality effects are far greater than any of these.[87]

LAG EFFECTS

Alternatively, some IT optimists have argued that lag effects, as opposed to measurement problems, explain the productivity paradox. In this view, such "general purpose technologies" as the steam engine, the dynamo, or the integrated circuit require long learning and dissemination periods before their full effects are felt. In the case of the dynamo, for example, forty years were required for the productivity potential of the new technology to be realized. Given this, we should expect IT to suffer an equally long period of weak productivity performance followed by substantial improvement.[88]

Lag effects, however, are also insufficient to bridge the gap between the economic determinists' view of IT and the economic evidence, for three reasons. First, recent IT productivity analyses incorporating lag terms provide no evidence of a significant effect.[89]

Second, even by dynamo standards, computers are hardly an immature technology. The first electronic computer was produced in the late 1940s; computers were in commercial use by bankers, brokers, and insurance companies by 1950; and by 1970 more than $100 billion worth of computers were already at work in the U.S. economy. Depending on how one dates its initial introduction, IT has thus either reached the forty-year mark already—or should at least be close enough to be showing some measurable effect.[90]

Third, and perhaps more important, the lag argument undermines the economic determinist RMA thesis' policy implications and renders "military revolution" moot as an issue of national security significance. If economic revolutions take forty years or more to mature, if those who partake early are rewarded with subpar economic returns, and if IT is still too young to show an important productivity payoff, then why should the U.S. military hasten to adapt prematurely to an economic revolution that apparently has not yet ripened? If an RMA's only policy implication is to wait and see what happens for perhaps another twenty years,[91] or maybe to experiment tentatively while awaiting further developments, then how is this different from finding that there is no revolution afoot at all? A forty-year-long "revolution" with no reward for early participation begs the distinction between revolution and evolution and renders the difference irrelevant from a policy perspective.

WHY IT MIGHT ACTUALLY BE UNPRODUCTIVE

Finally, there are a number of reasons why IT's poor productivity could be real, not just a measurement error. Many are described in the literature;[92] I will provide four illustrative examples here: high costs, diminishing benefits, managerial difficulties created by IT, and perceptual biases.

First, IT is more expensive than generally realized, and IT's nature promotes systematic overspending relative to actual utilization. Hardware costs average about $3,000 per personal computer (PC)—$1,000 a year over a PC's three-year average life span. However, a study of U.S. corporate practice shows it costs about $13,000 a year to make a PC functional—more than ten times the price of the equipment itself.[93] And while the per unit cost of computer hardware is falling rapidly, equipment is only a fraction of the total cost of using IT. The costs of other, larger system components are constant or increasing. Moreover, the computing power required to perform the same basic business functions is constantly increasing as software writers produce ever larger, ever more demanding programs. The result is roughly constant equipment costs over time, with much of the nominal increase in computing power absorbed in increases in software complexity.[94]

Compounding this problem is the fact that few IT users exploit more than a fraction of the capacity purchased at this cost. For example, cutting edge word-processing software is distinguished from earlier models mainly by the availability of advanced features such as macros, grammar checkers, or multiuser annotation capabilities. Few users employ such cost-increasing features, yet they make it necessary for all to upgrade in order to maintain compatibility. This upgrade thus represents a recurring cost with no compensating improvement in output for most users. Such externalities are widespread in IT.[95] As another example, users with an occasional need for graphics manipulation must often upgrade their hardware to accommodate this single application's speed or memory demands. On an average day, when the machine is used only for word processing, this results in an unnecessarily capable—and expensive—machine being underutilized. Such "specialized complements" are also common in IT.[96]

Second, there may be steeply diminishing marginal benefits to computerization. IT's biggest productivity improvements have been in areas where whole classes of routine, repetitive human activity could be automated, such as in telephone operation or simple clerical functions. Few such operations remain to be automated. More complex activities such as managerial analysis, on the other hand, may be enhanced by better data availability, but cannot generally be automated—and the evidence to date suggests that large increases in data availability do not necessarily translate into corresponding increases in decision quality. On the contrary, the sheer ease of data creation and transmission have created major problems with information overload.[97]

Third, effective management oversight of IT expenditure is complicated by the same measurement problems described above. When the real output of IT is opaque, managers must make purchasing decisions on intuitive grounds. Evidence of actual business practice suggests that few firms apply to IT the kind of formal analytical methods they use to assess other capital investments. Instead, decisions are often driven by competitors' behavior, fear of falling behind the technological state of the art, or vague impressions of the importance of adopting new methods.[98] Each will tend, ceteris paribus, to err on the side of overexpenditure.

Finally, it should be acknowledged that our casual perceptions are not necessarily good guides to IT's actual effectiveness. IT has become an everyday element of most offices, and we are often impressed by its increasing role in our lives. Studies have shown, however, that individuals often overestimate computers' effects on their own activities. British grocery store managers thought that computerized scanning devices saved on labor costs. However, personnel records showed that the devices increased the total hours worked. Internal Revenue Service agents' perceptions of new laptop computers' effects on the timeliness and quality of audits were also greatly exaggerated. Software users consistently prefer multiple options for command entry, yet analyses show that extra choices actually slow learning and performance.[99] The real cost of IT is also often underestimated by its users. Most of these costs described above are opaque to the individual user, but they loom large both for corporate bottom lines and for national productivity.[100] Casual impressions are thus often inaccurate—and always inadequate when more systematic data are available, as is the case for the productivity effects of IT.

At a minimum, the case for major IT-driven productivity acceleration has thus not been made. A growing economics literature provides little reason to conclude that IT is revolutionizing the productive basis of the economy on a scale comparable to that of agriculture or the substitution of machine for muscle. Most studies show weak productivity performance for IT; counter-arguments based on measurement error or lag effects fall short (especially for the economic determinist RMA literature's unusually aggressive claims for IT); and there are other plausible explanations implying that the shortfall in IT productivity is real and not illusory.

Research is, of course, ongoing. Future results could yet prove to be more optimistic for IT. But only an extraordinary reversal would support the economic determinist RMA thesis. Simply put, the scale of productivity effect implied by advocates of this theory is at or beyond the most optimistic extreme of the current economics literature.[101] Overall, the results are thus substantially inconsistent with the economic determinist RMA thesis.

Contingent Innovation RMA: Observable Propositions

The contingent innovation thesis, by contrast, holds that RMAs occur when far-sighted innovators see unrecognized potential in new technologies and create radical new doctrines and organizations to exploit it. Again, change per se is not enough. All organizations change over time, including both the agents and the victims of revolution. Stasis is a straw man. The emphasis in the RMA literature is on the scale and pace of change. Incrementalist gradualism causes new technology to be grafted inappropriately onto old-fashioned tactics and organizations. Only bold, radical innovation can harness the potential of revolutionary technology.[102]

Although authors vary in their identification of past RMAs, virtually all agree on at least one key case: blitzkrieg, which serves as the defining example of the phenomenon. This case thus approximates an Ecksteinian critical case for the contingent innovation theory—if it is to hold anywhere, it should hold here.[103]

In particular, this theory holds that Germany's radical successes during the period 1939 to 1941 were the result of its adoption of sweeping organizational and doctrinal changes to exploit the potential of the tank, the airplane, and the radio. Because the French and British were unwilling (or unable) to do more than adapt old organizations and ideas to the new equipment, they failed to keep pace and were overwhelmed.[104]

By contrast, the non-RMA essential continuity theory holds that no radical German departure was needed. Extreme combat results are attributable not to innovation per se, but to major asymmetries in the combatants' ability to cope with complexity. Armies that have mastered the complex demands of modern war—including combined arms, dispersion, cover, concealment, small unit independent maneuver, depth, and reliance on large reserves—are likely to need only incremental updating of their doctrines and organizations as technology changes.

The scale and pace of German innovation is thus an important indicator for the relative consistency of the two theories with the case evidence. Supranormal scale or pace are required by the contingent innovation theory and are central to its policy implications. Although incrementalist gradualism is not strictly required by the essential continuity theory,[105] it would be consistent with it—and inconsistent with the contingent innovation model.

In addition, the essential continuity theory implies two other testable claims for this case. First, for decisive battlefield victories like Germany's from 1939 to 1941, the theory requires a major German advantage in the specific dimensions of skill enumerated above. Second, the theory implies that the 1939–41 results should have been more decisive than prior twentieth century battles fought between comparably skill-mismatched opponents. While the contingent innovation RMA thesis is silent on these points, if either implication were shown false, this would tend to weaken the essential continuity alternative.

Contingent Innovation RMA: Evidence

WAS GERMAN 1939–41 DOCTRINE OR ORGANIZATION
RADICALLY INNOVATIVE?

Under the influence of Sir Basil H. Liddell Hart and Maj. Gen. John F. C. Fuller, a conventional wisdom emerged following World War II that German doctrine represented a radical departure created by a handful of tank visionaries and opposed by a reactionary high command.[106] More recent scholarship suggests quite the opposite, however.[107]

Contrary to the contingent innovation RMA school's implications, the doctrine the Germans took into World War II was an incremental adaptation of the methods they had used in the latter half of the First World War. This is not to argue that the Germans were not innovative—but the nature of the change that occurred has been mischaracterized in the RMA debate. Rather than abandoning older principles in favor of a radical new system of tactics, the Germans retained the basic doctrinal ideas they developed between 1915 and 1917, updating them to incorporate new equipment, but with little change in the underlying concepts of strategy, tactics, or organization.

At the operational and strategic level, for example, German doctrinal ideas from 1939 to 1945 were little different from those of 1914 or even 1870. The battle of annihilation, obtained by encircling enemy forces in the field and designed to afford rapid, decisive offensive victory, was the basis of German strategy and operations from Helmuth von Moltke the elder through Alfred von Schlieffen, Helmuth von Moltke the younger, Heinz Guderian, Erwin Rommel, and Erich von Manstein.[108] Although the means of encirclement evolved from flanking envelopments by marching infantry to breakthrough battles exploited by tanks, the concept itself was the consistent foundation of German strategy and operational art for at least seventy years prior to the advent of blitzkrieg.[109]

At the tactical level, most of the basic principles of German World War II doctrine had emerged by 1917. Between 1915 and 1917 the German army developed an offensive tactical system based on combined arms integration, independent small-unit maneuver, deep penetration without regard for flank security, initiative by low-level commanders, careful use of terrain, and close coordination of movement with suppressive fires. The defensive system stressed depth, maintaining a strong reserve, and counterattacking to stifle breakthroughs.[110] The resulting "elastic defense" held the Allies at bay through the ever-larger offensives of 1916–17, while the corresponding "stormtroop tactics" created offensive breakthroughs at Caporetto in October, 1917; the Second Battle of the Somme in March, 1918; at the Lys River in April, 1918; and on the Chemin des Dames in May, 1918.[111]

Interwar German doctrine updated and adapted these tactics but did not significantly depart from them. Immediately following the war the Germans undertook a rigorous analysis of their experience and concluded that their 1917–18 tactical principles were basically sound. Their first postwar manual, *Leadership and Battle with Combined Arms,* published in 1921 and 1923,[112] departed from prior practice mostly by assuming that open warfare would, with effective tactics, predominate from the outset (whereas the western front's preexisting trench stalemate was a point of departure for 1917 doctrine). It also provided detailed treatments of tank and aircraft use. The latter discussions built upon and extended the existing tactical concepts to incorporate new technology; they did not discard them to substitute a new way of fighting.[113]

Leadership and Battle was updated with the publication of the 1933 *Troop Leadership* manual.[114] This was, in fact, the last major German doctrinal publication prior to 1945, and served as the foundation for German tactics throughout the war.[115] However, *Troop Leadership* differed only incrementally from its predecessor. Large sections of text were lifted directly from the 1923 document, whose basic principles were again unchanged. The main differences were an updated treatment of tank tactics to account for newer technology, an increase in the scale assumed for armored formations, and greater relative emphasis on motorized warfare.[116] As James Corum put it: "Despite the specific evolution of tactics found in *Troop Leadership,* the greater part of that regulation, down to the organization of the document itself, is drawn with minimal changes from *Leadership and Battle.*"[117]

Nor did German military organization depart radically from its precedents.

The German emphasis on combined arms drove their organizational designs from at least 1917. The assault battalion structure of March, 1918, for example, combined infantry, mortars, artillery, machine guns, and flamethrowers down to the company level.[118] This philosophy yielded the panzer division's tank-infantry-artillery integration as a natural evolutionary outgrowth once tanks had become a sizable presence in the German force structure. It was hardly an unprecedented novelty created only by their willingness to innovate radically in the face of technological change.[119]

In its strategic, tactical, and organizational fundamentals, German doctrine in World War II was thus a lineal, incremental adaptation of a system developed mostly in the First World War.[120] By contrast, other military forces have departed much more radically from past ideas in times of great technological change without inducing correspondingly revolutionary gains in effectiveness.

Britain's Royal Air Force, for example, adopted during the interwar period a truly radical strategic bombing concept that rejected the very foundation of British First World War air doctrine (i.e., that the airplane's main role was to provide reconnaissance for ground forces and defend friendly airspace). In the new doctrine, wars were to be won, or ideally deterred, by the threat of offensive bombing against hostile cities and industry. Both air defense and the diversion of aircraft to tactical support of ground forces were held to be self-defeating, allowing hostile bombers to get ahead in the all-important race to destroy the opposing population's will to resist. This doctrine was a much more radical departure than was Germany's *Troop Leadership*. Its failure either to deter or defeat German aggression in 1939–40 forced England to fall back first on traditional tactical support of ground forces in France, then to an essentially defensive air strategy in the Battle of Britain.[121]

Similarly, the U.S. Army responded to the development of atomic weapons by abandoning its traditional doctrine of integrated, combined arms maneuver and adopting instead a new system of primary reliance on atomic fires and rejection of direct-fire ground combat in any role other than support of atomic weapon use. The Pentomic Division that resulted was a radical departure from precedent—far more radical than the panzer division. While the latter applied traditional combined arms concepts to a new arm, the Pentomic Division embodied a new concept of victory through atomic firepower, and in fact rendered the U.S. Army incapable of conducting combined arms operations in the absence of atomic weapons. Although a very innovative response to a new technology, it was surely not a revolutionary improvement in effectiveness, and was abandoned by 1961.[122]

In fact, Germany's own opponents during the period 1939 to 1941 were in some ways more radically innovative than the Germans. For example, the British

Army's 1940 armored division organization was based on the assumption that the tank could be used independently in massed formations.[123] This was a greater departure from First World War practice than was the German view that tanks required support from other arms to be effective. Yet it was hardly more successful despite its being more innovative.

Contrary to the emphasis in the RMA literature, blitzkrieg was thus not the result of radical doctrinal innovation. In fact, the differences between German 1917 and 1939 practices mostly took the form of updating preexisting doctrine to accommodate new technologies—precisely the kind of gradualist, evolutionary change that the contingent innovation RMA school would reject today as dangerously unimaginative or shortsighted. By contrast, other doctrines both more and less innovative than Germany's have failed. This in turn challenges the RMA literature's contention that the key distinction between success and failure in times of revolutionary transition is an organization's willingness to overcome inertia and innovate radically enough.[124]

DID GERMANY COPE BETTER WITH COMPLEXITY THAN ITS OPPONENTS DID?

Germany's incrementalism thus tends to contradict the contingent innovation RMA thesis. It is consistent, however, with the essential continuity theory. What about the latter's other implications for this case? In particular, was the German army better skilled in the key dimensions enumerated above, and were the 1939–41 results more decisive than earlier twentieth century battles between armies of comparably mismatched skill?

In fact, the German army of 1939–41 is widely thought to have been among the most tactically and operationally skilled armies of the twentieth century.[125] It proved highly capable in each of the critical tasks enumerated above. German offensive doctrine and training emphasized the coordinated use of independent small units to exploit local cover and concealment, the use of suppressive fire to permit movement, and close combined arms cooperation.[126] German defensive doctrine emphasized depth and reserves. The general training emphasis on low-level initiative and independent operation greatly facilitated the implementation of such principles.[127]

By contrast, the French, British, and Soviet armies against whom the Germans fought during this period are widely thought to have been seriously deficient in these respects. Their small-unit tactics were formulaic and rigid, fire and movement was often poorly coordinated, and combined arms interaction was limited at best.[128] The French manned the key sector around Sedan with poorly trained reservists disposed in shallow, static positions with minimal reserves.[129] When attacked, these units broke and fled. The Soviets, too, provided little or no depth to defensive positions, and withheld only limited forces in mobile reserve.[130]

The result was a significant imbalance in the combatants' skill in carrying out the tasks enumerated above. The German attackers proved highly adept and thus were shielded from the worst effects of improvements in Allied weaponry. On the other hand, the Allies were much less adept and thus were much more exposed to increasingly lethal German technology. The result, according to the essential continuity theory, was a series of decisive German battlefield successes.

WERE 1939–41 OUTCOMES MORE DECISIVE THAN PRIOR SKILL MISMATCHES? Finally, the essential continuity theory implies that less-advanced technology should mean less extreme consequences for any given skill differential. While a complete test of this proposition will require development of a more precise operational measure of skill, some insight can be gained by considering a reasonably comparable prior case.

In the spring of 1918 Germany launched a series of offensives. These operations featured many of the same mistakes described above.[131] In particular, the British and French defenders were deployed in shallow, static positions with very modest fractions of the available forces withheld as mobile reserves.[132] If the essential continuity thesis is correct, then we should expect to see the German attack succeed, but to a much smaller degree given the lesser ability of earlier weapon technology to exploit such mistakes.

In fact, the Germans managed to break through the Allied defenses three times in succession. These breakthroughs—in the Second Battle of the Somme (Mar. 21–Apr. 9), at the Lys River (Apr. 7–29), and at the Chemin des Dames (May 27–June 6)—yielded penetrations of 40, 10, and 24 miles, respectively. They also marked the end of the trench stalemate on the western front.[133] None, however, could be exploited decisively. In each case, the Allies eventually managed to reassemble a defensive front across the gap the Germans had created. Moreover, the cost of creating these breakthroughs was enormous. In the Second Battle of the Somme the Germans suffered some 250,000 casualties. Lys River cost them 350,000 more.[134] While the results were far more successful than any previous western front offensive since 1914—no other attack since then had reached even the defender's rear defense line—they were far less successful than Germany's 1939–41 experience.

When Germany invaded France in 1940, panzer columns penetrated more than two hundred miles in ten days—an advance of about five times the 1918 maximum, and at a rate more than twice as fast.[135] German losses in the 1940 campaign totaled 157,000—a casualty rate (as a fraction of forces committed) of less than one-tenth of that suffered in the Second Battle of the Somme.[136] Most important, the 1940 campaign knocked France out of the war and ejected British forces from the continent, whereas the 1918 campaign failed to obtain a strategically decisive outcome.

Against broadly similar Allied mistakes in 1918 and 1940, German attackers thus proved able to succeed in both cases, but with much greater effect and at much lower cost in 1940. This is consistent with the essential continuity theory's implications, and thus tends to corroborate the theory.

Essential Continuity: Observable Propositions

The German 1939–41 case study offers some corroborative evidence for the essential continuity theory. A broader assessment, however, can be obtained by considering an additional case comparison (one for which the RMA thesis offers no determinate prediction), and by exploiting available data for an indirect large-n test.

In the absence of a more precise or comprehensive operational measure of skill, case analysis must be restricted to extrema where classification is unambiguous. The German case above offers one such extremum; the Arab-Israeli Wars offer another. Like the German army, the Israeli army is widely considered to be among the most skilled of the twentieth century.[137] By contrast, the Egyptian and Syrian armies in the Middle East wars have generally been regarded as unskilled and poorly suited to the management of complex operations—at least for the period from 1948 to 1967.[138] The essential continuity theory thus implies that as weapon technology became more lethal between 1948 and 1973, Israeli loss rates should have remained relatively stable (since Israeli skill would enable them to escape the worst effects of more lethal Arab weaponry). Egyptian and Syrian loss rates, by contrast, should have increased markedly.

At the large-n level, a direct test would require a more comprehensive operational measure of skill and a database of corresponding measurements, neither of which is yet available.[139] An indirect test can be obtained, however, by making two assumptions: first, that the relative frequency or war-proneness of skilled and unskilled armies have not changed radically over time;[140] and second, that time can be used as a proxy for technological sophistication (i.e., technology can be treated as a systemic variable whose value advances continuously over time). For these assumptions, the theory would predict relatively constant mean combat results over time, but increasing variance. This means that in wars between skilled and unskilled armies, the former should fare ever better and the latter ever worse, producing gradual divergence under the pressure of advancing technology. However, wars between skilled armies and wars between unskilled ones should produce little change in outcomes over time (the former because each can limit its exposure to the other's technology, the latter because neither can),[141] with the result that mean outcomes across a heterogeneous admixture of opposing skill levels should change less quickly than their variance.

Essential Continuity: Evidence

For the Arab-Israeli cases, the results are generally consistent with the theory. Between 1948 and 1973, weapon lethality increased markedly: the mean antitank weapon penetration range given in figure 11.5, for example, increased by nearly a factor of ten (from 229 meters in 1945 to 2,048 meters in 1975). Israeli loss rates rose during the same period, but gradually—from 7.5 battle deaths per thousand soldiers per month in the 1948 War of Independence, to 8.9 in the 1956 Sinai War, to 15.6 in the 1967 Six-Day War, to 18.5 in the 1973 October War. This represents a total increase of 8.1 deaths per thousand.[142] Egyptian loss rates rose much more rapidly: from 6.6 battle deaths per thousand soldiers per month in 1948 to 108 in 1956, and to 185 in 1967. This represents a total increase of more than 170 deaths per thousand soldiers, or a factor of almost thirty over the entire period. The Syrian loss rate rose by more than 130 deaths per thousand: from 50 in 1948 to 184 in 1967—an increase of nearly a factor of four.[143] Between 1948 and 1967, Israeli loss rates thus rose by less than 10 percent of either the Egyptian or the Syrian increase.[144]

An exception to the general trend is the 1973 October War. Syrian loss rates remained relatively high at 116 (compared to the Israeli rate of 18.5). However, the Egyptian rate fell from 185 in 1967 to 28 in 1973. While still about 50 percent higher than the comparable Israeli figure, this represents a major departure from the general Arab trend. In part this is due to the unusual tactical circumstances of the 1973 war: Israel, not the Arabs, was taken by surprise in the initial attack, and found itself engaged in hasty, poorly coordinated counterattacks. In part, however, it is also due to a very different behavioral pattern by the Egyptians, who carefully planned their operations and drilled their troops thoroughly in a limited repertoire of key functions (especially, dismounted antitank defense from prepared, covered and concealed positions). Although the Egyptians in 1973 were certainly not as broadly capable an organization as were, say, the Germans in World War II, they were thus able to develop the ability to implement more complex techniques in at least a few especially important areas. Taken in combination with Israel's failure to exploit proper combined arms methods in their Sinai counterattacks, this enabled the Egyptians to improve their performance substantially relative to their earlier experience.[145] While further research is required to develop a full characterization of Egyptian skills as demonstrated in the 1973 war, there is reason to suspect that the

Table 11.1. Battle Deaths per Thousand Soldiers per Month, Mideast Wars

	Egypt	Syria	Israel
1948	6.6	50.0	7.5
1956	108.0		8.9
1967	185.0	184.0	15.6
1973	28.0	116.0	18.5

case may still be consistent with the general prediction of lesser exposure for armies able to exploit more complex countermeasures.

At the large-*n* level, figures 11.8 to 11.11 plot loss exchange ratios (initiator battle deaths divided by defender battle deaths), loss rates (friendly battle deaths per thousand soldiers per month), loss infliction rates (hostile battle deaths per thousand soldiers per month), and war duration for all international wars between 1816 and 1994, as provided by the University of Michigan Correlates of War data set.[146]

While the results vary by measure, all display modest changes in mean over time, and all but one (loss infliction rate) display statistically significant increases

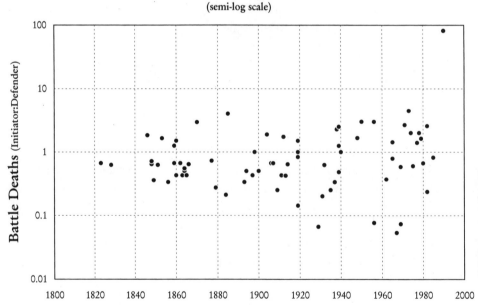

Fig. 11.8. Loss exchange ratio (initiator:defender battle deaths) as a function of time. Data from University of Michigan Correlates of War dataset.

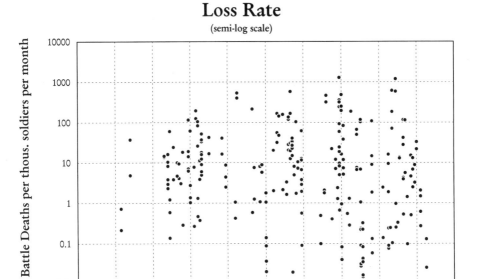

Fig. 11.9. Loss rate (battle deaths per thousand soldiers per month) as a function of time. Data from University of Michigan Correlates of War dataset.

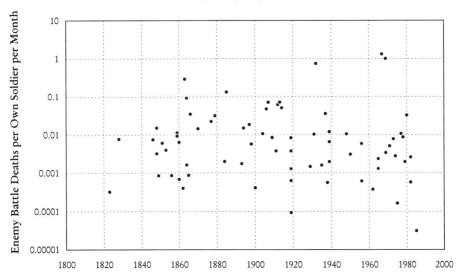

Fig. 11.10. Loss infliction rate (enemy battle deaths per thousand friendly soldiers per month) as a function of time. Data from University of Michigan Correlates of War dataset.

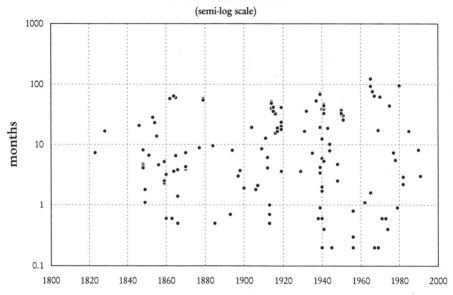

War Duration

(semi-log scale)

Fig. 11.11. War duration (months). Data from University of Michigan Correlates of War dataset.

in variance.[147] More specifically, the null hypothesis of no change in variance between 1900 and 1994 can be rejected at the .01 level for loss exchange ratios, the .1 level for loss rates, and the .0005 level for war duration (but only the .28 level for loss infliction rate).[148] Only two of the four measures show statistically significant changes in mean: loss rate, for which the null hypothesis of no change in mean from 1900 to 1994 can be rejected at the .09 level; and war duration, for which the null hypothesis can be rejected at the .06 level.[149] For these two, only one (loss rate) displays an increase in mean greater than that of its increase in variance over the 1900–94 interval; over the complete 1816–1994 interval available in the data, however, this measure too shows greater increase in variance than mean.[150]

Overall, then, three of the four large-*n* measures show the predicted increase in variance; similarly, three of the four show larger increases in variance than in mean, as predicted by the theory, while for the longer time interval available in the data (but not strictly within the twentieth century bounds of the theory), all four measures behave as predicted. While these results are not uniformly confirmatory, they are thus reasonably supportive on the whole. However, it should be emphasized that the large-*n* analysis is at best an indirect test since (pending development of more complete data) it depends on unverified assumptions as to the distribution of skill and technology over time.

Together with the small-*n* comparisons above, these results provide at least provisional plausibility for the new theory. The small-*n* analyses show that at least some important cases display the predicted (intuitive) increase in vulnerability for unskilled armies as weapon lethality has increased, and the predicted (counterintuitive) decline or relative continuity in vulnerability for skilled armies. While this cannot yet be considered a decisive corroboration, it is at least broadly consistent with theoretical prediction.

Conclusions and Implications

The case for a coming revolution is thus weaker than generally thought. Of the two main causal arguments for revolution, the economic determinist RMA school bases its case on a view of the present as an ongoing civil economic revolution resulting from new IT. Yet economic data show little evidence for a revolutionary productivity effect from IT. In fact, aggregate U.S. productivity growth has fallen throughout the postwar period, with the information sector lagging behind even the performance of the economy as a whole. While measurement issues may account for some of the apparent productivity slowdown, they are unlikely to be responsible for an unmeasured difference between negative growth and revolutionary expansion.

The contingent innovation school is premised on the need for major doctrinal and organizational change to exploit new technology's potential. Yet for the key case cited in the literature, blitzkrieg, German doctrinal and organizational change was actually incremental and conservative. In fact, interwar Germany did precisely what RMA advocates warn against today: it updated a preexisting concept of war to incorporate new technology without discarding its traditional strategy, tactics, or principles of military organization. If incremental, evolutionary updating of old ideas is consistent with the key cited example of revolution, then the theory is either at odds with the evidence or must be expanded to a degree that would substantially alter its policy implications.

An alternative, nonrevolutionary theory is at least as well supported by the evidence. In particular, I have described a new theory that projects future warfare as an incremental extension of a century-long pattern of growth in the importance of skill differentials between combatants. Skilled military forces (i.e., those that can cope with increasing complexity) have been able to limit their exposure to the growing lethality of modern weapons. However, military forces less skilled in managing complex undertakings have seen their vulnerability climb as technology has advanced. Wars between the skilled and the unskilled have thus grown progressively more one-sided over time. Outcomes between highly skilled opponents have changed much less in spite of major changes in technology, however. The future, as an extension of this trend, is thus less likely to see a new pattern of U.S. dominance via information supremacy and deep precision strike than it is to witness increased variance in results across opponents of varying skill.

While exhaustive testing of this theory must await development of data on skill indicators, an initial set of tests based on partial or indirect evidence suggests at least first-order empirical plausibility for the new theory. Armies widely held to be highly skilled (the Germans and the Israelis) show declining or only slowly increasing loss rates over time in spite of major increases in weapon range and lethality. On the other hand, armies widely held to be unskilled (the Syrians and the Egyptians prior to 1973) show rapidly increasing loss rates. At the large-n level, if we assume a roughly constant proportion of skilled to unskilled armies in the international system over time, then this theory predicts roughly constant mean combat outcomes over time, but increasing variance. Available data is mostly consistent with this prediction.

None of the three theories thus show perfect consistency with the data, but of the three, the essential continuity thesis displays significantly smaller divergence between prediction and observation. Each RMA school faces a substantial burden of contradictory evidence; essential continuity proved generally a better fit to the data on the basis of the preliminary plausibility probe provided here. Further testing is required, but in the meantime, there is reason to believe that continued gradual, incremental change may be at least as likely as military revolution.

Implications

If this conclusion holds up under continued testing, it will have significantly different implications for policy and scholarship than the orthodox RMA views. As examples, I briefly sketch two areas of scholarly divergence—offense-defense theory and realist theories of great power emergence—and four areas of policy divergence—defense budget priorities; force structure; research, development, and system acquisition; and military doctrine.

OFFENSE-DEFENSE THEORY

For scholarship on offense-defense theory, my findings imply that future regional warfare will be less offense-dominant than many RMA advocates have suggested. Perhaps more important, my argument also implies that the scholarly literature has miscoded the offense-defense balance for at least the first half of the twentieth century. In fact, offense-defense theorists and RMA advocates hold a similar view of twentieth century military history through the end of the Cold War. Both groups recognize three distinct eras for land warfare: defense dominance from 1900 to the beginning of the Second World War; offense dominance from the emergence of blitzkrieg through the advent of nuclear weapons; and defense dominance through at least the breakup of the Soviet Union.[151] My theory, by contrast, sees no systematic shift in the offense-defense balance between 1900 and August, 1945. Throughout, we would expect to see increasing amplitude in combat outcomes but no net change in mean results.

GREAT POWER EMERGENCE AND THE NATURE OF POWER

For realist theories of great power emergence, my conclusions imply that the accelerated transition foreseen by many RMA advocates is unlikely. Moreover, my conclusions also challenge the broader RMA contention that the nature of power is shifting away from traditional geopolitical factors such as size, population, or industrial capacity, and toward technological know-how or "soft" factors such as ideology or cultural influence.[152] Much of the latter argument is based on the assumption that warfare and society are both in the midst of a third wave information revolution in which information mastery will lead to international influence in ways not previously possible without mass military power. My argument, by contrast, sees much less divergence between new and old. While global communication will continue to expand, the sources of military strength are changing much less rapidly. To the extent that coercive force remains relevant, traditional indicators of power are thus likely to remain relevant as well. By the same token, my theory suggests that traditional understandings of power have substantially underestimated the importance of organizational factors and their increasingly significant role in allowing some states to cope more effectively than others with the demands of increasing military complexity. Although there is more continuity in warfare than many would suggest, this does not mean that existing theories have described that continuity adequately.

DEFENSE BUDGET PRIORITIES

It is widely argued that the Defense Department faces a "bow wave" problem in which today's weapon development programs are creating future spending obligations that planned budgets cannot meet. More broadly, continuing pressure to limit defense spending creates powerful incentives to cut back on at least one of the budget's three major components (readiness, force structure, and modernization) in order to preserve the others. Some RMA advocates have expressed concern that modernization will be the victim and, as a result, a revolutionary opportunity will be lost.[153]

Nevertheless, we should be wary of proposals to protect modernization at the expense of readiness. This is not to say that modernization should be halted: weapons, like any other capital stock, wear out and must be replaced. The issue is the relative pace of modernization. The above analysis suggests that trading slower modernization for lesser cutbacks in training, schools, and quality-of-life accounts (those parts of the budget that help create and retain skilled personnel) would be a better choice than the reverse.[154] At the margin, a less-skilled military force is more dangerous than less-advanced technology. The decay of today's combat skills would not only forfeit the ability to exploit current technical advantages against less skilled opponents, it would also enable a future challenger to turn the tables by acquiring better technology and use it to its full potential against inadequately skilled Americans. Neither is a risk worth taking.

FORCE STRUCTURE

Many RMA advocates have called for a radical restructuring of the U.S. military away from direct-fire ground forces and toward heavier reliance on air and deep-strike missile systems.[155] The analysis here, on the other hand, suggests that such a restructuring could be very risky. Sometimes it would be highly effective: against unskilled, mistake-prone armies, a mostly air and deep-strike-oriented U.S. force would in fact be the ideal solution. However, such an imbalanced U.S. force would be at a grave disadvantage against a skilled opponent better able to limit its exposure. By giving up direct-fire ground capability in exchange for more deep-strike systems, such a force would be much weaker than today's against an opponent able to escape destruction at extreme range and close with our own forces. Such a restructuring would thus strengthen U.S. capability mostly where it is already so strong as to be nearly beyond challenge (i.e., against error-prone opponents) by creating weaknesses elsewhere. Unless we are certain we will never again face skilled opposition, this could be a dangerous approach.

The analysis above thus suggests that new technology ought not to change the gross balance between deep-strike and close combat forces—but it does not mean that the latter's nature should stay the same. In particular, as the vulnerability of massed armor in the open increases, it is likely that combat between skilled armies will shift increasingly toward dispersed operations in covered terrain. Yet U.S. Army modernization and force structure planning continues to emphasize antiarmor capability against massed opponents in open terrain.[156] A balanced U.S. force structure will provide increasingly ample air and missile capability against such targets as technology advances. The focus of army close combat planning thus ought to shift toward increased emphasis on operations in covered, built-up terrain and lesser emphasis on antiarmor capability in open country.

RESEARCH, DEVELOPMENT, AND SYSTEM ACQUISITION

An emphasis on exploiting the errors of mistake-prone opponents and preparing for warfare in covered terrain against more skilled enemies also implies some different directions for research and development and system acquisition. In particular, it suggests that pilot programs to explore remote surveillance against targets in wooded and built-up areas merit higher priority and accelerated development relative to other ongoing surveillance initiatives. Similarly, new precision munitions effective against dispersed targets in such terrain also warrant greater relative attention. If they could be made effective at reasonable cost, such developments could have sweeping consequences. The only technical development in the foreseeable future that could cause a truly revolutionary change in warfare—that is, one that would break the twentieth century pattern of slow change in outcomes between skilled opponents—would be one that could make terrain, dispersion, and combined arms irrelevant. If deep-strike systems really *could* destroy any target anywhere regardless of its apparent exposure or concentration, this would overturn the ability of skilled armies to limit their vulnerability to hostile firepower and bring about a truly new situation. It is far from clear that such developments are attainable—but the attempt warrants greater attention than it is now receiving.

MILITARY DOCTRINE

Finally, much of the RMA literature advocates radical doctrinal change, and argues that the chief obstacle to exploiting the RMA is the inherent conservatism of military organizations.[157] But if my theory is correct, radical doctrinal change would be neither necessary nor desirable. It would be unnecessary because warfare would not be on the verge of revolution. It would be undesirable because many of the proposed innovations would rest on technologies that would only be effective enough against unskilled opponents. Against tougher opposition, doctrines dependent on such technologies could be highly problematic.

In fact, it is not the case that our only real risk is to underinnovate in the face of technological progress, or that our main challenge is simply to induce unwilling organizations to change. While there are historical examples of military forces that adapted too slowly, there are also examples of ones that changed too fast or too much. The interwar Royal Air Force and the U.S. Army in the Pentomic era have already been noted. In addition to them one could cite the French *Jeune École* navalists of the 1880s, European air war visionaries of 1900–

14, or the U.S. Air Force's hasty conclusion that nuclear weapons had rendered conventional air support of ground forces obsolete in the late 1940s.[158] All represent visionary, forward-looking thinkers who decided that a revolution was at hand when it was not. In the cases of the Royal Air Force, the Pentomic Division, and the atomic U.S. Air Force, this was the result of large, professional military bureaucracies adapting too quickly for their own—or their nations'—good. For the Royal and U.S. Air Forces these excessive adaptations cost lives in subsequent conventional land wars in France and Korea.

This is not to suggest that doctrine should stand still. American military doctrine has changed regularly since World War II and will surely continue to do so.[159] Ensuring that this continuing evolution is sound and sufficient is an important, challenging job for the defense planning community—both military and civilian. My point is that this normal process of incremental adaptation to changing technology is entirely appropriate to the times. To retain methods that have worked well in prior conflicts is not a sign of hopeless shortsightedness, nor is novelty per se a sign of vision or foresight. The measure of an analysis is its deductive rigor and its support in the evidence—not its nonconformity or the scale of its apparent departure from current practice.

In fact, interwar Germany is in many ways a better model than the RMA literature realizes.[160] The doctrine Germany took to war in 1939 was the product of a military bureaucracy that carefully considered its experience in the last war, retained most of it as valid, updated it as necessary to account for changing technology, tested the results rigorously in extensive field trials, and put tremendous emphasis on training and education throughout the ranks. It was not a case of maverick visionaries introducing radical innovations in the face of opposition from a hidebound senior leadership.

As in the interwar years—and the rest of the twentieth century—we face changing technology and the need to adapt. And, just like during the interwar years and the rest of the twentieth century, we face the challenge of knowing not just how much change is enough, but also how much is too much, and of deciding how to reach such a conclusion. The Reichswehr is hardly the only possible model, but the United States in the late 1990s could do a lot worse than to follow the example of such a corps of rigorous empirical gradualists.

Notes

A version of this essay appeared in *Security Studies* 8, no. 1 (autumn, 1998) and is used here by permission of Frank Cass & Co., Ltd.

This analysis was supported by the Institute for Defense Analyses Central Research Program. The opinions expressed are those of the author, and do not necessarily represent the positions of IDA, its management, or sponsors. The author would like to thank Richard Betts, Tami Davis Biddle, Jeffrey Cooper, Steven David, Peter Feaver, Ben Frankel, David Graham, Richard Harknett, Wade Hinkle, Lawrence Katzenstein, Michael Leonard, Thomas Mahnken, Brian McCue, Maj. H. R. McMaster, James Ralston, Brad Roberts, Alex Roland, Victor Utgoff, and Lt. Col. James Warner for helpful comments on earlier drafts. Responsibility for all errors and omissions remains the author's alone. Previous versions were presented at the *Security Studies*/U.C. Davis/Office of Net Assessment Conference on the Revolution in Military Affairs, Monterey, Calif., Aug., 1996; the International Studies Association 1997 Annual Meeting, Toronto, Mar., 1997; and the American Political Science Association 1997 Annual Meeting, Washington, D.C, Sept., 1997.

1. See, for example, John J. Mearsheimer, "Numbers, Strategy, and the European Balance," *International Security* 12, no. 4 (spring, 1988): 174–85; Richard K. Betts, "Conventional Deterrence: Predictive Uncertainty and Policy Confidence," *World Politics,* Jan., 1985, pp. 153–79; Seymour J. Deitchman, *Military Power and the Advance of Technology* (Boulder, Colo.: Westview, 1983); *Crisis in the Persian Gulf: Sanctions, Diplomacy and War, Hearings Before the Committee on Armed Services, House of Representatives* (Washington, D.C.: GPO, 1991), HASC 101–57, pp. 314–61, 431–78, 889–917.

2. See, for example, William J. Perry, "Desert Storm and Deterrence," *Foreign Affairs* 70, no. 4 (fall, 1991): 66–82; and idem., interview, *Defense News,* May 1–7, 1995, p. 38; William E. Odom, "Storming Past a New Threshold in Warfare," *Christian Science Monitor,* Apr. 4, 1991, p. 19; idem., *America's Military Revolution* (Washington, D.C.: American University Press, 1993); Ray Cline, "Warfare's New Era," *Washington Times,* Feb. 27, 1991, p. G1; Richard J. Dunn III, *From Gettysburg to the Gulf and Beyond: Coping with Revolutionary Technological Change in Land Warfare* (Washington, D.C.: Institute for National Strategic Studies, National Defense University, 1992), McNair Paper 13, esp. pp. 79–91.

3. See, for example, Steven Metz and James Kievet, *The Revolution in Military Affairs and Conflict Short of War* (Carlisle Barracks, Pa.: U.S. Army War College Strategic Studies Institute, July, 1994), pp. 2–5; A. J. Bacevich, "Preserving the Well-Bred Horse," *National Interest,* fall, 1994, pp. 43–49; Richard K. Betts, "The Downside of the Cutting Edge," *National Interest,* fall, 1996, pp. 80–83; and Martin van Creveld, *The Transformation of War* (New York: Free Press, 1991), which anticipates many of these arguments, although written just prior to the Gulf War.

4. See, for example, Andrew F. Krepinevich, Jr., "Cavalry to Computer: The Pattern of Military Revolutions," *National Interest,* fall, 1994, pp. 30–42; Alvin and Heidi Toffler, *War and Anti-War: Survival at the Dawn of the 21st Century* (Boston: Little, Brown, 1993); Eliot Cohen, "A Revolution in Warfare," *Foreign Affairs* 75, no. 2 (Mar.-Apr., 1996): 37–54; James R. Blaker, *Understanding the Revolution in Military Affairs: A Guide to America's 21st Century Defense* (Washington, D.C.: Progressive Policy Institute, 1997); Michael G. Vickers, *Warfare in 2020: A Primer*

(Washington, D.C.: Center for Strategic and Budgetary Assessments, 1996); Michael J. Mazarr, project director, *The Military-Technical Revolution: A Structural Framework* (Washington, D.C.: Center for Strategic and International Studies, 1993); Comdr. James R. FitzSimonds and Comdr. Jan M. Van Tol, "Revolutions in Military Affairs," *Joint Force Quarterly* (spring, 1994): 24–31; Daniel Goure, "Is There a Military-Technical Revolution in America's Future?" *The Washington Quarterly* 16, no. 4 (autumn, 1993): 175–92; Jeffrey Cooper, *Another View of the Revolution in Military Affairs* (Carlisle Barracks, Pa.: U.S. Army War College Strategic Studies Institute, 1994); idem, "Another View of Information Warfare," in Stuart J. Schwartzstein, *The Information Revolution and National Security* (Washington, D.C.: Center for Strategic and International Studies, 1996), pp. 109–31; Paul Bracken, "The Military After Next," *The Washington Quarterly* 16, no. 4, (autumn, 1993): 157–74; Gen. Gordon R. Sullivan and Lt. Col. Anthony M. Coroalles, *The Army in the Information Age* (Carlisle Barracks, Pa.: U.S. Army War College Strategic Studies Institute, Mar., 1995); Martin C. Libicki, *The Mesh and the Net: Speculations on Armed Conflict in a Time of Free Silicon* (Washington, D.C.: National Defense University, Mar., 1994), McNair Paper no. 28; John Arquilla and David Ronfeldt, "Cyberwar is Coming!" *Comparative Strategy* 12: 141–65. Some hold that an RMA is available only to the United States—while we may fail to realize its potential if we choose the wrong policies, no other state is really in the running. See, for example, Joseph Nye and William Owens, "America's Information Edge," *Foreign Affairs* 75, no. 2 (Mar.-Apr., 1996): 21–36. On strategic information warfare, see, for example, Roger C. Molander et al., *Strategic Information Warfare: A New Face of War* (Santa Monica: RAND, 1996); Winn Schwartau, *Information Warfare* (New York: Thunder's Mouth Press, 1994); and Michael Vlahos, "The War After Byte City," *The Washington Quarterly* 20, no. 2 (spring, 1997): 41–72.

Another major strain in this literature holds that while the revolution is mostly ahead of us, no radical changes in current U.S. policies will be necessary to bring it about—incremental updating of current practice is sufficient. While the radical change school is mostly (but not entirely) civilian, the incremental change school is mostly (but not entirely) military. See, for example, Antulio J. Echevarria and John M. Shaw, "The New Military Revolution: Post-Industrial Change," *Parameters* (winter, 1992–93): 70–77; David Jablonsky, "U.S. Military Doctrine and the Revolution in Military Affairs," *Parameters* (autumn, 1994): 18–36; Gen. Gordon R. Sullivan and Lt. Col. James M. Dubik, *Land Warfare in the 21st Century* (Carlisle Barracks, Pa.: U.S. Army War College Strategic Studies Institute, Feb., 1993); U.S. Army Training and Doctrine Command, *TRADOC Pamphlet 525-5: Force XXI Operations* (Fort Monroe, Va.: U.S. Army TRADOC, Aug. 1, 1994 [hereafter cited as TRADOC]); and Lt. Gen. Frederick J. Brown, USA (Ret.), *The U.S. Army in Transition II: Landpower in the Information Age* (Washington, D.C.: Brassey's, 1993). The distinction between this school and the revolution-is-now literature described in note 2 is mostly semantic. Both see a present and future of U.S. military dominance as long as the United States continues its current policy course. The choice of a dividing line between the nonrevolutionary present and the revolutionary future is essentially arbitrary, and the policy implications of the two schools are essentially the same.

5. Among those on record as supporting some version of the RMA thesis include three serving secretaries of defense, at least one deputy secretary of defense, the

current undersecretaries of defense for Policy and Acquisition, the current chairman and recent vice chairman of the Joint Chiefs of Staff, the chiefs of staff of the army and the air force, and a wide variety of other Defense officials from the assistant secretary level down. See, for example, Bradley Graham, "Battle Plans for a New Century," *Washington Post,* Feb. 21, 1995, pp. 1ff; John Barry, "The Battle Over Warfare," *Newsweek,* Dec. 5, 1994, pp. 27ff; Jeff Erlich, "One on One: Interview with Secretary of Defense William Perry," *Defense News,* May 1–7, 1995, p. 38; and "Deutch Gets Report Card Letter on the Revolution in Military Affairs," *Inside the Navy,* Oct. 24, 1994, p. 11.

6. Stephen Biddle, "Victory Misunderstood: What the Gulf War Tells Us About the Future of Conflict," *International Security* 21, no. 2 (fall, 1996): 139–79.

7. For the coming RMA school, "Victory Misunderstood" addressed one important argument—that new technology's effects in the Gulf War demonstrate the potential for a coming RMA—and concluded that this argument was based on a misunderstanding of technology's role in the 1991 outcome. This essay is intended to broaden the analysis to include other, non–Gulf War evidence adduced in the coming RMA literature, and to assess this evidence's adequacy to support the RMA position overall.

8. This is not necessarily to argue that military revolutions have never occurred—my argument here is only that none have occurred in the twentieth century, and none is likely at the beginning of the twenty-first. The general validity of revolutionary discontinuity as a model of earlier historical change is beyond the scope of this paper.

9. See, for example, Andrew Krepinevich, "Recasting Military Roles and Missions," *Issues in Science and Technology* 11, no. 3 (spring, 1995): 41–48; Andrew Krepinevich and Michael Vickers, "Embrace New Air Power Age," *Defense News,* Nov. 18–24, 1996, p. 25; Cohen, "Revolution in Warfare," pp. 37, 47–50; Blaker, *Understanding the Revolution,* pp. 4, 16, 19, 21; Vickers, *Warfare in 2020,* pp. 1, 7, 8, 9, 14; Mazarr et al., *Military-Technical Revolution,* pp. 34–35; Goure, "Is There a Military-Technical Revolution," p. 178; Stuart Johnson and James Blaker, "The FY 1997–2001 Defense Budget," *Strategic Forum,* no. 80 (July, 1996): 3–4; Adm. William Owens, "The Emerging System of Systems," *Military Review* 75, no. 3 (May-June, 1995): 15–19; Martin C. Libicki and James A. Hazlett, "Do We Need an Information Corps?" *Joint Forces Quarterly* (autumn, 1993): 88–97; Richard J. Newman, "Warfare 2020," *U.S. News and World Report,* Aug. 5, 1996, pp. 34–41; Terry Atlas, "U.S. Plans for War on Digital Battlefield: Military Counting on Smart Weapons," *Chicago Tribune,* Sept. 22, 1996, pp. 1ff.; and Jeff Erlich, "Officers Propose Counter to QDR," *Defense News,* May 19–25, 1997, pp. 4ff.

10. See, for example, Cohen, "Revolution in Warfare," p. 51; Krepinevich, "Cavalry to Computers," p. 42; and Earl H. Tilford, Jr., *The Revolution in Military Affairs: Prospects and Cautions* (Carlisle Barracks, Pa.: Strategic Studies Institute, U.S. Army War College, 1995), p. 16. Some hold that the United States should use RMA military capabilities to deter the emergence of a competing superpower (or a "peer competitor" as the literature terms it). See, for example, Blaker, *Understanding the Revolution,* p. 14.

11. See, for example, Cohen, "Revolution in Warfare," pp. 44–46; Vickers, *Warfare in 2020,* pp. i, 2, 5; and Blaker, *Understanding the Revolution,* p. 15. Conversely, some argue that the RMA will shift the offense-defense balance toward defense. See, for example, Cooper, *Another View,* p. 31.

12. On the importance of organizational innovation in an era of RMA, see, for example, Andrew Krepinevich, "Ten Reasons Why the U.S. Military May Fail to Respond Effectively to the Need for Change" (paper presented to the Center for Strategic and Budgetary Assessments 1996 Annual Conference on "Defense Innovation: Meeting the Challenges of a New Century").

13. The new theory builds upon the explanation of the Gulf War outcome provided in "Victory Misunderstood," but expands upon and generalizes it. While the two are consistent, the presentation here provides a much more complete articulation.

14. I will not provide a detailed resume of this literature in its entirety here, but will focus on issues of causation and evidence. For a more complete review, see Stephen Biddle, *Revolutionary Change in Warfare* (Alexandria, Va.: Institute for Defense Analyses, 1995), IDA P-3123, pp. 4–21.

15. See, esp., Tofflers, *War and Anti-War*, pp. 18–25; also Bracken, "Military After Next," p. 162; Eliot A. Cohen, "What to do about National Defense," *Commentary* 98, no. 21 (Nov., 1994); Sullivan and Coroalles, *Army in the Information Age*, pp. 1, 3; TRADOC, pp. 1-1, 2-5; Cooper, *Another View*, pp. 17, 30–31; Echevarria and Shaw, "The New Military Revolution: Post-Industrial Change," pp. 70–77; Brown, *U.S. Army in Transition*, pp. 22, 72; and Jablonsky, "U.S. Military Doctrine," pp. 19–20.

16. As the Tofflers, perhaps the most influential exponents of this view, put it: "The way we make war reflects the way we make wealth. . . . Starting with the very invention of agriculture, every revolution in the system for creating wealth triggered a corresponding revolution in the system for making war. . . . A revolutionary new economy is arising based on knowledge, rather than conventional raw materials and physical labor. This remarkable change in the world economy is bringing with it a parallel revolution in the nature of warfare" (*War and Anti-War*, pp. 3, 35, 5). On the properties of "third wave" economies and societies, see the Tofflers, *War and Anti-War*, pp. 18–25; and, esp., idem, *The Third Wave* (New York: Bantam, 1980).

17. See, for example, Krepinevich, "From Cavalry to Computer," pp. 36, 38; Goure, "Is There a Military-Technical Revolution," p. 175; FitzSimonds and Van Tol, "Revolutions in Military Affairs," pp. 24–25, 27; Mazarr et al., *Military-Technical Revolution*, pp. 18, 33, 57; Cooper, *Another View*, p. 26; and Dunn, *From Gettysburg to the Gulf*, pp. 11–20, 24. This view is also reflected implicitly in, for example, Brig. Gen. Morris J. Boyd and Maj. Michael Woodgerd, "Force XXI Operations," *Military Review* (Nov., 1994): 17–28. While individual authors (in either school) vary widely in their classification of historical cases, a few other examples appear in the majority of accounts—especially Napoleonic warfare; the exploitation of gunpowder, railroads, and the telegraph; and carrier aviation. See Biddle, *Revolutionary Change*, pp. 8–9.

18. French 1937 doctrine, for example, was made more offense-minded than its 1921 predecessor by the addition of text describing the attack as *"le mode d'action par excellence."* Similarly, French strategy adapted to motorization by planning to rush forces well forward into Belgium, using the new vehicles' speed to attain more distant positions before the Germans could reach them. These were hardly radical departures (the new text on the offensive was balanced with cautionary emphasis on the lethality of defensive artillery, while the rapid advances were designed to establish a traditional defensive line in a new place), but neither did

doctrine stand still—and the French in the interwar period are widely described as among the most cautiously conservative armies of the 20th century. See Eugenia Kiesling, "If It Ain't Broke, Don't Fix It," *War in History* 3, no. 2 (Apr., 1996): 208–23.

19. Krepinevich, "Cavalry to Computer," p. 31. Elsewhere he implies, for example, that reorganization of the Joint Chiefs of Staff, the strengthening of the regional commanders-in-chief, or the army's development of AirLand Battle doctrine were not sufficiently radical changes to qualify the Gulf War as fully revolutionary (p. 40).

20. Mazarr et al., *Military-Technical Revolution,* pp. 33, 57. See also, for example, Blaker, *Understanding the Revolution,* who argues that to realize the RMA's potential will require "deep, fast, and rampant innovation" to "transform [U.S.] defense posture" (pp. 29, 30); Cohen, "Revolution in Warfare," who describes the needed change as "radical" (pp. 38, 48, 52), a "fundamental reordering of American defense posture" (p. 37) and a "drastic shrinking of the military, a casting aside of old forms of organization and creation of new ones, a slashing of current force structure" (p. 37); Goure, "Is There a Military-Technical Revolution," who describes the necessary doctrinal and organizational changes as "extensive remodeling of the military-technical structure of U.S. forces," and "profound . . . military innovation" (pp. 182, 186); Vickers, *Warfare in 2020,* whose requirements include a "fundamental rethinking" of the entire U.S. military posture and a massive reduction in ground forces (pp. 14, 16); and Adm. William A. Owens, "Foreword," in Schwartzstein, *Information Revolution,* who argues that the RMA will demand "big changes," and "deep, fast, and widespread innovations," whose radical nature will induce "anxiety" in existing organizations (p. ix). See also FitzSimonds and Van Tol, "Revolutions in Military Affairs," p. 26; Boyd and Woodgerd, "Force XXI Operations," pp. 18, 26; Sullivan and Coroalles, *Army in the Information Age,* pp. 18–21; Erlich, "Officers Propose Counter to QDR," pp. 4ff.; and Bracken, "Military After Next," pp. 157–58, which argues that radical change will be needed, but not necessarily soon.

As noted above, an alternative school of RMA advocates holds that no radical change is necessary, either because the RMA has already arrived, or because incremental change in current U.S. policy is enough to induce it (see references in notes 2 and 4 above). The argument that the RMA is already here has been addressed elsewhere (see Biddle, "Victory Misunderstood"). The argument that the RMA is yet to arrive but can be obtained without unusual policy departures, on the other hand, poses a distinction whose relevance is unclear. If revolution and nonrevolution imply the same policies of incremental change, then why does it matter whether the same events are dubbed "revolutionary" or not? In principle, simply knowing what to expect is valuable, but this knowledge is usually pursued to assist in decision making of some sort. While there may be decisions that hinge on this distinction per se, none have been articulated in this literature. By contrast, the radical-change RMA camp articulates a clear and pressing case for policies we would not want—and probably could not get—unless the times are truly revolutionary in a specific, meaningful sense. I will thus focus on the latter here.

21. See, for example, Cohen, "Revolution in Warfare," p. 52; Goure, "Is There a Military-Technical Revolution," pp. 177, 182; Mazarr et al., *Military-Technical Revolution,* p. 60; Cooper, *Another View,* p. 28; Krepinevich, "Ten Reasons," pp. 1–2;

Bracken, "Military After Next," pp. 158–59; and Sullivan and Coroalles, *Army in the Information Age,* pp. 18–21.

22. A variety of alternative explanations of the role of technology in nineteenth and twentieth century warfare exist, several of which imply very different interpretations of observed events than either RMA school. These include offense-defense theory, the historiography on the emergence of total war, and William McNeill's argument that military history since about 1000 A.D. is properly characterized by a process of continuous incremental change and not a periodic revolution (or "punctuated equilibrium") model as implied by the RMA literature. While the differences between these schools and the RMA argument are clear—and testable—with respect to the historical record, their projections for future warfare are less well specified. I will therefore focus here on the two RMA variants and the alternative theory described above as the clearest anticipatory projections in the literature to date, although I expect to consider the entire range of alternative theories on the role of technology in twentieth century warfare in future work. On offense-defense theory, see, for example, Stephen Van Evera, *Causes of War,* vol. 1 (Ithaca, N.Y.: Cornell University Press, forthcoming), chaps. 5, 6; Sean Lynn-Jones, "Offense-Defense Theory and Its Critics," *Security Studies* 4, no. 4 (summer, 1995): 660–91; Charles Glaser, "Realists as Optimists," *International Security* 19, no. 3 (winter, 1994–95): 50–90; Robert Jervis, "Cooperation Under the Security Dilemma," *World Politics* 30, no. 2 (Jan., 1978): 167–214; and George Quester, *Offense and Defense in the International System* (New York: John Wiley and Sons, 1977). On the technological roots of total war, see, for example, Walter Millis, *Arms and Men* (New Brunswick, N.J.: Rutgers University Press, 1956); and Richard Preston, Alex Roland, and Sydney Wise, *Men in Arms: A History of Warfare and its Interrelationships with Western Society* (New York: Harcourt Brace, 1956), pp. 209–44. For McNeill's argument, see *The Pursuit of Power: Technology, Armed Force, and Society since A.D. 1000* (Chicago: University of Chicago Press, 1982).

23. As a point of departure, I will focus here on tactical and operational level phenomena. The same general issues, however—complexity, variations in states' ability to cope with it, and its importance for the outcomes of wars—are likely to pertain to the strategic and politico-economic management of national war efforts as well. See, for example, Paul Kennedy, "Introduction," in Paul Kennedy, ed., *The War Plans of the Great Powers, 1880–1914* (London: Unwin Hyman, 1979), pp. 1–22.

24. Of course, technology has changed in many other respects as well, many of which have made warfare more complex—whether at the battlefield level, or with respect to strategy, economic preparations for conflict, or the political management of war. Among the most consequential of these changes have been the improvements in transportation, communications, administrative techniques, and public health that enabled a tremendous increase in the size and geographical scope of armies in the second half of the nineteenth century; and the systematic application of science to war-making in the twentieth. The former increased the managerial complexity of operating and maintaining armies; the latter led to more sophisticated, complicated equipment whose use demanded increased role specialization and internal organizational complexity and encouraged the development of increasingly complicated civil-military oversight mechanisms. The treatment below is thus illustrative, not exhaustive. On the growth of armies,

see, for example, Martin Van Creveld, *Technology and War* (New York: Free Press, 1989), p. 161; on the application of science to warfare, see, for example, Bernard and Fawn M. Brodie, *From Crossbow to H-Bomb: The Evolution of the Weapons and Tactics of Warfare* (Bloomington: Indiana University Press, 1962), pp. 124–51, 172–308; idem., *Technology and War,* esp. pp. 217–34; Millis, *Arms and Men,* pp. 265–303; on its consequences for complexity, see Chris Demchak, *Military Organizations, Complex Machines: Modernization in the U.S. Armed Services* (Ithaca, N.Y.: Cornell University Press, 1991); Martin Binkin, *Military Technology and Defense Manpower* (Washington, D.C.: Brookings, 1986), pp. 53–69; on its consequences for civilian management of the military, see McNeill, *Pursuit of Power,* pp. 262–361.

25. Representative opposing tanks are the German PzKw IVh for 1945, the Soviet T-55 for 1975, T-62 for 1985, and T-72 for 1995 and 2005. Penetration ranges for U.S. weapons against the PzKw IVh, T-55, and T-62 are taken from John Ellis, *Brute Force: Allied Strategy and Tactics in the Second World War* (New York: Viking, 1990), table 62; R. M. Ogorkiewicz, *Technology of Tanks,* vol. I (Coulsden, Surrey: Jane's, 1991), p. 111; F. M. Von Senger und Etterlin, *German Tanks of World War II,* trans. of *Die deutschen Panzer 1926–45* (Munich: J. F. Lehmans Verlag, 1968), trans. by J. Lucas, pp. 21–28, 34–74, 194–210; and John Milsom, *Russian Tanks: 1900–1970* (New York: Galahad Books, 1970), pp. 160–81. Penetration ranges for U.S. weapons versus the T-72 are inferred from Gulf War experience, as described in, for example, Rick Atkinson, *Crusade: The Untold Story of the Persian Gulf War* (Boston: Houghton-Mifflin, 1993), pp. 447, 466; Robert Scales et al., *Certain Victory: The U.S. Army in the Gulf War* (Washington, D.C.: Office of the Chief of Staff, 1993), p. 293; and maximum missile ranges as given in Ted Nicholas and Rita Rossi, *U.S. Missile Data Book, 1996* (Fountain Valley, Calif.: Data Search Associates, 1995). Figures given represent ranges at which the specific weapon can penetrate the specific armor and assume frontal arc engagement with shooter and target at equal elevation and cant.

26. In principle, artillery can overcome cover by firing over it. Concealment, however, is an even greater problem for artillery firing over a terrain mask than for shorter range systems firing at targets they can see themselves. Artillery in *indirect fire* (where shooter and target are not intervisible) requires remote target acquisition to identify its targets, compute their locations, and communicate this data back to the gunners. For targets behind a terrain mask, target acquisition will often be at a distance from the target (e.g., by aerial observation). This combination of distance and remote communication has been highly problematic for much of the twentieth century. Distance aggravates the effects of foliage or urban concealment, while communications systems have often been unreliable, noninteroperable, or imprecise with respect to target location (alternatively, the communicator may be imprecise—until very recently, a major problem was forward observers' gross inaccuracy in calculating their own locations [Rupert Pengelley, "HELBAT Strikes Back," *International Defense Review,* May, 1981, pp. 555–78]). Although some of these problems have been greatly eased in recent years, foliage and urban concealment are likely to remain as serious limitations for the foreseeable future. See the discussion below.

27. L. G. Starkey et al., *Capabilities of Selected U.S. and Allied Antiarmor Weapon Systems* (Alexandria, Va.: Weapon System Evaluation Group, May, 1975), WSEG Report 263, declassified Dec. 31, 1983, p. 36. For more rolling, broken terrain in

the Fulda Gap region of Germany, only 13 percent of the terrain within a thousand meters is visible from a typical weapon site (idem., *Capabilities*, p. 35). See also Richard Simpkin, *Race to the Swift: Thoughts on Twenty-First Century Warfare* (New York: Brasseys, 1985), p. 69.

28. Alan Vick et al., *Enhancing Air Power's Contribution Against Light Infantry Targets* (Santa Monica, Calif.: RAND, 1996), p. 49, and assuming five to ten minutes to reach and occupy the new firing position, recompute firing data, and commence firing.

29. Starkey et al., *Capabilities*, p. 49; data is for M113/TOW combination ca. 1975. Other systems have differing reload rates and times of flight, though all suffer rate-of-fire reduction when forced to take cover from counterfire.

30. Assuming a battalion of eighteen ca. 1970 122 mm howitzers using airbursts given perfect accuracy and fire distribution. See W. J. Schultis et al., *Comparison of Military Potential: NATO and Warsaw Pact* (Alexandria, Va.: Weapon System Evaluation Group, June, 1974), WSEG Report 238, declassified Dec. 31, 1982, p. 67.

31. On tank losses to dug-in infantry antitank defenses, see, for example, John Weeks, *Men Against Tanks* (New York: Mason/Charter, 1975), esp. pp. 68–73, 100–104. On the dynamics of combined arms interaction generally, see, for example, Jonathan House, *Toward Combined Arms Warfare: A Survey of 20th Century Tactics, Doctrine and Organization* (Fort Leavenworth, Kans.: U.S. Army Combat Studies Institute, 1984); G. D. Sheffield, "Blitzkrieg and Attrition: Land Operations in Europe, 1914–45," in *Warfare in the Twentieth Century: Theory and Practice,* ed. Colin McInnes and G. D. Sheffield (London: Unwin Hyman, 1988), pp. 51–79; Shelford Bidwell, *Modern Warfare: A Survey of Men, Weapons, and Theories* (London: Allen Lane, 1973), pp. 149–50, 170–71; and John English, *On Infantry* (New York: Praeger, 1984), pp. 110, 112–13, 142, 200, 202.

32. Note that this discussion is limited to land force weapons, broadly defined (i.e., including helicopters, but excluding fixed wing aircraft). For a similar definition, see Simpkin, *Race to the Swift,* pp. 117–32. Land weapons are capable of using fine-grained terrain features for concealment in exchange for a reduction in velocity. Fixed-wing aircraft cannot travel slowly enough to avail of this degree of terrain feature, but are capable of very high maximum speeds; they thus rely more heavily on maximizing speed to limit exposure than land weapons as defined here.

33. For a systematic formal analysis of the relationship between velocity and casualties, see Stephen Biddle, "The Determinants of Offensiveness and Defensiveness in Conventional Land Warfare" (Ph.D. diss., Harvard University, 1992), pp. 67–77.

34. This is a central conclusion of ibid. See, for example, pp. 17–19, 187–95, 318–21.

35. See, for example, Headquarters, Department of the Army, *FM 100-5, Operations* (Washington, D.C.: GPO, 1982), pp. 19–21.

36. Robert Helmbold, *Rates of Advance in Historical Land Combat Operations,* CAA-RP-90-1 (Bethesda, Md.: U.S. Army Concepts Analysis Agency, 1990), p. 4–10, fig. 4-3b; 1970s tank speeds are taken from fig. 11.1.

37. See, for example, J. B. A. Bailey, *Field Artillery and Firepower* (Oxford: Military Press, 1989), pp. 132–34, 169–71, 184–86; and Shelford Bidwell and Dominick Graham, *Firepower: British Army Weapons and Theories of War, 1904–1945* (Boston: Allen and Unwin, 1985), pp. 21, 253–57.

38. Such methods were resisted with particular stubbornness by many early-century officer corps whose training and social background made them especially reluctant to trust the lower ranks to act independently. See, for example, Timothy Travers, *The Killing Ground: The British Army, The Western Front, and the Emergence of Modern Warfare, 1900–1918* (London: Unwin Hyman, 1987), pp. 51–53. On "bounding overwatch" in particular, see Headquarters, Department of the Army, *FM 71-1, The Tank and Mechanized Infantry Company Team* (Washington, D.C.: GPO, 1988); on the morale implications of dispersion under cover and the resulting "empty battlefield," see Richard Holmes, *Acts of War: The Behavior of Men in Battle* (New York: Free Press, 1986).

39. As in the techniques for tank-infantry intercommunication improvised in World War II. See Michael D. Doubler, *Closing with the Enemy* (Lawrence: University Press of Kansas, 1994), pp. 16–17, 47–51.

40. In fact, the demands created by dispersion in the defense are in many ways even greater than on the offense. Such "elastic" defenses are premised on a willingness to give up ground early in order to halt the attack in depth. This means that forward positions at the point of attack are sure to be overrun. Soldiers occupying these positions typically know this, and must either be able to conduct a fighting withdrawal under fire, or at least sell their lives as dearly as possible in order to buy time for the redeployment of the reserve. Withdrawal under fire is among the most technically demanding maneuvers in modern land warfare; conscious self-sacrifice in defense of an untenable position requires a very high order of discipline and motivation. On the demands of withdrawal under fire, see, for example, *FM 100-5*, pp. 158–60. Such defenses also place heavy demands on senior leaders. Their design is a balancing act. Too much force in forward prepared positions leaves the defense without sufficient reserves to halt the attack once slowed; too little (or too shallow a forward zone) means the attack will not be delayed long enough for a larger reserve to arrive in time. Since the use of the reserve is the linchpin of the defense as a whole, timing and locating its commitment is crucial. If used in a counterattack it must strike the attacker's weakest point at the attacker's moment of greatest extension (if misdirected against a locally strong position or committed at the wrong moment, such defenses can fail catastrophically). If used to reinforce the defenses at the attacker's point of main effort it must not be committed prematurely against a feint, or while the attacker retains sufficient reserves to redirect his main effort elsewhere (Biddle, "Determinants," pp. 87–102).

41. Demchak, *Military Organizations.*

42. For other examples, see the theory-testing discussion for the essential continuity thesis, below.

43. On Iraqi errors, see, for example, Murray Hammick, "Iraqi Obstacles and Defensive Positions," *International Defense Review,* Sept., 1991, pp. 989–91; Robert H. Scales, Jr., "Accuracy Defeated Range in Artillery Duel," *International Defense Review,* May, 1991, pp. 473–81; Scales et al., *Certain Victory,* pp. 117–18, 261–62, 293, 360; Col. Michael D. Krause, *The Battle of 73 Easting, 26 February 1991: A Historical Introduction to a Simulation* (Washington, D.C.: U.S. Army Center of Military History and the Defense Advanced Research Projects Agency, Aug. 27, 1991), pp. 17–18, 28; Gordon and Trainor, *The Generals' War,* pp. 287–88, 295; Freedman and Karsh, *The Gulf Conflict,* pp. 389–90; and Jeffrey Record, *Hollow Victory* (Washington, D.C.: Brassey's, 1993).

44. See Eliot A. Cohen, director, *Gulf War Air Power Survey* (Washington, D.C.: GPO, 1993).

45. See Gus Pagonis, *Moving Mountains: Lessons in Leadership and Logistics from the Gulf War* (Boston: Harvard Business School Press, 1992).

46. Krause, *Battle of 73 Easting*, pp. 11–12; J. R. Crooks et al., *73 Easting Re-Creation Data Book* (Westlake, Calif.: Illusion Engineering, 1992), IEI Report DA-MDA972-1-92, appendices, shoot history by vehicle for Eagle, Ghost, Iron Troops; personal communication with Maj. H. R. McMaster, USA, Sept. 8, 1995.

47. Consider, for example, the results of the French failures in Aug., 1914, which produced the loss of most of Allied Belgium and critical industrial territory near the German border, but which still cost the German invader tens of thousands of casualties and left most of the theater of war in Allied hands. See, for example, Bernadotte E. Schmitt and Harold C. Vedeler, *The World in the Crucible, 1914–1919* (New York: Harper and Row, 1984), pp. 41–69.

48. As in the Arab armies' defeat by the Israelis in 1967. See, for example, Chaim Herzog, *The Arab-Israeli Wars* (New York: Random House, 1982), pp. 143–92. Note, esp., the effects of Egyptian maldeployment, mistakes regarding terrain passability, and air force unreadiness (idem., *Arab-Israeli Wars,* pp. 152, 157, 159, 161).

49. While any of these weapons can be fired blindly against concealed targets, their effectiveness in this mode is limited to temporary suppressive effects—that is, to forcing a partly exposed target (such as a machine gunner about to fire) to withdraw into complete cover (e.g., to duck below the edge of a foxhole). To kill a target by anything other than a very lucky shot, such weapons require a clear line of sight.

50. Witness the difficulty of striking concealed ground targets in Bosnia, even given the current state of the art in remote surveillance, target acquisition, and weapon guidance technologies. See, for example, Tony Capaccio, "An Army Bosnia Review Rates JSTARS a 'White Elephant,'" *Defense Week,* Nov. 25, 1996, pp. 1ff; idem, "NATO Strikes Must Pierce the Fog of War," *Defense Week,* Feb. 14, 1994, pp. 1ff; Capt. Kristin M. Baker, untitled, *Military Intelligence* (Oct.-Dec., 1996): 27–29; Lt. Col. Collin A. Agee, untitled, *Military Intelligence* (Oct.-Dec., 1996): 6–12; and Peter Brooks and Edward Smith, "Evaluation of Airborne Surveillance Systems," *IDA Research Summaries* 3, no. 1 (winter-spring, 1996): 4–5.

51. Vick et al., *Enhancing Air Power's Contribution,* pp. 13–30; Brooks and Smith, "Evaluation of Airborne Surveillance Systems," pp. 4–5; and Dominick Giglio, "Overview of Foliage/Ground Penetration and Interferometric SAR Experiments," *SPIE Proceedings* 2230 (1994), pp. 209–17. Note that forward observers at close range can often see part way into a forest or town, but they cannot see through an extended mask, and lose effectiveness as range increases.

52. On the capabilities of modern counterprojectile radars, see, for example, Scales, "Accuracy Defeated Range," pp. 473–81; on "shoot and scoot" tactics and other means for reducing artillery vulnerability to counterbattery fire, see, for example, Bailey, *Field Artillery and Firepower,* pp. 93–114; and Headquarters, Department of the Army, *FM 6-20-1, Field Artillery Cannon Battalion* (Washington, D.C.: GPO, 1983), pp. 1-39–1-48.

53. COMINT and SIGINT may enable an analyst to deduce a unit's general location, but they only rarely provide specific locations of nonemitting weapons

with the precision needed for effective targeting (esp. for targeting armored vehicles). The latter requires some additional source of information. See Scales, "Accuracy Defeated Range," pp. 478–79; and Vick et al., *Enhancing Air Power's Contribution,* pp. 19–20.

54. See Stephen Biddle et al., *New Approaches to Planning for Emerging Long Term Threats,* vol. 1 (Alexandria, Va.: Institute for Defense Analyses, 1994), IDA P-2896, pp. 26–27, 54.

55. On the DARPA FOLPEN (foliage penetrating radar) initiative, see James Ralston, "Ultra-Wideband Radar Program Review," briefing slides, Institute for Defense Analyses, Feb. 20, 1996; Giglio, "Overview of Foliage/Ground Penetration and Interferometric SAR Experiments"; and Vick et al., *Enhancing Air Power's Contribution,* pp. 17–20. Note also that FOLPEN would provide no capability against targets in other forms of cover. While ground-penetrating radar is receiving increasing attention (largely as a means of locating buried landmines or underground bunkers), built-up areas would pose difficult problems for any developmental remote sensor type.

56. Victor Utgoff and Ivan Oelrich, "Confidence-building with Unmanned Sensors," in *Technology and the Limitation of International Conflict,* ed. Barry Blechman (Lanham, Md.: University Press of America, 1989), pp. 13–31.

57. John W. Sherman III, "Aperture-antenna Analysis," in *Radar Handbook,* ed. Merrill I. Skolnik (New York: McGraw-Hill, 1970), pp. 9-1–9-40. Synthetic aperture radars (SARs) treat the flight path of an airplane as the aperture of the radar, integrating signals and reflections at differing points along the path as though made up of a single antenna. Such approaches require that the aircraft's flight path be offset from the direction of surveillance, however (most current SARs use flight paths roughly perpendicular to the direction of surveillance). For a SAR-carrying munition to strike a target, it must eventually attain a flight path directly toward its target, and must therefore eventually lose SAR guidance when the terminal attack phase of the engagement is reached. While this would not necessarily make SAR impractical (e.g., an initial SAR search phase could be used to provide target coordinates for satellite navigation to impact), it would complicate the design of such a weapon.

58. Infrared, for example, is attenuated significantly by live foliage, whereas laser and television guidance would both be highly problematic (Vick et al., *Enhancing Air Power's Contribution,* pp. 22–24). Munition guidance might thus have to be provided by reference to an external coordinate system (such as the global positioning system [GPS]), in whose terms target locations could be described and transmitted to the munition. This in turn places extreme demands on system accuracy. Since initial target location errors cannot be overcome by terminal homing, such a weapon would suffer compounding of inaccuracies arising from the surveillance device and from the guidance system of the munition itself. On the relative accuracy of terminal guidance and GPS/inertial systems, see David Fulghum, "Small Smart Bomb to Raise Stealth Aircraft's Punch," *Aviation Week and Space Technology,* Feb. 27, 1995, pp. 5off.

59. See, for example, R. M. Ogorkiewicz, "Automating Tank Fire Controls," *International Defense Review,* Sept., 1991, pp. 973–74; and idem "Latest Developments and Trends in Main Battle Tanks," *Armada International,* Apr., 1987, pp. 8–26. The U.S. Army is already funding an advanced technology development program in hit avoidance that includes research in integrated laser warning, radar

warning, and passive missile warning systems; jammers; obscurants; and onboard counterfire systems. See "Army Weaponry and Equipment," *ARMY,* Oct., 1993, p. 319.

60. See, for example, Gen. John Shalikashvili, chairman, Joint Chiefs of Staff, *Joint Vision 2010* (Washington, D.C.: Department of Defense, 1996), pp. 15–16.

61. On the complexity implications of "close coupling" see Charles Perrow, *Normal Accidents: Living With High-Risk Technologies* (New York: Basic Books, 1984), pp. 62–100.

62. See, for example, Shalikashvili, *Joint Vision 2010,* pp. 9–10, 13–14, 16.

63. While some have argued that control of territory can be made unnecessary by coercive use of airpower to punish the opposing leadership or society, available research provides very little evidence to support such a contention. See, esp., Robert Pape, *Bombing to Win* (Ithaca, N.Y. Cornell University Press, 1996).

64. On deep attack and complexity, see, for example, Bailey, *Field Artillery and Firepower,* pp. 314–15. On "systems of systems," see, esp. Owens, "Emerging System of Systems," pp. 15–19.

65. Note that for the special case of unskilled opposition, U.S. military capability may look almost as imposing as RMA advocates say. This in turn suggests that for at least some potential opponents, resort to other, nontheater warfare responses, such as terrorism, low-intensity conflict (LIC), or use of weapons of mass destruction (WMD) may be increasingly likely. See, for example, Betts, "Downside of the Cutting Edge," pp. 80–83. More broadly, a related argument holds that the main future threat to U.S. national security lies not in deliberate interstate warfare but rather in the undirected chaotic overflow of refugees, internal warfare, social disorder, ecological destruction and disease resulting from the collapse of failed states in the developing world. See Robert Kaplan, "The Coming Anarchy," *The Atlantic,* Feb., 1994, pp. 44–76; for a counterargument, see Jeremy Rosner, "Is Chaos America's Real Enemy?" *Washington Post,* Aug. 14, 1994, pp. C1ff.

While there is much merit to the argument that future opponents will seek out lower-intensity or WMD responses to U.S. theater warfare strengths, this does not release us from the need to prepare for theater conflicts. First, only by remaining powerful in this form of warfare do we induce opponents to resort to LIC, which is ultimately less threatening to U.S. interests than is successful aggression in more traditional theater wars. (WMD use, on the other hand, is hardly less threatening than conventional theater warfare, but for this reason our opponents are likely to pursue such weapons anyway—America's unpreparedness for theater warfare would probably not halt proliferation.) Second, many regional powers will maintain sizable conventional armies as a means of threatening local neighbors, even if such forces offer little in a war with the United States; this implies a continuing need for preparedness on our part. Third, the possibility that a peer competitor might eventually emerge is a serious (though unlikely) security threat. Some degree of continuing U.S. preparation for theater warfare hedges against this possibility and helps maintain fragile organizational competencies that have proven difficult to rebuild from scratch in the past. None of this, of course, is to argue that we are either under- or overprepared for such wars today, or that any specific force level is needed for such preparedness. My point is that a continuing focus on the future of theater warfare remains an appropriate (and necessary) element of sound U.S. defense planning.

66. As these theories rest on very different bodies of evidence and argument, it is difficult to structure comparative tests for which determinate predictions can be inferred for all three theories at once. Given this, I will provide a separate series of tests for each theory. Only one of these, a critical case test of the contingent innovation and essential continuity theories, provides a direct, head-to-head comparison. The others enable us to assess relative consistency of prediction and observation, but require a more complex judgment given that the nature of the tests differs across theories.

67. As Massachusetts Institute of Technology economist Erik Brynjolfsson put it, "Productivity is the fundamental economic measure of a technology's contribution." Erik Brynjolfsson, "The Productivity Paradox of Information Technology," *Communications of the Association for Computing Machinery* 36, no. 12 (Dec., 1993): 67–77. Likewise, Stephen S. Roach, chief economist at Morgan Stanley, describes productivity growth as "at the crux of economic success. . . . It is the only way a nation can increasingly generate higher lifestyles for its households and separate itself competitively from its peers." Quoted in W. Wayt Gibbs, "Taking Computers to Task," *Scientific American* 277, no. 1 (July, 1997): 82.

68. *War and Antiwar,* p. 37. See also, for example, Echevarria and Shaw, "New Military Revolution: Post-Industrial Change," pp. 70–77; Sullivan and Coroalles, *Army in the Information Age,* pp. 1, 3; Jablonsky, "U.S. Military Doctrine," pp. 19–20; TRADOC, pp. 1-1, 2-5; Cooper, "Another View of Information Warfare," esp. p. 114; and Arquilla and Ronfeldt, "Cyberwar is Coming!" p. 162; Brown, *U.S. Army in Transition,* pp. 22, 72. On the Tofflers's influence on the RMA debate, see Robert J. Bunker, "The Tofflerian Paradox," *Military Review* 75, no. 3 (May-June 1995): 99–102; Steven Metz, "A Wake for Clausewitz," *Parameters* (winter, 1994–95): 127, 131; also Daniel Goure, "The Impact of the Information Revolution on Strategy and Doctrine," in Schwartzstein, *The Information Revolution and National Security,* p. 218; and Eliot Cohen, "Recent Books," *Foreign Affairs* 73, no. 3:156.

69. It has been argued that measurement difficulties render productivity data invalid for assessing IT, but for the purposes of the RMA debate, current economic data are sufficient. See discussion below.

70. For useful reviews, see Diane D. Wilson, "IT Investment and its Productivity Effects," *Econ. Innov. New Techn.* 3 (1995): 235–51; Thomas K. Landauer, *The Trouble with Computers* (Cambridge: Massachusetts Institute of Technology Press, 1996), pp. 13–46; Paul Attewell, "Information Technology and the Productivity Paradox," in *Organizational Linkages: Understanding the Productivity Paradox,* ed. Douglas H. Harris (Washington, D.C.: National Academy Press, 1994), pp. 13–53; Brynjolfsson, "Productivity Paradox of Information Technology," pp. 67–77; and Gibbs, "Taking Computers to Task," pp. 82–89.

71. These data are taken from *U.S. Department of Commerce, Bureau of Labor Statistics Data* [Online], Major Sector Productivity and Costs Index, http://stats.bls.gov:80/cgi-bin/surveymost?pr.

72. See, for example, Catherine J. Morrison and Ernst R. Berndt, *Assessing the Productivity of Information Technology Equipment in U.S. Manufacturing Industries* (Cambridge, Mass.: National Bureau of Economic Research, Jan., 1991), NBER Working Paper 3582; Martin Neil Baily and Alok Chakrabarti, *Innovation and the Productivity Crisis* (Washington, D.C.: Brookings, 1988); Gary W. Loveman, "An Assessment of the Productivity Impact of Information Technologies," MIT Management in the 1990s Working Paper 88-054, July, 1988; also pub. in Thomas J.

Allen and Michael S. Scott Morton, *Information Technology and the Corporation of the 1990s: Research Studies* (New York: Oxford University Press, 1994), pp. 84–110; P. Weill, "The Relationship Between Investment in Information Technology and Firm Performance: A Study of the Value Manufacturing Sector," *Information Systems Research* 3, no. 4 (1992): 307–33; Stephen S. Roach, "America's Technology Dilemma: A Profile of the Information Economy," Special Economic Study, Morgan Stanley & Co., Apr., 1987; Richard H. Franke, "Technological Revolution and Productivity Decline: Computer Introduction in the Financial Industry," *Technological Forecasting and Social Change* 31 (1987): 143–54; and P. Osterman, "The Impact of Computers on the Employment of Clerks and Managers," *Industrial and Labor Relations Review* 39 (Jan., 1986): 175–86. An exception is T. F. Bresnahan, "Measuring the Spillovers from Technical Advance: Mainframe Computers in Financial Services," *American Economic Review* 76 (Sept., 1986): 742–55, which finds positive returns to IT investment in a sample of financial services firms between 1958 and 1972 (note that this predates the IT revolution as the RMA literature defines it). Note that analyses using indirect measures (e.g., information worker wage structure or firm operating cost efficiency) sometimes found more positive results. See Alan B. Krueger, "How Computers Have Changed the Wage Structure: Evidence From Microdata, 1984–89," *Quarterly Journal of Economics* (Feb., 1993): 33–59; P. Alpar and M. Kim, "A Microeconomic Approach to the Measurement of Information Technology Value," *Journal of Management Information Systems* 7, no. 2 (fall, 1990): 55–69; and S. Y. Harris and J. L. Katz, "Organizational Performance and Information Technology Investment Intensity in the Insurance Industry," *Organization Science* 2, no. 3 (1991): 263–96.

73. Loveman, "An Assessment," p. 85.

74. Also: "There appears to have been an overinvestment in [information technology] capital in 1986 in the sense that marginal benefits are less than marginal costs." Morrison and Berndt, *Assessing the Productivity of Information Technology,* pp. 16, 17–18.

75. William J. Baumol et al., *Productivity and American Leadership: The Long View* (Cambridge: Massachusetts Institute of Technology Press, 1989), esp. pp. 143–62.

76. See, for example, Ernst R. Berndt and Catherine J. Morrison, "High-Tech Capital Formulation and Economic Performance in U.S. Manufacturing Industries: An Exploratory Analysis," *Journal of Econometrics* 65 (1995), 9–43; Stephen D. Oliner and Daniel E. Sichel, "Computers and Output Growth Revisited: How Big is the Puzzle," *Brookings Papers on Economic Activity* 2 (1994): 273–334; A. Barua, G. H. Kriebel, and T. Mukhopadhyay, "Information Technologies and Business Value: An Analytical and Empirical Investigation," *Information Systems Research* (1993): xx; Daniel E. Sichel, *The Computer Revolution: An Economic Perspective* (Washington, D.C.: Brookings, 1997); Paul A. Strassman, *The Squandered Computer: Evaluating the Business Alignment of Information Technologies* (New Canaan, Conn.: Information Economics Press, 1997); and Landauer, *Trouble with Computers,* pp. 79–194.

77. Erik Brynjolfsson and Lorin Hitt, "Paradox Lost? Firm-Level Evidence of High Returns to Information Systems Spending," MIT Working Paper, Mar., 1993, and Feb., 1994. Similar findings are reported in: Frank R. Lichtenberg, *The Output Contributions of Computer Equipment and Personnel: A Firm-Level Analysis* (Cambridge, Mass.: National Bureau of Economic Research, Nov., 1993), NBER Working Paper 4540.

78. Brynjolfsson and Hitt, "Paradox Lost?" pp. 13–14; Brynjolfsson, "Productivity Paradox of Information Technology," p. 70; Wilson, "IT Investment," p. 245. In fact, data problems are a significant shortcoming of the IT productivity econometric literature as a whole (Brynjolfsson, "Productivity Paradox of Information Technology," p. 70), which contributes to the difficulty of resolving the productivity paradox decisively in either direction (at least for economists' primary concern—explaining the downturn in U.S. productivity growth—if not for the RMA's more aggressive contention of a revolutionary *increase*. See below).

79. Erik Brynjolfsson and Lorin Hitt, "Information Technology as a Factor of Production: The Role of Differences Among Firms," *Econ. Innov. New Techn.* 3 (1995): 183–99.

80. Landauer, *Trouble with Computers,* pp. 35–36; Wilson, "IT Investment," p. 245; Lichtenberg, *Output Contributions,* pp. 7–8, 10; Strassman, *Squandered Computer,* pp. 97–107; Brynjolfsson and Hitt, "Information Technology," pp. 188–90. Note that many of these problems pertain to the Lichtenberg study, which uses essentially the same data, as well (Lichtenberg, *Output Contributions,* pp. 17–22).

81. See, esp., Zvi Griliches, "Productivity, R&D, and Basic Research at the Firm Level in the 1970s," *American Economic Review* 76 (1986): 141–54. It has also been argued that shortcomings in the calculation of the U.S. Consumer Price Index (CPI) have systematically overestimated inflation prior to 1987, thus misattributing as inflation some real increases in economic output and hence biasing productivity data downward. See, for example, Robert J. Gordon, *Problems in the Measurement and Performance of Service-Sector Productivity in the United States* (Cambridge, Mass.: National Bureau of Economic Research, Mar., 1996), NBER Working Paper 5519, pp. 4–5.

82. Note that the debate in the economics literature concerns mostly the ability of measurement error to explain the totality of the *decline* in U.S. productivity growth and not its potential to account for an unmeasured, radical *increase* in aggregate productivity growth rates under the influence of new IT investments. See, for example, Gordon, *Problems,* pp. 40–46.

83. Landauer, *Trouble with Computers,* p. 98.

84. See, for example, the argument in ibid., pp. 99–101.

85. See, for example, Morrison and Berndt, *Assessing the Productivity;* and Roach, "America's Technology Dilemma."

86. Morrison and Berndt, *Assessing the Productivity,* p. 12. Similarly, Roach finds that from the 1970s to 1986, output growth per information worker underperformed that of production workers by a factor of about 10 in manufacturing, almost 25 in durables, about 6 in mining, and 2 in transportation ("America's Technology Dilemma: A Profile of the Information Economy," table 7, as reproduced in Loveman, "An Assessment," p. 87).

87. On quality and productivity measurement for IT, see, for example, Martin Neil Baily and Robert J. Gordon, "The Productivity Slowdown, Measurement Issues, and the Explosion of Computer Power," *Brookings Papers on Economic Activity* 19, no. 2 (1988): 347–420; and Landauer, *Trouble with Computers,* pp. 95–101. Gordon later concluded that the difficulties were more significant than he argued here, but mostly as a result of CPI estimation and base-year index bias problems (see *Problems,* pp. 1–5). He ultimately finds that these are still unlikely to account for the entirety of the U.S. productivity slowdown, and that in fact, correction of the base-year index bias problem actually *increases* the magnitude

of U.S. productivity slowdown after 1987 (i.e., in a period of very high IT investment) (*Problems,* p. 5).

88. See, for example, P. A. David, "Computer and Dynamo: The Modern Productivity Paradox in a Not-Too-Distant Mirror," Center for Economic Policy Research, Stanford, Calif., 1989; Brynjolfsson, "Productivity Paradox," p. 75; Elhanan Helpman and Manuel Trajtenberg, *A Time to Sow and a Time to Reap: Growth Based on General Purpose Technologies* (Cambridge, Mass.: National Bureau of Economic Research, Sept., 1994), NBER Working Paper 4854; and Charles Jonscher, "An Economic Study of the Information Technology Revolution," in Allen and Morton, *Information Technology,* pp. 5–42.

89. Berndt and Morrison, "High-Tech Capital," pp. 38, 40.

90. Landauer, *Trouble with Computers,* pp. 14, 101–105, 378n. Moreover, even if IT eventually does attain the dynamo's productivity effect, it is far from clear that this would imply an RMA by the standards given in the literature—which finds no RMA-inducing fundamental shift in the mode of production associated with electrification.

91. David estimates that another twenty years may be required for IT to show its true productivity payoff ("Computer and Dynamo," as cited in Landauer, *Trouble with Computers,* p. 102).

92. See, esp., Landauer, *Trouble with Computers,* pp. 115–94; Attewell, "Information Technology," pp. 24–49; National Research Council, "Conclusions," in *Organizational Linkages,* ed. Harris, pp. 291–301; Strassman, *Squandered Computer,* pp. 118–32; and Gibbs, "Taking Computers to Task," pp. 82–89.

93. These costs include $1,730 a year for network connection and software; $4,680 in technical support; and $5,590 for user time spent learning software, rearranging disk files, waiting for system repairs, assisting coworkers, proofing data files and printouts, installing software, game playing, and other nonproductive "futzing" (Gibbs, "Taking Computers to Task," p. 87).

94. As Microsoft Vice President Nathan Myhrvold put it: "Software is a gas. It expands to fill its container" (quoted in Gibbs, "Taking Computers to Task," p. 87). See also Strassman, *Squandered Computer,* pp. 118–27; Landauer, *Trouble with Computers,* pp. 115–17.

95. Richard Nelson, "Recent Evolutionary Theorizing About Economic Change," *Journal of Economic Literature* 33, no. 1 (Mar., 1995): 74; Landauer, *Trouble with Computers,* pp. 188–90; Gibbs, "Taking Computers to Task."

96. Nelson, "Recent Evolutionary Theorizing," p. 74.

97. Landauer, *Trouble with Computers,* pp. 123–24, 141–57, 205–10.

98. Loveman, "An Assessment," pp. 103, 104; Landauer, *Trouble with Computers,* pp. 90, 183–84, 187–88; Brynjolfsson, "Productivity Paradox," p. 75 and 75n; Wilson, "IT Investment," p. 236.

99. Wilson, "IT Investment," pp. 243–44; Attewell, "Information Technology," 30; Landauer, *Trouble with Computers,* pp. 155–56; 388n.

100. An SBT Accounting Systems study concluded that user time lost to "futzing" alone cost the economy more than $100 billion a year (Gibbs, "Taking Computers to Task," p. 87). These costs have come as an unwelcome surprise to many business executives. See, for example, Paul Strassman, "Next Blow to IS' Image: The Cost of Owning PCs," *Computerworld,* Mar. 10, 1997. See also idem., *Squandered Computer,* pp. 118–27.

101. No such extreme claim is advanced in any of the economics literature discussed

above. Note that although the economics literature on IT and productivity is large and growing, it is wholly unreferenced in the RMA debate. Remarkably, there appears to have been no effort to assess the implications of ongoing economic research for the economic claims advanced by RMA advocates. At a minimum, none of the RMA sources above cite any part of this literature. While some authors cite parts of the management practice literature (notably Peter Drucker's work), systematic economic analysis is essentially absent.

102. See references in notes 19–21 above.

103. Harry Eckstein, "Case Study and Theory in Political Science," in *Strategies of Inquiry*, ed. Fred I. Greenstein and Nelson W. Polsby (Menlo Park, Calif.: Addison-Wesley, 1975), pp. 79–137.

104. See, for example, Krepinevich, "From Cavalry to Computer," pp. 36, 38; FitzSimonds and Van Tol, "Revolutions in Military Affairs," pp. 24–25; Goure, "Is There a Military-Technical Revolution," p. 175; Mazarr et al., *Military Technical Revolution*, pp. 18, 33, 57; Cooper, *Another View*, p. 26; and Blaker, *Understanding the Revolution*, p. 6. Note that none of these references attempt a sustained analysis of blitzkrieg. Rather, the case is used as an illustration to establish the historical reality of the phenomenon as described, typically on the basis of an extremely abbreviated summary history. This demonstration of historical precedent is important to the credibility of the overall thesis, which would otherwise rest on speculation alone, but it hardly provides a basis for detailed comparison of actual events and the literature's explicit claims about those events. Yet while the explicit description of blitzkrieg is quite thin, its use conveys a variety of implicit claims about German interwar military planning. My analysis will focus on these claims by comparing the RMA theory that blitzkrieg is held to illustrate with the actual details of the case, rather than comparing the actual history with RMA advocates' version of it, which is too thin to support systematic analysis.

105. The theory is specified in terms of a military's ability to handle complex battlefield operations, not in terms of innovation per se. If radical innovation were required for a previously inept military to acquire such abilities, then radicalism would be consistent with the theory. For an already skilled organization, however, radical change would be unnecessary (and possibly counterproductive).

106. See, for example, Sir Basil H. Liddell Hart, *The Other Side of the Hill* (London: Cassell, 1948); idem., *The Liddell Hart Memoirs* (New York: G. P. Putnam's Sons, 1965); and idem, *History of the Second World War* (New York: G. P. Putnam's Sons, 1970); John F. C. Fuller, *Armament and History* (New York: Charles Scribner's Sons, 1945), pp. 140–41; Robert O'Neill, "Doctrine and Training in the German Army, 1919–1939," in *The Theory and Practice of War*, ed. Michael Howard (Westport, Conn.: Praeger, 1965; reprint, Bloomington: Indiana University Press, 1970), pp. 143–67; Charles Messenger, *The Art of Blitzkrieg* (London: Ian Allen, 1976); and Bryan Perret, *The History of Blitzkrieg* (London: Robert Hale, 1983). For a review and critique of this literature, see J. P. Harris, "The Myth of Blitzkrieg," *War in History* 2, no. 3 (Nov., 1995): 335–52. On problems with Liddell Hart's analysis in particular, see John Mearsheimer, *Liddell Hart and the Weight of History* (Ithaca, N.Y. Cornell University Press, 1988); and Brian Bond, *Liddell Hart: A Study of His Military Thought* (New Brunswick, N.J.: Rutgers University Press, 1977), pp. 90, 94–95, 98, 113, 173.

107. See, esp., Harris, "Myth of Blitzkrieg," pp. 335–52; James S. Corum, *The Roots of Blitzkrieg: Hans von Seeckt and German Military Reform* (Lawrence: University

Press of Kansas, 1992); Manfred Messerschmidt, "German Military Effectiveness Between 1919 and 1939," in *Military Effectiveness,* vol. 2, *The Interwar Period,* ed. Allan R. Millett and Williamson Murray (Winchester, Mass.: Allen and Unwin, 1988), pp. 218–55; Matthew Cooper, *The German Army 1933–39: Its Political and Military Failure* (London: Macdonald and Jane's, 1978), pp. 113–21.

108. See, for example, Gunther Rothenberg, "Moltke, Schlieffen, and the Problem of Strategic Envelopment," in *Makers of Modern Strategy: from Machiavelli to the Nuclear Age,* ed. Peter Paret (Princeton, N.J.: Princeton University Press, 1986), pp. 296–325; Jehuda Wallach, *The Dogma of the Battle of Annihilation* (Westport, Conn.: Greenwood, 1986); and Harris, "Myth of Blitzkrieg," pp. 335–52.

109. This is not to suggest, as some have done, that German interwar thinkers were unwilling to question or modify the Moltke/Schlieffen canon, or that the resulting German doctrine fit Schlieffen's prescriptions in all details. In the 1920s, Hans von Seeckt, for example, differed with Schlieffen's writings on the importance of mass armies, technical education for officers, and detailed mobilization planning. Perhaps most important, von Seeckt, as noted above, concluded that breakthrough battles would be necessary to obtain encirclement, as opposed to the envelopments favored by Schlieffen. See Corum, *Roots of Blitzkrieg,* pp. 51–55, 66–67. German doctrine thus did not stand still—but neither did it depart radically from its preexisting foundations in the latter interwar period, as the RMA school suggests.

110. On German tactics in World War I, see Bruce Gudmundsson, *Stormtroop Tactics: Innovation in the German Army, 1914–1918* (New York: Praeger, 1989); Timothy Lupfer, *The Dynamics of Doctrine: Changes in German Tactical Doctrine During the First World War* (Fort Leavenworth, Kans.: U.S. Army Combat Studies Institute, 1981); G. C. Wynne, *If Germany Attacks: The Battle in Depth in the West* (London: Faber and Faber, Ltd., 1940; reprint, Westport, Conn.: Greenwood, 1976); Wilhelm Balck, *Development of Tactics, World War,* trans. by Harry Bell (Fort Leavenworth, Kans.: General Service Schools Press, 1922); and Jonathan M. House, *Toward Combined Arms Warfare: A Survey of Twentieth Century Tactics, Doctrine, and Organization* (Fort Leavenworth, Kans.: U.S. Army Combat Studies Institute, 1984).

111. On the role of German doctrine in World War I combat outcomes, see, for example, C. R. M. F. Cruttwell, *A History of the Great War, 1914–1918* (Oxford: Clarendon Press, 1934), p. 505; Cyril Falls, *The First World War* (London: Longmans, 1960), pp. 314–19; Rod Paschall, *The Defeat of Imperial Germany, 1917–1918* (Chapel Hill, N.C.: Algonquin, 1989); Barrie Pitt, *1918: The Last Act* (New York: Norton, 1962), pp. 43–44, 60–61; Gudmundsson, *Stormtroop Tactics,* pp. 155–70; Wynne, *If Germany Attacks;* and Lupfer, *Dynamics of Doctrine.*

112. *Heeresdienstvorschrift 487: Führung und Gefecht der verbundenen Waffen* (Berlin: Verlag Offene Worte, 1921, 1923).

113. *Leadership and Battle* continued, for example, to emphasize combined arms, "fluid squad fire and maneuver tactics," and initiative and flexibility by junior commissioned and noncommissioned officers. The new infantry branch manual of 1922 "incorporated all of the tactical developments of 1917 and 1918." See Corum, *Roots of Blitzkrieg,* pp. 40, 42–43.

114. *Heeresdienstvorschrift 300: Truppenführung* (Berlin: Verlag Offene Worte, pt. 1, 1933, pt. 2, 1934).

115. Corum, *Roots of Blitzkrieg,* p. 140; Harris, "Myth of Blitzkrieg," p. 345.

116. Corum, *Roots of Blitzkrieg*, pp. 199–200; Messerschmidt, "German Military Effectiveness," p. 244.

117. Corum, *Roots of Blitzkrieg*, p. 200.

118. Gudmundsson, *Stormtroop Tactics*, p. 159. On the general emphasis on combined arms integration in German organizational design, see also Corum, *Roots of Blitzkrieg*, pp. 43–48, 202, 207–10; and House, *Toward Combined Arms Warfare*, pp. 35, 57–58.

119. This does not mean it was inevitable—other outcomes were certainly possible—but neither was it a radical departure from past practice. As James Corum put it: "Even though the panzer division was Guderian's creation in 1935, it was less a quantum leap than a natural evolution from the army's tactics in the 1920s" (*Roots of Blitzkrieg*, p. 202). Neither was German willingness to group tanks together in independent divisions (rather than parceling them out among infantry divisions as supporting weapons) a fundamentally novel approach. Germany had long preferred to concentrate elite units or special weapons at the point of attack, rather than spreading them throughout their entire force structure. This tendency can be seen, for example, in their concentrated use of the elite *stosstruppen* formations in the spring of 1918, as well as their willingness in 1939–45 to support separate elite units with special access to weapons and equipment (e.g., the Grossdeutchland and Hermann Goering divisions, or the Waffen SS panzer and *panzergrenadier* divisions) at the cost of starving regular units—even regular panzer divisions—for resources. Nor was the idea of grouping tanks together in division-size units unique to Germany. Both France and Britain had also done so by 1940. In fact, the superiority of German over French or British division organization was not in any greater willingness to use tanks in large, independent formations, it was in the Germans's superior ability to integrate tanks with infantry and fire support. On *stosstruppen* employment, see, esp., Gudmundsson, *Stormtroop Tactics*, pp. 155–70; on German elite units in World War II, see, for example, George Stein, *The Waffen SS: Hitler's Elite Guard at War, 1939–45* (Ithaca, N.Y. Cornell University Press, 1966).

120. As J. P. Harris put it: "The German army at the outbreak of war had no radically new theory of war called Blitzkrieg or called anything else. In essence the operational thinking of the German army had changed surprisingly little since the First World War, indeed since the late nineteenth century. Nor, for that matter, had German strategic thinking changed. The Germans had always had a marked preference for short, decisive campaigns, it was just that they could not generally manage to achieve short-order victories in First World War conditions. . . . The notion that the German conduct of the Second World War was informed by a Blitzkrieg doctrine, concept, or strategy is largely spurious" ("Myth of Blitzkrieg," pp. 344, 352). Or, in Bruce Gudmundsson's assessment: "By the time that the German attack against the West was carried out in the spring [of 1940], the fundamentals of the blitzkrieg at both the tactical and operational level had been present in the German army for almost a quarter century" (*Stormtroop Tactics*, p. xii).

121. See, esp., Tami Davis Biddle, "Rhetoric and Reality in Air Warfare: The Evolution of British and American Ideas About Strategic Bombing, 1917–1945" (Ph.D. diss.: Yale University, 1995), pp. 137–228, 302–490, 491–538; Sir Charles Webster and Noble Frankland, *The Strategic Air Offensive Against Germany, 1939–45*, vol. I (London: HMSOffice, 1961), pp. 52–64, 144–54; Malcolm Smith, *British Air*

Strategy Between the Wars (Oxford: Clarendon, 1984); Richard Overy, "Air Power and the Origins of Deterrence Theory Before 1939," *Journal of Strategic Studies* 15, no. 1 (Mar., 1992); Anthony Verrier, *The Bomber Offensive* (London: Batsford, 1968), pp. 33–78.

122. On the Pentomic Division and associated U.S. Army doctrinal changes, see Andrew Bacevich, *The Pentomic Era* (Washington, D.C.: National Defense University Press, 1986); and Robert Doughty, *The Evolution of U.S. Army Tactical Doctrine, 1946–76*, Leavenworth Paper 1 (Fort Leavenworth, Kans.: U.S. Army Combat Studies Institute).

123. House, *Toward Combined Arms Warfare*, p. 89; Robert Citino, *Armored Forces: History and Sourcebook* (Westport, Conn.: Greenwood, 1994), pp. 49–50.

124. Some may argue that even if blitzkrieg were not a radical departure from previous German practice, it was still revolutionary because it produced a radical outcome. Of course, this is not what the contingent innovation school argues (for an exception, see Cohen, "Revolution in Warfare," pp. 46–47, which describes German interwar military innovation as "evolutionary"). It is somewhat more consistent with the view that the U.S. has already achieved an RMA, without any major doctrinal or organizational change. For counterarguments to this thesis, see Biddle, "Victory Misunderstood." To argue, however, that an RMA has not yet been realized but can be achieved by ordinary, gradualist, incremental adaptation is to render moot the RMA thesis as a current-day policy concern. If the policy implications of RMA and non-RMA are the same—gradual incremental adaptation to continuously changing technology—then why does it matter whether we declare the late twentieth century a revolution or not? The importance of the RMA debate lies in its policy consequences; if these are defined away, the distinction degenerates to mere semantics.

125. For representative assessments, see Martin Van Creveld, *Fighting Power: German and U.S. Military Performance, 1939–1945* (Westport, Conn.: Greenwood, 1982); and Trevor N. DuPuy, *A Genius for War: The German Army and General Staff, 1807–1945* (London: MacDonald and Jane's, 1977). Note that German skills did not extend to the strategic level of war, or the politico-economic management of a war economy. See Russell F. Weigley, "The Political and Strategic Dimensions of Military Effectiveness," in *Military Effectiveness*, vol. 3, ed. by Millett and Murray, pp. 341–64. As the theory above is specified primarily in terms of battlefield outcomes rather than grand strategic or political ones (these have been the primary focus of the RMA debate as well), it is thus the Germans's tactical and operational abilities that are most germane for purposes of theory testing here. The larger question of the ability of military force to satisfy national political objectives may follow a similar pattern, however. It may be that the political, economic, and strategic complexity of war has also grown over time, thus winnowing the politically and strategically skilled from their contemporaries as well. This might help account for the fact that while German battlefield victories became more decisive from 1914–18 to 1940, Germany's ultimate defeat in the Second World War was even more destructive for German society than was its defeat in the First. Unfortunately, the latter question is beyond the scope of the current inquiry.

126. See, for example, DuPuy, *Genius for War*, pp. 256–57, 267; U.S. War Department, *Handbook on German Military Forces* (Baton Rouge: Louisiana State University Press, 1945), TM-E 30-451, pp. 217–28; Robert Allan Doughty, *The Breaking Point:*

Sedan and the Fall of France, 1940 (Hamden, Conn.: Archon, 1990), pp. 30–32; W. Heinemann, "The Development of German Armored Forces, 1918–40," in *Armoured Warfare,* ed. H, P. Harris and F. H. Toase (New York: St. Martin's, 1990), pp. 68–69. Note, however, that German practice in these respects improved significantly between the Polish campaign and the invasion of France. See, for example, Florian K. Rothbrust, *Guderian's XIXth Panzer Corps and the Battle of France* (New York: Praeger, 1990), pp. 17–26.

127. See, for example, U.S. War Department, *Handbook on German Military,* pp. 229–36; Timothy A. Wray, *Standing Fast: German Defensive Doctrine on the Russian Front During World War II* (Fort Leavenworth, Kans., U.S. Army Command and General Staff College, 1986), pp. 21, 76–89; and Paddy Griffith, *Forward into Battle* (Chichester, Sussex: Anthony Bird, 1981), pp. 92–93.

128. See, for example, Eugenia Kiesling, *Arming Against Hitler: France and the Limits of Military Planning* (Lawrence: University Press of Kansas, 1996), pp. 139–43, 167, 169–70; Doughty, *Breaking Point,* pp. 27–30, 32; Williamson Murray, "British Military Effectiveness in the Second World War," in *Military Effectiveness,* vol. 3, ed. Millett and Murray, pp. 107–29; Shelford Bidwell and Dominick Graham, *Firepower: British Army Weapons and Theories of War, 1904–1945* (Boston: Allen and Unwin, 1982), pp. 207–47; and John E. Jessup, "The Soviet Armed Forces in the Great Patriotic War," in *Military Effectiveness,* vol. 3, ed. Millett and Murray, pp. 268–73.

129. French positions on the Meuse were prepared in only two to four kilometers depth; about 30 percent of the available maneuver battalions were withheld in reserve (Doughty, *Breaking Point,* pp. 101–26), and assuming comparable reserve withholds across Second Army's two corps and four forward-committed divisions. By contrast, German defenses in Normandy four years later were as much as fifteen kilometers deep, or more than three times the French figure. See Martin Blumenson, *Breakout and Pursuit* (Washington, D.C.: Office of the Chief of Military History, 1961), p. 191. Against the 1944 British offensive in Operation Goodwood, some two-thirds of the available German maneuver battalions were withheld in reserve, or more than twice the French figure. See Martin Samuels, "Operation Goodwood—The Caen Carve-Up," *British Army Review* (Dec., 1990): 5–6.

130. See, for example, John Erickson, *The Road to Stalingrad,* vol. 1 (New York: Harper and Row, 1975), pp. 68, 80–81; and Alan Clark, *Barbarossa: The Russian-German Conflict, 1941–5* (New York: Morrow, 1965), pp. 37–40. Prepared positions in the "Stalin Line" defending the Soviets' pre-1939 borders, for example, were only two kilometers deep (idem., *Road to Stalingrad,* p. 71).

131. For overviews of the spring 1918 offensives, see, for example, Sir James E. Edmonds, *Military Operations, France and Belgium, 1918* (London: MacMillan, 1935); Martin Middlebrook, *The Kaiser's Battle* (London: Allen Lane, 1978); John Terraine, *To Win A War: 1918, The Year of Victory* (London: Sidgewick and Jackson, 1978), pp. 59–102; and Pitt, *1918,* pp. 75–154.

132. On British and French force employment in 1918, see, esp., Biddle, "Determinants," pp. 268–75, 303–305, 326–30.

133. Pitt, *1918,* pp. 96, 116, 142.

134. Middlebrook, *Kaiser's Battle,* p. 347; George Bruce, ed., *Harbottle's Dictionary of Battles* (New York: Van Nostrand Reinhold, 1979), p. 151.

135. The maximum German advance rate in 1918 on the western front was the twenty miles they penetrated between May 27 and May 29 at the Chemin des Dames

(the offensive eventually gained another four miles by its high-water mark on June 6) (Pitt, *1918,* p. 142). This implies a 1918 maximum advance rate of ten miles per day, vice the 1940 maximum of a little over twenty miles. For 1940 advance distance and time, see L. F. Ellis, *The War in France and Flanders, 1939– 1940* (London: HMSO, 1953), pp. 35, 153, map 2.

136. For German strength and losses in 1940, see Philip Karber et al., *Assessing the Correlation of Forces: France, 1940* (McLean, Va.: BDM Corporation, 1979), BDM/ W-79-560-TR, p. 2–3; and Bruce, *Harbottle's Dictionary,* p. 95, respectively. For German 1918 strength and casualties, see Middlebrook, *Kaiser's Battle,* pp. 50 and 347.

137. See, for example, Anthony H. Cordesman and Abraham R. Wagner, *The Lessons of Modern War,* vol. 1 (Boulder, Colo.: Westview, 1990), pp. 351, 354–55; and Edward Luttwak and Daniel Horowitz, *The Israeli Army, 1948–1973* (Cambridge, Mass.: Abt, 1975).

138. See, for example, Cordesman and Wagner, *Lessons of Modern War,* pp. 1:351–55; and Herzog, *Arab-Israeli Wars,* pp. 152, 157, 159, 161. Prior to the 1973 war, Anwar Sadat undertook a military reform program aimed at professionalizing the Egyptian officer corps. Although this did not produce an army trained to Israeli standards, it did provide a major improvement over their skills prior to the 1970s. See George W. Gawrych, "The Egyptian High Command in the 1973 War," *Armed Forces and Society* 13, no. 4 (summer, 1987).

139. A variety of indicators are potentially suitable for developing such skill data, ranging from the simple and relatively coarse (such as hours of training prior to initial deployment, or per year thereafter), to the more complex and discriminating (e.g., the U.S. Army's training readiness standards, which describe competencies and establish standards in great detail). Unfortunately, existing cross-national databases lack information of either sort, hence a significant data development effort will be needed for a more complete test. Alternatively, a theory of complexity management might be used to predict such skills as a function of other independent variables, such as a state's human capital, culture, or civil-military relations. These data could then be adopted as indicators for empirical testing of a meta theory linking the causes and the consequences of the ability to manage complexity. While theoretical development is ongoing in this area, the results are not yet sufficiently advanced to support such an application here. This does *not* mean that tests cannot be undertaken immediately—indeed, several are provided here—but it does mean that for the time being these tests must be limited to a small-n sample of cases, and to indirect testing strategies relying on some a priori assumptions about underlying distribution of skill in the international system as a whole. On the U.S. Army's training readiness standards, see Robert Holz et al., eds., *Determinants of Effective Unit Performance: Research on Measuring and Managing Unit Training Readiness* (Alexandria, Va.: U.S. Army Research Institute for the Behavioral and Social Sciences, 1994). On theories of organizational skill in managing military complexity, see Stephen Biddle and Robert Zirkle, "Technology, Civil-Military Relations, and Warfare in the Developing World," *Journal of Strategic Studies* 19, no. 2 (June, 1996): 171–212; Demchak, *Military Organizations;* also Stephen Peter Rosen, "Military Effectiveness: Why Society Matters," *International Security* 19, no. 4, (spring, 1995): 5–31; and Kenneth M. Pollack, "The Influence of Arab Culture on Arab Military Effectiveness" (Ph.D. diss., Massachusetts Institute of Technology, 1996).

140. Note that this assumption does not require that the average skills of armies fifty years ago be equal to those of today's organizations, it instead requires that the relative proportion of skilled and unskilled *according to the standards of the day* be relatively constant over time.

141. It is also likely that unskilled armies will be less able to exploit their own weapons' increasing potential (Biddle and Zirkle, "Technology"). This will also tend to reduce change in mean outcomes over time for wars between unskilled opponents.

142. Casualty rates are derived from J. David Singer and Melvin Small, *Correlates of War Project: International and Civil War Data, 1816–1992* [Computer File] (Ann Arbor, Mich.: Inter-University Consortium for Political and Social Research, 1994) (hereafter cited as COW database). For Israel, the derivation used mobilized strength as given in Larry H. Addington, *The Patterns of War since the Eighteenth Century* (Bloomington: Indiana University Press, 1984), p. 303, rather than prewar active duty military personnel as given in the COW database.

143. Casualty rates are derived from the COW database. Data on rates of advance are less complete and display mixed results. The COW database provides no data on advance rates. The U.S. Army's CDB90 database is less systematic and less comprehensive but it does include rate-of-advance data for some battles. For documentation, see Robert Helmbold, *A Compilation of Data on Rates of Advance in Land Combat Operations*, CAA-RP-90-04 (Bethesda, Md.: U.S. Army Concepts Analysis Agency, 1990). CDB90 provides no data at all for the 1948 war. In 1956, the Egyptian army yielded ground at an average rate of 27.2 kilometers per day for the engagements covered in the database; this increased to 59.02 in 1967, but declined to 22.71 in 1973 following Sadat's reforms (see below). Data for Israeli advances against Syrian defenses are available for 1967 and 1973 (with a single data point for 1982). In 1967, the Syrians yielded the Golan Heights in a single days' fighting, producing an average rate of advance of 18.3 kilometers per day for the participating units; this fell to 2.3 kilometers per day for the Israeli counterattack in the Golan in 1973. The single data point for 1982 provides a rate of 12 kilometers per day (all advance rate data are derived from the Army CDB90 database). The advance rate results for Egyptian opponents are thus broadly consistent with the theory's predictions, although the 1973 case warrants careful attention, as argued in more detail below. The data for Israeli advance rates against Syrian defenses are inconsistent with theoretical prediction, although variations in tactical circumstances may account for some of the difference. For example, in 1973, the Israeli advance took the form of a frontal counterattack following an extended, desperate defensive struggle over the same ground, whereas in 1967, the Israelis attacked what had been a mostly quiet front. Pending closer examination, however, it is unclear how much of the difference in results is attributable to this extraneous variation in tactical context.

144. Similarly, one observes very similar patterns if the German case is broadened from the specific campaigns considered above to the overall outcomes of the two World Wars. Although weapon range and lethality increased dramatically from 1914 to 1945, German aggregate casualty rates actually *fell* from 40.6 battle deaths per thousand soldiers per month in World War I to 18.7 in World War II (COW database). Similarly, available data on rates of advance yielded by German defenders show a decline of almost 60 percent between 1914 and 1945, even as the average rated speed of their opponents' primary combat arms increased by almost a factor of ten (assuming an average road speed of 4 MPH for a walking

infantryman in 1914, and an average road speed for tanks of about 30 MPH in 1945, as per fig. 11.1) (CDB90 database).

145. On Egyptian operations in the 1973 October War, see, for example, Cordesman and Wagner, *Lessons of Modern War*, pp. 1:14–116; and Chaim Herzog, *The War of Atonement: October, 1973* (Boston: Little, Brown, 1975). On Egyptian skills, see Gawrych, "Egyptian High Command."

146. By contrast with the economic determinist RMA school, whose propositions about past warfare span many centuries, the essential continuity thesis as described above is limited to the twentieth century. Inasmuch as the COW database affords a wider perspective, the complete data are provided here, but the theory per se makes no firm claims as to its behavior prior to 1900. It is likely that at least some of the essential continuity thesis' provisions pertain to earlier periods as well since, for example, the lethality increase described above began well prior to 1900. Other consequences deriving from this may also be discernible in earlier data, although no systematic attempt has been made to establish this.

147. Changes in mean are modest relative to the spread in the data: as noted below, OLS regression analysis to estimate changes in mean dependent variable values as a function of time explain no more than 3 percent of the variance for any of the four dependent variables.

Note that changes in variance are not necessarily evident by inspection in the scatter plots provided by figs. 11.8–11.11. The change in the outer envelope of the data spread is very small in figs. 11.9 and 11.10, even though in the case of fig. 11.9 (as noted below) the increase in variance is statistically significant at the .1 level. In all four figures, distribution of the data within the envelope is nonuniform with respect to time, but this is often difficult to see due to the size of the data set, which produces numerous overstrikes obscuring individual data points. The formal hypothesis testing provided below is thus a more reliable indicator of the behavior of the data than simple visual inspection.

148. For the longer time interval 1816–1994, all four measures show statistically significant increases in variance: at the .00008 level for loss exchange ratio, the .0003 level for loss rate, the .07 level for loss infliction rate, and in excess of the .00001 level for war duration.

Significance levels were obtained using the Goldfeldt-Quandt test. See, for example, Robert Pindyck and Daniel Rubenfeld, *Econometric Models and Economic Forecasts*, 2d. ed. (New York: McGraw-Hill, 1981), pp. 148–50. Note that in this case, the hypothesis of interest concerns the heteroskedasticity of the data set itself, rather than the heteroskedasticity of residual terms from a regression equation. Hence, rather than the F statistic being the ratio of the error sum of squares for the low group and the high group, it is the ratio of the sum of squared deviations from the mean of each group.

149. Note that for the longer time interval 1816–1994, the only measure to display a significant change in mean is loss rate (at the .08 level).

Changes in mean were determined by OLS regression for the log of each outcome measure as a function of time (logarithms were required to obtain normally distributed residuals). Significance levels are for t tests on the estimated time coefficients. In none of the four regressions was more than 3 percent of the variance explained. Significance levels for rejection of the null hypothesis of no change in mean were .40 for loss exchange ratio and .30 for loss infliction rate.

150. For loss rate, the estimated increase in mean from 1900 to 1994 is 133 percent; the increase in variance between the first 5 data points and the last 5 is only 12 percent. For war duration (the other statistically significant increase in mean), the estimated increase from 1900 to 1994 is 62 percent; the increase in variance between the first 5 data points and the last 5 is 217 percent. (Note that for the longer 1816–1994 interval, even loss rate displays greater change in variance than mean: the change in variance from the first 10 data points to the last 10 is 124 percent; the change in estimated mean from 1816–1994 is 81 percent.)

151. See, for example, Stephen Van Evera, "Causes of War" (Ph.D. diss., University of California, Berkeley), p. 159; idem., "The Cult of the Offensive and the Origins of the First World War," *International Security* 9, no. 1 (summer, 1984): 58–107; Jack Snyder, *The Ideology of the Offensive* (Ithaca, N.Y. Cornell University Press, 1984), pp. 9, 15, 20–22 (note that Snyder and Van Evera treat the *perceived* offense-defense balance between 1900 and 1914 as offense-dominant, although the objective balance was quite the opposite); Quester, *Offense and Defense,* pp. 100–54, which treats 1900–14 as a period of high perceived preemptive incentive, although weapon technology was otherwise highly defensive; and Sean M. Lynn-Jones, "Offense-Defense Theory and its Critics," *Security Studies* 4, no. 4 (summer, 1995): 660–94.

152. See, for example, Nye and Owens, "America's Information Edge," pp. 21–36; and Cohen, "Revolution in Warfare," pp. 47, 51.

153. As described in Goure, "Is There a Military-Technical Revolution," p. 178; Johnson and Blaker, "FY 1997–2001 Defense Budget," pp. 3–4. See also, for example, Richard J. Newman, "Warfare 2020," *U.S. News and World Report,* Aug. 5, 1996, pp. 34–41; and Jim Hoagland, "Ready for What?" *Washington Post,* Mar. 28, 1996, p. A27. For an argument that some modernization and force structure should be reduced to provide resources for accelerated acquisition of RMA systems, see Owens, "Emerging System of Systems," pp. 15–19. Note that other RMA advocates emphasize long term research and development rather than immediate modernization. See, for example, Bracken, "Military After Next"; Frank Kendall, "Exploiting the Military Technical Revolution: A Concept for Joint Warfare," *Strategic Review* (spring, 1992): 23–30.

154. An alternative approach would be to preserve both the readiness and modernization accounts and take the necessary cutbacks in reduced force structure. The feasibility of this approach depends on the frequency of U.S. troop deployments, the number of wars the military is expected to fight simultaneously, and force requirements for fighting such wars. With the current requirement to be able to fight and win two, nearly simultaneous major regional conflicts (MRCs) as well as to participate in frequent peacekeeping and other overseas deployments, a major reduction in force structure could conflict with troop quality by reducing retention rates. Many skilled personnel are already leaving the military rather than accept the quality-of-life penalties associated with long deployments in austere environments. A full analysis of this trade-off is beyond the scope of this paper (the force structure discussion below focuses on the nature rather than the size of the needed forces), but it should be noted that one key issue is the size of the force required to win an MRC—an issue for which proper analysis probably requires new analytic methods, as argued below.

155. See, for example, Vickers, *Warfare in 2020,* pp. 1, 8, 9, 14; Blaker, *Understanding the Revolution,* pp. 16, 19–20, 22; Cohen, "Revolution in Warfare," p. 45; Mazarr

et al., *Military-Technical Revolution,* pp. 34–35; and Maj. Terry New, "Airpower Enters Decisive Era," *Defense News,* May 6, 1991, p. 28.

156. See, for example, William J. Perry, *Annual Report of the Secretary of Defense to the President and the Congress* (Washington, D.C.: GPO, Mar., 1996), pp. 149–52, 153.

157. See references in notes 19–21 above.

158. Led by Adm. H. L. T. Aube, the *Jeune École* held that the era of the battleship and the major fleet action had ended, to be replaced by fast torpedo boats and commerce raiding. See Theodore Ropp, *The Development of a Modern Navy: French Naval Policy, 1871–1904,* rev. ed., ed. Stephen S. Roberts (Annapolis, Md.: Naval Institute Press, 1987); McNeill, *Pursuit of Power,* pp. 262–65; Van Creveld, *Technology and War,* pp. 204–205. The European pre-1914 air war visionaries were a group of mostly civilian commentators who held that the era of mass land warfare had ended because aerial bombing of cities would make resistance intolerable. See Michael Paris, *Winged Warfare: The Literature and Theory of Aerial Warfare in Britain, 1859–1917* (Manchester: Manchester University Press, 1992); Robert Wohl, *A Passion for Wings: Aviation and the Western Imagination, 1908–1918* (New Haven, Conn.: Yale University Press, 1994); Timothy Travers, "Future Warfare: H. G. Wells and British Military Theory, 1895–1916," in *War and Society,* ed. Brian Bond and Ian Roy (New York: Holmes and Meier, 1975), pp. 67–87; Tami Davis Biddle, "Aviation in World War I," in *World War I Reconsidered,* ed. Mary Habek, Geoffrey Parker, and J. M. Winter (New Haven, Conn.: Yale University Press, forthcoming). On the USAF's overadaptation to the atomic bomb, see Caroline Ziemke, "In the Shadow of the Giant: USAF Tactical Air Command in the Era of Strategic Bombing, 1945–1955" (Ph.D. diss., Ohio State University, 1989).

159. Post–World War II U.S. Army doctrines, for example, include combined arms maneuver, the Pentomic Division and associated doctrine, the Reorganized Armor Division (ROAD) and associated doctrine, the Active Defense, and AirLand Battle. See Doughty, *Evolution;* John L. Romjue, *From Active Defense to AirLand Battle: The Development of Army Doctrine, 1973–1982* (Fort Monroe, Va.: TRADOC Historical Office, 1984).

160. This is not to suggest that all aspects of interwar or 1939–45 German military practice are worthy of emulation. In addition to the Reichswehr's and the Wehrmacht's military shortcomings at the strategic and grand strategic levels, their moral failings in cooperating with Nazism and the Final Solution are clearly grave errors to be avoided. My point here is only that there are valuable lessons in the nature of German tactical and operational level doctrine development from which the U.S. military of today can profit. On German military limitations, see Weigley, "Political and Strategic Dimensions"; on German military complicity in Nazism, see Omer Bartov, *Hitler's Army: Soldiers, Nazis and War in the Third Reich* (New York: Oxford University Press, 1991).

Contributors

Stephen Biddle, formerly of the Institute for Defense Analysis, is now professor at the University of North Carolina.

H. W. Brands is the Ralph R. Thomas Professor in Liberal Arts at Texas A&M University.

Alexander L. George is professor emeritus of international relations at Stanford University.

Father J. Bryan Hehir is the head of the Harvard Divinity School and a faculty associate at the Weatherhead Center for International Studies.

Andrew Kohut is the director of the Pew Research Center in Washington, D.C., and is a former president of the Gallup Organization.

Andrew Krepinevich is executive director of the Center for Strategic and Budgetary Assessments and lectures in security studies at the Johns Hopkins University and Georgetown University.

James M. Lindsay is a senior fellow at the Brookings Institution.

Charles Moskos, a former draftee, is professor of sociology at Northwestern University.

Williamson Murray is formerly of the Marine Corps Research Center, Marine Combat Development Command.

Bruce Russett is the Dean Acheson Professor of International Relations and Political Science at Yale University.

Tony Smith is the Cornelia M. Jackson Professor and Chair of the Department of Political Science at Tufts University.

Susan L. Woodward is a senior research fellow at the Centre for Defence Studies, King's College London.

Index

Quadrennial Defense Review (QDR), 201, 203, 208–10
Quemoy, 61

race: affirmative action, 185; "Black Failure," 182–83; and the military, 182–86; nondiscrimination, 183–86; U.S. Army, 183
Ramsey, Paul, 26
Reagan, Ronald, 62, 86
realism, 219
Reimer, Dennis, 100
Republic of Fear, The, 95
Republic of Ireland, 36
Reserve Officer Training Corps (ROTC), 181
Respublica Christiana, 15–16
Review and Extension Conference of the Treaty on Nonproliferation of Nuclear Weapons (NPTREC), 20
Revolution in Military Affairs (RMA), 209; Arab-Israeli Wars, 253; contingent innovation, 221–22, 247–53; economic determinism, 220–21, 238–45; essential continuity, 222; information technology, 238–39, 241–46; World War II, 252, 253
Rice, Donald, 94
Ridgeway, Matthew, 61
rogue states, 208
Roosevelt, Franklin, 141, 142, 166, 167
Roosevelt, Theodore, 39, 141
ROTC, 181
Russia, 171, 176. *See also* Soviet Union
Russian-Chinese Alliance, 50
Rwanda, 3, 27–28, 33, 67, 69, 180

Sacirbey, Mohamed, 123
Sarajevo, 114, 124–25
Saudi Arabia, 143, 156, 168, 177, 180
Shultz, George, 62–64, 71, 90
Schwarzkopf, Norman (Gen.), 98
Serbia, 36, 43, 113, 121, 124, 126–27, 147
Serrano, Jose, 42
sexual abuse/harassment: Aberdeen Proving Ground, Md., 186, 188; consensual sex, 187; and the military, 186–88; Tailhook, 186, 187; zero tolerance, 188
Shalikashvili, John (Gen.), 89, 203

signal intelligence (SIGNIT), 233
Sikhs, 121
Silajdžić, Haris, 123
skill variations, 232
Slovenia, 112, 118–21
Solana, Javier, 111
Somalia, 27, 36, 30, 39, 40, 41, 54, 66–67, 69, 88, 98, 104, 116, 144–45, 150, 152, 153, 171, 175, 179, 180, 190, 191
South Africa, 20
Soviet Union, 3, 20, 21, 27, 34, 39, 40, 46, 47, 49, 50, 51, 54. *See also* Russia
space assets, 205–206
Spain, 169, 175
Sri Lanka, 40
Stabilization Force (SFOR), 129
stable peace, 73–74
Stalin, Joseph, 96
stealth, 202
strategic information warfare, 218
strategic pause, 202
Suarez, Francisco, 15, 16
Sudan, 27
Suez Crisis, 74
sunrise systems, 219
sunset systems, 219
suppressive fire, 229
Switzerland, 42

Taft, William Howard, 142
Taiwan, 61, 205
technology, 201, 202, 218, 219
terrorism, 208
Tibet, 40
Toffler, Alvin and Heidi, 221, 238
Tonkin Gulf Resolution, 142, 143, 153
Truman, Harry S., 61, 77, 142, 150
Turkey, 85, 96

United Nations (UN), 18, 27, 28, 44, 52–55, 66–67, 77, 80, 88–89, 112, 115, 119, 121, 123–25, 129, 144, 146, 168; peacekeeping, 125–29, 131–32, 147–50, 172; Security Council, 20, 30, 54, 89, 113, 122, 124, 126; U.S. Congress, 148–49
unmanned aerial vehicles, 212
urban war, 207
Urquhart, Brian, 28
USS *Harlan County,* 145